国家自然科学基金项目"基于共享体验的旅游者忠诚度研究：
理论拓展与实证检验"（71704072）成果

心理学视角下的游客满意度研究

Tourist Satisfaction: A Psychological Perspective

孙旭华　著

By Xuhua（Michael）Sun

东南大学出版社
SOUTHEAST UNIVERSITY PRESS
·南京·

内容提要

本书以游客相对稳定的人格特质与不同旅游情境中所产生的情绪反应作为切入点,将大五类人格维度和积极与消极情绪整合成影响游客对目的地整体满意度的前因变量,以中国大陆赴澳大利亚游客为例,采用结构方程建模分析并揭示了游客满意度形成的心理机制。研究结果证实了游客人格和情绪反应对游客满意度的共同影响,情绪反应是游客人格特质与游客满意度之间的充分中介变量,从而进一步拓展了游客满意度的理论模型。这将有助于相关企业制定出更迎合游客人格取向的营销策略。本书可作为旅游管理、公共管理、消费者行为及中国市场等研究方向学者的参考用书,亦适用于高等院校管理专业及英语专业的本科生和研究生,以及旅游从业人员及爱好旅游人士学习与参考。

图书在版编目(CIP)数据

心理学视角下的游客满意度研究 / 孙旭华著 . — 南
京 : 东南大学出版社,2020.12(2021.3 重印)
　ISBN　978 - 7 - 5641 - 9233 - 4

　Ⅰ.①心…　Ⅱ.①孙…　Ⅲ.①旅游地-顾客满意度-
商业心理学-研究　Ⅳ.①F590.8

中国版本图书馆 CIP 数据核字(2020)第 224803 号

心理学视角下的游客满意度研究　Xinlixue Shijiaoxia de Youke Manyidu Yanjiu

著　者	孙旭华	**责任编辑**	刘　坚
电　话	(025)83793329　**QQ**:635353748	**电子邮件**	liu-jian@seu.edu.cn
出版发行	东南大学出版社	**出 版 人**	江建中
地　址	南京市四牌楼 2 号(210096)	**邮　编**	210096
销售电话	(025)83794561/83794174/83794121/83795801/83792174/83795802/57711295(传真)		
网　址	http://www.seupress.com	**电子邮件**	press@seupress.com
经　销	全国各地新华书店	**印　刷**	江苏凤凰数码印务有限公司
开　本	787mm×1092mm　1/16	**印　张**	16.5　**字　数**　415 千字
版　次	2020 年 12 月第 1 版	**印　次**	2021 年 3 月第 2 次印刷
书　号	ISBN　978 - 7 - 5641 - 9233 - 4		
定　价	68.00 元		

Preface

This book provides a comprehensive overview of tourist satisfaction research. The complexity of tourist satisfaction under a variety of individual and socio-cultural contexts challenges researchers in the field on their conceptulisations and methodologies because tourist satisfaction appears to be influenced not only by cognitive associations but by psychological interactions among its determinants. I intend to offer the readers insights into, and fine-grained analysis of this domain which I have been researching for years.

Tourist satisfaction is a complicated psychological construct with both cognitive and affective determinants. Previous studies on tourist satisfaction mainly take a cognitive approach from the perspective of service quality, and fail to pay due attention to its psychological predictors represented by tourist personality and affective responses. Due to personality discrepancies, the same travel experience at a destination may elicit different types of affective responses among different tourists. However, the role of individual differences in shaping those experience-engendered affective responses remains underexplored in the tourism literature. Thus, an in-depth examination of the relationships among such psychological constructs as personality, affect, and satisfaction is required to better understand the joint impact of personality traits and affective responses on tourist satisfaction.

By linking enduring personality traits with situational affective responses to develop a conceptual model for tourist satisfaction, this book aimed to reveal the psychological mechanism underlying the tourist satisfaction formation in the context of mainland Chinese package tourists to Australia. Employing structural equation modelling analysis, it investigated the structural relationships among tourist personality as measured by the Big Five Inventory, affective responses characterised as either positive or negative, and overall tourist satisfaction with travel experiences at a destination. To achieve the research objectives of this study, a sequential mixed-method approach consisting of two research stages was adopted in the research design. The qualitative exploration phase involving four sessions of focus group discussions provided an insight into tourists' salient positive and negative affective responses, thus guiding the development of the questionnaire design for the second stage. In the quantitative investigation phase, a total of 493 valid questionnaires were collected to examine how tourist personality, coupled with experience-elicited affective responses, influenced tourist satisfaction.

The results corroborated the joint impact of tourist personality and affective responses on tourist satisfaction. A major finding of this study was that affective responses acted as fully mediating variables between tourist personality and tourist satisfaction. Mediated by positive affective responses, extraversion, agreeableness, openness, and conscientiousness can predict tourist satisfaction; mediated by negative affective responses, agreeableness, neuroticism, and openness can also explain tourist satisfaction. The structural relationships among the exogenous variables and endogenous variables in the final model explained 55% of the total variance of negative affect, 44% of the total variance of positive affect, and finally both personality and affect explained 60% of the total variation in overall satisfaction. The strong statistical power of the final model suggested this study could serve as a basis for further research into psychological and affective determinants of tourist satisfaction.

Theoretically, this book advances the development of the tourist satisfaction model by incorporating tourist personality and affective responses as two important predictor variables of tourist satisfaction. It reveals how the personality characteristics of tourists can explain the overall satisfaction of tourists to destinations mediated by positive or negative affective responses, thus further enriching the research literature on tourist satisfaction. In addition, these findings extend the understanding of personality-affect relationships and how affective responses influence tourist satisfaction. Practically, a comprehensive understanding of the psychological mechanism underlying the formation of tourist satisfaction will assist industry practitioners in effectively managing tourist satisfaction through travel experiences generating positive affective responses.

This book provides a multifaceted analysis of the psychological antecedent variables which would determine or predict tourist satisfaction. It would also be of particular significance to organisations wanting to develop more appropriate marketing strategies to suit individual personality orientation. Based on extensive fieldwork and investigation, this book will be welcomed by students and scholars of tourism, hospitality, management studies, and Chinese studies.

Finally, I would like to take this opportunity to extend my sincere gratitude to Prof. Sam Huang and Prof. Graham Brown for their guidance and encouragement, which has always inspired me to set high standards of research excellence. I acknowledge the institutional support I received from the University of South Australia Business School and Nanjing University of Finance & Economics. Finally, I dedicate this book to my family for their love, tolerance, and continuous support.

Xuhua (Michael) Sun
December 2020

序　言

本书对游客满意度研究进行了全面的回顾和梳理。游客满意度不仅受其认知联想的影响，而且受其心理决定因素之间的相互影响，因此，在不同的个人、社会及文化背景之下，游客满意度研究的复杂性对学者们在理论概念及研究方法上提出了挑战。我想聊以此书把自己对于这个领域多年研究的见解和分析与诸君共飨。

游客满意度是一种复杂的心理建构，既有认知因素，又有情感因素。以往关于游客满意度的研究主要是从服务质量的视角，采用认知的方法，却忽视了以游客个性和情感反应为代表的心理变量的影响。由于个性差异，在同一目的地的相同旅游体验可能在不同游客之间导致不同类型的情感反应。然而，在旅游文献中，个体差异如何影响旅游体验所激发的情感反应仍然没有得到充分的研究。因此，只有深入探究人格、情感和满意度等心理变量之间的关系，才能更好地理解人格特质和情感反应是如何共同影响游客满意度的。

本书通过把相对稳定的人格特质与不同情境中所产生的情感反应联系起来，建立了一个全新的旅游满意度概念模型，旨在揭示中国大陆赴澳大利亚游客满意度形成的心理机制。本书采用结构方程建模分析并研究了"大五类"的游客个性、积极或消极的情感反应，以及游客对目的地整体满意度之间的关系。为了实现本论著的研究目标，研究设计中采用了先定性后定量的混合研究法。定性探索阶段通过四组焦点小组访谈，深入了解游客旅游过程中显著的积极和消极情感反应，从而服务于第二阶段定量研究中的问卷设计。在定量研究调查阶段，共收集了493份有效问卷，以此考察游客个性与情感反应对游客满意度的影响。

研究结果证实了游客人格和情感反应对游客满意度的共同影响。本研究的一个主要发现在于情感反应是游客个性与游客满意度之间的充分中介变量。外倾性、宜人性、开放性和尽责性的人格在积极情感反应介导下可以预测游客的满意度；宜人性、神经质和开放性的人格在消极情感反应介导下可以解释游客的满意度。结构模型中外生变量和内生变量之间的关系解释了消极情感反应总方差的55%，积极情感反应总方差的44%，人格和情感共同影响并解释了整体满意度总方差的60%。最终模型的强大统计能力表明，本研究可作为进一步研究游客满意度心理和情感两大变量的基础。

本书在理论上，通过将游客个性和情感反应作为游客满意度的两个重要预测变量，推进了游客满意度模型的发展。它揭示了游客的个性特征如何在积极或消极情感反应的介导下，解释游客对目的地的整体满意度，从而进一步丰富了游客满意度的研究文献。此外，这些发现延伸了对人格与情感之间关系的理解，以及情感反应如何影响游客满意度。在实用层面上，全面了解游客满意度形成的心理机制将有助于行业从业者通过管理游客的情感反应来有效地调节游客满意度。

本书为预测游客满意度的前因心理变量提供了一个多方面的分析，这将有助于相关企业制定出更适应个性取向的营销策略。在大量实地调查的基础上，本书对旅游、接待、管理研究和中国研究的学生及学者有较大的学习、参考意义。

最后，我想借此机会，向 Sam Huang 和 Graham Brown 两位教授表示衷心的感谢，感谢他们的指导和鼓励，一直激励着我高标准严格要求自己，努力攀登科研高峰。感谢南澳大学商学院和南京财经大学给予我的支持。最后，我把这本书献给我的家人，感谢他们的厚爱、宽容和一贯的支持。

孙旭华
2020 年 12 月于古都南京

Contents

1

The Landscape of Tourist Satisfaction Research: An Overview

This chapter commences with the research background to justify and contextualise the study. It outlines the three constructs (i. e. tourist satisfaction, personality traits, and affective responses) of the proposed conceptual framework, highlighting the need to expand the current tourist satisfaction literature to consider the impact that both personality traits and affective responses have on the formation of tourist satisfaction in the context of mainland Chinese outbound tourists to Australia. It discusses the purpose and specific objectives of the study, the methodology used, as well as its theoretical contributions. Furthermore, the chapter presents conceptual definitions of the major terms and the organisation of the whole book.

Tourist Satisfaction

Despite the voluminous academic writings on the subject of satisfaction and the industry obsession with satisfaction scores, perhaps it is time to think more closely about what satisfaction means in day to day conversation (something that is OK)—and figure out another more suitable term to capture what tourists truly seek(Bowen & Clarke 2009, p. 155).

Visitor satisfaction has been regarded as one of the key measures of success for a tourist destination but, having reviewed both academic writings and industry practices in the tourism satisfaction literature, Bowen and Clarke(2009) concluded that satisfaction research needs to be further extended to achieve a more comprehensive and sophisticated understanding of tourist satisfaction. More recently, Pearce and Packer (2013) echoed their comments and called on researchers to address the dynamic nature of tourist satisfaction.

In social sciences, customer satisfaction can be defined as "an attitude-like judgment following a purchase act or based on a series of consumer-product interactions" (Fournier & Mick 1999, p. 5) or an emotional response to an act of consumption (Westbrook & Reilly 1983). It has been acknowledged that a high level of customer satisfaction will lead to positive word-of-mouth and enhance the customer's repurchase intentions as well as the willingness to recommend (Homburg, Koschate & Hoyer 2005). Hence, the concept and level of satisfaction has become one of the critical indicators used to measure the success of marketing strategies, which is particularly vital to business success in today's competitive environment. Similarly, deriving from "customer satisfaction" in consumer behaviour studies, tourist satisfaction is one of the most essential and most frequently examined concepts in the tourism and hospitality industry because it serves as a decisive factor in sustaining and upgrading any tourism products and services (Gursoy, McCleary & Lepsito 2007). Tourists' overall satisfaction has an effect on destination choice, the consumption of tourism products and services, and destination loyalty (Yoon & Uysal 2005), which is of great significance to successful destination marketing.

Tourist satisfaction and the variables that determine satisfaction have been extensively debated in the tourism literature (Yüksel & Yüksel 2001); however, as yet there is no general agreement on a standard model or framework. Traditionally, tourist satisfaction has been perceived as a response to post-trip cognitive appraisals (Bowen 2001). For instance, the expectancy-disconfirmation paradigm (Oliver 1980), as the most widely-adopted model for satisfaction formation, has dominated satisfaction research for more than three decades (Neal & Gursoy 2008). According to the framework, tourists are satisfied when perceived performance meets or exceeds expectations and dissatisfied when performance fails to meet expectations. Nevertheless, this traditional measurement is limited by its strong reliance on cognitive evaluation processes, and its disregard for affect- and personality-related antecedents in satisfaction research (Oliver 1993; Kozak 2000; Pearce 2005).

During the past decade, more and more tourist behaviour researchers reach a consensus that it is insufficient to model satisfaction assessment merely through a cognitive approach (e. g. Sirakaya, Petrick & Choi 2004; Chang 2008; Del Bosque & San Martín 2008). As a consequence, there has been an increasing demand to understand tourist satisfaction from an affective perspective, albeit still in combination with cognitive influences (De Rojas & Camarero 2008). Correspondingly, the cognitive-affective approach has been recognised as an appropriate paradigm to evaluate the satisfaction process in tourism literature (e. g. Bigné, Andreu & Gnoth 2005; Del Bosque & San Martín 2008). In such a dual system process, the cognitive approach involves the evaluation of actual perceptions and comparison with prior expectations, whereas the affective approach functions when actual perceptions reach or exceed prior expectations, thus resulting in feelings of delight or pleasure. This cognitive and affective sequence indicates the cognitive evaluations can serve as antecedents to affective dimensions of tourist satisfaction.

Recently, the primacy of affective responses has been theorised and demonstrated empirically in tourist satisfaction formation (e. g. Faullant et al. 2011). From an affective neuroscience perspective, Pearce (2012) confirmed that affective responses, evoked by neural stimulation, do occur automatically without being preceded by the individual's cognitive judgments. This is a neglected dimension of tourist satisfaction research, which calls for a need to model tourists' affective responses as the antecedents of tourist satisfaction (Prayag, Hosany & Odeh 2013). In addition, Pearce and Packer (2013), from the viewpoint of contemporary developments in mainstream psychology, highlighted seven challenges for researchers interested in the domain of tourist satisfaction, among which the top two issues resided in recognising the nature and essence of tourist satisfaction as well as its core affective components. These suggested research directions address two earlier studies. One is by Pearce (2009) who characterised an emerging trend of monitoring affect in tourist satisfaction studies; the other is by Coghlan and Pearce (2010) who focused on tracking affective components of tourist satisfaction. Not surprisingly, these new voices have illuminated the path to accessing an under-researched area within tourist behaviour studies, and the necessity of conducting an in-depth study of the affective dimensions of tourist satisfaction. In other words, affective variables can not be excluded for modelling the antecedents of tourist satisfaction (Del Bosque & San Martín 2008; Coghlan & Pearce 2010; Prayag, Hosany & Odeh 2013; Prayag et al. 2015).

To bridge the gap in the tourist satisfaction literature, the current research seeks to empirically investigate the affective components of tourist satisfaction. Although more recent trends have regarded affective responses which tourists experience as the determinant factor in shaping tourist satisfaction (e. g. De Rojas & Camarero 2008; Pearce & Packer 2013), measuring and evaluating affective components of tourist satisfaction are challenging and difficult. The reason for this is that tourist satisfaction, perceived as a specific type of attitude with affective, cognitive and implicit behavioural elements (Pearce & Packer 2013), may change frequently at multiple levels during a variety of encounters throughout a package tour. Hence, tourist satisfaction in this study is conceptualised as a summative overall construct, adopting the affective approach to evaluate tourists' satisfaction with accumulated specific travel experiences at a destination.

To be precise, tourist satisfaction is a complicated psychological response with both cognitive and affective determinants (Mano & Oliver 1993), as well as "other undiscovered psychological and physiological dynamics" (Chang 2008, p. 108). Due to the discrepancy in tourists' personality, one type of scene or product at a destination may elicit different types of affective responses from different people. It is because of distinct variables represented by personality traits and affective responses that the judgment of the determinants in satisfaction formation can be individualistic and diverse (Gountas & Gountas 2007). Therefore, an in-depth examination of the interrelationships among such psychological constructs as personality, affect, and satisfaction is required for a better understanding of consumer psychology in tourism and hospitality (Crouch 2004). With few exceptions (Faullant et al. 2011), research into the joint impact of personality and affect on tourist satisfaction remains underexplored. This study aims to fill the gaps in existing literature by exploring the impact of both tourist personality and affective responses on the formation of overall tourist satisfaction.

Personality Traits

The most popular typology of personality traits, the Five Factors model (FFM or Big Five model) measures the most salient aspects of personality (Yamagata et al. 2006). The model addresses openness to experience, conscientiousness, extraversion, agreeableness, and neuroticism (Goldberg 1990, 1992) as five overarching domains or dimensions of human personality, each being represented by six specific facets. Research into consumer behaviour that has used the FFM has found a connection between individuals' personality and their preferences for certain brands, indicating that personality type is an important parameter for product choice (Aaker 1997; Matzler et al. 2005). Correspondingly, understanding the role of an individual as a consumer has been a long-standing focal point in the study of consumer behaviour (Lee 2009). Not surprisingly, in the context of tourism and hospitality, tourist personality would have significant implications on tourist behaviour and satisfaction evaluations (Reisinger & Mavondo 2004), and research on tourist personality would practically contribute to tourism marketing.

A review of the role of personality in the tourism and hospitality research identified that there is no more appropriate or helpful factor than personality in predicting and explaining tourist behaviour (Ross 1994). For instance, Gountas and Gountas (2007) confirmed a direct relationship between the consumer's personality orientation, emotional characteristics and self-reported satisfaction of the service experiences. Personality orientation has been identified to be an antecedent to travellers' emotional states (either positive or negative), and both personality and emotions influence consumers' appraisals of service satisfaction and their intentions to repurchase. Sohn and Lee (2012) explored to what extent service providers' emotional labour is affected by personality traits, as measured using HEXACO (i. e. honesty-humility, neuroticism, extraversion, agreeableness, conscientiousness, and openness) personality factors in the service industry. Four HEXACO personality factors, extraversion, agreeableness, conscientiousness, and openness were found to have a positive effect on emotional labour. Faullant et al. (2011) reported that two basic emotions, fear and joy, can be influenced by neuroticism and extraversion respectively; coupled with cognitive evaluations, they affect tourist satisfaction. In short, the mechanisms behind the relationships between personality and affect are less well articulated in the tourism literature.

Interestingly, Pearce and Packer (2013) sought to build up some new links between mainstream psychology and tourism research, and proposed a caveat that single trait theories of personality should be used with caution in tourism studies. Patterned responses to tourism settings can be better interpreted by all the core and stable dimensions of the FFM as driving forces, instead of simply viewing isolated dimensions of personality traits, for the latter would lose its predictive power (Pearce & Packer 2013). Therefore, in this study, all five dimensions of the FFM are employed as five independent variables in the research framework. In addition, it has been generally acknowledged that personality discrepancies cause tourists to experience different responses to affective influences (Gountas & Gountas 2007). One of the research objectives is to examine how each dimension of the FFM contributes to the formation of tourists' positive and negative affective responses. Built upon these personality-affect relationships, the ultimate objective is to systematically investigate the leading psychological antecedent variables (i. e. personality traits and affective responses) which would determine or predict tourist satisfaction.

Affective Responses

Affect refers to an instinctive reaction to stimulation (Zajonc 1980). One's affective response is a general ongoing subjective experience which refers to the entirety of the concept (Russell & Barrett 1999). The level of affective response can have an immediate and direct influence on behaviour in an unconscious way, and its effect can be prolonged between a few weeks to a few months (Wright & Staw 1999). As a consequence, it is reasonable to assume that affective responses play an important role in shaping overall satisfaction. Westbrook (1980) suggested that dis/satisfaction can be partially explained by enduring personality traits as well as by temporary affective responses, and that optimistic customers are more likely to be satisfied, compared to pessimistic ones.

In psychology, affect is a generic term to describe a wide range of phenomena, including emotion, mood and feeling (Cohen & Areni 1991). In some extant literature there is considerable ambiguity about the differences between the terms affect and emotion, and a major problem in both psychology and marketing remains the interchangeable use of these two terms (Bagozzi, Gopinath & Nyer 1999). Therefore, it calls for some elaboration on the common understanding of affect and emotion. Pearce (2009) argued that affect is seen as summarising those feelings that are consciously accessible. One's affective state is a general ongoing subjective experience. By contrast, emotion is widely regarded as the more specific of the two terms and is usually linked with a reaction to a specific object, event, or experience (Fredrickson 2001). Both affect and emotion have a subjective experience component; for emotion the subjective experience is one component of the responses involved, whereas for affect the subjective experience is the entirety of the concept (Russell & Barrett 1999). Emotion is often characterised by having a shorter duration than the more general term of affect. Momentary emotions are, to a certain extent, a reflection of one's general affective level

(Watson, Clark & Tellegen 1988). An emotion is an affective state, but not all affective states are emotions. In summary, for the purpose of this study, emotion is seen to be conceptually distinct from affect; however, affect, in general, arises from cumulative occurrences of transient emotional states.

Past studies use different approaches to conceptualise affect, among which, the PANAS approach (Watson & Tellegen 1985) appears to be the most popular. This paradigm focuses on two broad and general dimensions of affective states, usually positive affect (PA) and negative affect (NA). The most commonly used measure of positive and negative affect in scholarly research is the PANAS scale (Watson, Clark & Tellegen 1988), consisting of 20 single-word items, such as excited, alert, determined for positive affect, and upset, guilty, and jittery for negative affect. The PANAS measure has been well-adopted in tourism studies relating to experience quality and satisfaction (Zins 2002), leisure activity preferences (Barnett 2006), travel motivation and travel intention (Jang et al. 2009), and tourist satisfaction models (Del Bosque & San Martín 2008).

Affect is difficult to capture in word(Thrift 2004). In tourism, individuals may experience positive and negative affective responses during the same stay because they have multiple interactions with the resources of the place. On the other hand, affective responses triggered by the travel experiences are proposed to leave affective traces in memory. Within a certain period, these traces are available for individuals to access and will be integrated into their satisfaction states (Cohen & Areni 1991). As an affective response can arise several times in the course of a package tour, the frequency of affective responses rather than their intensity or duration is evaluated in order to identify the salient affective responses in the present study. This method is sensible (Oliver 1997) when various emotions or affects have to be assessed over a time period. Evaluating the frequency of an affective response is more measurable than capturing its intensity which could vary between an experience and another.

The review of relevant literature reveals abundant research for understanding affect, especially in its structure, dimensionality, and intensity. However, little research has used affect to understand subsequent psychological consequences in the tourism academia (Jang et al. 2009). Furthermore, empirical studies investigating the dimensions of tourists' affective responses toward destinations remain scant (Hosany & Gilbert 2010; Yüksel, Yüksel & Bilim 2010). Given the gap identified by Cohen and Cohen (2012) about the need to better understand affect in tourism and hospitality, this study focuses on the tourists' affective responses to their travel experiences. Although many previous studies investigate affective responses in a post-purchase or post-consumption situation, the accumulated tourists' affective responses during the travel consumption period will contribute to the final evaluation of tourist satisfaction.

Tourists' affective responses and overall satisfaction appear to be context specific (Farber & Hall 2007). It is necessary for the researcher to specify the context in studying these two psychological constructs. In addition, while affective responses and satisfactory states are experienced at specific time points in the travelling process, they can generally be assessed in retrospect and a holistic evaluation can be produced (Hosany & Gilbert 2010). Consequently, retrospective measures are employed in this study to generate holistic evaluations of tourists' affective responses. The target population of this study is mainland Chinese outbound tourists in the context of visiting Australia on group package tours for leisure purposes.

Purposes & Objectives

By introducing a conceptual tourist satisfaction model through the affective processing mechanism, the book aims to reveal the psychological processes underlying satisfaction formation in the context of mainland Chinese outbound tourists to Australia. The overall purpose of this study is to explore the structural relationships between tourist personality, affective responses, and tourist satisfaction. It aims to investigate how tourists' personality traits, in conjunction with their affective responses generated by neural stimulation or triggered by travel experiences, influence their level of overall satisfaction with a destination.

Specifically, this study endeavours to achieve the following five objectives:

1) to identify and document Chinese outbound tourists' salient positive and negative affective responses during their trip to Australia;

2) to identify the underlying structure of Five Factors model (FFM) personality traits as applied to Chinese respondents in the context of outbound travel to Australia;

3) to examine how each dimension of the FFM contributes to the formation of tourists' positive and negative affective responses;

4) to test how positive and negative affective responses associated with specific and holistic experiences of a travel trip influence tourists' overall satisfaction with a destination; and

5) to examine how tourists' personality traits, coupled with positive and negative affective responses, can contribute to the formation of tourist satisfaction with a destination.

The current study links enduring personality traits to affective responses, and examines the roles of personality traits and affective responses in satisfaction formation in the context of Chinese outbound tourism to Australia. It is anticipated that the theoretical discussion of this book may provide some preliminary insights into both customer relationship management and destination management in the context of tourism and hospitality.

Research Strategy

To achieve the purpose and objectives of the research, this study adopts a sequential mixed-method approach of combining qualitative and quantitative components. With qualitative exploration serving quantitative investigation in the mixed-methods design, this study undertakes in-depth exploration and provides a comprehensive understanding of Chinese outbound tourists' salient affective responses to long-haul package tours to Australia, as well as the structural model of tourist personality, affective responses and tourist satisfaction. The step-by-step procedures in data analysis and results reporting reflect the methodological rigor in this research.

In the first phase of the study, four semi-structured group discussions ($N = 32$) were conducted in Nanjing, China to identify and categorise participants' affective responses. All 32 participants paid their first visit to Australia by consuming the same travel product, i. e. 8-day package holiday tour, sequentially visiting Sydney, Brisbane, Gold Coast, and Melbourne. Therefore, the qualitative phase of the study is exploratory in its specific research context. During this stage, the initial assumptions about tourists' affective responses gathered from the literature were discussed with the participants within three days of their returning home. Demographic data were also gathered at this stage, including gender, age, occupation, education and personal annual income. All focus group interviews were voice-recorded and then transcribed. A thematic analysis was conducted on the written Chinese transcriptions to identify the salient affective responses. NVivo 10, qualitative data analysis computer software, was used to help categorise and organise the data. The qualitative study was expected to help identify some previously unknown factors, and salient positive and negative affective responses would be eventually confirmed and incorporated into the subsequent survey questionnaire design.

Following the qualitative exploration, a quantitative component was integrated into the research strategy to investigate the interrelationships between personality traits, affective responses, and tourist satisfaction in the conceptual framework. In the second phase of the study, a questionnaire survey was administered on respondents' return flight to China in order to guarantee the optimal time frame for data collection. At that time, the tourists' affective responses were still recent and easily accessible. The sample frame included Chinese outbound tourists from the Jiangsu Province, China, because it is one of the primary outbound tourist-generating markets in China. All respondents travelled to Australia prior to the implementation of the new China Tourism Law, and all were first-time visitors, which eliminated any bias arising from the previous experiences. The questionnaire resulted in 493 useable responses which formed the basis for the data analysis. The statistical methods involved in data analysis covered descriptive statistics, confirmatory factor analysis (CFA), and structural equation modelling (SEM). Descriptive statistics were used to gain an overall picture of the characteristics of Chinese outbound tourists to Australia. CFA was employed to test whether the collected quantitative data fit the hypothesised measurement model. SEM was adopted to examine the causal relationships among eight latent constructs in the model (i. e. extraversion, agreeableness, conscientiousness, neuroticism, openness, positive affect, negative affect, and satisfaction).

Theoretical Significance of the Study

From a theoretical perspective, firstly, this study advances the framework for tourist satisfaction by integrating personality traits as measured by the Big Five Inventory (BFI; John & Srivastava 1999) and affective responses characterised as either positive or negative. Most previous studies have concentrated largely on cognitive approaches to assess whether the perceived quality meets or exceeds expectation, while other studies define satisfaction as an affective state derived from travel experiences. Few recent studies have incorporated both cognitive and affective antecedents to model tourist satisfaction (e. g. Del Bosque & San Martin 2008). However, aside from cognitive and affective variables, multiple other factors may contribute to different levels of satisfaction, such as tourists' psychological features, demographic information or socioeconomic characteristics. More efforts are needed to examine the satisfaction process. More concretely, an in-depth examination of these variables and their interrelationships in the process of tourist satisfaction formation is required for a better understanding of the conceptual underpinnings of satisfaction.

A variety of psychological factors can be identified from past studies, among which the current study refines two constructs hypothesised to influence tourist satisfaction, i. e. affective responses and personality traits. Correspondingly, many contributions in the marketing literature have taken personality traits and emotions into consideration (Mooradian & Olver 1997); however, their relevance and impact on customer satisfaction, especially in the tourism setting, are as yet only little understood. In addition, although many other interrelated psychological influences may exist concurrently, it is generally admitted that the FFM personality domains account for an important portion of the variance in explaining or predicting tourist behaviour. A review on the role of personality in the tourism and hospitality research identifies that the majority of the tourism literature which employs the FFM either for data analysis or as part of the research framework has focused on analysing service staff personality (Leung & Law 2010) rather than tourist personality. To date there has been surprisingly little research employing the FFM to evaluate tourist satisfaction. Therefore, by exploring the joint impact of personality traits and affective responses on the formation of overall satisfaction in the context of mainland Chinese outbound tourists to Australia, this study is designed to develop and empirically test a model explaining tourist satisfaction with a destination. This study is unique and significant because it theorises the structural relationships between such psychological constructs as

personality, affect, and satisfaction in tourism study.

Secondly, this research identifies and develops a short Chinese 16-item Big Five Inventory (BFI-SC), an abbreviated version of the well-established 44-item Big Five Inventory, which assesses each of the five personality dimensions with three or four items on a 7-point Likert scale from 1 (strongly disagree) to 7 (strongly agree). BFI-SC can contribute to quick, but reliable estimation of the FFM personality constructs as applied to Chinese respondents in the context of outbound travel to Australia. The increasing acceptance of the FFM as a model for delineating the structure of core personality traits has called for the need to assess the FFM personality dimensions in both cross-cultural and cross-disciplinary settings (e. g. Rammstedt 2007; Denissen et al. 2008). Although the 44-item BFI has been a widely-used instrument, it has proven to be too lengthy and constraining for many research purposes, for example in the survey context. Therefore, the need for brief but efficient measures of the FFM continues to grow. The current study evaluates the factor structure and reliability of the Chinese version of the 44-item BFI (BFI-C) and reduces it to a 16-item measure of the Big Five dimensions with the satisfactory psychometric properties, which proves to be applicable to the sample of Chinese outbound tourists to Australia. Short instruments can "eliminate item redundancy and therefore reduce the fatigue, frustration, and boredom associated with answering highly similar questions repeatedly" (Robins et al. 2001, p. 152). Therefore, the brevity of the 16-item BFI-SC may be more appealing to future researchers wishing to apply this scale to their own study. This scale will also contribute to the current personality literature on the BFI across the different cultures.

Thirdly, this study addresses the differentiation between affect and emotion, for there is considerable ambiguity about the differences among these two terms in psychology and marketing. Therefore, it calls for some elaboration on the clear conceptualisations of these terms in tourism and hospitality. Findings from the qualitative stage in this study mainly support previous research on consumers' affective responses (e. g. Jun et al. 2001) and help conceptualise affective responses in the context of Chinese outbound tourists to Australia. It will not only enrich the tourism literature on positive and negative affective responses associated with the specific and overall experiences of a travel trip, but also contribute to a good theoretical understanding of consumer behaviour in general.

Conceptual Definitions

Personality was described by Lee (2009) as a dynamic and organised set of characteristics that lead to relatively consistent and enduring responses to one's own environment. It should be noted that personality as a central concept in this book refers to the trait model of personality, as opposed to personality development.

Personality traits are often defined as enduring "dimensions of individual differences in tendencies to show consistent patterns of thoughts, feelings and actions" (McCrae & Costa 2003, p. 25).

FFM is short for Five-Factor Model, representing the taxonomy of personality traits and also commonly referred to the *Big Five*. It includes five dimensions, i. e. openness to experience, conscientiousness, extraversion, agreeableness, and neuroticism.

Openness to experience (simplified as *openness* in the book) is considered to encompass aesthetic sensitivity, awareness of one's emotions, vivid imagination, preference for novelty and variety and intellectual curiosity (Costa & McCrae 1992).

Conscientiousness is the tendency to show self-discipline, act dutifully, and aim for achievement. Governed by their conscience, conscientious people are responsible, reliable, well organised, punctual, diligent, and ambitious (Barrick & Mount 1991).

Extraversion is generally described with adjectives such as energetic, enthusiastic, dominant, optimistic, companionable, communicative, and fun-loving. Individuals who are low in the extraversion trait can be described as shy, reserved, quiet, silent, and withdrawn (Costa & McCrae 1992; Barnett 2006).

Agreeableness is linked with words such as friendly, trustful, warm-hearted, cooperative, and reconcilable. Opposing terms are cold, unfriendly, vindictive, cynical, non-cooperative, fractious, and manipulative (McCrae & John 1992).

Neuroticism often refers to nervous, pessimistic, anxious, very emotional, and insecure individuals with the tendency to readily experience unpleasant emotions, such as anger, depression, or vulnerability (Costa & McCrae 1992).

Affect, in psychology, is a generic term to describe a wide range of phenomena, including emotion, mood and feeling (Cohen & Areni 1991). It is seen as summarising those feelings that are consciously accessible (Pearce 2009). One's affective response is effectively a general ongoing subjective experience which refers to the entirety of the concept (Russell & Barrett 1999). For the purpose of this study, affect is seen to be conceptually distinct from emotion; in general, it arises from cumulative occurrences of transient emotional states. Similarly, *affective responses* are conceptualised to be the summations of emotional happenings in this study.

PANAS represents the positive affect (PA) and negative affect (NA) schedule, consisting of 20 single-word items, *excited*, *alert*, *determined*, *interested*, *attentive*, *enthusiastic*, *inspired*, *proud*, *active*, and *strong* for positive affect, and *upset*, *guilty*, *distressed*, *ashamed*, *hostile*, *irritable*, *nervous*, *scared*, *afraid* and *jittery* for negative affect (Watson, Clark & Tellegen 1988). Affective responses are conceptualised as positive affective response (often interchangeable with positive affect in this study) and negative affective response (often interchangeable with negative affect in this study).

Tourist satisfaction refers to an affective state that is the emotional reaction to travel experiences (Spreng, MacKenzie & Olshavsky 1996). The current study conceptualises tourist satisfaction as a summative overall construct, adopting the affective approach to assess mainland Chinese package tourists' holistic satisfaction with Australia as a destination.

Chinese outbound tourism in this research specifically refers to mainland Chinese outbound tourism; accordingly, Chinese outbound tourists in this book are confined to mainland Chinese outbound tourists.

Organisation of This Book

This book is composed of eight chapters. As an introductory chapter to the whole study, Chapter 1 provides the research background and justification for the study, and then proceeds to shed light on the overall purposes and specific objectives of the study. It also addresses the research strategy and the significance of the study from the perspectives of theoretical contributions. Conceptual definitions of terms regarding the major constructs and variables in the study are presented at the end of this chapter. Chapter 2 provides an overview of Chinese outbound tourism development, highlighting mainland Chinese outbound travel to Australia. Furthermore, it discusses the practical significance of the study. Chapter 3 reviews the literature relevant to Chinese outbound tourism research, personality, affect, and satisfaction as well as both personality-affect and affect-satisfaction relationships independently. It also illustrates the development of the proposed conceptual framework and presents the hypothesised relationships between the research constructs. Chapter 4 provides an overview of research design and methods. A sequential mixed-method approach is employed to collect both qualitative and quantitative data through the focus group interview and the questionnaire survey respectively. Based on the description of the qualitative data collection and analysis procedures, Chapter 5 reports the qualitative study findings to identify Chinese group tourists' salient positive and negative affective responses during their trip to Australia. Chapter 6 elaborates on the quantitative investigation implemented in this study. SEM analysis is employed to examine how tourist personality, coupled with experience-engendered affective responses, influence tourist satisfaction. It reports the results following each step of the data analysis procedures, and presents the results of hypothesis testing. Chapter 7 discusses and interprets major findings of the study. Theoretical contributions and practical implications are evaluated in Chapter 8 to highlight the significance of this research, and it concludes with a summary of the study in terms of the five research objectives. Limitations of the study and suggestions for future research are also addressed.

2

Mainland Chinese Outbound Tourism Development

This chapter commences with the research background to contextualize the overall research problem, which is followed by the practical justifications for the book. It provides an outline of mainland Chinese outbound tourism development, highlighting mainland Chinese outbound travel to Australia. Furthermore, it discusses the practical significance of the study.

Overview of Chinese Outbound Tourism

Since the implementation of the economic reform and the opening-up policy in 1978, mainland China's economy has achieved a great leap forward over the recent three decades, which results in the rising levels of Chinese residents' discretionary income and living standards. On the other hand, the strategy of the China National Tourism Administration (CNTA) for outbound tourism was adjusted in 2005 from tight restriction to normative regulation (Xie & Li 2009). With a view to regulating outbound tourist flow, the Chinese government extended the Approved Destination Status (ADS) system to foreign countries and regions as destinations for Chinese citizens. To date, China has become a major tourist-generating market with 150 countries/areas listed in the ADS scheme and over 120 ADS agreements being in effect. Influenced by these major accelerators, mainland Chinese outbound tourism has developed from scratch, and evolved through a process from tours for visiting friends and relatives (VFR) in Hong Kong and Macao, to cross-border tours, and to self-financed travel to long-haul destination countries (Du & Dai 2005); the purpose of outbound tourism progressed from VFR travel to business travel and then to sightseeing and leisure travel. In general, Chinese outbound tourism (COT) follows an organized, planned, and controlled policy as appropriate principles of development (Zhang 2006), taking a path different from those in developed countries, and spanning a continuum from politics-oriented to economy-centered, and eventually to market-driven practices.

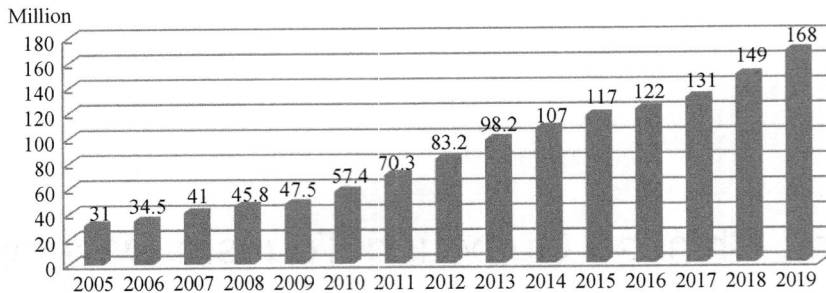

Figure 2.1　Growth of Chinese Outbound Travel Market（2005－2019）

Data Source：CNTA（2006－2020）.

The global marketplace of tourism has witnessed a rapid development of COT after the turn of the century. As illustrated in Figure 2.1, the volume of overseas trips by Chinese travellers has grown from 31 million in 2005 to 168 million in 2019, which has grown more than fivefold. The United Nations World Tourism Organization (UNWTO) forecast that by 2020, China would become the fourth largest source market in the world, generating 100 million tourist arrivals worldwide (UNWTO 2001). However, it reached that target well in 2014. According to the China Tourism Academy (CTA)'s latest forecast, the number of overseas trips by Chinese travellers is estimated to rise to 200 million annually by 2020 (China Daily 2013). Many countries have recognized the boom of COT and identified China as a key market in their national strategic plans for inbound tourism development, not only in terms of the number of tourist arrivals by Chinese travellers, but also because of the volume of Chinese tourists' overseas consumption. Overtaking both the second largest spender United States and the top spender Germany ranked in 2011, China became the top international tourism spender in the world in 2012, with the tourists' overseas expenditure surging to a record of 102 billion US dollars, a remarkable year-on-year increase of 40 percent (UNWTO 2013b). In 2013, Chinese outbound tourists contributed 120 billion US dollars to the prosperity of the global tourism industry, an increase of 20 percent over the previous year (CTA 2014). In 2018, the figure soared into 277.3 billion US dollars. Thus, China has been elevated to the position as the undisputed biggest global outbound tourism source market, contributing enormously to the development of global tourism as a whole.

Evolution of Chinese Outbound Tourism

With its remarkable achievements, COT has established a successful paradigm which may have significant implications for other countries. A reflexive and evaluative review of its development is presented to accentuate some distinctive Chinese characteristics which are not readily explainable using the established tourism theories and law of development. So far, the development of COT can be summarized into four phases.

The initial development phase (1983–1996) was characterized by the dynamics of strong political orientation and partial economic consideration. The beginning of COT can be traced back to the year of 1983 when Guangdong Provincial Travel Corporation experimented with organizing tours for visiting relatives in Hong Kong. In 1984, the State Council approved the organization of VFR tours to Hong Kong and Macao for mainland Chinese residents, which was regarded as the prelude to the outbound tourism among Chinese citizens. In November 1987, CNTA and the Ministry of Foreign Trade and Economic Cooperation gave sanction to eligible travel agencies in Dandong, a border city in Liaoning Province, to operate day trips to the border city of Sinuiju in the Democratic People's Republic of Korea. It represented the beginning of travelling to border areas for Chinese citizens. In the wake of this successful attempt, border regions such as Heilongjiang, Inner Mongolia, Liaoning, Jilin, Xinjiang, Yunnan, and Guangxi were authorized to operate cross-border travel respectively with the Russian Federation, Mongolia, Burma, Vietnam, and other neighbouring countries. Early travel to foreign countries by Chinese citizens was approved exclusively for visiting relatives as well. In 1988, the State Council sanctioned Chinese citizens' travel to Thailand for visiting relatives, provided that their relatives would provide a guarantee for them and pay for their expenses. Two years later, Singapore and Malaysia were added to the list. Such a regulation aimed at preventing the outflow of scarce foreign currency. In 1995, the ADS scheme was adopted by the Chinese government to approve eligible foreign countries and regions as destinations for Chinese citizens. Only licensed travel agencies were entitled to organize outbound group package tours to the ADS countries, with a fixed quota annually. This practise liberalized and yet still restricted Chinese citizens' travelling overseas. In summary, such an early stage of outbound travel market was dominated by tourists for visiting relatives and friends, as well as delegations and study groups, with a record of only five million overseas trips in 1996.

The second phase (1997–2004), known as the early rapid growth stage with a balanced mix of being both politically- and economically-governed, witnessed the gradual and cautious relaxation of the government control over COT, as evidenced by the number of Chinese outbound tourists amounting to approximately 29 million in 2004. On 1 July 1997, having been approved by the State Council, "Provisional Measures on the Administration of Self-financed Outbound Travel by Chinese Citizens" was jointly promulgated by CNTA and the Ministry of Public Security, thereby officially inaugurating the outbound travel by Chinese citizens (WTO 2003; Arlt 2006). China's strategies for tourism market development were defined as "vigorously developing inbound travel, actively developing domestic travel, and moderately developing outbound travel". In practical terms, outbound tourism in China received the government's approval to proceed, albeit in a planned-and-controlled course. Additionally, the State Council issued "Measures of Having Days Off for Annual Festivals and Commemoration

Days" in 1999, which promoted the formation of three gold week-long holidays (Spring Festival, May Day, and National Day). Supplemented by the practice of giving two days off a week since 1995, these measures enabled Chinese citizens to enjoy more leisure time both locally and abroad. Similarly, some enterprises in mainland China began to organize overseas package tours as incentives for their customers and employees, which further facilitated the development of outbound tourism. In such circumstances, holiday economy gradually developed into a more balanced tourism economy. On the other hand, China's accession to the World Trade Organization and the deeper integration into the global economy in 2001, known as an epoch-making landmark in China's reform and opening-up, have proved to be pivotal in contributing to the country's economic development. All these factors provided the necessary preconditions for the development of COT: increasing disposable income, the loosening of travel restrictions, sufficient leisure time, and the acquired wish of Chinese people to see the world through travelling abroad. During this period, outbound tourism was neither advocated nor restricted (Mak 2013). The organized package tour became the predominant travel pattern among all Chinese outbound leisure travellers. Outbound tourists were allowed to exchange Chinese currency only for those of ADS countries in order to control the outflow of foreign currency. In conclusion, the second phase is characterized by the transition from political-oriented to economic-centred policy practices regarding the evolution of COT.

COT's early development culminated with the advent of the new guidelines for Chinese tourism development issued by the CNTA on August 18, 2005, thus marking the third development phase (2005–2010). The CNTA modified China's strategic priorities for tourism market development into " comprehensively developing domestic travel, actively developing inbound travel, and methodically developing outbound travel". More exactly, the policy for outbound tourism development was shifted from " control or restriction" to " standardization or regulation" (Zhang 2006, p. 8), which has been deemed to be a milestone of great significance ushering in COT's " leap forward" in development. Acknowledged as the burgeoning stage with social considerations in tourism over economic and political ends, these six years saw the accelerated development of COT, as evidenced by its gaining more experiences and broad scope in the global tourism market with Chinese outbound tourists surging from 31 million in 2005 to more than 57 million in 2010. Liberalization of international travel restrictions can be well documented by the simplified bureaucratic procedures in obtaining private passports in China as well as the macroscopic readjustment and control of foreign currency exchange. On one hand, Chinese residents in big or medium cities have been able to apply for private passports with their ID cards and residence booklets since 2005. On the other hand, the State Administration of Foreign Exchange launched a series of new policies to relax limitations on mainland Chinese citizens' exchange for hard currency. In addition, on 21 July 2005, the government allowed Renminbi to discreetly appreciate by 2. 1 percent, which served as another financial stimulus to outbound tourism (McKinnon 2007). Since 2006, UnionPay, a bankcard association in China, has extended its coverage to Asia-Pacific Region, Europe, Americas, and Australia. It allowed Chinese tourists greater ease in consuming goods and services abroad, thus facilitating the growth of COT (China UnionPay 2013). With 34. 52 million outbound tourists annually in 2006, China emerged as one of the fastest growing outbound markets in the world and the largest one in Asia-Pacific Region. In response to balancing cooperation in trade and culture with other nations as well as fulfilling Chinese citizens' growing wanderlust to explore foreign lands, China had signed up for the ADS scheme with all developed countries by the end of 2010, which further indicated COT's incremental influence on the global tourism industry. It can also be attributed to the relaxation of visa regulations by many destination countries, and especially to the favourable social environment in China, such as "improvements in education literacy and popularity of information technology" (Mak 2013, p. 20). Therefore, COT within this period started to function properly to serve socio-cultural ends more than economic and political ones in its development agendas.

The fourth phase (2011 to the present), known as a market-driven development stage with the public support by the government, witnessed another breakthrough in the development of COT, as characterized by its growing sophistication and further segmentation in the existing markets. With a broad geographical coverage worldwide of the ADS countries, China generated 70. 3 million, 83. 2 million and 98. 2 million outbound tourists respectively in 2011, 2012 and 2013. Advancing from the quantitative growth to its qualitative development, it has been deemed to be the second wave of COT (Arlt 2013). With the liberation of individual travel schemes to more destination countries, combined with the influence of Western values on Chinese people, this wave has been fuelled by the "new Chinese tourists" (NCTs) who, with their increasing travel-savvy, prefer individual travel to group tours. A growing number of affluent NCTs look for experiences and individuality rather than sightseeing merely through the inclusive package tours; a substantial proportion of NCTs may have lived or studied abroad before, which boosts their confidence in exploring and experiencing exotic cultures more than just a snapshot. Similarly, China's increasing number of outbound travellers has attracted overseas tourist destinations to aggressively promote their tourism products and services in the Chinese market, which can also serve as a powerful pulling factor to Chinese tourists. Stimulated by these promotional campaigns, Chinese tour operators have been focusing on the niche market and designing special interest products to cater to more sophisticated demand from NCTs. In addition, particular attention has been paid to Chinese tourists' conspicuous consumption abroad. Chinese travellers, called "walking wallets" by some Westerners, set an astounding record of expenditure on the luxury goods during the 2012 London Olympics. Consequently, the term "Peking Pound" was coined to represent Chinese spending power

(China Daily 2014). Recently in 2013, the State Council issued "the Outline for National Tourism and Leisure (2013 – 20)", which is bound to facilitate the development of COT by institutionalizing the taking of paid annual leave and allowing Chinese citizens more freedom and flexibility of where and when to travel (China Daily 2013). Significantly, it has marked COT's embarking on a new era in its national agenda. With the accelerating trend of globalization and the popularity of information technology, Chinese tourists' propensity to travel abroad is expected to continue rising in the coming decades.

As a late mover in the global outbound tourism industry, the rapid development of COT can be attributed to following three dimensions: substantial economic growth, gradual political liberalisation, and sociocultural enhancement (TRA 2013; UNWTO 2013b). Specifically, unprecedented economic growth has resulted in the improved living standards of Chinese people and a rising number of Chinese middle class with higher disposable incomes; other economic factors involve appreciation of Renminbi, a huge trade surplus, and foreign exchange reserves. Political factors are closely related to the growing support by Chinese government for outbound tourism (Zhang & Heung 2002), including the relaxation of restrictions on foreign travel, improved world situation and bilateral diplomatic relationship, and easier access to passports, visas, and hard currency. Social factors include rapid urbanisation, long-term accumulated outbound tourism demand, improved literacy and widespread information technology (Mak 2013), the strong desire to travel around the world as a way to broaden horizons, and increasing leisure and the extension of paid holidays (UNWTO 2013b).

In summary, strong evidence shows that the government has played a crucial role in promoting the COT development. In return, the development of COT in the past three decades has made a far-reaching impact on the establishment of the globalized market economy system in China, as well as the advancement of better international understanding and world peace. The development pattern of COT, coupled with its multiple roles in China's social, economic and political arenas, has significantly enriched the world tourism knowledge base.

Approved Destination Status (ADS) Scheme

The overarching purpose of this section is to provide a general overview of the ADS scheme and to shed light on the unique role which it has been playing in the development of COT. The ADS scheme is based on a bilateral tourism arrangement whereby the Chinese government approves selected foreign countries and regions as destinations for self-financed Chinese citizens to undertake guided package leisure tour in groups with a special visa. ADS agreements embrace a strict regulatory framework that governs many facets of travel arrangements including passport application, visa processing, tour group itineraries, supervision of tourists, and destination marketing (Herrmann & Dang 2009). For instance, only ADS countries can be publicly organized or promoted as a destination for tourism groups in the Chinese market. However, this restriction does not have a bearing on the individual Chinese passport holder who can be free to travel abroad as long as he or she has sufficient financial resources and the individual tourist visa granted by the destination countries.

The ADS regime was initially introduced partly as a means of cautiously guarding the growth of COT, and particularly monitoring foreign exchange leakage. Therefore, the Chinese government originally imposed stringent controls on the approval of ADS recipient countries. It has been indicated that a country can be granted ADS and thereby be entitled to receive Chinese leisure travellers in groups on the premise that she must abide by the following seven guidelines: 1) the country should generate outbound tourists to China; 2) the country should maintain a favorable political relationship with China; 3) the country should have attractive tourist resources and suitable facilities for Chinese travellers; 4) the safety of Chinese travellers, together with freedom from discrimination, should be guaranteed; 5) the country should be easily accessible from China by transportation; 6) the expenditure of tourists from the destination country in China should be balanced with the counterpart of Chinese tourists in that country; 7) the number of tourists from the destination country and from China should only increase reciprocally (Arlt 2006; Guo, Kim & Timothy 2007). These preconditions were proposed to ensure that tourists could be exchanged on an equal basis so that neither side would suffer from any economic loss. Notably, the last two conditions were obviously impractical, thus demonstrating the Chinese government's intention of controlling the leakage of capital and foreign currency by implementing the ADS scheme. This is aligned with China's strategy of developing outbound tourism moderately at the preliminary stage of COT.

Table 2.1 Number of ADS Countries/Regions, 1983－2013

Year	Number of ADS Countries/Regions
1983	2
1990	5
1992	6
1999	9
2000	14
2002	19
2004	63
2005	108
2007	132
2009	134
2010	139
2011	140
2012	146
2013	150

Data Source: CNTA (2014). The Yearbook of China Tourism Statistics

As shown in the Table 2.1, the number of ADS countries and regions in the chronological sequence, the ADS scheme served as a major instrument for the Chinese government to implement its organized, planned, and controlled policy, known as the general guideline for the development of COT (Zhang 2006). Organized indicates that mainland Chinese residents must be organized in groups when they travel to any destination countries for leisure purposes; planned signifies that outbound tourism development should be planned in order to monitor its scale and keep it balanced with the development of both inbound and domestic tourism; controlled shows that the Chinese government will take a firm grip on the volume of outbound tourism, and that a quota system is established for the number of tourists permitted to visit each of countries with ADS.

Chinese citizens were first allowed to visit Hong Kong and Macao in 1983 for the sole purpose of visiting relatives and friends. Then the ADS system was introduced in 1995 as an attempt to restrict the number of Chinese tourists spending hard currency abroad. However, it was not until 1997 that Chinese outbound leisure tourism was officially recognised. In the same year following this historical milestone, the first ADS agreement with Australia and New Zealand was signed up, for their seemingly closer economic and diplomatic relationship with China. As the first Western destinations approved for ADS, Australia and New Zealand started to host Chinese leisure groups in 1999. It was regarded as the development milestone of the ADS scheme for its expansion beyond South-east Asia. ADS allowed Tourism Australia, on behalf of the Australian government, to promote Australia as a leisure travel destination in China, consequently contributing to a large increase in the number of Chinese tourists. The success story of the ADS between China and Australia provided other countries with the practical implications of a signed bilateral ADS agreement. Subsequently, Malta, albeit without large overseas Chinese communities, followed suit and became the first European country to implement ADS in May 2002, to be followed by Egypt, Turkey, Germany, South Africa and many more, in hopes of attracting the flood of Chinese outbound tourists. Most European countries were granted ADS in 2004. Although the majority of Chinese tourists would choose the USA as their preferential destination for outbound travel (Cai, O'Leary & Boger 2000), it was not until the year of 2008 that the Chinese government signed up for an ADS agreement with the US counterpart. It can be attributed to the fact that the Chinese government may use the ADS policy in the political and diplomatic arenas to diminish her foreign trade conflicts and issues with other countries. In 2010, China signed the ADS agreement with Canada, which recorded that all developed countries were on the list of ADS. So far, China has become the top tourist-generating market with 150 countries/areas listed in the ADS scheme and over 120 countries have implemented ADS agreements with China. It indicates that Chinese tourists can travel freely to most major tourist destinations in the world. The boom of Chinese outbound tourists all over the world has convinced the international communities of China's economic growth as well as its comprehensive national strength.

Acknowledged as an unprecedented tourism policy in the world, the ADS scheme is adopted to approve the signed country as the destination for the Chinese leisure travellers. It is an innovation of China's outbound tourism policy in the specific period (Zhang 2006). The unique feature of the ADS scheme is selective and this mechanism underlying itself is a paradox, liberalizing yet restricting. Motivated by Chinese citizens' increasing appetite for outbound tourism, China has been developing the ADS scheme to liberalize travel restrictions on its citizens' outbound global mobility, whilst simultaneously maintaining the control over the mobility of its citizens via a strict regulatory ADS framework. This preferential and incremental mechanism has profited both ADS countries and China economically. The ADS regime has facilitated the rapid development of COT, which makes China stand out as the most eye-catching force in terms of the global tourism economy. The four practical benefits of the ADS agreement are listed as follows: 1) ADS visa applications would be preliminarily assessed and eventually submitted by designated Chinese travel agencies on behalf of all members of a tour group, so the travellers do not have to visit the embassies or consulates and save all the paper works themselves. In the meantime, this has dramatically decreased the administrative workload and expenses concerned with assessing visa application; 2) for travelling to ADS countries, private passports can be used and hard currency can be exchanged; 3) the time for the visa acquisition can be reduced. The visa is issued within 48 hours versus 15 working days by the non-ADS tourist visa; 4) there is no need any more for Chinese citizens to travel abroad in the disguise of visiting business partners or attending fairs.

Apart from above-mentioned economic and practical benefits, the ADS scheme, since its inception, aims to enhance positive political and diplomatic relations between destination countries and China, and to limit illegal immigration. It is commonly agreed that the ADS means more than economic interests. In fact, it has also been employed as political and diplomatic leverage to reward or sanction countries in international relations. It should be noted that the ADS is awarded to countries that are politically friendly to China and without discriminatory policies toward Chinese tourists. The successful operation of the scheme for nearly two decades has contributed to favourable diplomatic relations between ADS countries and China. In general, the ADS mechanism can be adopted as the carrot-and-stick approach for the Chinese government to negotiate and authorize tourism arrangements so as to gain political advantage. With China's establishment of the world's top outbound tourism market, China will influence the shaping of the structure of the global tourism industry. It is understood that the Chinese government utilizes granting ADS to a country as a concession to support the applicant country. In return, China may gain more political favours from applicant countries to build up its national "soft power" in the international political arena. It has been claimed that ADS excluded countries that maintained diplomatic relations with Taiwan (Tse & Hobson 2008). This political act of China regarding the "Taiwan issue" can best exemplify its use of the ADS regime as a tool in handling its diplomatic and international relations with other countries.

The global tourism market witnessed the flood of Chinese tourists in the past decade, for the ADS scheme facilitates the travel of organised tour groups from China to the approved destination countries. Since the advent of the ADS agreement, there has been a big concern raised by some ADS recipient countries about how to minimize the rate of overstaying and especially the risk of the attempted illegal immigration in the host country. Joint efforts in immigration control can be seen from both governmental agencies and non-governmental organizations. For the receiving countries, only the group visa applications from China's authorized travel agencies can be accepted for further processing. ADS visas were valid only for the duration of the group tour with no possibility of extension or status change upon arriving in the host country. For the Chinese government, special emphasis has been laid on this issue to achieve a favourable international image. Only authorized travel agencies approved by the CNTA could operate overseas tour package to the ADS countries. A travel agency who has had too many overstayers is held accountable. As a punishment, they will be fined and their ADS may be revoked by the CNTA. In addition to government rules, Chinese travel agencies also develop their own controls to discourage overstays accordingly. Though not required by either government, Chinese travel agencies unilaterally require sizable monetary bonds from potential tourists to be refunded upon their return to China. Tour guides also keep the passports and tickets of tour members. On the other hand, the tour operators in the host countries will endeavor to monitor and supervise the conduct of tourists. The combination of formal and informal controls resulted in relatively few visa violations. Most importantly, with China's economy growing and living standards improving, there will be gradually fewer push factors for emigrating from China in an illegal way. Chinese tourists now constitute the most valuable source market for many ADS countries. Hence, for both sides, the ADS scheme has been recognized as an unprecedented success.

As for the ADS agreement, major considerations were given to political, diplomatic(Zhang 2006; Huang 2010) and economic areas (Mak 2013). Although the Chinese government may use the ADS agreement to exert diplomatic pressure, it is still subject to demands by its citizens to maintain its openness to international tourism. One of China's objectives in developing the ADS scheme was to stimulate and promote the internationalization of Chinese society. Allowing overseas travel increases the exposure of Chinese people to other cultures and enhances China's integration into the global community. With the improvement of the bilateral relationship and establishment of mutual confidence, efforts should be made to further facilitate travels among the

ADS countries. Obviously, from a long-term perspective, the ADS scheme is only a transitional measure. Once the majority of the world countries are granted the ADS, the function of the ADS arrangement would lose its original significance and the scheme itself obsolete.

Mainland Chinese Outbound Travel to Australia

The ADS scheme was extended to Australia in 1999, and Australia, together with New Zealand, became the first approved Western destination where Chinese citizens were allowed to travel on private passports for leisure group holidays. At the initial stage, as stipulated in the agreement, only 39 Chinese travel agencies were authorized to organize and operate the outbound group travel to Australia (Arlt 2006). Additionally, from 1999 to June 2004, the validity of the ADS agreement between China and Australia was limited to travellers from three designated cities only, i. e. Beijing, Shanghai and Guangzhou. In July 2004, it was expanded to cover residents living in the nine approved regions of Beijing, Shanghai, Guangdong, Tianjin, Hebei, Shandong, Jiangsu, Zhejiang, and Chongqing. Since August 2006, the ADS group travel to Australia has been fully opened to Chinese citizens. Overall, the ADS agreement between China and Australia has liberalised mutual visits, boosted tourist exchanges, and strengthened cultural cooperation, thus contributing to the sound development of the bilateral relationship between the two countries.

Despite the decline in Chinese visitor arrivals in 2003 and in 2008 arising from the outbreak of SARS and other influenza, Figure 2. 2 has shown the pronounced development of COT to Australia in the past 15 years. Specifically, Chinese visitors jumped from 190,000 in 2002 to 626,000 in 2012, recording an annual compound growth rate of 13 per cent (TRA 2013); in 2012, China surpassed the United Kingdom to become Australia's second largest inbound market in terms of visitor arrivals after New Zealand and the largest market for total expenditure with a spending of $ 4. 17 billion. The majority of growth in Chinese visitors has occurred in the last decade and China became the top source of international visitors to Australia according to the annual statistical report of 2017 − 2018, overtaking New Zealand. Visitor arrivals from China rose to 1,430,000 in 2018 − 2019, a fourfold increase since 2009. Chinese visitors contributed about A $12 billion to the Australian economy. The average spend per Chinese trip was A$9,235, forming a marked contrast to A$5,943 for Germans, A$5,219 for Americans, A$4,614 for Japanese, and A$A2,032 for New Zealanders. International tourism accounts for about a quarter of Australia's total tourism market. That means, in the greater scheme of things, Chinese travellers help create 0. 6% of Australia's annual GDP in 2018 − 2019. China has progressively become and will remain Australia's most valuable inbound market for the next decade.

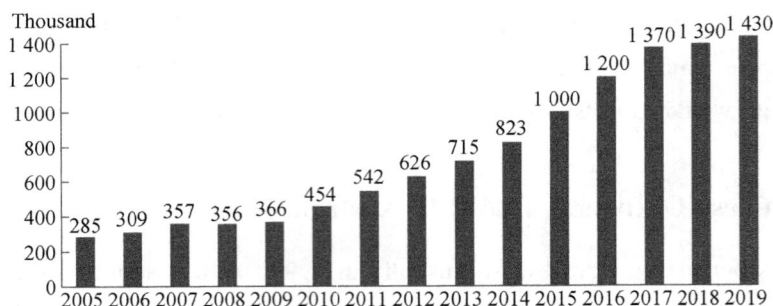

Figure 2.2 History of Visitors from China into Australia (2005 – 2019)

Data Source: Australian Bureau of Statistics (2020).

The following features have been identified from the recent profile of Chinese tourists to Australia. The period ranging from December to February (Christmas, the New Year, and the Spring Festival) tends to be the traditional peak season for Chinese outbound travellers to Australia. After that, there will be a sharp drop in the number of Chinese travel groups to Australia from March to June. However, there is also another high season in July and August for Chinese parents to take school students to travel in Australia. In general, the 45 – 59 demographic was the largest Chinese visitor segment to Australia; the group travel remains the prevailing segment in the market, particularly for those first-time visitors to Australia, while the free independent travel (FIT) and semi-FIT continue to increase as many Chinese tourists are becoming more experienced and sophisticated in travel product selection. 2018 saw an increase of 11.6 per cent in total visitor arrivals from China as compared to 2016. Among them, 74 per cent were for a leisure segment (55 per cent for holiday and 19 per cent for VFR), 17 per cent for education, 4 per cent for business, 2 per cent for employment, and 3 per cent for other purposes (see Figure 2.3). The changing composition of travellers can be evidenced by the fact that business traveller arrivals experienced a decline of 6.8 per cent, while the share of leisure and private travel increased. It has been noted that repeat visitors accounted for 47 per cent of total visitors. Having visited Australia previously, they would seek more unique experience rather than joining in a standard group tour.

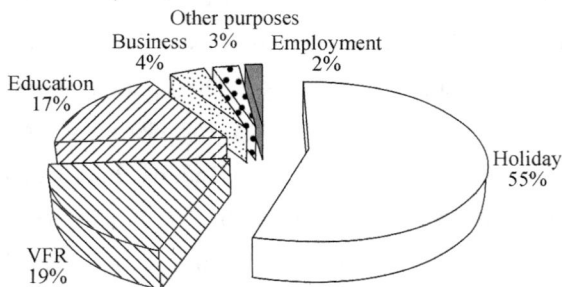

Figure 2.3 Composition of Chinese Visitors by the Purpose of Their Visit in 2018

Data Source: Tourism Research Australia(2019).

There are many reasons why Australia is selected as the destination of Chinese outbound tourists for this study. As a tourist destination, Australia enjoys great popularity not only for its beautiful natural environment, spectacular coastal scenery, and interesting local wildlife, but also for its food and wine experiences, unique multicultural environment, and niche activities including surfing, diving, hot air ballooning, fishing and golf (Huang & Gross 2010). In the range of travel experiences provided by Australia, the focus on the affective dimension in the concept of satisfaction is particularly relevant given that the majority of activities are based upon the tourists' involvement in and experience with nature-based tourism (Chhetri, Arrowsmith & Jackson 2004). Australia has proved to be one of Chinese travellers' most favoured tourist destinations, particularly for its good value for money and large overseas Chinese community, as well as its positive diplomatic relationship with China; the visa application procedures for Chinese visitors to Australia have been improved to be more flexible, simplified and service-orientated (Arlt 2006). Besides, Australia's being situated in the southern hemisphere provides Chinese visitors with opportunities to experience the season opposite to that of their residences. Australia, as an English-speaking country, is attractive to Chinese tourists who are open-minded and willing to experience western culture and lifestyle, totally different from their home environment. All these factors can serve as the pull factors for Chinese leisure travellers.

According to the results of an international visitor survey by Tourism Australia, the top five trip attributes that Chinese visitors value most are Australia's unspoilt natural environment, a laid-back and easy-going lifestyle, iconic attractions (Sydney Opera House, the Great Barrier Reef, koalas and kangaroos), good food and wine, and friendly and open locals. In the last decade, Tourism Australia was dedicated to utilizing traditional travel advertising and powerful social media to deliver genuine word of mouth (WOM) with a particular focus on the Chinese group leisure tourists. Two marketing campaigns launched successively by Tourism Australia, "Where the bloody hell are you?" and "There's nothing like Australia", have been tailored to specific Australian locations and distinctive experiences. Influenced by these communication and promotional strategies, many Chinese travellers would use the online resources to research and plan their trips to Australia, such as official tourism websites, specialized travel websites, and social networking websites like Tencent Weixin, Sina Weibo, Sina Blog, and Renren. It is noteworthy that the use of online sources by the Chinese travellers is well above the average among all the international visitors. They also seek recommendations from their friends and relatives who have previously visited or have been living in Australia. Besides, travel agents are still an important source of information, especially for first-time travellers to Australia. Chinese travelling in a group under an ADS visa must book their tours through an approved ADS travel agent. The majority of package tours are organized and operated by Aussie Specialist Travel Agents, while some customised travel products can also be booked through online travel agencies, such as Ctrip. com and Tuniu. com. Therefore, there is a growing trend toward FIT or semi-FIT in Chinese outbound market to Australia, with travel agents providing visas, flights and accommodations and travellers arranging the rest of their holidays themselves.

As a "must visit" holiday destination, Australia ranks high on the Chinese traveller's desired destination list. However, Australia's share of Chinese outbound travel has "decreased from one per cent in 2002 to 0.7 per cent in 2012" (TRA 2013, p. 13), partly because of the extensive popularity of other two long-haul destinations among Chinese citizens, i. e. the USA and Europe. Recognising the potential of Chinese outbound market and the increased competition amongst destinations for Chinese travellers, Tourism Australia has implemented its geographic strategy to expand market share not only in primary cities of Beijing, Shanghai and Guangzhou but also in secondary cities which include Chengdu, Chongqing, Hangzhou, Nanjing, Qingdao, Tianjin, Shenyang, Shenzhen, Suzhou, Wuhan, and Xiamen. The current marketing and distribution will have covered up to 30 cities by the end of 2020 (Tourism Australia 2012). In alignment with its geographic strategy, Tourism Australia provided funding support to Chinese carrier partners as both China Eastern and Sichuan Airlines launched new routes to make additional direct flights between Chinese secondary cities and the existing destinations in Australia, such as Nanjing-Sydney and Chengdu-Melbourne. Consequently, following a robust 2011 with growth of 52 per cent, capacity from China to Australia increased 16 per cent in 2012. As Australia continues to win market share of total capacity from China, its competitiveness as a long-haul destination will be enhanced.

The researcher has also analyzed the different Australian tourism products and services provided by the major nationwide outbound tour operators in China, e. g. China Travel Service (CTS), China International Travel Service (CITS), and China Youth Travel Service (CYTS), some major local outbound tour operators, e. g. Nanjing Zhongbei Friendship Travel Service (NZFTS), Shanghai Citic Travel Service (SCTS), and Jiangsu Sainty Travel Service (JSTS), and online travel agencies, e. g. Ctrip, Qunar, and Tuniu. In summary, Chinese tourists generally prefer tour packages involving multi-destinations for the first time visit to Australia. For the long-haul outbound travel, they take short breaks among different destinations and tend to have a schedule packed with activities. The duration of package tours to Australia varied from 6 to 12 days and their price ranged from RMB 6,999 to RMB 19,800 before the introduction of the new China Tourism Law on 1 October 2013. The itineraries for Chinese travel groups were mainly along the east coast of Australia. A comprehensive assessment of Australia's current destination appeal revealed that the top five appealing destinations to Chinese travellers covered Sydney, Gold Coast, Tropical North Queensland (Cairns), Melbourne, and Kangaroo Island (Tourism Australia 2013a). All itineraries included a city, nature-based, beach or cultural and heritage, and indigenous experience. Chinese tourists ranked the most appealing Australian experiences in order of preference as follows: wildlife, beach / coastal / harbor, niche (surfing / diving / fishing / golf), food and wine, wilderness / rainforest, outback / indigenous, city and shopping experiences (Tourism Australia 2013a). Interestingly, many travellers from three primary cities are showing growing enthusiasm for FIT travel. Several tailor-made itineraries covering West Australia (Perth), South Australia (Adelaide), Tasmania (Hobart), Northern Territory (Darwin and Uluru), etc., are designed for those experienced FITs seeking individualized experiences than packaged holidays.

Recognising the importance of the Chinese market and its potential for further growth, Tourism Research Australia (TRA) undertook research into the antecedents and consequences of satisfaction among Chinese visitors with a view to ensuring the attractiveness of Australia's tourism offering to the Chinese market (TRA 2014). Wang and Davidson (2009) previously used an expectancy disconfirmation approach to examine Chinese leisure tourists' satisfaction across a range of tourism experiences, and found that food, shopping, and tour itinerary were areas where Australia underperformed on satisfaction. Whilst Wang and Davidson's approach is useful, this study considers tourist satisfaction from a different perspective. Pearce and Packer (2013) proposed that tourism provides a genuine situation in which psychological theories and concepts can be examined and corroborated. Based on the aforementioned information, it can be concluded that Chinese outbound tourism boasts a steady and healthy growth, thus producing a rich and broad context for testing two underlying psychological forces (i. e. personality traits and affective responses) in determining the formation of overall tourist satisfaction. This study examines such psychological variables as personality and affect that influence Chinese outbound tourists' overall satisfaction with Australia. It could have practical implications for other destination countries that plan to tap into the Chinese outbound tourism market. Such a study is also conducive to the sustainable development of Australian tourism.

Practical Significance of the Study

In tourism, the overall satisfaction with a destination is a summary of satisfactory states accumulated over various individual experiences. However, measuring tourist experience and evaluating tourist satisfaction are challenging and difficult, as tourist experience takes place in phases (e. g. trip planning, travel to and from the destination, the destination experience). Although there is a voice that an understanding of satisfaction with each aspect of the trip must be the basic parameter used to evaluate overall satisfaction with the destination, most satisfaction studies in tourism have been conducted after the travel experience and looked into overall opinions expressed by tourists regarding the general tourist experience. Similarly, numerous travel experiences can collectively contribute to the travellers' overall satisfaction. This viewpoint has been empirically evidenced by Neal & Gursoy (2008) who conducted a multifaceted analysis of tourism satisfaction and found that tourists' level of satisfaction or dissatisfaction with different phases of their travel experiences affect their overall satisfaction with travel and tourism services. Tourist satisfaction should be evaluated as a system process and researched from a multidimensional perspective. Not surprisingly, among the tourism literature, an assessment of tourist satisfaction has been attempted using various perspectives and theories. Therefore, the present study sought to systematically examine the primary antecedent variables which would determine or predict tourist satisfaction, specifically outbound tourists' overall satisfaction with a destination.

As extant research has failed to identify the psychological underpinnings of tourist satisfaction related to outbound tourism, this study aims to investigate two underlying psychological forces (i. e. personality traits and affective experiences of Chinese outbound tourists to Australia) that determine the formation of overall tourist satisfaction. In addition, the utility of employing the Five-Factor Model (FFM) and the conceptualization of positive and negative affect (PANAS approach) as an organizing structure for understanding how personality and affect impact satisfaction was tested. It proposes that the level of overall tourist satisfaction can be collectively influenced by tourist personality traits and affective responses triggered by their specific travel experiences. A conceptual framework is developed to delineate the interrelationships among tourist personality, affective responses, and tourist satisfaction. All proposed relationships were tested jointly by a structural equation model. The study is of practical significance since satisfaction can be a manageable process through personalized marketing efforts as well as affective experiences management efforts. The results of this study can be used to enhance knowledge and understanding of the psychological determinants of tourist satisfaction, providing a more effective means for segmenting the market and managing overall satisfaction.

From a practical perspective, a study on mainland Chinese visitors' satisfaction with Australia as a tourist destination is not only valuable to Australian tourism marketing and planning organisations, but also provides useful information to other destination countries who want to expand their market share of Chinese outbound travel. This study provides insights into the motivators of satisfaction and the causes of dissatisfaction among Chinese tourists; consequently, it could help Australian industry practitioners better understand Chinese visitors so that they can make appropriate decisions to target and attract this important market segment.

Specifically, this study provides practical contributions in the following respects. Firstly, different personality traits were found to have a positive or negative impact on tourists' affective responses associated with specific and holistic experiences of a travel trip. Linking the product features to tourist personality, tourism marketers need to provide Chinese travellers with some tailor-made tourism products and services designed to accommodate their varying needs and travel preferences. Secondly, identifying the underlying causes of generating positive or negative affective responses could help decision-makers adopt proactive measures to minimise the negative effects of these psychological factors, thereby resulting in the maximum satisfaction level.

Thirdly, if the interrelationships between personality, affect, and satisfaction are clarified, it would assist tourism marketers in developing appropriate tourism products and launching effective campaigns that will generate positive WOM, enhance tourist loyalty to destination, and eventually secure more repeat visitors. Since this study only included respondents who were first-time visitors to Australia, the findings would have great implications for Australian marketers, because these visitors' overall satisfaction with Australia would determine their intention to revisit. The profile of Chinese visitors to Australia in 2019 has indicated that repeat visitors account for 47% of total visitors. In the long term, Australia is likely to remain a destination for repeat visitations from mainland China among all ADS destinations due to its unspoilt natural environment and laid-back lifestyle, coupled with its close economic and political connections with China. To sum up, in today's competitive environment, industry practitioners would be able to better serve an emerging market if they have a better understanding of the market and target customers. Such knowledge would be of particular significance in identifying predictor variables of tourist satisfaction and developing more appropriate marketing strategies to suit individual personality orientation.

Chapter Synopsis

This chapter has presented a comprehensive review on the evolution of mainland Chinese outbound tourism, the Approved Destination Status (ADS) scheme, and in-depth analysis of mainland Chinese outbound travel to Australia. Tourism provides a genuine situation in which psychological theories and concepts can be examined and corroborated. Chinese outbound tourism boasts a steady and healthy growth, thus producing a rich and broad context for testing two underlying psychological forces (i. e. personality traits and affective responses) in determining the formation of overall tourist satisfaction. This study examines the impact of personality traits and affective responses on Chinese outbound tourists' overall satisfaction with Australia. It is not only valuable to the sustainable development of Australian tourism, but also conducive to other destination countries who want to expand their market share of Chinese outbound travel.

3

Theoretical Foundations: Personality, Affect, and Satisfaction

This chapter provides a comprehensive review of the literature which underpins the study. It commences with a review of the development of outbound tourism from China which provides the contextual background for the research. It subsequently presents a detailed discussion of the three key research constructs, i. e. personality, affect, and satisfaction. Personality research in tourism and hospitality has drawn on theories from psychology and measurements as used in consumer behaviour. The next section differentiates affect from the other related concept of emotions, explaining the way the term affective responses is conceptualised in this study. It provides a rationale for the selection of the positive and negative affect schedule (PANAS) among all other approaches to conceptualising and operationalising emotion/affect, and then focuses on the PANAS literature and the underlying theories. It also provides a systematic review of the application of emotions/ affect in tourism studies. Stemming from theories about satisfaction in marketing and consumer behaviour, the use of satisfaction in tourism studies is subsequently reviewed.

Based on a clear understanding of the three research constructs, the remainder of the chapter is devoted to a further review of the relevant literature pertaining to the interrelationships between personality and affect, and between affect and satisfaction in order to formulate research propositions and inform the conceptual framework underlying this study. More specifically, the objective of this chapter is to elaborate on the rationale for proposing 12 research hypotheses from the literature review, and to develop the structural model of how tourist personality and affective responses influence overall tourist satisfaction in this study. The scope of inquiry focuses on not only the existing tourism and marketing literature, but also the broader literature in general psychology, education, and sociology.

Chinese Outbound Tourism Research

In the past two decades, the global tourism marketplace has witnessed a burgeoning growth in outbound tourism from China—the Sleeping Tourism Giant as described by Hall (1997). China has been identified as a major tourist-generating market attracting research attention in the worldwide academia. With such an unprecedented growth of tourism, there are many emerging issues, challenges, and opportunities, many of which have global implications. Destination marketers are looking to academia for guidance on how best to respond to this opportunity. For instance, Australian tourism and hospitality practitioners frequently ask: What kind of experiences should be delivered to Chinese tourists to maximise their satisfaction? Many researchers have thus embarked on a series of studies with the main aim of enabling global destinations to gain a better understanding of Chinese outbound tourism and Chinese tourists' needs and consumer behaviour.

With the rapid growth of outbound tourism, the scope of academic studies on COT has developed from being scarce and sketchy (Cai, Boger & O'Leary 1999) to being abundant and diverse, covering issues such as the developmental characteristics of COT (Cai, Li & Knutson 2007; Guo, Kim & Timothy 2007), profiles of Chinese travellers (Kim, Cai & Jung 2004; Xiang 2013), travel motivations (Huang & Hsu 2005; Kau & Lim 2005; Li 2007), Chinese outbound tourists' attitudes and behaviours (Ryan & Zhang 2007; Sparks & Pan 2009; Hsu, Cai & Li 2010; Wang & Davidson 2010), destination image and preferences (Kim, Guo & Agrusa 2005; Chen & Tsai 2007; Chow & Murphy 2008; Huang & Gross 2010), and tourist satisfaction (Truong & King 2009; Wang & Davidson 2009; Song et al. 2011). A meta-review of research papers on COT published in English academic literature reveals five major review articles, summarised in Table 3.1 evaluating the existing COT research and advocating future research to be more concerned with the source market as well as COT's social impacts, legal and ethical aspects (Tse 2015).

Table 3.1   A Summary of Five Chinese Outbound Tourism Review Studies

Study	Review Period	No. of Papers	Sources of Papers	Topic of Review	Key Findings
Cai, Li & Knutson (2007) Research on China Outbound Market: A Meta-Review	1995 – 2006	30	20 top-ranked tourism & hospitality journals	China's outbound tourism market	Identifying three main research streams: market overview, destination specific from secondary data, and destination specific from primary consumer data; implications for future research

Continued

Study	Review Period	No. of Papers	Sources of Papers	Topic of Review	Key Findings
Keating & Kriz (2008) Outbound Tourism From China: Literature Review and Research Agenda	1996 – 2008	22	Eight academic online databases	Chinese outbound tourism; push factors; pull factors; internal moderators; external moderator; destination image & choice	Suggesting that a new model for travel planning be developed to capture the nuances of destination choice in the Chinese context; providing an agenda for future research
Tse (2015) A Review of Chinese Outbound Tourism Research and the Way Forward	1995 – 2013	80	Key online databases of 21 hospitality & tourism journals	Destination-related research; tourist-related research; source market related research	Advocating future Chinese outbound tourism research to be more concerned with the source market; the social impacts of Chinese outbound tourism on its own people and destinations; and its legal and ethical aspects
Keating, Huang, Kriz & Heung (2015) A Systematic Review of the Chinese Outbound Tourism Literature	1983 – 2012	148	Three premier tourism journals	Publication outlet; research themes; most prominent authors; evolutionary analysis	Three distinct stages: crawling out (1983 – 1992), scurrying about (1993 – 2002), and walking erect (2003 – 2012). COT will increasingly generate new theory within the broader international tourism domain
Jin & Wang (2016) Chinese Outbound Tourism Research: A Review	2000 – 2014	161	16 top tourism and hospitality journals	research scopes, methods and themes	Identifying current patterns and future trends: to shift from an advocacy stance to the sustainable and ethics platforms under research paradigms that are more fertile for cross-cultural research

China's Outbound Tourism (Arlt 2006) is the first book in English entirely devoted to the specific topic of COT. Based on an analytic framework under which COT can be studied, Arlt goes far beyond describing COT's development situation and providing the relevant statistics, and analyses the topic in a very comprehensive manner (Tse 2007), thus contributing to shaping the landscape of COT. Within the last decade, research has sought to understand COT in terms of diverse research themes. The meta-review of the existing academic inquiries reveals that research interests in the domain of COT research focus mainly on tourist behaviour.

One important topic of interest in tourist behaviour as a traveller-orientated research focus is to gauge Chinese outbound tourists' satisfaction with destinations or services. Several studies have investigated the satisfaction level of mainland Chinese visitors to Hong Kong (Heung 2000; Zhang & Chow 2004; Song et al. 2011). A review of literature shows that the majority of approaches view Chinese outbound tourists' satisfaction as a cognitive progress. For instance, based on the expectancy disconfirmation theory, Heung (2000) examined mainland Chinese travellers' satisfaction with hotel services in Hong Kong. Adopting the importance-performance analysis model, Zhang and Chow (2004) assessed the performance of Hong Kong's tour guides as perceived by mainland Chinese outbound visitors. Song et al. (2011) assessed Chinese tourists' satisfaction with three service sectors—hotel, retail, and local tour operators—in Hong Kong. Later, using the same tourist satisfaction index, Li et al. (2012) compared mainland Chinese tourists' satisfaction with Hong Kong and the United Kingdom as their travel destination. Following the traditional cognitive approach to tourist satisfaction evaluations, Wang and Davidson (2009) used the expectancy disconfirmation paradigm to examine Chinese leisure tourists' satisfaction across a range of tourism experiences in Australia. In addition, other studies analysed the visitor satisfaction of Chinese tourists to the Gold Coast in Australia (Li & Carr 2004), Singapore (Kau & Lim 2005), Taiwan (Lin & Lin 2006), Vietnam (Truong & King 2009), and Korea (Lee, Jeon & Kim 2011). Judging by the aforementioned studies on tourist satisfaction, they centre on measuring outbound Chinese tourists' satisfaction purely through a cognitive approach. A review of existing studies on Chinese outbound tourism reveals that little attention has been paid to either Chinese outbound tourists' satisfaction from an affective perspective or Chinese outbound tourists' overall satisfaction with a destination as determined by individual personality traits and affective responses as vital elements in destination marketing. This study thus endeavours to provide some insights into these questions.

Other topics of interest in tourist behaviour focus on research areas ranging from Chinese travellers' motivation (e.g. Ryan & Mo 2002; Pan & Laws 2003; Huang & Hsu 2005; Johanson 2008; Hua & Yoo 2011), Chinese outbound tourists' constraints or barriers to travelling outside the mainland (e.g. Hsu & Lam 2003; Sparks & Pan 2009; Li, Zhang, Mao & Deng 2011), travel expectations and preferences (e.g. Kim, Guo & Agrusa 2005; Chow & Murphy 2008; Agrusa, Kim & Wang 2011; Li et al. 2011), destination image and perceptions (e.g. Huang & Gross 2010; Wang & Davidson 2010; Hsu & Song 2012; Stepchenkova & Li 2012), and attitudes and behaviours (Ryan & Zhang 2007; Sparks & Pan 2009; Hsu, Cai & Li 2010; Wang & Davidson 2010). It is worthwhile noting that Ong and du Cros (2012), from a sociological perspective, identified nostalgia and aesthetics as Chinese backpackers' affective responses elicited by their travel experiences of visiting post-colonial Macau, instead of prompting anti-colonial feelings towards Macau's colonial past. Except this, most of studies related to the Chinese outbound tourists' travel behaviour failed to set foot in tourists' affective domains and their resultant effect on tourist behaviour. Furthermore, a review of the existing literature on Chinese outbound tourism also reveals that empirical studies linking Chinese outbound tourists' personality with their travel behaviour are rare. Thus, further academic inquiries can be directed at integrating the affective determinants of tourist satisfaction with other psychological variables, like personality, to establish a more comprehensive theoretical framework for understanding tourist satisfaction in the context of Chinese outbound tourism.

One of the earliest studies on Chinese outbound travel market, Wang and Sheldon(1996) identified four main categories of destination regions/countries in the developmental process of Chinese outbound travel market: (1) Hong Kong and Macau; (2) other border countries; (3) the seven countries of the Association of South East Asian Nations (ASEAN), i. e. Thailand, Singapore, Malaysia, Indonesia, the Philippines, Vietnam, and Brunei; and (4) the rest of the world. More specifically, the Chinese outbound travel market successively covered Hong Kong, Macau, Singapore, Malaysia, Thailand, Japan, South Korea, Vietnam, Australia, New Zealand, Canada, the United States, and Europe, which reflects more or less the trend of the ADS development (Tse 2015). When Australia and New Zealand were first recognised as ADS countries in 1999, there was an emerging interest in understanding how these destination markets appealed to Chinese tourists. By profiling Chinese visitors to Australia, early studies were devoted to identifying their travel preferences, lifestyles, and travel benefits sought in Australia as a burgeoning travel destination beyond Asia (Yu & Weiler 2001; Ryan & Mo 2002). Visitor arrivals from China to Australia reached 840,000 in 2014 (Tourism Australia 2015), making China the second-largest source market to Australia after New Zealand. Mainland China has been acknowledged as one of the major significant markets by the Australian inbound tourism industry. More studies are needed with regard to the nature of this market and the challenges Australia is likely to face in the near future, and the implications for Australian tourism product suppliers and marketers, who will need to maintain and enhance their attractiveness to Chinese visitors.

In summary, apart from studies on tourist behaviour, COT research themes have covered tourist market analysis, business practice, development and trends, and the macro-environment. These research themes complement each other to provide a comprehensive understanding of COT. With the rapid development of COT, researchers started to examine the macro-environment that acted as a push factor for its development. Chinese socioeconomic and political factors play important parts in promoting the outbound tourist flows. From a sociological perspective, COT is the best form that "can be used to demonstrate touristic consumerism in urban China" (Wang 2004, p. 51). Tourism products and services are no longer consumed in a sheer economic way, but rather consumed in cultural and social ways (Wang 2004). As a consequence, besides demographic characteristics, a comprehensive review of Chinese tourist segments must consider their psychological, social, cultural, and economic backgrounds in a holistic and dynamic manner. The global marketplace of tourism will continue to witness the growing demand from Chinese consumers. Therefore, a more contemporary and in-depth understanding of Chinese outbound tourists and their travel behaviour is direly needed. With the increasing number of Chinese outbound tourists in the international tourism market, critical academic inquiry is needed to understand the underlying mechanism pertaining to the formation of tourist satisfaction. The current study is designed to address this critical question by investigating the impact of tourist personality and affective responses on tourist satisfaction in the context of Chinese outbound tourists to Australia.

Personality

People continuously spend their time trying to understand what the human personality is (Cervone & Pervin 2010). In general, personality is perceived as a dynamic and organised set of characteristics which would lead to relatively consistent and enduring responses to one's own environment across varied situations (Lee 2009). In psychology, eight theories have been developed to interpret human personality (Friedman & Schustack 2009): psychoanalytic perspective (which focuses on unconscious influences and sexual drives), neo-analytic/ego perspective (which addresses the self's management of emotions, internal and external drives), biological perspective (which looks at inherited tendencies and limits), behaviourist perspective (which analyses the roles of learning experiences on personality shaping), cognitive perspective (which captures active human thought processes), humanistic/existential perspective (which pays attention to the spiritual nature of individuals), interactionist perspective (which recognises that inner tendencies are modified when they interact with environmental factors), and lastly trait perspective (Tan & Tang 2013). Among these, the trait perspective is often adopted to assess individual personality (Jin, Lee & Gopalan 2012). In regards to the current study, it should be noted that personality as a main research construct refers to personality traits.

Defining Personality Traits

Personality traits are defined as enduring "dimensions of individual differences in tendencies to show consistent patterns of thoughts, feelings, and actions" (McCrae & Costa 2003, p. 25). Personality traits refer to a complex and differentiated mental structure that accounts for regularity and consistency in behaviour (Kassin 2003). Within these definitions, the term "tendencies" stresses that traits are only dispositions, not absolute determinants. Traits can describe personality characteristics rather than addressing the underlying causes of personality development or why personality exists. The terms "consistent patterns" and "regularity and consistency" indicate that traits are reasonably stable over time and relatively consistent across different situations. These inner psychological features lead to differences among individuals, thus reflecting how a person responds to his or her environment. In this sense, personality traits have been found to be influential factors that predict long-term patterns of behaviour (Yoo & Gretzel 2011).

Nevertheless, trait theories have been much criticised for underestimating the effect of specific situations on people's behaviour, thus often serving as poor predictors of behaviour (Funder 2009). An individual may score high on assessments of a specific trait, but he or she may not always behave that way in every situation. For instance, emotionally stable people may feel overwhelmingly excited after winning a close game with great efforts. Researchers may predict behaviour averaged across many different situations with greater precision than those from single instances (Epstein 1979). The relevance of personality assessment in behaviour research was revealed as follows: "the more of a trait people have, the more likely they are to show the behaviour it disposes toward, and thus the more frequently we are likely to see it. Similarly, the more the trait characterises them, the more intensely they act and react in relevant situations" (McCrae & Costa 2004, p. 25-26). Therefore, personality traits can endure for long periods and characterise individuals as behaving in a certain manner (McCrae & Costa 2003).

In previous studies, it has been demonstrated that the situation can moderate the correlations between personality and contextual behaviour (e. g. Hattrup & Jackson 1996; Hough & Schneider 1996). There is also support for the position that the expression of personality can be constrained by certain cues conceptualised as strong situations by Mischel (1977). In a strong situation, certain behaviour is desired as correct response or enhanced as normative expectation; such a strong situation purports to direct how to perform desired behaviour (Beaty, Cleveland & Murphy 2001). For instance, an individual who is normally introverted and withdrawn might revolt against the exercise of tyranny for his/her colleague who is being bullied or treated brutally. In such a strong situation, the individual behaviour is driven by what is expected and desired behaviour rather than by their typical personality traits. In contrast, a situation that lacks these features is referred to as weak. A weak situation "does not provide clear incentive, support or normative expectations of behaviour" (Beaty, Cleveland & Murphy 2001, p. 128). For instance, as people are propelled to live and work at a faster pace in modern society, leisure holidays are in high demand as an avenue for them to escape from work (Easterbrook 2003), thus providing a setting in which they can relax and be themselves. The behaviour of vacation/leisure travellers at a destination will usually be driven by their innate personality characteristics, because individual tourists do not share a common perception of what behaviour is expected of them in a relaxing travel environment. In these weak situations, when environments are ambiguously structured in terms of appropriate behaviour, behaviour is more dependent on individual predispositions; the strength of the situation is based on " the consistency of individuals' perceptions of appropriate behaviour" (Beaty, Cleveland & Murphy 2001, p. 128).

To sum up, in strong situations, behaviour can be directed by normative behaviour, as opposed to personality characteristics, while in weak situations, behaviour can be generated in terms of the individuals' own perceptions of appropriate behaviour, which is reflective of their personality orientations. Therefore, the strength of a situation is particularly important to consider when collecting personality data. The current study utilises the trait perspective to operationalise tourist personality in the controlled setting of Chinese outbound tourists' 8-day holiday package tours to Australia. The majority of activities are based upon the tourists' involvement in and experience with nature-based tourism (Chhetri et al. 2004). Tourists regard the nature-based tour in Australia as an avenue to escape from work and seek relaxation, through which they intend to return to their original nature. Following this line of thought, environments are ambiguously structured in terms of appropriate behaviour. In such a weak situation, tourist personalities are relied on to predict behaviour. The personality traits of individual tourists will be assessed according to his or her perceptions of their own average behaviour, thus enhancing generalisability of the findings across different weak situations.

The Five-Factor Model of Personality

In the last two decades, consensus has emerged among personality researchers that the most prominent aspects of an individual's personality can be delineated with a five-factor model (FFM), also known as the Big Five (Goldberg 1990). The FFM, the most popular typology of personality traits, measures the most salient aspects of personality (Yamagata et al. 2006). The model addresses extraversion, neuroticism, agreeableness, conscientiousness, openness to experience (openness as its short form in this book) (Goldberg 1990, 1992) as five overarching dimensions of human personality, each being represented by specific traits or facets. Characterising these core constructs of personality in natural English-language trait adjectives, the FFM is very useful for personality ratings and questionnaires (see Table 3.2 for a summary of the Big Five prototypes defining facets and identified characteristics), based on Goldberg (1990) and Watson and Clark (1992). McCrae and Costa (1997) replicated and corroborated the FFM in cross-cultural personality studies, and thus argued that it is universal and valid for use in multiple cultural settings.

Table 3.2　Big Five Prototypes Defining Facets and Identified Characteristics

Personality Traits	Facet Scales	Central Trait Adjectives	
		High	Low
Extraversion	Warmth, activity, assertiveness, gregariousness, positive emotions, excitement-seeking	sociable, gregarious, assertive, talkative, energetic, outgoing, outspoken, dominant, enthusiastic, active	quiet, reserved, shy, silent, withdrawn, retiring
Neuroticism	Anxiety, angry hostility, depression, vulnerability, impulsiveness, self-consciousness	tense, anxious, nervous, moody, depressed, angry, embarrassed, emotional, worried, insecure	stable, calm, contented
Agreeableness	Trust, modesty, altruism, compliance, tender-mindedness, straightforwardness	good-natured, sympathetic, appreciative, forgiving, courteous, helpful, generous, cooperative	cold, unfriendly, fault-finding, quarrelsome, hard-hearted, thankless
Conscientiousness	Order, dutifulness, competence, deliberation, self-discipline, achievement-striving	dependable, responsible, organised, hardworking, achievement-oriented	careless, disorderly, frivolous, irresponsible, undependable
Openness	Ideas, values, actions, fantasy, feelings, aesthetics	imaginative, cultured, curious, original, broad-minded, intelligent, inventive, having wide interests	simple, shallow, commonplace, unintelligent, having narrow interests

Adapted from Goldberg (1990) and Watson & Clark (1992)

Although trait terms are valuable for describing how people act in everyday life (Fleeson 2004), the FFM is not without its critics. The term "model" reveals a sort of theoretical attempt to "generate psychological phenomena of interest" (Block 1995, p. 188). However, providing a purely descriptive and simplified classification of personality and little explanation of the underlying causes of personality, the FFM lacks convincing theories or hypotheses underpinning the FFM personality taxonomy. It is merely a common framework for various and diverse phenotypic attributes of personality (John & Srivastava 1999). The following sections will provide an overview of each dimension of the five personality traits in the FFM: extraversion, neuroticism, agreeableness, conscientiousness, and openness. These five personality terms stand for the major personality constructs. Within each personality construct lies a subset of characteristics labelled facets. This will enable a clearer understanding of what each personality construct represents. While this study explores personality traits on a construct level, it will empirically investigate the impact of each trait construct on positive/negative affect and holistic tourist satisfaction.

Extraversion

Extraversion(as opposed to introversion) represents "differences in preference for social interaction and lively activity" (McCrae & Costa 2003, p. 46). It is generally described with adjectives such as energetic, enthusiastic, dominant, optimistic, companionable, fun-loving, and communicative. Individuals who are high on extraversion tend to be sociable, talkative, outgoing, warm-hearted, assertive, ambitious, and to experience positive affect (Besser & Shackelford 2007). Extraversion is characterised by showing a keen interest in other people and external events. For example, extraverted students may enhance social interactions in the classroom but it may also impede learning because they can be distracted in class (Nguyen et al. 2005). By contrast, individuals who are low on extraversion are generally described as shy, reserved, quiet, silent, passive, and withdrawn (Costa & McCrae 1992; Barnett 2006). Sociability theory suggests that extraverts tend to be happier than introverts because they engage in more social activities and enjoy social activities relatively more than introverts (Huang et al. 2014).

Extraversion is considered to encompass six facets, including *warmth* (outgoing), *gregariousness* (sociable), *assertiveness* (forceful), *activity* (energetic), *excitement-seeking* (adventurous), and *positive emotions* (enthusiastic). Extraverts are predisposed to be talkative and sociable in nature, and likely to experience pleasant interactions with others because of their personality nature of warmth and gregariousness. Being warm-hearted, they enjoy the company of others (Rose et al. 2010). Assertiveness as another facet of extraversion, indicates that forceful individuals tend to express opinions and leadership to influence others, and strive to excel above others in competition. The final three facets, activity, excitement-seeking and positive emotions, refer to situations that can lead to an active and exciting life. Being energetic, enthusiastic and bold, extraverts venture into the unknown with confidence (John & Srivastava 1999). Prior studies have documented robust relationships between extraversion and overall positive affect (Srivastava et al. 2008).

Neuroticism

Neuroticism (as opposed to emotional stability) refers to "the proneness of the individual to experience unpleasant and disturbing thoughts and to have corresponding disturbances in thoughts and actions" (McCrae & Costa 2003, p. 46). Characterised as nervous, pessimistic, anxious, and very emotional, individuals high in neuroticism are prone to experience unpleasant emotions, such as anxiety, anger, depression, or vulnerability (Costa & McCrae 1992). They are more self-conscious, vulnerable, temperamental, and tend to worry a great deal (McCrae & Costa 2003). On the contrary, individuals who score low on neuroticism are calm, relaxed, even-tempered, and contented (Barnett 2006). The "characteristics associated with neuroticism suggest that such individuals will not engage in relationships that require long-term commitments on their part and demand high social skills, trust in others and initiative" (Raja et al. 2004, p. 351). Individuals with neurotic characteristics tend to experience a higher degree of uncertainty when making a decision and feel regretful about making an improper choice, thus avoiding situations that demand taking control (Huang et al. 2014).

Neuroticism is considered to encompass six facets, including *anxiety* (nervous), *angry hostility* (irritable), *depression* (discontented), *self-consciousness* (shy), *impulsiveness* (moody), and *vulnerability* (not self-confident). Neuroticism is associated with adjustment and emotional resilience when under stress and pressure. Individuals who are high in neuroticism tend to be irritable, discontented, shy, sensitive to ridicule, easily embarrassed, and have high anxiety level, which means they may pay more attention to the potential negative outcomes of a situation or an event (Rose et al. 2010). Hence, neuroticism is sometimes thought to be useful for some very detail-oriented jobs. *Depression* is prone to feelings of sadness, hopelessness, loneliness, guilt and self-inferiority. Neurotic tendencies can have negative effects on subjective and psychological well-being (Grant, Langan-Fox & Anglim 2009). *Anxiety*, *angry hostility*, *depression* and *self-consciousness* represent emotional states of a neurotic individual, while *impulsiveness* and *vulnerability* reveal more about his or her behavioural states. *Impulsiveness* is "the tendency to give in to temptations and be overcome by desires" (McCrae & Costa 2003, p. 48), which may result in vulnerability, suggesting an inability to cope with stress, emotional breakdown, and panic in times of danger.

Agreeableness

Agreeableness (as opposed to antagonism) is often defined as how an individual is able to get along with others, representing the tendency to be soft-hearted rather than ruthless, trusting rather than suspicious, and helpful rather than uncooperative (Santrock 2009). Agreeableness is linked with words such as friendly, trustful, cooperative, reconcilable, and sympathetic towards others; opposing terms are cold, unfriendly, vindictive, cynical, non-cooperative, fractious, and manipulative (McCrae & John 1992). Agreeableness is considered to encompass six facets, including *trust* (forgiving), *straightforwardness* (not demanding), *altruism* (warm), *compliance* (not stubborn), *modesty* (not show-off), and *tender-mindedness* (sympathetic). Being trustworthy themselves, agreeable individuals have a propensity to trust others and are featured as *straightforwardness*. Their nature of *altruism* is perceived to be one critical personality attribute of employees who interact with customers (Barrick et al. 2003). Agreeablenss was found to have a positive influence on emotional labour; in the meantime, people who are high on agreeableness tend to be associated with helping colleagues (Kamdar & Van Dyne 2007). Being unassertive, agreeable individuals possess the personality attribute of compliance (McCrae & Costa 2003); being humble, agreeable individuals exhibit modesty in controlling the relationship between understanding the situation and performing the required duty in the workplace (Sohn & Lee 2012). They also tend to show tender-mindedness and are willing to be involved with charities and volunteering causes (McCrae & Costa 2003).

Conscientiousness

Conscientiousness refers to the tendency to show self-discipline, act dutifully, and aim for achievement (Costa & McCrae 1992; Rose et al. 2010). Governed by their conscience, people who are highly conscientious tend to possess characteristics of being responsible, diligent, reliable, well-organised, punctual, ambitious and persevering (Barrick & Mount 1991). In contrast, individuals who are low on conscientiousness tend to be negligent, disorganised, late, aimless and unreliable (McCrae & Costa 2003); they are impulsive and seek immediate gratification (Barnett 2006). Conscientiousness is considered to encompass six facets, including *competence* (efficient), *order* (organised), *dutifulness* (responsibility), *achievement-striving* (thorough), *self-discipline* (not lazy), and *deliberation* (not impulsive). Conscientious individuals tend to view themselves as being competent in seeking out information to ensure high performance. Conscientious employees are often more motivated to pursue excellence and achieve success through their hard work, which calls for a high sense of responsibility and self-displine. The personality attributes of being organised, rule-following, detail-oriented, and achievement-striving can be powerful predictors of professional competencies and job performance (Viswesvaran et al. 2001; Salgado 2002). Hence, conscientious individuals prefer to plan ahead. The facet of deliberation indicates that they think in advance before taking action to consider the potential outcomes of their actions (McCrae & Costa 2003).

Openness

Openness refers to individuals' receptiveness to new ideas, approaches, and experiences (McCrae & Costa 1997). It embraces aesthetic sensitivity, awareness of one's emotions, vivid imagination, preference for novelty and variety, and intellectual curiosity (Costa & McCrae 1992). It has been proposed that open individuals, being more intellectually curious and behaviourally flexible, are more motivated to engage in gaining new knowledge and experiences (Besser & Shackelford 2007). People who are high on openness are original, curious, and artistic, imaginative rather than practical; independent rather than conforming; and prefer variety to routine. By contrast, people who are low on openness tend to be characterised as conventional, and have less interest in seeking diverse experiences (McCrae & Costa 2003).

Openness is considered to encompass six facets, including *fantasy* (imaginative), *aesthetics* (artistic), *feelings* (excitable), *actions* (wide interests), *ideas* (curious), and *values* (unconventional). Fantasy, as the predominant facet in the dimension of openness, represents a vivid imagination and an inclination to develop elaborate daydreams (McCrae & Costa 1997). Aesthetics is seen as sensitivity to or appreciation of art and beauty; therefore, openness has been closely related to success in artistic jobs (Barrick et al. 2003). Open individuals tend to seek and value diverse feelings, therefore they are eager to take action to experience something new. Sensation-seeking and the need for variety and novelty are characteristics of openness. For example, open tourists are more inclined to travel to an unknown destination. Being open to ideas and values are related to intellectual curiosity and independence of judgment (McCrae & Costa 2003). For instance, open individuals are curious about both inner and outer worlds, and they are more willing to explore novel ideas and entertain unconventional values.

These five broad superordinate dimensions of the FFM are well-established in the personality literature. Research on personality structure used to be a core concern of personality psychology throughout its history, while recent emphases have been laid on the prediction of consequential outcomes from the FFM (Ozer & Benet-Martinez 2006). Specifically, further refinement of these factors has focused on the structure of the external correlates of the factors rather than solely on the structure of the factor indicators (Ozer & Benet-Martinez 2006). A plethora of prior studies have utilised this model to explain workplace variables, such as job performance (e. g. Barrick & Mount 1991; Hogan & Holland 2003), job satisfaction (e. g. Judge et al. 1998; Mount, Ilies & Johnson 2006), occupation choice (e. g. Barrick, Mount & Gupta 2003; Jin, Watkins & Yuen 2009), emotional labour (e. g. Gursoy, Boylu & Avci 2011; Sohn & Lee 2012), knowledge sharing (e. g. Mooradian & Matzler 2006; Matzler et al. 2008), and organisational commitment (e. g. Panaccio & Vandenberghe 2012; Spagnoli & Caetano 2012). Besides, prior studies have documented robust relationships between the FFM personality traits and consumer behaviour, including customer service (e. g. Brown et al. 2002; Tan, Der Foo & Kwek 2004), shopping behaviour (e. g. Carver & Scheier 2008; Huang & Yang 2010), and even online behaviour (e. g. Landers & Lounsbury 2006; Acar & Polonsky 2007). The FFM personality traits have also been found to be an influential predictor for subjective well-being (e. g. Gutiérrez et al. 2005), and even the individuals' life span and life satisfaction (e. g. John & Gross 2004; Joshanloo & Afshari 2011).

Successful prediction of such consequential outcomes is a demonstration of the practical importance of personality that demands attention. Research in consumer behaviour that used the FFM has found a connection between individuals' personality and their brand preferences and brand loyalty, indicating that personality is an important parameter for product choice and customer loyalty (Lin 2010). Correspondingly, in the context of tourism, tourist personality may have significant implications on destination choice and destination loyalty. Over the last two decades, there has been a significant increase in the number of empirical studies published in the domain of tourist behaviour research. Nevertheless, tourist behaviour literature has given limited consideration to the role that tourist personality plays in predicting tourist behaviour responses. Research on tourist personality would practically contribute to tourism marketing. In the next section, the extant studies on the link between personality and tourist behaviour are reviewed to identify the research gap.

The Link between Personality and Tourist Behaviour

As mentioned above, personality traits play a pivotal role in the domain of consumer behaviour. Similarly, differences in personality traits may contribute to different interpretation of a travel episode as well as discrepancies in travel experiences. In tourism research, Plog is the first researcher on the personality types for market segmentation purposes, attempting to predict travel patterns and travel motivation from a personality perspective (Madrigal 1995). Based on a personality continuum ranging from allocentrism to psychocentrism, Plog (1974) proposed a tourist typology, including five distinct types of tourists: the allocentric, near-allocentric, mid-centric, near-psychocentric, and psychocentric. Intellectually curious and eager to explore the world, allocentrics prefer exotic destinations and unstructured vacation itineraries rather than package tours, and more involvement with local cultures. In contrast, psychocentrics tend to visit familiar destinations in group package tours as well as those well-established areas with virtually no elements of adventure or risk-taking during their travel. Many studies have since applied Plog's (1974) travel personality framework to understand destination choice and travel style preferences (Basala & Klenosky 2001; Chandler & Costello 2002; Litvin 2006).

Plog (2001) asserted that the life cycle of destinations can be linked with the psychographic curve in terms of the types of travellers who visit there the most. Changes in the type of tourists attracted to a destination based on their personality can help to shed light on why destinations rise and fall in popularity. Some scholars have questioned the model's applicability and validity for predicting or describing life cycle evolution because it relies only on the psychographic profile of visitors (McKercher 2005) and is not realistic (Chen, Mak & Mckercher 2011). For example, Smith's (1990) study on examining Plog's model of tourism destination preferences across seven countries fails to establish a link between tourists' personality types and destination preferences. Plog's model of motives is merely useful as a description but not as an explanation for motivation and behaviour (Leiper 1995; Pearce & Packer 2013). In addition, the model as a psychographic tool is limited because it does not consider multiple-motivated behaviour and is unable to explain why different types of tourists visit a single destination (Jiang et al. 2012).

Since Plog initiated the psychocentric-allocentric model to explain travel motivation and travel patterns, the impacts of personality on tourist behaviour have been examined in numerous studies (e. g. Nias 1985; Frew & Shaw 1999). For more than three decades, academics have attempted to elucidate tourist behaviour by developing different frameworks for tourist typologies (Swarbrooke & Horner 2004). However, some studies report that the relationship between personality and leisure behaviour is not very robust (Nias 1985), while others suggest that personality has been recognised as a significant predictor of tourist behaviour in various contexts, including vacation destination choices, leisure activities and other travel-related decisions (Yoo & Gretzel 2011). To a large extent, personality has been evidenced to be positively associated with travel motivations, destination preferences, tourist perceptions, degree of activity participation, and level of involvement with cultures (e. g. Gretzel et al. 2004; Reisinger & Mavondo 2004b; Lepp & Gibson 2008). The researcher agrees with Ross (1994) who stated that there could be "no more appropriate or useful study than personality as it illuminates tourist behaviour" (p. 31).

Because of the universality of the FFM, as shown in other studies previously cited, the model has been adopted in tourism research to interpret different tourism-related behaviour. Based on a comprehensive review of prior studies on personality in the context of tourism and hospitality, Leung and Law (2010) noted that the majority of the tourism literature which uses the FFM either for data analysis or as part of the research framework often focuses on analysing service staff personality (e. g. Liu & Chen 2006; Barrash & Costen 2007; Teng 2008) rather than tourist personality. Although the quality of service provided by the staff in the tourism industry can serve as a major determinant of tourist satisfaction (Teng, Huang & Tsai 2007; Sohn & Lee 2012), analysing tourist personality can help develop a better understanding of their travel behaviour and identify individual needs and wants, thus providing tailor-made services accordingly.

More recently, only a small number of studies in tourism employed the FFM to measure tourist personality. For instance, Yoo and Gretzel (2011) investigated the influence of personality traits on travel behaviour relating to the use of consumer-generated media (CGM); travellers' personality traits have been found to significantly affect perceived barriers to content creation, motivations to engage in CGM creation, and specific creation behaviour. In a study examining the causal relationships between experience, personality, and attitude on the behaviour of scuba divers, personality was found to have a significant direct relationship with both divers' attitude and underwater behaviour (Ong & Musa 2012). Moreover, in another study of how personality traits influence tourism information search and feedback behaviour, although personality alone was found not to fully elucidate tourism information search behaviour, hierarchical regression analysis confirmed the usefulness of FFM personality traits in this regard (Tan & Tang 2013). Faullant et al. (2011) analysed the relationships between personality, basic emotions, and satisfaction in the context of mountaineering experience, and confirmed that extraversion and neuroticism as two broad fundamental personality traits, together with cognitive appraisals, influence tourist satisfaction. With the exception of this study, to the best of researcher's knowledge, prior research has not documented the impact of FFM personality traits on tourist satisfaction.

In tourism, the measurement of personality mostly focuses on specific traits such as extraversion and neuroticism, venturesomeness (Plog 2002; Weaver 2012) and especially sensation-seeking in the context of recreation and adventure experiences (e. g. Pizam et al. 2004; Galloway et al. 2008; Lepp & Gibson 2008), rather than the full use of well-established scales such as the FFM (Cohen, Prayag & Moital 2014). Extraversion and neuroticism have been the most frequently recognised and studied personality traits that can influence tourist behaviour (e. g. Matzler et al. 2008; Faullant et al. 2011; Gursoy, Boylu & Avci 2011; Huang, Gursoy & Xu 2014). However, in attempting to build up some new links between mainstream psychology and tourism research, Pearce and Packer (2013) warned that single trait theories of personality should be applied to tourism research with caution. Patterned responses to tourism settings can be better interpreted by all the core and stable dimensions of the FFM as driving forces, instead of simply viewing isolated dimensions of personality traits, for the latter would lose its predictive power (Pearce & Packer 2013). To address this limitation in previous studies, the current study employs all five dimensions of the FFM as independent exogenous variables to investigate how the FFM personality traits predict tourist satisfaction.

Affect

Affect is an instinctive reaction to stimulation occurring (Zajonc 1980). The level of affective response can have an immediate and direct influence on behaviour in an unconscious way, and its effect can be prolonged between a few weeks to a few months (Wright & Staw 1999). In psychology, affect is a generic (an umbrella) term to describe a wide range of phenomena, including emotion, mood and feeling (Cohen & Areni 1991; Hosany & Gilbert 2010). In some extant literature there is considerable ambiguity about the differences between the terms affect and emotion. Because of the semantic similarity between these two concepts, a major problem in psychology, marketing, and tourism remains the interchangeable use of these two terms (e. g. Bagozzi et al. 1999; Hosany & Gilbert 2010). Many psychologists argue that these are two different concepts presented in the dynamic course of human behaviour (e. g. Pearce 2009). Therefore, it calls for some elaboration on the common understanding of the differences and linkages between affect and emotion.

Differentiation between Affect and Emotion

The term "affect" is normally used to characterise general subjective experiences, with emotions and moods as instances of the feeling states (Izard 1977; Gardner 1985). Pearce (2009) argued that affect is perceived as a generalised summary of those feelings that are consciously accessible. One's affective state is effectively a general ongoing subjective experience. By contrast, emotion is widely regarded as the more specific of the two terms and is

usually linked with a reaction to a specific object, event, or experience (Fredrickson 2001). Emotions can be interpreted as episodes of intense feelings that are attributable to a specific stimuli or object (Cohen & Areni 1991). Both affect and emotion have a subjective experience component—for emotion the subjective experience is one component of the responses involved, whereas for affect the subjective experience is the entirety of the concept (Russell & Barrett 1999). From this perspective, emotions can be perceived as a subset of the larger realm of affect (Russell & Barrett 1999). Emotion is often characterised by having a shorter duration than the more general term of affect. Emotions are direct, intense mental reactions to a specific event or stimulus (Beedie, Terry & Lane 2005), and are therefore transient and situational in nature. Momentary emotions are, to a certain extent, reflections of one's general affective level (Watson, Clark & Tellegen 1988). An emotion is an affective state, but not all affective states are emotions. In summary, emotion is seen to be conceptually distinct from affect; however, affect, in general, refers to an average of emotions experienced over a certain period of time (Nawijn et al. 2013), and it arises from cumulative occurrences of transient emotional states.

Similarly, emotional responses are characterised by episodes of intense feelings associated with a specific referent (Cohen & Areni 1991); therefore, affective responses can be conceptualised to be the summations of emotional responses/happenings. For example, emotional responses would be relevant for describing the specific experiences of an episode, such as encountering wildlife or being robbed during the trip; however, an individual's prevailing style on a trip has close associations with his or her holistic affective responses. An emotional response is one of short duration that includes a clearly identifiable physiological response such as the elevation of heart rate or pupil dilation (Pearce 2011). For the purpose of this study, following Pearce's position that affect can be the summation of emotional happenings, affective responses are conceptually distinguished from emotional responses, which represents a more generalised evaluation of affective states lasting for a relatively longer time. The frequencies and dynamics of each specific short-lived emotional response can contribute to shaping overall affective responses.

The Measurement of Affect/Emotion

A coherent stream of research over the past two decades has placed increasing emphasis on the role of affect/emotion in marketing and consumer behaviour. Early research mainly focused on consumers' emotional responses to advertising (e.g. Edell & Burke 1987; Holbrook & Westwood 1989). Other studies have examined emotions generated by product consumption and services (e.g. Derbaix & Pham 1991; Chebat & Michon 2003; Laros & Steenkamp 2005). Scholars have also investigated emotion's impact on global evaluative variables such as satisfaction and behavioural intentions (e.g. Zeelenberg & Pieters 2004; Ladhari 2007;

Martínez Caro & Martínez García 2007; Martin et al. 2008).

Although self-report measures may arise in some biases that responses are vulnerable to tendencies like wanting to appear consistent or to provide socially desirable answers (Verplanken & Orbell 2003), self-report measures are still widely employed in the psychological literature to effectively and efficiently capture affective responses (Parrott & Hertel 1999; Diener 2000), because of their convenient use and straightforward interpretation (Laros & Steenkamp 2004). Typically, scholars use self-report responses to verbal or written questions to assess respondents' emotional reactions to a stimulus. These are referred to as Measures of Affect or Measures of Emotion.

Traditionally, researchers have often adopted or adapted scales from psychology such as the Pleasure, Arousal, and Dominance Scale (PAD) (Mehrabian & Russell 1974), the Differential Emotion Scale (DES1) (Izard 1977), the Psychoevolutionary Theory of Emotions (PTE) (Plutchik 1980), and the Positive Affect and Negative Affect Scale (PANAS) (Watson et al. 1988) to understand customer or tourist experiences (e. g. Richins 1997; Hosany & Gilbert 2010; Lee & Kyle 2013). In the marketing literature, Richins (1997) proposed the Consumption Emotion Set (CES) to conceptualise and operationalise emotional states triggered in a variety of product and service consumption contexts. However, existing taxonomies from psychology and marketing fail to take tourism and destination-specific characteristics into consideration (Hosany & Gilbert 2010). To capture the range of tourists' emotional responses toward destinations, Hosany and Gilbert (2010) developed the Destination Emotion Scale (DES2). Likewise, Lee and Kyle (2013) developed the Festival Consumption Emotions (FCE).

With regard to the theoretical approaches to measure affect/emotions, they are conceptualised either as continuous underlying dimensions (valence based) such as PAD, PANAS, DES2, and FCE or as a taxonomy of discrete emotions (emotion specificity) such as joy and anger in DES1, PTE, and CES.

The PAD Paradigm

In environmental psychology, Mehrabian and Russell (1974) suggested that a human's affective responses to varied person-environment interactions be conceptualised in terms of three uncorrelated bipolar dimensions: pleasure-displeasure, arousal-non-arousal, and dominance-submissiveness. Pleasure refers to the extent to which a person is happy, content, relaxed, or satisfied in the situation. The arousal state refers to the extent to which a person feels excited, stimulated, interested, or alert in the situation. Dominance refers to the degree to which a person feels controlled, influential, important, or dominant in the situation. In the PAD paradigm, each of these dimensions can range from high to low (e. g. high arousal) and each also has a positive and a negative element.

From an evolutionary perspective, Russell and Pratt (1980) adopted the factor analysis to identify eight dimensions underlying emotional responses to the physical environment from 105 affective items, i. e. pleasant-unpleasant, relaxing-distressing, exciting-gloomy, and arousing-sleepy. The eight-descriptor model was consistent with two primary emotional dimensions of pleasure and arousal. In subsequent examinations of the PAD paradigm, the dimension of dominance was omitted because of its poor performance as a predictor in explaining variations in consumer emotions (Sherman, Mathur & Smith 1997).

The PAD scale has been adapted to measure affective responses to product/service consumption experiences(e. g. Havlena & Holbrook 1986; Wirtz, Mattila & Tan 2000; Yüksel & Yüksel 2007; Jang & Namkung 2009), to different service environments (e. g. Donovan et al. 1994; McGoldrick & Pieros 1998; Wirtz & Bateson 1999; Yüksel 2007; Lee 2014), or to tourism destination settings (e. g. Bigné & Andreu 2004; Bigné, Andreu & Gnoth 2005; Yüksel & Akgül 2007). However, the PAD scale does not purport to capture emotions per se but rather to measure the perceived pleasure, arousal, or dominance engendered by a set of environmental stimuli (Wirtz, Mattila & Tan 2000). Specific emotional responses such as happiness, excitement, anger, or fear can not be unequivocally distinguished from a person's PAD scores. Thus, the PAD scale is best used when a researcher is interested in measuring the dimensions underlying emotional responses and does not need to know the specific emotions being experienced by study participants.

DES1 and PTE

Izard's(1977) DES1 contained 10 subscales that represent the basic emotions of *interest*, *joy*, *anger*, *disgust*, *contempt*, *sadness*, *fear*, *shame*, *guilt*, and *surprise*; this approach is often utilised to examine post-purchase emotions in customer satisfaction research (Westbrook & Oliver 1991). Similar to DES1, Plutchik's (1980) PTE identified a briefer framework than that of Izard, and viewed all emotions as stemming from eight basic categories of *fear*, *anger*, *joy*, *sadness*, *disgust*, *acceptance*, *expectancy* (*anticipation*), and *surprise*; this approach does not attempt to determine the underlying causes of emotions while it concentrates on grouping according to similarity. From a biological perspective, both DES1 and PTE argue that basic emotions are derived from survival instincts (Barsky & Nash 2002). These two approaches measure emotions that individuals express to increase their ability to survive.

These scales have been used to understand consumers' emotional responses to product consumption and some type of marketing stimuli(e. g. Holbrook & Westwood 1989), but they are not designed to capture the entire domain of emotional experience or to assess the interpersonal aspects of consumption. Emotions as measured by DES1 and PTE can best be characterised in terms of two independent dimensions: positive and negative. However, a disadvantage of these two existing emotional scales is that there is an overemphasis on negative emotion. It has been argued that DES1 and PTE tend to reflect negative emotions (Mano & Oliver 1993) or cover the entire range of fundamental emotional responses to physical environments (Richins 1997). Researchers have criticised the above approaches because negative emotions seem to be predominant over positive ones, and many everyday emotions are omitted. For example, love, hate, envy, relief, and pride do not appear in these models (Barsky & Nash 2002). In addition, tourists' positive affect was rated significantly higher than negative affect on holidays (Nawijn 2011b). Thus, these two scales are inappropriate for measuring affect/emotions in the tourism context.

PANAS

A coherent stream of research over the past two decades has placed increasing emphasis on the role of affect in marketing and consumer behaviour. Watson, Clark, and Tellegen (1988) focused on positive affect (PA) and negative affect (NA), and developed the PANAS, consisting of 20 single-word items, such as *excited*, *alert*, *determined*, *interested*, *strong*, *enthusiastic*, *proud*, *inspired*, *attentive*, and *active* for positive affect, and *upset*, *guilty*, *distressed*, *scared*, *hostile*, *irritable*, *ashamed*, *nervous*, *afraid*, and *jittery* for negative affect. Although there is no agreement on the best approach to measure affect (Bagozzi et al. 1999), the PANAS approach is the most popular conceptualisation, which has been well validated in studies relating to product and service satisfaction (Mano & Oliver 1993), and post-purchase behaviour (Mooradian & Olver 1997). Building on the PANAS, Thompson (2007) developed an internationally reliable short-form measurement, the I-PANAS-SF, comprising two 5-item scales. For positive affect, items are *active*, *alert*, *attentive*, *determined*, and *inspired*, while for negative affect, items are *afraid*, *ashamed*, *hostile*, *nervous*, and *upset*.

Two dominant dimensions consistently emerge in studies of affective responses. Briefly, PA reflects the extent to which a person feels enthusiastic, active, and alert. High PA is a state of high energy, full concentration, and pleasurable engagement, whereas low PA is characterised by sadness and lethargy. In contrast, NA is a general dimension of subjective distress and unpleasant engagement that subsumes a variety of aversive mood states, including anger, contempt, disgust, guilt, fear, and nervousness, with low NA being a state of calmness and serenity(Watson, Clark & Tellegen 1988). Watson and Tellegen (1985) viewed affective dimensions in terms of positivity and negativity: positive affect represents the extent to which a person has a zest for life, and negative affect refers to the extent to which a person reports feeling upset or unpleasantly aroused (Jun et al. 2001). However, the full 20-item PANAS has one drawback for many cross-cultural settings. As demonstrated in validation studies (Crawford & Henry 2004), it contains some words that either are colloquial to North America or are ambiguous in "international" English.

CES

Despite the widespread application, in recent years, researchers have questioned the applicability, reliability, and validity of psychological emotion scales in consumer studies (Laros & Steenkamp 2005; Schoefer & Diamantopoulos 2008). Emotion taxonomies from psychology fail to measure emotions in a consumption context because consumer experiences are situation-specific (Richins 1997). Furthermore, adapting scales from psychology may lead to issues of content validity (Haynes, Richard & Kubany 1995). Realising the need for a more comprehensive theory to understand consumption emotions and improve measurement validity, Richins (1997) developed the CES to capture emotions elicited in diverse product and service consumption contexts, including 47 emotion descriptors grouped into 16 dimensions, namely, *anger*, *worry*, *sadness*, *fear*, *shame*, *romantic love*, *excitement*, *optimism*, *joy*, *surprise*, *discontent*, *love*, *envy*, *loneliness*, *peacefulness*, and *contentment*. She found that positive emotions such as joy, pride, and contentment were strongly experienced while few negative emotions were reported in all three product consumption situations.

However, the CES has still received some criticism. For instance, Bagozzi, Gopinath, and Nyer (1999) questioned the discriminant validity of the scale. The two dimensions of romantic love and love from the CES scale are very similar. More recently, Huan and Back (2007) adapted the CES to uncover dimensions of consumption emotions in the lodging industry. As opposed to a 16-dimensional structure, Huan and Back (2007) identified seven dimensions and called the generalisability of Richins's (1997) CES in other settings into question.

DES2 and FCE

Given that specific emotions are sensitive to context (Richins 1997), Hosany and Gilbert (2010) further noted that affect/emotion scales from psychology and marketing are context specific and fail to capture the richness of tourist and destination characteristics. Existing emotion scales overlook the complexity of positive emotions (Fredrickson 1998), which is commonly associated with tourism experiences (Nawijn et al. 2013). Thus, the aforementioned measures may not be suitable for all tourism product consumption situations (Hosany & Gilbert 2010). In response to these issues, some recent efforts have focused on identifying and validating the dimensions of emotions specific to the tourism context. The theorisation of emotions has received unprecedented attention in contemporary tourism literature.

Realising the need to measure the diversity and complexity of tourists' emotional responses to destinations, Hosany and Gilbert (2010) developed the DES2, a parsimonious scale with 15 items representing three emotional dimensions of *joy*, *love*, and *positive surprise*. Measured with five items (cheerful, delight, enthusiasm, joy, and pleasure), *joy* is associated with positive outcomes such as the realisation of one's goals (Lazarus 1991). The pursuit of pleasure is a core facet of the tourist experience (Currie 1997; Nawijn 2011a). The dimension of love is measured with five items (affection, caring, love, tenderness, and warm-hearted). The dimension of *positive surprise*, measured with five items (amazement, astonishment, fascinated, inspired, and surprise), is often characterised as a neutrally valence emotion arising from unexpected occurrences (Meyer, Reisenzein & Schützwohl 1997). More recently, using data collected from international tourists visiting two distinct destinations, Thailand and Petra, Hosany et al. (2015) further confirmed the DES external validity. It is worth mentioning that the DES2 only captures positive valence emotions without negative occurrences in tourists' retrospective evaluations of the destination. It has raised the issue relating to a lack of empirical evidence underpinning the construct validity of emotions.

Recently, a handful of tourism researchers have attempted to identify the structure of emotions elicited during tourism-related experiences(Han, Back & Barrett 2010). Building on the growing number of studies on emotions conducted in tourism context, Lee and Kyle (2013) developed a FCE scale capturing festival visitors' emotional experiences in situ. Emotions elicited at festival settings were identified in four dimensions: *love*, *joy*, *surprise*, and *negative*, which includes the three dimensions of the DES2 and a negative emotion dimension.

Conceptualising Affective Responses in the Study

As addressed in section 2.3.1, the term *affect* in this study refers to *affective responses* in a tourist destination context characterised by a series of episodes of intense emotional responses associated with a specific travel experience. In general, the retrospective evaluation of past affective experiences requires recall and overall assessment that involves integrating all—or only some—moments of that experience (Fredrickson 2000). Consequently, retrospective evaluations of overall affective responses are based on the temporal integration of the emotional responses to a certain number of single "moments" (Schäfer et al. 2014). From this point of view, the overall evaluation of experienced affective responses should strongly depend on the cumulative occurrences of relatively short-lived emotional responses. As Richins (1997) proposed that emotions are context specific, retrospective measures are employed in this study to generate Chinese package tourists' holistic affective responses to their 8-day travel experiences in Australia, which can be best predicted by the average of all single emotional responses to specific travel episodes. Prior studies have established that people have emotional responses to their immediate physical and social environment (e.g. Farber & Hall 2007). Accordingly, this study seeks to capture the emotional responses to travel episodes that shape Chinese package tourists' holistic affective responses to the whole travel experiences during the trip to Australia.

Researchers have generally operationalised the measurement of affect/emotions using either a discrete/basic (specific emotions) or valence (positive and negative) approach (Faullant et al. 2011). Consensus has emerged that the two approaches do not conflict (Laros & Steenkamp

2004) and studies in tourism use both. However, measurement of affect/emotions in tourism has favoured the valence-based approach (Prayag et al. 2015), because it can give a more parsimonious account of affective experiences (Lazarus 1991). Summary dimensions such as positive and negative emotions (Del Bosque & San Martín 2008; Lee et al. 2008; Grappi & Montanari 2011) are commonly used in tourism research. In many studies, the two dimensions, either positive or negative, capture a large portion of the variance in emotion ratings (Bagozzi et al. 1999). Additionally, it has been shown to relate to other variables in the conceptual frameworks, such as tourist satisfaction and post-purchase behaviour (e.g. Bigne et al. 2005; Del Bosque & San Martin 2008; Grappi & Montanari 2011; Yuksel & Yuskel 2007). During the same stay individuals may experience positive and negative affective responses because they have multiple interactions with the resources of the destinations. Positive and negative emotions have been found to vary throughout the tourism experience (Nawijn 2011a), but negative emotions in particular tend to remain the same over the duration of the holiday (Lin et al. 2014). Positive affect toward destinations is emphasised in the literature while negative affect is not often addressed (Trentelman 2009). Consequently, as a well-established affect measurement, the PANAS approach is adopted in this study when various affective responses have to be measured during a specified timeframe. Affective responses are conceptualised into a two-dimensional construct: positive and negative affective responses.

Specific Affective Responses in Tourism Research

Affect is often conceptualised as generally high-order dimensions, either positive or negative, but there has also been an interest in more specific emotions. A number of studies have established the validity and applicability of the differential affect/emotion scale across various consumption settings. Considering that consumption emotions differ in character and intensity from emotions that are experienced in other contexts, Richins (1997) developed the CES to delineate an array of consumption emotions. Pearce and Packer (2013) proposed that Richins' list of potential emotional responses could be extended to capture how tourists feel about their individual travel experiences, including *happy*, *contented*, *optimistic*, *pleased*, *worried*, *frustrated*, *tense*, *lonely*, *unfulfilled*, *discontented*, *irritated*, *sad*, and *depressed*.

Stemming from the structure of consumption emotions, many recent studies have attempted to understand the role of affect/emotion in the context of tourism and hospitality. For example, prior studies investigate the influence of emotions on the decision to purchase tourism and leisure services(e.g. Kwortnik & Ross 2007), the determinants of post-consumption emotions (Muller et al. 1991), the relationship between emotions and overall satisfaction (e.g. De Rojas & Camarero 2008; Del Bosque & San Martín 2008), tourist behavioural intentions (e.g. Bigné, Andreu & Gnoth 2005; Yüksel & Akgül 2007; Lee et al. 2008; Grappi & Montanari 2011), and emotions as a segmentation variable for leisure and tourism markets (e. g. Bigné & Andreu 2004; Barnett 2006). Other studies focus on emotional experience associated with festivals (e. g. Grappi & Montanari 2011; Lee et al. 2008), shopping (e. g. Yüksel 2007; Yüksel and Yüksel 2007), restaurants (e. g. Han & Jeong 2013), theme parks (Bigné, Andreu & Gnoth 2005; Ma et al. 2013), holidays (Nawijn et al. 2013), and adventure tourism (e. g. Faullant, Matzler, and Mooradian 2011).

A growing body of work on tourism consumption emotions has emerged in the past decade, with a number of studies focusing on the felt emotions characterised as either positive or negative. Zins (2002) employed the PANAS to identify six salient positive affects (*active*, *alert*, *attentive*, *satisfied*, *enthusiastic*, and *pleased*) and seven salient negative affects (*nervous*, *scared*, *upset*, *angry*, *unhappy*, *afraid*, and *in bad mood*) among complaining and non-complaining travellers. Bigné et al. (2005) reported visitors' positive emotions at a theme park, such as *satisfied*, *happy*, *pleased*, *joyful*, *delighted*, and *entertained*. Tsaur et al. (2007) observed that zoo operators who utilised media featuring animal sounds and images to engender positive emotions among visitors; these positive emotions can be described as *joyful*, *relaxed*, *surprised*, *excited*, *warm/friendly*, and *enjoyable*. Kwortnik and Ross (2007) demonstrated that tourists experience a variety of positive affects on holiday because people's vacations are engineered to be *comfortable* and *enjoyable*. Pictured destinations evoke positive emotions (*pleasantness*, *relaxation*, *arousal*, and *excitement*) (Yüksel & Akgül 2007). Based on the previous studies and the findings of focus group interviews, Del Bosque and San Martín (2008) utilised four positive affects (*pleased*, *enchanted*, *impressed*, *and surprised*) and four negative affects (*bored*, *displeased*, *disappointed*, *and angry*) to investigate the impact of emotions on tourist satisfaction with a destination in Spain. By conducting an exploratory study, Jang et al. (2009) identified six positive affects (*full of life*, *satisfied*, *in good spirits*, *calm and peaceful*, *cheerful*, *and extremely happy*) and six negative affects (*nervous*, *so sad nothing could cheer you up*, *restless or fidgety*, *everything was an effort*, *worthless*, and *hopeless*) among Taiwanese seniors, thus providing empirical support to understand psychological aspects of senior travellers.

Whilst other studies of affect in tourism have been conducted from the perspective of consumer behaviour (e. g. Bigné & Andreu 2004), Tung and Ritchie (2011) highlighted the importance of understanding a tourist's emotions during a memorable experience, whether they are positive (*happy* and *excited*) or negative (*fearful*, *angry*, and *frustrated*). Using examples from a select number of tourists on dynamic volunteer tourism expeditions, Coghlan and Pearce (2010) documented nine positive emotions (*happy*, *contented*, *optimistic*, *pleased*, *excited*, *fulfilled*, *encouraged*, *calm*, and *peaceful*), among which *happy*, *contented*, *optimistic*, and *pleased* are frequently recorded at high levels, whereas emotions such as *worried*, *frustrated*, *tense*, *lonely*, *unfulfilled*, *discontented*, *irritated*, *sad*, and *depressed* do occur among some volunteers, but generally at lower levels. In the festival context, Lee et al. (2008) employed four items each to capture both positive (*pleased*, *satisfied*, *excited*, and *energetic*) and negative (*bored*, *sleepy*, *annoyed*, and *angry*) affects and found these emotions mediate the impact of the festival environment on loyalty to the festival. Similarly, Grappi and Montanari (2011) adopted four items (*happy*, *pleased*, *energetic*, and *excited*) to measure positive emotion and three items (*bored*, *angry*, and *annoyed*) for negative emotion at an Italian festival, and identified the role of emotions in mediating the effects of environmental factors on attendees' re-patronising intention. More recently, Nawijn et al. (2013) used nine positive affects (*interested*, *joyful*, *grateful*, *amused*, *content*, *proud*, *awed*, *loving*, and *hopeful*) and eight negative affects (angry, sad, afraid, ashamed, contemptuous, embarrassed, guilty, and disgusted) to trace vacationers' emotions daily during their holidays using a diary. Interestingly, from an affective neuroscience perspective, Pearce (2012) attempted to explain individuals' affective experiences in returning to previous places of significance and familiarity in their lives.

Based on the extensive review of specific positive and negative affective responses in tourism research, it can be concluded that further research on affect/emotions in tourism should be conducted (e. g. Cohen & Cohen 2012). Empirical studies on the role of affect/emotions in the context of tourist destinations remain scant (Hosany & Gilbert 2010). Apart from positive affect, negative affect can be associated with tourist destinations as well; future research should not only continue to examine the positive affective dimensions associated with different types of tourist experiences at a destination, but also the structure of negative affective responses to travel experiences at a destination. To address such a gap, this study aims to identify and document Chinese package tourists' salient positive and negative affective responses during their trip to Australia.

Satisfaction

Satisfaction is a positive reaction resulting from favourable appraisals of consumption experiences (Babin & Griffin 1998). Customer satisfaction is one of the core concepts not only in the field of marketing and consumer behaviour (Oliver 1997), but also in tourism management in particular (Hui, Wan & Ho 2007). Numerous researchers have examined customer satisfaction theories systematically in the areas of tourist shopping (e. g. Yüksel & Yüksel 2007), heritage organisations (e. g. De Rojas & Camarero 2008), theatrical performance (e. g. Song & Cheung 2010), hotel and restaurant service (e. g. Sánchez-García & Currás-Pérez 2011), and international package tour (e. g. Hosany & Witham 2010; Lee, Jeon & Kim 2011). Different theories from the general consumer behaviour literature have been applied or adapted to understand tourist satisfaction (e. g. Del Bosque & San Martín 2008; Song et al. 2012). Studies generally show that the concept of tourist satisfaction is different from that of customer satisfaction in other industries (Sun & Kim 2013).

A meta-review of tourist satisfaction literature reveals four major review studies (summarised in Table 3.3) which evaluate the previous tourist satisfaction research and provide some signposts that further research is warranted to achieve a more comprehensive and sophisticated understanding of tourist satisfaction (Bowen & Clarke 2009). Ryan (1995) offered a clear, concise guide to issues, concepts, and problems in researching tourist satisfaction, especially providing a thorough grounding in research design and techniques in relation to the tourist attitudes, perceptions, behaviour and levels of tourist satisfaction. It covered the nature of research itself, the design of a research project, qualitative and quantitative research, questionnaire design and implementation, different types of data, correlations, multiple regression analysis, and the coding and significance of data. It made extensive references to the use of statistical software packages, including NCSS, MINITAB, and SPSS. Kozak (2000) conducted a critical review of approaches to measure satisfaction with tourist destinations, thus highlighting the importance of tourist satisfaction measurement in carrying out destination performance research. He suggested that the measurement and management of tourist satisfaction within the context of destination marketing consider the methodological weaknesses of past research and the possibility of their improvement. Specifically, these major improvements are categorised into eight groups: scale development, attribute generation, quality of life, sample selection, consideration of multiple members' opinions, asking of summary questions, consideration of differences between first-time and repeat tourists, and data collection.

Table 3.3　A Summary of Four Tourist Satisfaction Review Studies

Study	Category	Key Words	Topic of Review	Key Findings
Ryan (1995) Researching Tourist Satisfaction: Issues, Concepts, Problems	Book	tourist behaviour & attitudinal measurement; research methodology	tourist attitudes, perceptions, behaviour & satisfaction	Containing twelve themed chapters and a concluding summary, it provides practical information on developing research projects and develops a theoretical basis for tourist behaviour and attitudinal measurement
Kozak (2000) A Critical Review of Approaches to Measure Satisfaction with Tourist Destinations	Journal article	measurement of satisfaction; research methodology	customer satisfaction measurement approaches; tourist satisfaction research	The study suggested that the measurement and management of tourist satisfaction within the context of destination marketing should consider the methodological weaknesses of past research and the possibility of their improvement

Continued

Study	Category	Key Words	Topic of Review	Key Findings
Bowen & Clarke (2002) Reflections on Tourist Satisfaction Research: Past, Present and Future	Journal article	satisfaction; research methodology	three concepts of satisfaction, quality and value; research methodologies & new research methods	The overall objective is to raise issues and to indicate answers—or at least provide some signposts—that will be of use to practitioners and academics alike as they seek to better understand tourist satisfaction
Bowen & Clarke (2009) Fulfilling the Promise: Tourist Satisfaction	Book chapter	antecedents of satisfaction; emotions	antecedents of satisfaction; attribution; emotions; satisfaction & other judgments	It can be concluded that satisfaction research needs to be further extended for achieving a more comprehensive and sophisticated understanding of tourist satisfaction

Bowen and Clarke (2002) provided an overview of some key considerations in the existing literature on tourist satisfaction. The overall objective was to raise issues and to develop answers that would be of use to practitioners and academics alike as they sought to better understand tourist satisfaction. Special emphasis is placed on the distinctiveness of the four concepts: satisfaction, quality, and value; the supposed components of satisfaction and related theoretical paradigms; the particular characteristics of tourism that provide the context for the development of satisfaction; and the need for innovation in research methodologies and methods. Seven years later, Bowen and Clarke (2009) once again conducted a review on both academic writings and industry practices in the tourist satisfaction literature with regards to five aspects: satisfaction and tourism supply, antecedents of satisfaction, attribution, emotions, and satisfaction and other judgements. They also highlighted the need for extending further satisfaction research to achieve a more comprehensive and sophisticated understanding of tourist satisfaction.

Such a review of considerable literature on tourist satisfaction has witnessed the research focus and trend direction developing from satisfaction measurements, research methodology, to antecedents of satisfaction and emotional judgments in tourist behaviour studies. Although numerous empirical studies have been dedicated to investigating determinant variables that affect tourist satisfaction, there is no clear consensus as to the best approach for understanding tourist satisfaction. Some researchers attach great importance to cognitive attributes when evaluating tourist satisfaction with destinations (e.g. Chen & Chen 2010; Wang & Davidson 2010; Lee, Jeon & Kim 2011; Song et al. 2011), while some adopt both cognitive and affective dimensions to assess tourist satisfaction with destinations (e.g. Bigné, Andreu, and Gnoth 2005; Del Bosque & San Martín 2008; De Rojas & Camarero 2008; Su & Hsu 2013). Some recent studies even suggest the supremacy of affective attributes in tourist satisfaction evaluations (e. g. Coghlan & Pearce 2010). More recently, Pearce and Packer (2013), from the viewpoint of contemporary developments in mainstream psychology, highlighted seven challenges for researchers interested in the domain of tourist satisfaction, among which the top two issues resided in recognising the nature and essence of tourist satisfaction as well as its core affective components. These suggested research directions address two earlier studies. One is by Pearce (2009) who characterised an emerging trend of monitoring affect in tourist satisfaction studies; the other is by Coghlan and Pearce (2010) who focused on tracking affective components of tourist satisfaction. Not surprisingly, these new voices have illuminated the path to accessing an under-researched area within tourist behaviour studies, and the necessity of conducting an in-depth study of the affective dimensions of tourist satisfaction. An in-depth literature review of tourist satisfaction for this study is addressed from the following three perspectives.

Cognitive Approach

Customer satisfaction, in association with service quality conceptually and methodologically, has been widely explored by scholars and practitioners over the past three decades. It can be regarded as a post-consumption judgment of the gap between the expected service and the actually perceived service (Anderson 1998). Theoretically, customer satisfaction is generally modelled as the outcome of a comparison process between expectations and perceived performance (Wirtz & Bateson 1999). Similarly, deriving from the research into customer satisfaction, tourist satisfaction, from a cognitive perspective, was conceptualised as the gap between tourist expectation and perception of a multitude of travel attributes. Several different theoretical foundations in satisfaction research can be tracked in the tourism literature. Among these, four theories or models—equity (Oliver & Swan 1989), norm (LaTour & Peat 1979), perceived overall performance (Tse & Wilton 1988), and the expectancy-disconfirmation theory (Oliver 1980)—are adopted by most tourism scholars to assess tourist satisfaction (e. g. Pizam & Milman 1993; Bowen 2001; Chang 2008; Neal & Gursoy 2008).

Equity Theory

Oliver and Swan (1989) used equity theory to examine consumer satisfaction. They argue that consumer satisfaction can be regarded as the relationship between the costs and anticipated rewards/benefits associated with the product or services purchased, with price, time, and effort as the key factors influencing the level of consumer satisfaction. If the rewards exceed the cost, consumers are likely to be satisfied, and vice versa (Sasser, Schlesinger & Heskett 1997). In other words, if travellers perceive that the rewards (benefits) they received from their travel experience outweighed the costs associated with it, they are likely to evaluate their travel experience as a satisfactory experience. Thus, it can be said that if tourists receive benefits or values based on their time, effort, and money for travel, the travel experience at a destination is worthwhile.

Norm Theory

Several researchers have adopted the norm theory suggested by Latour and Peat (1979), in which norms act as reference points for evaluating the product. Satisfaction is reached once those norms are met, and dissatisfaction occurs as a result of disconfirmation relative to these norms. It is similar to the expectancy-disconfirmation paradigm. Yoon and Uysal (2005) argued that tourists are likely to compare their experiences at a travel destination with the past one at other alternative destinations they visited, and then use their past experiences to form a subjective norm (reference point) to evaluate their satisfaction with the new destinations. It has been criticised because of tourists' inability to trace their past experiences and establish accurate assessment standards for specific destinations or travel experiences if they only take two or even less frequent vacations a year (Kozak 2000).

Perceived Performance Model (PPM)

To examine satisfaction, Tse and Wilton (1988) developed the Perceived Performance Model (PPM). This model suggests that consumers' satisfaction or dissatisfaction with a product can be determined by only evaluating the actual performance. According to this model, consumer satisfaction or dissatisfaction is only a function of the actual performance, regardless of consumers' expectations. Accordingly, tourists' evaluation of their satisfaction with travel experiences can be made without considering their prior expectations. This model is effective when tourists do not know what they want to enjoy and experience and do not have any knowledge about their destination circumstances, and only their actual experiences are evaluated to assess tourist satisfaction (Pizam, Neumann & Reichel 1978). However, the PPM has received a considerable amount of criticism, because the absence of the expectation variable makes it "impossible to interpret high levels of customer satisfaction as the results of low expectations or superior quality of service provider" (Fuchs & Weiermair 2004, p. 215). The results of measuring expectations can serve as a benchmark to determine the optimum level of performance, thus improving the quality of tourist experiences (Song et al. 2011).

Expectancy-disconfirmation Paradigm (EDP)

The most widely adopted model of customer satisfaction evaluation has been the expectancy-disconfirmation paradigm (Oliver 1980), which has dominated satisfaction research for more than two decades (e. g. Oliver 1997; Fournier & Mick 1999). The EDP posits that satisfaction is a summary judgment based on the comparison between product performance and its prior expectation (Oliver 1993). In the model, the discrepancy between performance and expectation determines the final stage of satisfaction (Oliver 1980). When you get what you expect, you have a confirmation; when you get more than expected, you have a positive disconfirmation; and when you get less than expected, you have a negative disconfirmation. According to the framework, consumers are satisfied when perceived performance meets or exceeds expectations and dissatisfied when performance fails to meet expectations.

The EDP, from the general consumer behaviour and satisfaction literature, has been widely applied and confirmed in researching tourist satisfaction. It postulates that tourists compare perceived travel experiences with some prior standards (expectations) and that the confirmation or disconfirmation of those expectations predicts tourist satisfaction (e. g. Hui, Wan & Ho 2007; Song et al. 2012). For instance, Chon (1989) indicated that tourist satisfaction is based on the discrepancy between previously held expectations and the perceived evaluative outcome of the experience, which is simply the result of a comparison between tourists' previous images of the destination and what tourists actually see, feel, and achieve at the destination.

Despite its prevalence in the literature, the EDP has been criticised by some researchers as not being able to provide a reliable measure of tourist satisfaction (e. g. Johns, Avcí & Karatepe 2004; Huang, Weiler & Assaker 2015). One shortcoming of the EDP is that tourists' retrospective expectations may be altered or updated by the receipt of further information about the destination, and it is thus difficult to measure their actual travel experiences at a destination as well as their revisit expectations, because perceptions would be determined by expectations (Yüksel & Yüksel 2001; Huang, Hsu & Chan 2010). Given that the discrepancy is a purely cognitive term, the other major concern of the EDP lies in its strong reliance on cognitive evaluation processes, and its disregard for affective and personality-related antecedents in the tourist satisfaction evaluation process (Farber & Hall 2007; Oliver 1993).

In summary, the above review of several cognitive approaches to tourist satisfaction study indicates that cognitive approaches are valuable in providing a broader social context in which to frame tourist satisfaction. However, it is contended that cognitive approaches remain insufficient for explaining tourist satisfaction without incorporating affective approaches (Del Bosque & San Martin 2008; Oliver 1993). The evaluation of tourist satisfaction needs to be considered in multiple dimensions. In particular, the integration of the cognitive and affective approaches is needed for the inquiry into tourist satisfaction. For instance, in the EDP, confirmation or disconfirmation of the previous expectancy with the perception after the travel experience would involve both cognitive and affective processing in the tourists' minds in leading to the final stage of satisfaction/dissatisfaction. Thus, on a theoretical basis, the EDP does seem to have informed the later development of cognitive-affective satisfaction theory (Huang, Weiler & Assaker 2015).

Cognitive-affective Approach

Several researchers have stressed that satisfaction is not a simple cognitive measure and is instead a complex affective state(Westbrook 1987; Oliver 1993). Initially, Westbrook (1980) equated satisfaction with emotion and later tested emotion as an antecedent of satisfaction (Westbrook & Oliver 1991). In a comprehensive model, Oliver (1993) included cognitive, affective, and attribute performance assessments as determinants of a global satisfaction measure. In assessing the state of satisfaction research, Fournier and Mick (1999) encouraged an expansion of the role of emotions. Mano and Oliver (1993) extended the theoretical and empirical evidence and concluded that:

The satisfaction response is not easily tied down. It does not respond as a pure affect nor does it exist in the absence of feeling. It is apparently a complex human response with both cognitive and affective components (p. 465).

The EDP might perform poorly in explaining satisfaction with travel experiences or service encounters, because service encounters are not easily reduced to concrete, multi-attribute evaluations (e. g. Jayanti 1998). The inclusion of the affective dimension in the conceptualisation of tourist satisfaction with destinations is particularly important due to its experiential nature. Because tourists interact with the tourism setting and personnel during the travel experience, understanding tourists' affective responses becomes critical in modelling satisfaction in a tourism setting.

The cognitive-affective model, which often seems to be more insightful in explaining the tourist satisfaction process, has been implicitly and explicitly applied (e. g. Oliver 1993; Yoon & Uysal 2005; Del Bosque & San Martin 2008). It posits the causal role of cognition as a necessary but not sufficient condition in order to elicit emotions (Lazarus 1991). A common agreement among researchers seems to be that affective evaluation depends on cognitive assessment while the affective responses are formed as a function of the cognitive ones (Yoon & Uysal 2005). The distinction and direction of the relationship between cognitive and affective components have been emphasised in the existing tourist satisfaction models. In such a dual system process, the cognitive path involves the evaluation of quality and comparison with expectations, whereas the affective path begins when experiences reach or exceed expectations leading to feelings of pleasure. This cognitive-affective sequence indicates the cognitive evaluations can serve as antecedents to affective dimensions of tourist satisfaction. For instance, in an attempt to analyse how visitor emotions in a theme park environment influence satisfaction and behavioural intentions, Bigné, Andreu, and Gnoth (2005) used CFA to conclude that the cognitive theory of emotions (i. e. emotions are engendered by visitors' disconfirmation of the theme park) better explains the effect of pleasure on satisfaction and loyalty, thus proposing a model that explains the cognitive-affective determinants of satisfaction. Del Bosque and San Martin (2008) carried out an exploration of the cognitive and affective psychological processes which an individual goes through during the pre-experience and post-experience stages and confirmed that emotions are affected by post-experience cognition (disconfirmation). The findings have corroborated the cognitive-affective approach for researching tourist satisfaction.

While past literature has concentrated on describing satisfaction based on the evaluations consumers make of perceived quality (confirmation/disconfirmation theories) from their expectations, more recent developments have regarded the emotions consumers experience as the determinant factors in creating satisfaction (Bowen & Clarke 2002; De Rojas & Camarero 2008; Meng, Turk & Altintas 2012). De Rojas and Camarero (2008) defined satisfaction as the sensations or feelings generated both by cognitive and emotional aspects of the goods and services, as well as an accumulated evaluation of various components and features. For a long period, it had been assumed that consumer decisions were based on the product quality, use, and benefits. Only in the last two decades has market research begun to study the emotions evoked by the stimuli of marketing (Laros & Steenkamp 2005) from an affective approach. These studies provide important insights into the role of affect in the process of tourist satisfaction formation. Instead of treating both cognitive and affective processes as being independent from one another (Mano & Oliver 1993; Oliver 1993), the studies link affect to disconfirmation process to better understand tourist satisfaction from a comprehensive perspective and provide a dynamic analysis of the influence of cognition and affect in tourist satisfaction research.

Traditionally, most studies examined the relationship between cognitive determinants and satisfaction without considering affective determinants (e. g. Wang, Hsieh & Huan 2000). Subsequently, an increasing number of studies have perceived satisfaction as a cognitive process leading to an emotional state (e. g. Crompton & Love 1995; Chhetri, Arrowsmith & Jackson 2004). However, there are still comparatively few studies simultaneously investigating cognitive and affective dimensions of tourist satisfaction, although a number of studies called for the need to examine the impact of both antecedents on satisfaction (Bowen & Clarke 2002; Meng, Turk & Altintas 2012). Neuropsychological research has confirmed that emotions play an important role in the brain functioning to determine among alternatives and there are interactions between cognition and affect in the brain (e. g. LeDoux 2000); however, there is little investigation into how cognitive and affective antecedents interact to affect tourist satisfaction. In conclusion, the contribution of the cognitive-affective model applied to tourist satisfaction is still under-theorised and under-researched (Huang, Weiler & Assaker 2015).

The Primacy of the Affective Approach

As addressed above, the cognitive and affective sequence shows a cognitive appraisal of tourist satisfaction and the creation of the affective responses to tourist satisfaction. Recent literature recommends that tourist satisfaction research put a high premium on tourists' emotional states during their experiences (e. g. Coghlan & Pearce 2010; Lee, Lee & Choi 2011; Tung & Ritchie 2011). As such, the cognitive-affective model seems to be further developed to merit continuing research attention. In general consumer behaviour literature, Wirtz, Mattila and Tan (2000) purely focused on the emotional role of satisfaction in the consumption of services. Similarly, in tourism literature, Faullant, Matzler and Mooradian (2011) highlighted affective considerations of tourist satisfaction and suggested an instance of an "emotions first, cognition second" (p. 1425) sequence in the satisfaction evaluation process. Thus, the primacy of affective approach has been recently theorised and demonstrated empirically in tourist satisfaction assessment.

A new school of thought regarding the primacy of the affective responses to tourist satisfaction, either in the affective-cognitive approach or in the purely affective approach, is an acknowledged and emerging research issue (Coghlan & Pearce 2010; Pearce 2012; Pearce & Packer 2013). Zajonc (1984) proposed that affective responses can be primary in the formation of summary evaluations, and that affect can occur without being preceded by cognitive recognition or processing. Zajonc and Markus (1985) argued that an emotion can be generated by biological, sensory or cognitive events. From the neuroscience perspective, Pearce (2012) confirmed that affective responses, evoked by neural stimulation, do occur automatically without being triggered by individuals' cognitive judgments. This is a neglected dimension of tourist satisfaction research. Some neuropsychological research has confirmed these recent theories (e. g. LeDoux 2000).

Unlike the above-mentioned two approaches, the primacy of the affective approach acknowledges and highlights tourists' affective considerations in explaining tourist satisfaction. Adopting such an approach, researchers have examined both the antecedents and consequences of tourist satisfaction (e. g. He & Song 2009; Coghlan & Pearce 2010; Hosany & Witham 2010). From the neuroscience perspective, the model of tracking affective dimensions of tourist satisfaction seems to look into tourist satisfaction from the tourist's inner mindset and thus offers more insights into the psychological mechanisms of tourist satisfaction.

Measurement of Tourist Satisfaction

Irrespective of how satisfaction is conceptualised (either cognitive, cognitive-affective, or purely affective), it is common for studies to measure satisfaction at the aggregated level (e. g. Lee, Yoon & Lee 2007; Chen & Chen 2010; Engeset & Elvekrok 2015) as opposed to the attribute level (Chi & Qu 2008; Eusébio & Vieira 2013). Measuring tourist experience and evaluating tourist satisfaction are challenging and difficult, as tourist experience takes place in phases (e. g. trip planning, travel to and from the destination, the destination experience). Tourist satisfaction research has adopted both attribute-based and overall approaches in operationalising and measuring tourist satisfaction as a complex psychological construct（Chi & Qu 2008；Hsu 2003；Huang et al. 2010）. Satisfaction research in tourism and hospitality has indicated that tourists' satisfaction with individual attributes of the destination leads to their overall satisfaction with the destination（e. g. Kozak & Rimmington 2000；Hsu 2003）. It is important to distinguish overall tourist satisfaction from tourist satisfaction with individual attribute of the destination.

Overall tourist satisfaction with a travel experience is a function of satisfactions with the individual attributes/elements of all the products/services that constitute to the experience, such as accommodation, weather, natural environment, social environment, attractions, restaurants （e. g. Pizam & Ellis 1999；Chi & Qu 2008）. Tourism researchers have been interested in measuring both overall tourist satisfaction with a particular destination（e. g. Kozak 2001； Alegre & Cladera 2006；Yu & Goulden 2006）and tourist satisfaction with a specific service encounter, such as with the accommodation sector（e. g. Heung 2000）, restaurants（e. g. Lin & Mattila 2010；Nam & Lee 2011）, travel agencies（e. g. Millán & Esteban 2004）, package tours（e. g. Lee, Jeon & Kim 2011）, interpreting services（Huang, Weiler & Assaker 2015）, and retail shops（Yüksel 2007）. Although there is a growing belief that an understanding of satisfaction with each aspect of the trip must be the basic parameter used to evaluate overall satisfaction with the destination（Gountas & Gountas 2007）, most satisfaction studies in tourism and other aspects of leisure have been conducted after the travel experience and have looked into overall opinions expressed by tourists regarding the general tourism experience. As a consequence, from the destination marketing perspective, understanding tourists' overall satisfaction with the destination and its determinants is of great significance in a practical sense.

Based on existing theoretical and empirical research in the fields of marketing and tourism, Gnoth et al.（2009）developed a conceptual model of tourist satisfaction at the destination level which could serve as a background for designing a universal, parsimonious, short and easily applicable measurement instrument. As to the research methodology, the research design covers qualitative, quantitative, and mixed research. Tourist satisfaction studies adopt many advanced statistical techniques（e. g. SEM）to test the relationship between tourist satisfaction and other casual factors. For instance, Hsu（2003）employed a multi-attribute approach to investigate mature motor coach travellers' satisfaction. Using half of the randomly selected data from the sample, she conducted an exploratory factor analysis（EFA）to identify 20 items；using the other half of the sample, she then ran a CFA to confirm the underlying structure. Of the six latent variables, flexible schedule, tour guide, and price and value were found to have significant effect on travellers' overall satisfaction.

Tourist satisfaction has been frequently examined with both antecedent and consequent constructs. The antecedent-satisfaction-consequence framework has been commonly evidenced in tourist satisfaction studies (e. g. Assaker & Hallak 2013; Palau-Saumell et al. 2013). In the majority of studies within the tourism context, either the expectancy-disconfirmation model or cognitive-affective model has been applied to identify and investigate the antecedents of tourist satisfaction; high levels of satisfaction with travel experiences lead to the positive consequences in tourist behaviour studies, such as intention to recommend and destination loyalty (e. g. Gountas & Gountas 2007; Hosany & Witham 2010; Prayag, Hosany & Odeh 2013). As a complex psychological phenomenon, the evaluation of tourist satisfaction is a complicated process that can be influenced by various cognitive and affective factors. For example, service quality and perceived value have been frequently adopted as determinants of satisfaction in the literature. While service quality is mostly treated as a cognitive response to a service offering (Anderson, Fornell & Lehmann 1994), perceived value may reflect more of the customers' emotions (Lee, Lee & Choi 2010). In a multicultural tourism experience, levels of tourist satisfaction can be influenced by their personality, lifestyle, motivations, previous experiences with knowledge of the destination, marketing methods, and image of the destination (Ryan 1997).

Conceptualising Tourist Satisfaction in the Study

The complexity of researching tourist satisfaction also lies in its conceptualisation. Past literature has demonstrated that researchers tend to employ three approaches of satisfaction conceptualisation to reveal the innate features of tourist satisfaction as a complicated psychological construct, i. e. attribute-based and global satisfaction concepts, and a multilayer satisfaction conceptual framework. An attribute-based conceptualisation (e. g. Tribe & Snaith 1998; Heung 2000) enables more in-depth understanding of satisfaction with regard to salient travel attributes and dimensions; a global concept of satisfaction (e. g. Heung, Wong & Qu 2002; Yoon & Uysal 2005; Gountas & Gountas 2007) is adopted more often when researchers study relationships between satisfaction and its determinant or dependent variables. It is important to distinguish overall satisfaction from satisfaction with individual attributes, because particular tourism attributes have a notable effect on overall tourist satisfaction (Seaton & Bennett 1996). Besides these two approaches of satisfaction conceptualisation, Huang, Hsu and Chan (2010) used employee performance or service quality to predict tourist satisfaction, and developed a multilayer conceptual framework for tourist satisfaction specifying satisfaction objects in the context of a package tour, which has largely complemented the satisfaction research.

Given the key role of customer satisfaction, a great deal of research has been devoted to investigating the antecedents of satisfaction (e. g. Tse & Wilton 1988; Yoon & Uysal 2005; Wang & Hsu 2010). Most early research work concentrated on satisfaction at the global level

(e. g. Oliver 1980). Afterwards, researchers started to pay attention to attribute-level conceptualisation of the antecedents of satisfaction (e. g. Oliver 1993). Under an attribute-level approach, overall satisfaction is a function of attribute-level evaluations. Attribute satisfaction has significant, positive, and direct effects on overall satisfaction; overall satisfaction and attribute satisfaction are distinct but related constructs (Oliver 1993). Attribute-level evaluations typically capture a significant amount of variation in overall satisfaction (e. g. Bolton & Drew 1991; Hsu 2003).

If satisfaction is conceptualised as an overall end-of-trip evaluation of the destination experience rather than conceptualised and measured at the level of specific destination attributes (Huang & Hsu 2009; Huang, Weiler & Assaker 2015), it seems that it can be better differentiated from positive emotions in the destination context and the relationship between the two concepts can be clearer. It is common for studies to measure satisfaction at the aggregated level (e. g. Lee, Yoon & Lee 2007; Chen & Chen 2010; Huang, Weiler & Assaker 2015) as opposed to the attribute level (e. g. Chi & Qu 2008; Eusebio & Vieira 2013). Accordingly, consistent with recent research in tourism (e. g. Assaker & Hallak 2013; Sun, Chi & Xu 2013; Engeset & Elvekrok 2015), tourist satisfaction is operationalised as a summative overall construct in this study.

Satisfaction research in tourism has indicated that tourists' satisfaction with an individual component of the destination may lead to their overall satisfaction with the destination(Mayer et al. 1998; Hsu 2003). Overall satisfaction with a travel experience is a function of satisfaction with various attributes of the destination, such as travel environment, natural and historic attractions, infrastructure, accessibility, entertainment, and events (Pizam & Ellis 1999; Kozak & Rimmington 2000). For example, instead of assessing satisfaction with one aspect of the service experience at one point in time, Neal and Gursoy (2008) proposed that travellers' overall satisfaction with travel and tourism services is a function of their satisfaction with pre-trip services, services at the destination and the transit route services. As a consequence, tourist satisfaction should be studied as a system process because several stages of the travel process collectively contribute to the overall tourist satisfaction. In addition, Huang, Hsu and Chan (2010) proposed a multilayer satisfaction framework to examine the relationship between tour guide performance and tourist satisfaction. Tourist satisfaction was investigated at three levels: satisfaction with tour-guiding service, with services provided by ground tour operators at a destination, and with overall tour experience at a destination. One theoretical contribution of the study lies in the multilayer conceptualisation of the satisfaction construct using employee performance or service quality to predict tourist satisfaction.

Based on the aforementioned discussion, the current study conceptualises and operationalises tourist satisfaction as a summative overall construct, adopting the affective approach to assess mainland Chinese package tourists' holistic satisfaction with Australia as a destination. In the range of travel experiences provided by Australia, the focus on affect in the concept of satisfaction is particularly relevant given that the majority of activities are based upon the tourists' involvement and experiences with nature-based tourism. As a consequence, overall tourist satisfaction, as one of three research constructs (i. e. tourist personality, affective response, and tourist satisfaction) in this study, should be taken as a whole in operationalising the conceptual model. Accordingly, Chinese package travellers' overall satisfaction with Australia as a tourist destination will be measured.

Personality and Affect

Although tourism research acknowledges the importance of studying emotions (Hosany & Gilbert 2010; Nawijn et al. 2013; Lee 2014), prior research fails to simultaneously examine the relationship between tourist personality and affective responses. Consumption-related affect/emotions—usually operationalised as broad, summary dimensions such as positive and negative emotions or, alternatively, pleasure and arousal—have been shown to be influenced by enduring personality traits and, in turn, to influence customer satisfaction.

In principle, personality is a relatively permanent or at least long-term matter of predispositions, while affect is a short-term matter of consciously accessible feelings (Yik & Russell 2001). Robust relationships have been identified between enduring traits and transient affect (Mooradian 1996). Some people are more inclined to be happy and relaxed, while others are more likely to be nervous or worried. A straight relationship between personality and emotions has demonstrated the existence of a direct effect that tourists' personalities have on their emotions as regards the changes in their emotional experiences during a vacation (Lin et al. 2014). Faullant et al. (2011) analysed the relationships between personality, basic emotions, and satisfaction in the context of the mountaineering experience, and their results show that two basic emotions—fear and joy—are influenced by neuroticism and extraversion respectively. In addition, their study showed that the consumption-related emotions, together with cognitive evaluations affect tourist satisfaction.

Many researchers have reached the consensus that one's affect can be predicted from or explained by one's enduring personality traits (e. g. Yik & Russell 2001; McNiel & Fleeson 2006; Srivastava, Angelo & Vallereux 2008). Therefore, the study of affect would be enhanced through clarifying the relationship between enduring personality and temporary affect. Yik and Russell (2001) provided ample evidence to support the Five Factors Model (FFM) as the powerful model for personality in predicting short-term affective states. In short, both empirical and conceptual considerations indicate reliable and meaningful links between personality and affect.

The role of individual differences in shaping those travel-related affective responses has not been adequately investigated and has not been tested empirically. Within personality research, there is also a pronounced emphasis on dispositions toward global positive and negative affect, rather than the frequency and intensity of experiencing particular emotional states (e. g. Pervin 1993; Shiota, Keltner & John 2006). Since issues may arise pertaining to how personality influences affect (e. g. Carver, Sutton & Scheier 2000; Lucas & Fujita 2000; Penley & Tomaka 2002), research has increasingly focused on the prediction of affect from personality (Yik & Russell 2001). The understanding of the nature of affect will depend on the degree to which it is more environment- or personality-dependent (Beaty, Cleveland & Murphy 2001). Therefore, it can be proposed that correlations between personality and affect would reveal the fundamental structure of affect. In addition, some personality dimensions might predict behaviour indirectly via their association with affect.

Affect or emotional predispositions are an extension of, or closely related to a range of personality traits (Watson, Clark & Tellegen 1988). In psychology, a number of studies have aimed at correlating personality traits with affective responses (e. g. Rusting & Larsen 1997; Giluk 2009; Miller, Vachon & Lynam 2009). The close relationship between personality and affect has been consistently documented. Many researchers agree that a link exists between personality and emotions. Having a good command of such a link would be extremely useful in developing appropriate marketing strategies to satisfy different personalised needs. Affective experiences influence consumers' behaviour and perception during consumption interactions (Gountas & Gountas 2007). Because emotion is also involved with a behavioural response derived from physiological arousal (Westbrook 1980), personal traits or enduring dispositions should be taken into account when assessing emotional responses (Chang 2008).

In tourism research, Lin et al. (2014) acknowledged and addressed the role of personality in influencing the change of emotions tourists experience during a vacation. When the impacts of personality on specific emotions were addressed, personality was found to determine the baseline levels of fear and sadness and moderate change in disgust across individuals' vacations. Gountas and Gountas (2007) identified direct relationships among tourism consumers' personality orientation, emotional characteristics, and self-reported satisfaction with their experience. Personality proved to be an antecedent to tourists' emotional states and both personality and emotions were found to have an impact on consumers' evaluations of their travel experiences.

Relating Extraversion &Neuroticism to Affect

A body of literature exists concerning personality traits influencing customer emotions and behaviour. The majority of research has found that the relationship between personality and affect is correlational. Each of the personality traits in the FFM — namely, extraversion, neuroticism, conscientiousness, agreeableness, and openness — has been linked theoretically and empirically to positive and negative affect respectively. For instance, Shiota, Keltner and John (2006) argued that positive emotion dispositions are differentially associated with self- and peer-rated Big Five Factors. In particular, many studies on the links between personality and affect have relied on the two dominant temperamental traits of extraversion and neuroticism (e. g. Eysenck 1992; Gross, Sutton & Ketelaar 1998; Lucas et al. 2000). Previous studies have demonstrated prominent correlations between extraversion and positive affect and neuroticism and negative affect with remarkable robustness, stability, and generality; these relationships have been replicated repeatedly in cross-disciplinary and cross-cultural studies (e. g. Rusting & Larsen 1997; Wilson & Gullone 1999; McNiel & Fleeson 2006; Srivastava, Angelo & Vallereux 2008; Miller, Vachon & Lynam 2009).

Since the neuroticism trait is associated with a sensitivity to risk, it reflects a person's propensity to experience psychological distress (Ross et al. 2009). Neuroticism is generally described using words such as fearful, anxious, pessimistic, worried, and insecure. Neurotic individuals are depressed, anxious, and unstable(Yoo & Gretzel 2011). Consequently, neurotic individuals feel a higher degree of uncertainty when making tourism choices, exaggerate the magnitude of adverse consequences, appear to be afraid of making a poor decision, and feel regretful about any inappropriate decision. In order to avoid making the wrong choice, neurotic individuals are likely to be highly involved throughout the destination selection and decision-making process (Matsumoto 2006).

Costa and McCrae (1980) found that the extraversion trait strongly correlates with positive affect and that neuroticism traits correlate strongly with negative affect. Extraverts are cheerful and enthusiastic, so positive affect forms a core aspect of this personality factor (Tellegen 1985; Tellegen & Waller 2008). Extraversion is related positively to positive thinking and positive reappraisals (e. g. Watson & Hubbard 1996). Individuals high in neuroticism are prone to experience negative emotions such as *depression*, *anxiety*, and *anger* (Velting 1999). Hopelessness and depression are predicted positively by neuroticism and negatively by extraversion (Velting 1999). Neurotic persons typically express negative affect when in stressful situations (Van Heck 1997). High scores on neuroticism represent individual differences in the tendency to experience distress, nervous tension, depression, guilt, low self-esteem, poor control of impulses, and somatic complaints (Miller, Vachon & Lynam 2009). Persons high in neuroticism tend to experience negative affect (McNiel & Fleeson 2006). Extraversion is distinguished by venturesomeness, affiliation, positive affectivity, energy, ascendance, and ambition (Penley & Tomaka 2002). Extraverts are inclined to favour social activities and intense personal interactions (Bakker et al. 2006). Using the Day Reconstruction Method, Srivastava et al. (2008) argued that extraverts enjoy interacting with others and experience positive affect during all the episodes from a single day. Most notably, the relationship between extraversion and positive affect was found to be partially mediated by extraverts' greater social participation. The findings support a transaction approach to personality, in which extraversion is seen as a style of actively engaging with the environment (Srivastava, Angelo & Vallereux 2008).

The correlations between extraversion and positive affect as well as between neuroticism and negative affect replicate across measures and methods (Lucas & Fujita 2000), indicating strongly that a tendency to experience positive affect or negative affect is one of the defining characteristics of extraversion or neuroticism respectively (Srivastava, Angelo & Vallereux 2008). The positive affect scale (Watson, Clark & Tellegen 1988) contains the items *active*, *enthusiastic*, and *inspired*; the extraversion scale embraces the statements "is talkative", and "generates a lot of enthusiasm". The negative affect scale contains the items *jittery*, *afraid*, *scared*, *nervous*, and *ashamed*; the neuroticism scale embraces the statements "can be tense", "get nervous easily", and "worries a lot". Similar connotations are found on both the personality and affect scales. In the tourism setting, Faullant, Matzler and Mooradian (2011) theoretically and empirically linked extraversion and neuroticism to the fundamental positive (*joy*) and negative (*fear*) affective responses respectively. Based on these findings and rationales, it is hypothesised that:

H1a: Extraversion has a positive impact on positive affect experienced at a destination.

H1b: Extraversion has a negative impact on negative affect experienced at a destination.

H2a: Neuroticism has a negative impact on positive affect experienced at a destination.

H2b: Neuroticism has a positive impact on negative affect experienced at a destination.

Relating Agreeableness &Conscientiousness to Affect

The relations between neuroticism/extraversion and affect are strong, robust, and clearly important; nevertheless, few studies have been conducted to examine the predictive utility of the three remaining factors (agreeableness, conscientiousness, and openness) on affect (Yik & Russell 2001). It has been suggested that these three factors are also significantly related to affect (McCrae & Costa 1991; Shiota, Keltner & John 2006; Ong & Musa 2012). For instance, instead of being tied solely to extraversion, positive affect stems primarily from individuals' interpersonal relationships with others (Watson & Clark 1992; Cheng & Furnham 2003). While extraversion may determine the quantity of these relationships, agreeableness dominates the quality of the relationships (DeNeve & Cooper 1998).

Agreeable people are generally good-natured, generous, cooperative, supportive, caring, considerate, and willing to share their interests with others(Barrick, Mount & Judge 2001). In addition, agreeable individuals are generally trusting and believe that others are honest and well-intentioned (Costa & McCrae 1992; Tan & Tang 2013). Therefore, in the context of a group-package tour, agreeable individuals are likely to approach group members with a sense of trust and care. In most cases, they would be favoured by their travel companions in the group. In the work setting, as agreeable individuals might regulate their emotions to maintain harmonious relationships with other colleagues, they would create a friendly environment, enjoy consideration from others, thus enhancing team cohesiveness and winning trust and respect from other team members (Panaccio & Vandenberghe 2012). The majority of agreeable people generally tend to suppress or ignore any minor negative affect engendered by their travel experiences and therefore tend to believe that the trip was a success (Barnett 2006).

Conscientious individuals tend to be dependable, responsible, self-disciplined, strong-willed, and achievement-oriented (Barrick, Mount & Judge 2001). In addition, conscientiousness has particularly been linked with self-esteem (Costa & McCrae 1992; Brown & Ryan 2003), which seems consistent with the need for self-esteem acting as one of travel motivations based on Maslow's hierarchy of needs. In general, hopelessness and depression can not be linked to conscientiousness (Velting 1999; Yoo & Gretzel 2011), and positive affect is predicted positively by conscientiousness (Cheng & Furnham 2003). Conscientiousness is related positively to positive thinking and positive reappraisals (Watson & Hubbard 1996; Zhang 2006). McCrae and Costa (1991) found that high levels of agreeableness and conscientiousness are associated with increased positive, and decreased negative affect. They interpreted these significant results as indicating that "loving and hardworking people have more positive experiences and less negative experiences because these traits foster social and achievement-related successes" (McCrae & Costa 1991, p. 28). It seems likely that higher levels of agreeableness and conscientiousness foster the types of interpersonal and achievement-related experiences that lead, in turn, to greater life satisfaction for many individuals (Besser & Shackelford 2007). Based on the aforementioned discussion and analysis, both agreeableness and conscientiousness were found to correlate positively with positive affect and negatively with negative affect. Thus, it is hypothesised that:

H3a: Agreeableness has a positive impact on positive affect experienced at a destination.

H3b: Agreeableness has a negative impact on negative affect experienced at a destination.

H4a: Conscientiousness has a positive impact on positive affect experienced at a destination.

H4b: Conscientiousness has a negative impact on negative affect experienced at a destination.

Relating Openness to Affect

Individuals who are categorised as open are intellectually curious, imaginative, broad-minded, unconventional, and more willing to explore new ideas (Barrick et al. 2001). Moreover, openness is related to aesthetic sensitivity, attentiveness to inner feelings, preference for variety, and independence of judgment(e. g. Costa & McCrae 1992; Yoo & Gretzel 2011). High open people display creativity, flexible thinking, and culture appreciation (Moutafi, Furnham & Crump 2006). Using data from a normal adult sample, Costa, McCrae and Holland (1984) found low but significant correlations between an openness marker and measures of positive and negative affect. Jeng and Teng (2008) investigated the relationships between personality and motivations for playing online games, and found that openness was positively related to discovery and role-playing motivations. Furthermore, openness is positively correlated with intelligence or fluid intelligence (Moutafi, Furnham & Crump 2006). Many studies also showed that pro-environmental attitudes were related to openness (e. g. Hirsh & Dolderman 2007; Hirsh 2010; Ong & Musa 2012). Individuals with high openness are characterised by their tendency to seek novelty, eagerness to gain new knowledge, care for the environment, and great passion for life, thus leading to positive affect and high life satisfaction. In psychology, positive relations were reported between openness and positive affective states (Costa & McCrae 1984; McCrae & Costa 1991; Watson & Clark 1992). Interestingly, high openness individuals tend to experience higher levels of positive affect more keenly than do other individuals (Costa & McCrae 1992).

Individuals who score high on openness may also be more open to affective responses to travel experiences than closed individuals. Aesthetic engagement with a landscape alone will result in differing levels of pleasure and comfort among people with the features of openness. Affective responses to travel experiences are highly dependent not only upon how the tourists perceive the viewed landscape based on its looks and perhaps sounds, but also of their historical knowledge or cultural awareness of the landscape itself (Chhetri, Arrowsmith & Jackson 2004). This analysis suggests that openness with aesthetic sensitivity will correlate positively with positive affect. Therefore, it is hypothesised that:

H5a: Openness has a positive impact on positive affect experienced at a destination.
H5b: Openness has a negative impact on negative affect experienced at a destination.

Affect and Satisfaction

Research on the role of affect in the formation of customer satisfaction has mostly examined and operationalised affect as high-order and broad dimensions: either positive/negative affect or pleasure and arousal (Faullant et al. 2011). Westbrook (1987) is credited with introducing the concept of affect into the cognitive process of customer satisfaction (Oliver 1980). Using Izard's (1977) emotional typology, Westbrook integrated affective responses with the expectancy-disconfirmation model and confirmed that positive and negative consumption-related emotions contributed significantly to the explanation of variance of overall satisfaction with automobiles and paid cable TV services, concluding that "affective variables alone explain almost as much variance in satisfaction judgements as do the cognitive belief variables" (Westbrook 1987, pp. 265-266). Mano and Oliver (1993) further investigated the impact of affect on satisfaction and found that satisfaction was positively correlated with pleasure and negatively correlated with displeasure, thus extending the theoretical and empirical evidence for the affective determinant of customer satisfaction. Both positive and negative affect could serve as concurrent antecedents to satisfaction; affective determinants are as important as cognitive determinants of satisfaction (Oliver 1993). Subsequently, the role of affect as a predictor of satisfaction judgements has received considerable attention, and the relationship between affect and satisfaction has been confirmed in marketing and consumer behaviour studies (e. g. Mooradian & Olver 1997; Bagozzi, Gopinath & Nyer 1999; Wirtz & Bateson 1999; Phillips & Baumgartner 2002; Ladhari 2007; Walsh et al. 2011).

In consumer behaviour research, affect/emotions arising from consumption experiences deposit affective memory traces, which consumers process and integrate to form post-consumption satisfaction judgements (e. g. Westbrook & Oliver 1991; Ladhari 2007). Similarly, in tourism, tourists processed affective responses elicited by travel experiences to shape post-trip evaluations of satisfaction. In the past decade, tourism researchers have attempted to examine the impact of affect/emotions on tourist satisfaction and behavioural intentions, and have confirmed relationship between affective responses and tourist satisfaction (e. g. Zins 2002; Gountas & Gountas 2007; Chang 2008; Del Bosque & San Martín 2008; Faullant et al. 2011; Su & Hsu 2013; Prayag et al. 2015). Specifically, significant relationships between affective responses and tourist satisfaction have been established in the contexts of shopping environment (e. g. Yüksel 2007; Yüksel & Yüksel 2007), the theme park experience (e. g., Bigné, Andreu & Gnoth 2005), the restaurant and dining service (e. g. Arora & Singer 2006; Han & Jeong 2013), the destination experience (e. g. Del Bosque & San Martín 2008; Hosany & Gilbert 2010; Prayag, Hosany & Odeh 2013), the heritage tourism (e. g. De Rojas & Camarero 2008; Su & Hsu 2013), and the festival environment (e. g. Lee et al. 2008; Grappi & Montanari 2011; Mason & Paggiaro 2012).

Positive Affect and Satisfaction

In the context of marketing and consumer behaviour, satisfaction is a key outcome of positive affective responses such as *pleasure*, *interest*, and *joy* (Oliver 1997). Westbrook

(1987) identified the specific positive affect/emotions (i. e. *joy* and *interest*) as the important predictors of tourists' satisfaction evaluations. In a later study, Westbrook and Oliver (1991) demonstrated that satisfaction was related to *pleasant surprise* and *interest*. Thus, it is logical to believe that in tourism, positive emotions such as *joy* (Faullant, Matzler & Mooradian 2011), *happiness*, *excitement*, and *pleasure* (Grappi & Montanari 2011) have a favourable influence on satisfaction. Adventure tourism such as mountaineering evokes powerful emotion (*joy*) that, coupled with cognitive appraisals, influence tourist satisfaction (Faullant et al. 2011). In a heritage tourism context, Prayag, Hosany and Odeh (2013) showed that *joy*, *love*, and *positive surprise* can generate satisfaction. In the theme park experience, Bigne et al. (2005) found a positive link between *arousal*, *pleasure* and satisfaction. *Pleasure* is also related to the formation of satisfaction in a restaurant setting (Lin & Mattila 2010). Satisfaction is a key outcome of positive affective responses and the lack of negative affective responses (Fallant et al. 2011; Hosany & Prayag 2013).

It remains unclear in the marketing literature whether satisfaction is phenomenologically distinct from many positive emotions (Bagozzi et al. 1999). Shaver et al. (1987) found that satisfaction shared much common variance with positive emotions such as *happiness*, *joy*, *delight*, and *enjoyment*. In other studies (e. g. Nyer 1997) positive emotion (*joy*) and satisfaction loaded on the same factor. A review of specific affective responses in tourism research indicated that *satisfied* was identified as one of the positive affect/emotions (e. g. Zins 2002; Bigné, Andreu & Gnoth 2005; Lee et al. 2008; Jang et al. 2009). The overlap between positive affect and satisfaction can be described as ambiguous and complicated due to satisfaction being neither a basic emotion nor a central affective category in leading theories on affect (Bagozzi, Gopinath & Nyer 1999).

In the context of overall destination experiences, some studies (e. g. Del Bosque & San Martin 2008; Hosany & Gilbert 2010) have established significant relationships between positive affect/emotions and satisfaction. Congruent with prior studies in consumer behaviour (e. g. Westbrook 1987; Westbrook & Oliver 1991) that have established surprise as a key component of satisfactory consumption experiences, Prayag et al. (2015) showed that *positive surprise* was related to overall satisfaction with the tourist destination. Positive affect largely enhances tourists' satisfaction level, which in turn has a significant influence on behavioural intentions (Prayag et al. 2015). Affective responses are key dimensions of travel experiences (Lee & Shafer 2002; Pearce 2012), serving as the most significant indicator of overall satisfaction. Following the same reasoning, the greater the level of the positive affect expressed by respondents, the greater the level of overall satisfaction with the destination. Based on the above discussions, many studies in the marketing and tourism literature confirm a positive relationship between positive emotions and satisfaction in various contexts and settings. Therefore, it is hypothesised that:

H6: Positive affect experienced at a destination positively affects satisfaction with the destination.

Negative Affect and Satisfaction

Tourism experiences are not devoid of negative affect. Negative affect is the result of failing to meet a minimum standard(Price, Arnould & Deibler 1995). The amount of negative affect felt plays an instrumental role in the magnitude of satisfaction levels (Martin & Tesser 1996). However, there is no consensus on the impact of negative affect on the evaluation of holiday experiences. In fact, mixed evidence exists on the relationship between negative emotions and satisfaction. Although some previous studies have found that tourists' negative affect/emotions significantly impact their satisfaction and intentions to recommend (e. g. Westbrook 1987; Phillips & Baumgartner 2002; Hosany & Prayag 2013), others found no effect between affect and satisfaction (Westbrook & Oliver 1991; Van Dolen et al. 2004). Lee and Kyle (2013) postulated that negative emotions such as *anger*, *sadness*, and *fear* were not much felt at festivals and most negative emotions were not evaluated differently when comparing on-site and post-visit experiences.

Not surprisingly, Nawijn (2011b) found that tourists' positive affect was rated significantly higher than negative affect on holidays. Hence, if tourists felt mostly negative emotions at a destination, their overall satisfaction with the travel experiences at that destination may be consequently reduced. The greater the level of the negative affect, the greater the level of overall dissatisfaction. Zins (2002) identified seven salient negative emotions (*nervous*, *scared*, *upset*, *angry*, *unhappy*, *afraid*, and *in bad mood*) among those complaining travellers and found that satisfaction will be negatively correlated with negative consumption experience emotions. By utilising four negative affects (*bored*, *displeased*, *disappointed*, and *angry*), Del Bosque and San Martín (2008) argued that the less frequent the negative affect during the tourist experience, the higher the level of satisfaction with the tourist destination. In adventure tourism such as mountaineering, fear is clearly experienced as a negative affect and it has a negative impact on customer satisfaction (Faullant et al. 2011). Employing three items (*bored*, *angry*, and *annoyed*) for measuring negative emotions at an Italian festival, Grappi and Montanari (2011) concluded that more negative emotions lead to less satisfaction. Negative emotions have been shown to decrease satisfaction levels (Phillips & Baumgartner 2002). In other studies, negative emotions seem to have a stronger impact on post-purchase evaluations when compared to positive emotions (e. g. Inman, Dyer & Jia 1997). Hence, it is hypothesised that:

H7: Negative affect experienced at a destination negatively affects satisfaction with the destination.

Conceptual Framework

A comprehensive literature review of personality, affect, and satisfaction, coupled with the relationships between research constructs calls for a deliberate scrutiny of tourist satisfaction with a destination as determined by tourist personality and affective responses as vital elements in the context of Chinese package tourists to Australia. The purpose of this study is to investigate how tourists' personality traits, in conjunction with affective responses triggered by travel experiences, influence their level of overall satisfaction with the travel destination.

As addressed in section 2.6, both quantitative (e. g. Hosany & Gilbert 2010; Lee, Jeon & Kim 2011) and qualitative (e. g. Bowen 2001) studies consistently confirm the role of affect/emotions in satisfaction formation. However, the overwhelming majority of survey-based satisfaction studies still fail to incorporate affect/emotions in their conceptual models (Cohen, Prayag & Moital 2014). Therefore, in response to such a limitation in the extant studies, a conceptual framework containing the affective variable is developed to delineate the relationships among personality, affect, and satisfaction. It is argued that personality traits are highly influential, leading to tourists' affective reactions and thus impacting tourist satisfaction. All the hypotheses attempt to explain the psychological processes underpinning the development of tourist satisfaction.

Specifically, this study endeavours to achieve the following five objectives:

1) to identify and document Chinese outbound tourists' salient positive and negative affective responses during their trip to Australia;

2) to identify the underlying structure of Five-Factor Model (FFM) personality traits as applied to Chinese respondents in the context of outbound travel to Australia;

3) to examine how each dimension of the FFM contributes to the formation of tourists' positive and negative affective responses;

4) to test how positive and negative affective responses associated with specific and holistic experiences of a travel trip influence tourists' overall satisfaction with a destination; and

5) to examine how tourists' personality traits, coupled with positive and negative affective responses, can contribute to the formation of tourist satisfaction with a destination.

It is anticipated that the theoretical discussion of this book may provide some preliminary insight on destination marketing management in a tourism context. All the hypothesised relationships are visually presented in Figure 3.1 to explain the interrelationships between psychological variables of the tourist in satisfaction formation. Thus, the main objective of this study is to empirically validate this conceptual model that has established relationships among the three constructs of personality (five dimensions), affect (positive and negative), and satisfaction.

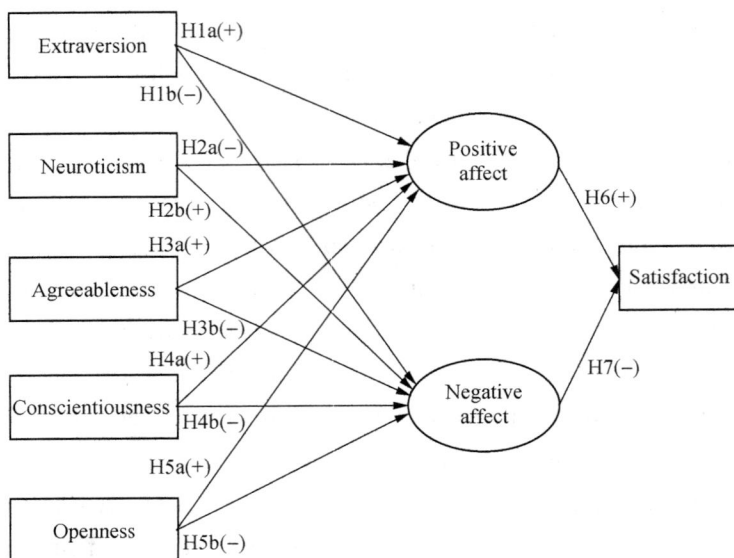

Figure 3.1   A Conceptual Model of Personality, Affect, and Satisfaction

Chapter Synopsis

This chapter has provided an in-depth critical review on the development of personality, affect, and satisfaction theories, and the research background (i. e. Chinese outbound tourism). With respect to the three research constructs, this chapter has identified the research gap in the literature while presenting an overview of extant literature in the relevant fields, thus laying a solid foundation for the development of the conceptual framework and hypotheses. It has provided a detailed discussion highlighting the importance of considering personality, individual differences, and affective responses triggered by travel experiences in tourist behaviour, specifically tourist satisfaction research.

A review of the extant literature on the relationships among personality, affect, and satisfaction was conducted in order to formulate the conceptual framework that guides the research. The links between the five dimensions of FFM and two broad dimensions of affect (positive or negative affect) were established to develop ten research hypotheses. In addition, two research hypotheses were constructed with regard to the relationship between affect and satisfaction. In the next chapter, the research methodology employed to investigate these hypotheses will be discussed.

4

Research Strategy

This chapter details the research methodology employed in this study. Following Creswell's (2009) suggestion for designing research, it addresses three essential stages, i. e. research paradigms, design or strategy, and methods of data collection and analysis. The objective of this chapter is to explain decisions about the selection of research methods and data analysis techniques for the present research. Specifically, the first section of this chapter outlines the philosophical paradigm that underpins the research—pragmatism. The second section introduces the design of the sequential mixed-method approach within the context of the research questions, and addresses issues related to the rationale of the research design, the sampling frame as well as ethical considerations. The third section expounds the qualitative exploration in which focus group discussions were conducted to collect qualitative data, and thematic analysis is applied to analyse data. The fourth section focuses on the quantitative investigation which comprises questionnaire survey, instrument development, pilot test, and SEM as its method of data analysis.

Research Paradigm

A research paradigm can be defined as the world view or belief system that guides researchers(Tashakkori & Teddlie 1998), which contains "basic assumptions, the important questions to be answered or puzzles to be solved, the research techniques to be used, and examples of what good scientific research looks like" (Neuman 2005, p. 65). In other words, it can be perceived as a cluster of beliefs that influence what should be studied, how research should be done, and how findings should be interpreted. Therefore, the selection of the most appropriate philosophical paradigm in relation to a particular discipline is of great importance to a researcher (Bryman 2008), for the choice of philosophical approach represents the researcher's values as reflected in their choice of data collection techniques. Positivism, interpretivism, and pragmatism have been generally used in social science (Bryman 2006). In this section, these three main research paradigms are discussed respectively, before determining pragmatism as the most appropriate paradigm for this study.

Positivism aims to explain social and physical reality through observable and testable facts as outlined in theory (Neuman 2005). Positivists consider social science as "an organised method for combing deductive logic with precise empirical observations of individual behaviour in order to discover and confirm a set of probabilistic causal laws that can be used to predict general patterns of human activities" (Neuman 2005, p. 66). Therefore, positivist researchers generally focus on collecting data about an observable reality and searching for regularities and casual relationships from the data to create law-like generalisations. Positivism relates to the philosophical stances of natural scientists, emphasizing the objectivity and strict processes and procedures of research so that the results are objective and are able to be generalised (Jennings 2001). More specifically, the positivism paradigm employs a deductive research approach to substantiate theories or test hypotheses using empirical data.

Interpretivism is taken to denote an alternative to the positivist orthodoxy, highlighting the significance of understanding the subjective meaning of social actions (Bryman & Bell 2011). Different from the positivists who start with a theory and test theoretical postulations with the collected data, interpretivists employ an inductive approach: starting with data they then endeavour to derive a theory about social phenomena from the observed data. By collecting and analysing participants' subjective viewpoints, researchers build broader themes and generate a theory interconnecting the themes through typically qualitative approaches (Creswell & Plano Clark 2007). In the interpretivist approach, researchers provide another perspective that defines the social world besides positivism; however, they provide only a narrow view of limited participants and the findings are the subjective interpretation of researcher (Glesne & Peshkin 1999). The personal beliefs or the feelings of the researcher affect every stage of the research process, from the choice of research area to the interpretation of results. Instead, in positivist research, the researcher must remain independent of the context to minimise the subjective bias.

Pragmatism as the philosophical paradigm, takes a middle or dual stance between positivism and interpretivism (Denscombe 2008). It is the underlying philosophy of mixed-methods, recognising that there are many different ways of interpreting the world and undertaking research, and that no single point of view can ever give the whole picture of social phenomena, and that there may be multiple realities (Denscombe 2008). It allows researchers to use mixed-methods as a third approach if the use of either the qualitative or quantitative research is not adequate for the research study. In essence, pragmatism acts as a bridge between contradicting paradigms, such as the positivist and interpretive social science paradigms. Pragmatism acknowledges the importance of both the positivist and interpretive social science stances, and provides a platform on which elements of both of these can work together to achieve comprehensive outcomes.

This study aims not only to investigate how tourists' personality traits, coupled with affective responses elicited by travel experiences, influence their overall satisfaction with a destination, but also to understand Chinese outbound tourists' salient positive and negative affective responses during their trip to Australia. Therefore, not only does this study require collecting quantitative data to corroborate hypotheses, thus identifying the general patterns of tourist behaviour, it also calls for collecting and analysing qualitative data to conceptualise tourists' affective responses to their travel experiences. Joint use of qualitative and quantitative data may help generate unique insights into a complex social phenomenon that are unlikely to emerge from either type of data alone. This research accentuates the importance of both positivist and interpretive perspectives in a single study. In light of this, a pragmatism paradigm was selected as the most desirable paradigm guiding this research.

Research Design

A research design, generally recognised as a framework or blueprint for an empirical research project, is essentially a comprehensive plan for data collection and analysis, detailing the procedures necessary for obtaining the information required to resolve research questions or examine specific hypotheses. Following the pragmatism paradigm, the methodology adopted in this study should allow for a qualitative exploration of Chinese outbound tourists' affective responses to their travel experiences in Australia, and a quantitative investigation of the causal relationships among the theoretical constructs (i. e. tourist personality, affective responses, and tourist satisfaction) as stipulated in the conceptual framework. Given the objectives and nature of this study, a sequential mixed-methods approach was adopted to integrate the qualitative phase and the quantitative phase in the present study. Four procedures were specified for the design of this research, comprising the data collection process, the sampling process, the instrument development process, and the data analysis process. These four dimensions show the interrelated levels of decisions that go into the process of designing research.

Mixed-Methods Design

As discussed in the pragmatism paradigm, the mixed-methods approach is characterised as "integrating elements of both quantitative and qualitative designs so that the strengths of each can be maximized" (Riddick & Russell 2008, p. 162). Denscombe (2008) has defined four features of this research approach:

1) Quantitative and qualitative methods within the same research project; 2) A research design that clearly specifies the sequencing and priority that is given to the quantitative and qualitative elements of data collection and analysis; 3) An explicit

account of the manner in which the quantitative and qualitative aspects of the research relate to each other, with heightened emphasis on the manner in which triangulation is used; 4) Pragmatism as the philosophical underpinning for the research (Denscombe 2008, p. 272).

Accordingly, the mixed-methods approach refers to "the collection or analysis of both qualitative and quantitative data in a single study in which the data are collected concurrently or sequentially"(Creswell 2009, p. 212). Mixed-methods research can be divided into either a concurrent or sequential mixed approach (Leech & Onwuegbuzie 2009). The concurrent approach suggests that both quantitative and qualitative data are collected at the same time while the sequential model indicates that the quantitative and qualitative data are collected sequentially across stages.

It is noticeable that there has been an immense growth in the use of the mixed-methods approach in recent years(Bryman 2006). The mixed-methods approach is emerging as a new paradigm to study complex phenomena in social science. Researchers have employed the mixed-methods approach with the desire to improve data accuracy, provide a holistic picture, overcome weaknesses of a single method, and build upon previous research which used a single method of data collection (Denscombe 2008). Most importantly, mixed-methods researchers are pragmatic and are primarily interested in applying the methods which enable them to answer their research questions.

The nature of the research problems and the development of related theories guided the design of this research (Creswell & Plano Clark 2007). With the emerging nature of the phenomena and limited systematic studies, the present research adopts the sequential mixed-methods approach. This two-phase mixed-methods design starts with collecting qualitative data to explore a phenomenon and identify variables, which then informs the subsequent composition of the survey instrument in the quantitative phase. As depicted in Figure 4. 1, focus group discussions were conducted in the first stage of data collection, while a questionnaire survey was implemented in the second stage of data collection.

Initially, a comprehensive literature review was performed, which located the dominant conceptual framework within its epistemological frameworks. The literature review indicates that Chinese outbound tourists' affective responses to their travel experiences in Australia as the phenomenon under study is poorly understood by extant theories in the context of the rapid development of Chinese outbound tourism, with limited research conducted systematically on the Chinese tourists' affective experiences when travelling overseas. Given the underexplored nature of this phenomenon, qualitative interviews were employed at the first stage of research to address the emerging important yet scarce research into Chinese outbound tourists' affective responses. It facilitated exploring the richness of the context to account for the phenomena and answer why and how these affective responses would be elicited among Chinese outbound tourists. However, this stage was predominantly explorative and it did not intend to test specific constructs highlighted in the conceptual framework. Rather, adopting thematic analysis, it analysed qualitative data to identify any unknown items for a more accurate measurement of the research constructs. The review of the qualitative data informed the conceptualisations of Chinese outbound tourists' affective responses and helped identify the items for the measurement of affective responses in the subsequent quantitative stage.

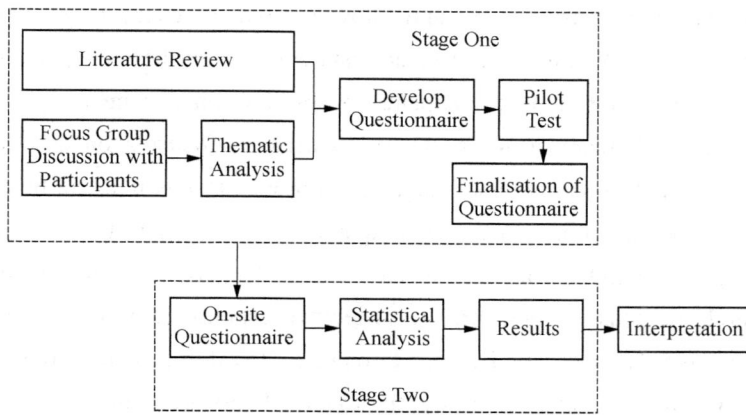

Figure 4.1　Mixed-methods Sequential Research Design of the Study

Based on the literature review and findings from the focus group discussions, a preliminary questionnaire was developed to examine the impact of both personality traits and affective responses on mainland Chinese outbound tourists' overall satisfaction with Australia as a tourist destination. Then a pilot study was conducted to test the questionnaire's length, format, and clarity. The questionnaire format was modified and finalised for use in the quantitative investigation of the conceptual model. SEM was performed to analyse the quantitative data to identify the survey study results. Eventually, findings from the qualitative and quantitative studies were interpreted with reference to the relevant literature.

Justifications for Mixed-Methods Design

With regard to the fact that researchers increasingly adopt the mixed-methods approach, the following section provides the rationale for the mixed-methods design in this research which included the qualitative phase followed by the quantitative phase. In the qualitative phase, focus group discussions were conducted with Chinese outbound tourists travelling to Australia to gain a better understanding of their affective responses elicited by their travel experiences in Australia. In the quantitative phase, a questionnaire survey was administered to investigate the impact of tourist personality and affective response towards tourists' overall satisfaction with a destination. The qualitative phase of this research informed the design of the questionnaire survey which subsequently examined and measured the variables as well as the relationships among the research constructs. In the design of this study, each research phase has a specific purpose; thus, the researcher can use the results from the qualitative method to help develop or inform the use of the quantitative method. The method applied in the quantitative stage is dependent on the previous qualitative stage because the results of the focus group interviews will inform the development of the research instrument in the subsequent stage.

Qualitative methods are useful for examining and developing an understanding of phenomena about which little is known, and allow for the discovery of in-depth information about the subject of study(Wellington & Szczerbinski 2007). Furthermore, qualitative research is usually inductive, allowing study participants to describe what is meaningful and salient to them. Qualitative research searches for personal knowledge, focusing on describing individual cases. Qualitative research is, thus, not designed to produce results that can be generalised to a larger population; rather a primary purpose of qualitative research is to provide a richness of detail about a smaller number of people and cases than is typically developed through quantitative research methods (Patton 2005). Affective responses are complex phenomena that cannot be comprehensively understood solely through a closed-ended questionnaire. To gain a more comprehensive understanding, it is essential to have focus group interviews with informants to explore the underlying reasons that cause the specific affective responses to their travel experiences in Australia.

The Five-Factor personality model and the PANAS have been well established in Western literature, but have not yet been studied systematically in China. To address such a gap, this research responds to the questions regarding whether such a dynamic context of Chinese outbound tourists to Australia will generate divergent findings to the research conducted in the English literature. Therefore, the mixed-methods approach is adopted because both qualitative and quantitative data can provide the researcher with more adequate answers (Denscombe 2008). In the case of this research study, mixed-methods was chosen to improve the accuracy of the research instrument, and in order to create a more holistic view of the phenomenon.

In addition, despite the rapid development of Chinese outbound tourism, few studies have been conducted to evaluate Chinese outbound tourists' satisfaction with destination countries determined by their personality traits and affective responses to their travel experiences. Consequently, rich, detailed, and explorative data are first needed to understand the conceptualisation of Chinese outbound tourists' affective responses elicited by their travel experiences. Following this exploratory process, a questionnaire survey is necessary to examine the relevance of tourist personality and affective responses in the formation of overall tourist satisfaction, thus generalising the conceptual framework of tourist satisfaction from the psychological perspective.

To sum up, the overall quality of the mixed-methods approach, if used appropriately, is greater than either qualitative or quantitative research alone (Creswell & Plano Clark 2007). It can answer questions that could not be answered by one method alone in one research project (Leech & Onwuegbuzie 2009). The researcher can use the strengths of one method to complement the weakness in the other and draw a convergence conclusion to produce more complete knowledge (Johnson & Onwuegbuzie 2004). It enhances the rigour, breadth, complexity, richness, and depth of any enquiry (Cameron & Molina-Azorin 2011). Given these reasons, the mixed-methods research design is chosen as the most suitable strategy for this study.

Sampling Frame

In statistics, a sampling frame is the source material or device from which a sample is selected. In this study, the purpose of sampling frames is to provide a means for choosing the particular members of the target population that are to be interviewed in the focus group discussions (FGDs) and survey. More specifically, the sampling frame consisted of Chinese outbound group tourists on a package tour to Australia for pleasure, departing from Jiangsu Province, China. In addition, random cluster sampling was adopted in the study.

Research Sites

Jiangsu Province was selected as the research site for conducting the interview and questionnaire survey due to its economic ranking, geographic location, and cultural background. Located in east China, Jiangsu Province, as a flourishing economic region, ranked second nationwide in GDP in 2014 (National Bureau of Statistics of China 2015). The per capita disposable income of urban residents averaged 32,538 *yuan* (US $5,254) in 2013 (Ministry of Commerce of the People's Republic of China 2014). With a long history and a rich cultural heritage, Jiangsu is well-known for being a fertile "land of fish and rice" since ancient times, and contains 13 prefecture-level cities, including Nanjing, Suzhou, Yangzhou, Zhenjiang, Changzhou, Nantong, Xuzhou, Huai'an, and the like (Figure 4.2). With a population of over 79 million, Jiangsu Province is a lucrative market which generated about 1.5 million outbound tourists in 2014 and ranked fifth in terms of the number of outbound tourists, right after Beijing, Guangdong Province, Shanghai, and Zhejiang Province (JSChina 2015).

Historically, Jiangsu Province has long been the birthplace of famous scholars and literati who were the main force of travel in ancient China (Guo, Turner & King 2002). People in Jiangsu therefore have a long-established tradition of travelling. Furthermore, as a major economic centre and focal point of trade and commerce in China, Jiangsu is widely regarded as China's most developed province measured by its Human Development Index (United Nations Development Programme 2013). Not surprisingly, a burgeoning Chinese middle class has quickly formed in Jiangsu Province. Those newly affluent are well-educated and therefore are more willing to be exposed to foreign cultures. Although Beijing, Shanghai, and Guangdong Province are still the primary regions generating outbound tourists, more and more people from second- and third-tier cities (such as Nanjing, the capital of Jiangsu Province, and Suzhou, the second largest city in the province after Nanjing) are participating in overseas travel. The survey of residents in Jiangsu could be a representative of the target study population.

Figure 4.2   Map of Jiangsu Province

Source: Adapted from www. chinahighlights. com/ jiangsu map. htm.

Target Population

Tourism Australia, in its most recent profile of Chinese visitors in the year 2012 and 2013, identified that peak travel periods are from December to February and July to August. This regular peak time made it possible to obtain the desired sample size within a timeframe. Outbound tourists from Jiangsu Province generally prefer group tours organised by local tour operators when taking a long-haul holiday tour. White-collar professionals and managers prefer holidays other than sightseeing tours and they are more likely to choose free and independent travel (FIT) products to suit their personality orientation and individual travel demands. Only group tourists were selected for this study since the package tour is the dominant form of travel to Australia for leisure, pleasure, and holiday purpose by mainland Chinese at present and will continue to be so in the near future.

The study confined the target population to package tourists paying their first visit to

Australia departing from Jiangsu Province and consuming the same travel product, i. e. an 8-day package holiday tour, sequentially visiting Sydney, Brisbane, Gold Coast, and Melbourne (see Appendix 1 for both English and Chinese versions of the itinerary). Four criteria had been pre-formulated before data collection in order to sample the most eligible participants for the study. The first screening criterion was that participants had to be mainland Chinese citizens aged over 18 who were visiting Australia as part of a group package tour. Secondly, the potential participants were asked whether they had visited Australia recently, and how many times they had visited Australia. Those who had visited Australia more than once were excluded from this study because their recent affective responses upon travelling in Australia might have been biased by their previous travel experiences. Thirdly, collecting retrospective information about affective responses can be problematic (Faullant et al. 2011); therefore, the timing for data collection was carefully chosen. To guarantee the optimal timeframe for data collection, the tourists were asked to participate in the FGDs within three days of their return home. The survey respondents were required to complete their questionnaires on their return flights to China. At that time, the respondents' travel experiences in Australia were still fresh in their minds and easily accessible. Fourthly, since the different travel experiences caused by factors such as the length of stay or the tour itinerary at a destination are likely to generate dynamic variations and fluctuations in affective responses among tourists (Kozak 2001), the sample only focused on the tourists who paid their first visit to Australia consuming the identical travel product, i. e. an 8-day package holiday tour, which was the most popular and favourable all-inclusive tourism product to Australia in the market, attracting the majority of the first-time visitors from China.

Generally speaking, the target population is selected in some manner that involves the various regions and socioeconomic strata the researcher intends to cover in the study. For a qualitative exploratory study, homogenous sampling can "bring focus to a sample, reduce variation, simplify analysis, and facilitate group interviewing" (Patton 2005, p. 127). Eligible FGD participants and survey respondents were mainland Chinese tourists departing from Jiangsu Province who for the first time took an 8-day package tour to Australia. To ensure the FGD participants met the selection criteria, evidence of travelling to Australia (e. g. passports and visa copies) was requested.

To access the sample in Jiangsu Province, the researcher contacted several local tour operators and one professional marketing research company. It is worth noting that the researcher's previous work experience in the tourism industry in Jiangsu Province contributed to his good connections with the tour organising agencies, thus facilitating his data collection. Four FGD sessions were conducted by the researcher with the support of several major tour operators which dominate the China-Australia leisure tourism in Jiangsu Province, for example, Nanjing Zhongbei Friendship International Travel Service (ZFITS) and Jiangsu Branch of Shanghai

CITIC International Travel Company (CITIC). ZFITS is an influential one in Jiangsu Market; while CITIC serves as the biggest wholesaler dealing with outbound tourism to Australia in East China. As the travel services authorised by the CNTA to handle outbound travel arrangement to ADS destinations for self-funded travellers, ZFITS and CITIC are credited as being in the "the Best 100" tourism companies and "5A Grade" travel agencies in China.

Ethical Considerations

As the research involved mainland Chinese outbound tourists as study participants, there was a range of ethical issues that needed to be acknowledged. Prior to conducting this study, the detailed ethics protocol, including the research aims, methodology, participants, and the recording and storage of the collected data, was submitted to the University of South Australia's Human Research Ethics Committee. The participant information sheets outlining the conditions of their involvement were distributed to all the participants, informing them about the nature and consequences of the research. In addition, written approval also needed to be gained from local travel agencies in China in order for the research to be carried out among their customers, namely outbound group tourists to Australia. Without these tour operators' endorsement and support for the research, it would be extremely difficult for the researcher to get access to any respondent. After obtaining approval from these sources, the research participants were recruited.

Based on their personal interests or understanding of the importance of this research, participants took part in the study on a voluntary basis and they were entitled to withdraw at any stage. At the qualitative stage of research, participants were required to sign consent forms prior to the researcher conducting each session of the FGDs. Since focus group participants were recruited among outbound tourists who just returned from their package tour to Australia, it was considered culturally appropriate to provide participants with a reward of RMB 150 (approximately US $25) for their contribution. In the stage of quantitative research, survey respondents were notified that returning the completed questionnaire suggested their willingness to participate and approval of using their completed questionnaires in subsequent data analysis. Respondents were given a souvenir as a small token of appreciation for their time spent filling in the questionnaire on their return flights back to China.

It is the researcher's responsibility to protect the confidentiality and privacy of participants who agreed to engage in a study(Josselson 2007). All participants at the time of initial contact were advised that the anonymity of their participation and the confidentiality of individual information would be guaranteed. Both qualitative and quantitative data were gathered on a confidential basis and were only analysed and reported from an overall point of view to present a profile structure of the complete sample, excluding any identification information of the participants. A summary of major findings of the study was offered to participants upon request. It should be emphasised that original notes, audiotapes, questionnaires, and electronic files containing the data would be retained for five years at the University of South Australia.

Qualitative Exploration

The main objective of the qualitative exploration was to explore in depth the salient attributes of Chinese outbound tourists' affective responses to their travel experiences in Australia. This was important since the items of affective responses on the questionnaire for the subsequent quantitative investigation would be based on the findings of the qualitative exploration. Therefore, given the emerging nature and inadequacies in understanding the tourists' affective responses to their travel experiences at a destination, the qualitative exploration was for the purpose of refining the measurement items and better conceptualising Chinese package tourists' affective responses to Australia as a tourist destination.

The qualitative exploration was carried out in three stages. In Stage 1 the questions were developed based on the literature and discussions with two supervisors. Stage 2 involved focus group interviews with 32 mainland Chinese outbound tourists to Australia. Each FGD was taped, with the agreement of each participant, and then summarised, including verbatim quotations, from the tape. Stage 3 involved analysing the qualitative data to help search for the words and phrases that tourists used to describe their affective responses during their travel to Australia. Then some of the questions for the questionnaire survey were eventually confirmed in light of the first round of interviews and analysis.

Focus Group Discussions

To begin with, this section provides information on how the qualitative research was designed. FGD is a form of qualitative research that involves a trained facilitator who guides a small group of subjects (typically 6 to 10 people) at one location to discuss a phenomenon of interest for a period of 1.5 to 2 hours. The moderator is responsible for setting the agenda and raising an initial set of questions for participants with the intention of gaining a holistic understanding of research questions based on participants' comments and discussions. Accordingly, FGD provides a useful tool to understand the importance of the context and explore the phenomenon under study from an overall perspective.

Second, it addresses the rationale and nature of adopting the FGD. Focus groups are particularly suited to this type of exploratory research, as qualitative data and in-depth insights are elicited through interaction in a group setting (Arthur & Nazroo 2003). Dynamic interactions in the focus group setting provided insight beyond the content themes. Group dynamics is the most distinctive methodological feature of FGD, which encourages members to build on each other's thoughts and ideas (Seal, Bogart & Ehrhardt 1998). Group dynamics stimulate memories, ideas, and experiences among participants, which will help researchers garner a deep understanding of the issues and facilitate the further relevant instrument construction. Ideally, participant comments will stimulate and influence others to think and share as well. Some people even find themselves changing their thoughts and opinions during the discussion. As the qualitative study explores a relatively under-researched area, there is no universal rule for the number of FGDs required for this study (Krueger & Casey 2009). It takes more than one focus group on any one topic to produce valid results—usually three or four. Consequently, four sessions of FGD, each with eight participants, could provide an adequate sample size for an exploratory qualitative study. Besides, adopting the purposive sampling performs an essential function in providing the researcher with the justification to make generalisations from the homogeneous sample that is being studied (Guest, Bunce & Johnson 2006).

Third, a briefing session paves the way for the success of a FGD and helps a researcher establish a rapport with participants (Denzin & Lincoln 2005). To access the target sample in Jiangsu Province, the researcher attended two briefing sessions organised by the travel agencies in Nanjing prior to the group departure to Australia. The researcher extended an invitation to all the tourists and kept them informed of what the study was about, and how they would contribute to the study. In addition, two research coordinators from ZFITS and CITIC volunteered to help recruit potential focus group participants through telephone calls and online means (e. g. bulletin board system, BBS travel discussion groups); the professional staff from Nanjing Stone Marketing Research Co. , Ltd. offered assistance in arranging the meeting venue, and coordinating meeting schedules for participants.

Research Instrument

This section details the research instruments adopted in the semi-structured FGD and describes how these were developed as research tools for data collection. A FGD guide outlining the FGD schedule and a list of questions were designed to guarantee that the collected data would be much more focused and easier to analyse. Additionally, advice and tips for conducting the focus groups were gained from research methods texts (Bryman 2008; Neuman 2005).

Structuring and amending the FGD questions play an important role in guaranteeing the appropriateness of the research questions(Bryman & Bell 2007). In the preparatory phase of the FGD, the researcher generated the preliminary draft of the FGD guide (see Appendix 2) based on the literature review of the relevant fields and his previous insights into the field of tourism marketing. Two fellow PhD students specializing in tourism management helped check the conciseness and comprehensibility of all the questions, and then provided some useful comments and suggestions. After the first revision, the FGD guide was assessed by the researcher's two supervisors for its wording and completeness. The FGD guide was finalised in terms of supervisors' suggestions and experiences. Overall, the interview protocol was arranged into four sections: 1) introduction, 2) semi-structured FGD questions, 3) closing, and 4) demographic questions. The detailed interview protocol can be found in Appendix 3.

Methods of Qualitative Data Analysis—Thematic Analysis

Thematic analysis can be regarded as a fundamental method of qualitative data analysis which entails identifying, categorising, and summarising iterative patterns or topics within the data through the marked codes(Braun & Clarke 2006). Compared with other qualitative analysis methods such as conversation analysis and discourse analysis or narrative analysis which are based on "particular theoretical or epistemological position" (Braun & Clarke 2006, p. 78), thematic analysis is methodologically flexible. Therefore, thematic analysis can be conducted with or without a pre-determined theoretical framework, to find out either what the reality of the world is or how the reality is constructed.

As thematic analysis is methodologically flexible, themes or patterns can be identified in either an inductive or deductive way(Braun & Clarke 2006) or by combining both approaches (Fereday & Muir-Cochrane 2006). With an inductive approach, themes emerge by reading and re-reading the data. When using a deductive approach the data are analysed based on a pre-existing coding framework (Patton 2005).

When analysing the interviews at this stage, a predominantly deductive approach was applied to identify themes of Chinese outbound tourists' affective responses to their travel experiences. Existing studies (see Chapter 2) have provided abundant knowledge about the characteristics of positive affect and negative affect in the domain of psychology and marketing, and tourists' affective experiences in leisure travel activities. Therefore, a draft coding framework for positive affective responses and negative affective responses could be pre-determined based on a systematic review of the literature. According to the occurrence frequencies of affective responses, sub-themes could then be generated from the rich qualitative data. Therefore, the thematic analysis in this research can be seen as both theory-driven and data-driven.

Thematic analysis can be used either to provide "a rich overall description" of the entire dataset or to give "a more detailed and nuanced account of one particular theme, or group of themes, within the data" (Braun & Clarke 2006, p. 83). Therefore, through thematic analysis, Chinese outbound tourists' holistic affective responses triggered by their travel experiences and detailed accounts of each theme of affective response were captured in the qualitative phase of this research.

Quantitative Investigation

The overall aim of the quantitative research phase was to understand the relationships among mainland Chinese outbound tourists' personality traits, affective responses, and overall satisfaction. The four steps of the quantitative investigation included: 1) developing the questionnaire, 2) data collection, 3) data analysis, and 4) interpretation of results.

Questionnaire Survey

The survey questionnaire consisted of four sections measuring three main constructs of personality traits, affective responses, tourist satisfaction, and demographic profile. The questions were developed on the basis of a review of the related literature as well as the findings of the focus group interviews, and were modified to be applicable to the research context and target respondents. The measurements of the research constructs were adopted from the Big Five Inventory Scale (John et al. 1991), the PANAS scale (Watson et al. 1988) and Oliver's (1997) satisfaction scale, respectively.

For the sake of consistency, all the questions, excluding the demographic ones, were followed by an answer scheme on a 7-point Likert scale(1 = strongly disagree to 7 = strongly agree). The survey was then administered on the respondents' return flights to gain their overall evaluations of their travel experiences in Australia. To ensure stable results of subsequent data analysis and to follow the principles of SEM—the main statistical technique to be used for data analysis—a sample size of 500 was deemed appropriate for this study.

With the approval of several major tour operators which dominate the China-Australia leisure tourism in Jiangsu Province, for example,ZFITS and CITIC, seven escort guides helped distribute and collect the questionnaires on their return flights to China. They also took the responsibility of explaining the items in the questionnaires and monitoring the quality of the returned questionnaires. In order to guarantee the reliability and validity of the collected quantitative data, before the launch of the survey, the researcher conducted a training session with the seven escort guides at which food was provided as an incentive to attend. They were instructed on how to complete the questionnaires.

Instrument Development

A survey instrument which included all the variables of interest was developed to investigate the hypotheses. The questionnaire incorporated measures of the BFI, PANAS, and overall tourist satisfaction. The questionnaire development followed these six steps: 1) Prior to the questionnaire development, a team of experienced travel professionals and academic researchers on Chinese outbound tourism were consulted for the development of measurements for Chinese visitors' affective experiences and travel behaviour in Australia. 2) Then the questions in the questionnaire were developed on the basis of a review of the related literature as well as expert opinions, and were modified to be applicable to the research site and target population. 3) A preliminary version of the questionnaire with four sections was subsequently designed to measure all variables. Sections A to C included measurements of personality traits, affective responses, and tourist satisfaction respectively; Section D was developed to obtain the demographic profiles of respondents. A preliminary draft of the questionnaire was developed and administered to the experienced travel professionals and academic researchers who helped make minor adjustments. 4) The questionnaire was translated into Chinese to minimise the language bias, following a blind translation-back-translation method (Brislin 1976). The retranslated English version was compared with the original English one to secure the accuracy of the translation. 5) The researcher had the questionnaire reviewed by a team of academic researchers and travel professionals to get some useful feedback and suggestions for further refinement. 6) The developed questionnaire was pretested on 32 respondents from FGDs to further establish its validity. Feedback from the panel and the pre-test were used to revise and finalise the survey instrument. 7) The results of the qualitative phase were supplemented to inform the finalisation of the survey questionnaire.

The research instrument developed for this study was divided into three main parts: measurement of FFM personality traits (Part A), measurement of affective responses (Part B), measurement of satisfaction (Part C), and demographic information (Part D). The full preliminary questionnaire can be found in Appendix 2. Specifically, Part A included John, Donahue and Kentle's (1991) BFI to measure extraversion, agreeableness, conscientiousness, neuroticism, and openness. Part B included PANAS to measure type of affective responses when travelling in Australia. Part C included Oliver's (1997) satisfaction scale to measure Chinese outbound tourists' overall satisfaction with Australia as a tourist destination. All items were measured on a 7-point Likert scale (1 = strongly disagree to 7 = strongly agree). Finally, Part D sought to obtain additional demographic information about the tourists' backgrounds, such as gender, age, occupation, education, monthly income, household size, and travel companion. All the changes pertaining to the measures used in this study are indicated in the following sections.

Measurement of Personality Traits (BFI)

Tourists' personality traits were assessed using John et al. 's (1991) Big Five Inventory (BFI). It was developed to evaluate the five personality traits where individual facets do not need to be assessed (John & Srivastava 1999). Forty-four items for personality traits—extraversion (8 items), agreeableness (9 items), conscientiousness (9 items), neuroticism (8 items), and openness (10 items) (see Table 4.1)—were measured on a 7-point Likert scale (1

= strongly disagree to 7 = strongly agree). Each item from five dimensions was a short sentence describing a kind of behaviour or state (e. g. I am moody), and respondents were instructed to indicate how much they agreed or disagreed with the statement. As a public domain alternative to the well-known proprietary measure of the Five Factor Model such as NEO PI-R by Costa and McCrae (1992), the BFI is suitable for informants who are unwilling to participate in lengthy surveys. However, despite its brevity, it shows "high levels of internal consistency reliability and of content validity" (Ashton 2007, p. 41). Scales based on the BFI items have demonstrated substantial internal reliability with its Cronbach's coefficient alpha of 0. 83, generally ranging from 0. 75 to 0. 85 for each personality dimension (John & Srivastava 1999). Its generalisability across languages and cultures can be shown at the authors' website: http:// www. ocf. berkeley. edu/ ~ johnlab/bfi. htm from which the validated translation of the questionnaire into Chinese can be publicly accessed. This pre-existing Chinese version of the BFI has been translated and back-translated again between Chinese and English in order to re-test and re-verify its accuracy before it was eventually utilised without any change in the survey.

The increasing acceptance of the FFM as a model for delineating the structure of core personality traits has been evidenced in both cross-cultural and cross-disciplinary settings(e. g. Rammstedt 2007; Denissen et al. 2008). The 44-item BFI was employed to measure personality traits among Chinese adults who had a smoking habit in the previous research, and was abbreviated into 29 items with internal reliability estimates (Cronbach's alpha) ranging from 0. 69 for agreeableness to 0. 81 for neuroticism (Leung et al. 2013). In another study, the BFI was used to assess personality traits among tourism information consumers in Taiwan. The Cronbach's alpha for the five traits ranged from 0. 81 to 0. 90, implying high reliability (Tan & Tang 2013). In order to generalise the dimensional structure of personality across the different culture, the well-accepted 44-item BFI was selected to assess respondents' personality traits in the current research context of Chinese outbound tourists to Australia.

Table 4. 1　Measurement for Each Personality Dimension in BFI (John et al. 1991)

Extraversion (8 Items)	
1.	is talkative
6.	is reserved (R)
11.	is full of energy
16.	generates a lot of enthusiasm
21.	tends to be quiet (R)
26.	has an assertive personality
31.	is sometimes shy, inhibited (R)
36.	is outgoing, sociable

Continued

	Agreeableness (9 Items)
2.	tends to find fault with others (R)
7.	is helpful and unselfish with others
12.	starts quarrels with others (R)
17.	has a forgiving nature
22.	is generally trusting
27.	can be cold and aloof (R)
32.	is considerate and kind to almost everyone
37.	is sometimes rude to others (R)
42.	likes to cooperate with others
	Conscientiousness (9 Items)
3.	does a thorough job
8.	can be somewhat careless (R)
13.	is a reliable worker
18.	tends to be disorganised (R)
23.	tends to be lazy (R)
28.	perseveres until the task is finished
33.	does things efficiently
38.	makes plans and follows through with them
43.	is easily distracted (R)
	Neuroticism (8 Items)
4.	is depressed, blue
9.	is relaxed, handles stress well (R)
14.	can be tense
19.	worries a lot
24.	is emotionally stable, not easily upset (R)
29.	can be moody
34.	remains calm in tense situations (R)
39.	gets nervous easily
	Openness (10 Items)
5.	is original, comes up with new ideas
10.	is curious about many different things
15.	is ingenious, a deep thinker
20.	has an active imagination
25.	is inventive
30.	values artistic, aesthetic experiences
35.	prefers work that is routine (R)
40.	likes to reflect, play with ideas
41.	has few artistic interests (R)
44.	is sophisticated in art, music, or literature

(R) indicates using the reverse-scored item.

Measurement of Affective Responses—PANAS

The PANAS assessed two broad affective dimensions: positive and negative affect (Watson, Clark & Tellegen 1988). The International PANAS Short Form (I-PANAS-SF) is a well-validated, brief, cross-culturally reliable 10-item version of the PANAS. For Positive Affect, items are Active, Alert, Attentive, Determined, and Inspired, with reported internal consistency reliability between .73 and .78 (Thompson 2007). For Negative Affect, items are Afraid, Ashamed, Hostile, Nervous, and Upset, with reported internal consistency reliability between .72 and .76 (Thompson 2007). The I-PANAS-SF was developed for general use in research situations where either time or space is limited, but also for use in international samples where English may not be the mother tongue.

The measurement items for affective responses were adapted from PANAS (Watson, Clark & Tellegen 1988), previous studies on affect, such as Jun et al. (2001) and Richins (1997), and findings of qualitative exploration. These items characterised the affective domains in the tourism specialisation concept. Affective responses were measured with unipolar scales because individuals may experience positive and negative affect during the same stay. In the qualitative exploration phase, the frequency of affect had been presented to reflect Chinese package tourists' salient affective responses to their travel experiences in Australia. In the quantitative investigation phase, the identified salient affective responses were examined by a large sample of population to confirm their content validity. Therefore, respondents were asked to indicate the extent to which they agreed or disagreed with the felt affective responses on a 7-Likert scale (1 = strongly disagree; 7 = strongly agree).

Measurement of Tourist Satisfaction

Tourist satisfaction was operationalised as a summative overall construct on a 5-item, 7-point Likert scale based on Oliver's (1997) scale: (1) this is one of the best outbound destinations I have visited, (2) I am satisfied with my decision to visit Australia, (3) my choice to visit Australia is a wise one, (4) I have really enjoyed myself on travelling in Australia, and (5) I am sure it is the right thing to visit Australia. Numerous studies used a summative overall scale to measure satisfaction (e.g. Bloemer & De Ruyter 1998; Bolton & Lemon 1999; Hsu 2003; Hsu & Kang 2007). These items had shown high reliability in representing satisfaction levels (e.g. Van Dolen, De Ruyter & Lemmink 2004; De Rojas & Camarero 2008; Yüksel, Yüksel & Bilim 2010).

Respondents' Demographic Profile

The characteristics of tourists are important factors to be taken into consideration when the researcher analyses satisfaction with destinations (Huh, Uysal & McCleary 2006). Therefore, demographic information and behavioural indicators were requested to characterise visitors, including gender, age, marital status, occupation, education, income, household size, and travel companion. In addition, participants were able to provide their outbound travel experiences in the past five years at the end of the questionnaire. The purpose of collecting demographic information was to have a clear understanding of the sample and to determine if any of the demographic variables would have a greater effect on the relationships being investigated in this study.

Pilot Test

Conducting a pilot study helps ensure that research questions are appropriate and that the research instrument functions smoothly (Bryman, Allan & Bell 2007). A pilot test was conducted in order to examine the internal consistency of the questionnaire items. It provides the opportunity to identify the potential difficulties with the questionnaire including ambiguities, bias, or missing attributes. The results of the pilot testing were used to adjust the questionnaire design, wording, and measurement scales in order to ensure the provision of valid information. The pilot sample is usually a small subset of the target population. After a successful pilot testing, the researcher may then proceed with data collection using the sampled population.

The pilot study was implemented to maximise the content validity of the questionnaire (DeVellis 2012). The first step was to have the questionnaire reviewed by a team of tourist behaviour researchers, plus two travel and tourism professionals. This process resulted in minor alterations made to specific wording of the items measuring tourists' affective responses when travelling in Australia to avoid confusion. In addition, the pilot test also resulted in several items being removed from the questionnaire due to the item redundancy. The pilot study also received expert feedback that a screening question should be included to identify first-time visitors to Australia as respondents, and that respondents eligible for the study should have just finished their visit to Australia. It was also advised to remove the question which restricts only tourists from the Yangtze River Delta as respondents eligible for the study. Next, a pilot study involving 32 participants of focus group discussions was then conducted. Data were utilised for the testing of validity and reliability of the measurement instruments. Overall, the pilot test confirmed that the measurements used for this study had achieved an adequate level of reliability and the content validity of the survey instrument was also deemed adequate.

Some respondents were confused by the phrase "affective experiences" in Part B. The rubrics for completing Part B were required to be more elaborate and specific. To make it more explicable, it was rephrased as follows: "Reviewing in retrospect your own holistic affective responses of the trip to Australia in the past week, please tick a number to indicate the extent to which you agree or disagree with the following statements (the number 1-7 indicating *strongly disagree* to *strongly agree*)." Moreover, there were some terms not familiar to many tourists. Words such as "jittery", "nostalgic", and "anticipating" are not part of the everyday vocabulary of most people, potentially causing confusion among respondents, yet they appeared in the preliminary questionnaire. A preliminary draft of the questionnaire was developed and administered to the experienced travel professionals and academic researchers who helped make further adjustments.

As suggested by Yoon and Uysal (2005), the evaluation of tourist satisfaction needs to be considered in multiple dimensions, and they adapted the universal scale of Oliver to measure this concept. This approach has also been adopted in other studies (e.g. Van Dolen, De Ruyter & Lemmink 2004; Bigné, Andreu & Gnoth 2005; Del Bosque & San Martín 2008). In this study, for the five measurement items of overall tourist satisfaction, the fifth item, *"I am sure it is the right thing to visit Australia"* was found to be redundant because the first item, *"This is one of the best outbound destinations I have visited"*, had the same literal meaning related to the travel decision. Therefore, the fifth item was removed to avoid redundancy. Thus, satisfaction was measured on a 4-item, 7-point Likert scale based on Oliver's (1997) scale: (1) I have really enjoyed the trip in Australia, (2) my choice to visit Australia was a wise one, (3) the travel experience in Australia was exactly what I needed, and (4) I am satisfied with my trip in Australia.

The Chinese questionnaire was edited and proofread by two researchers, who are both proficient in English and Chinese, to ensure the accuracy of the items translated from English. Prior to the main survey, a pilot test with focus group participants was undertaken after each focus group discussion. Most informants completed the entire questionnaire in 15 minutes or less. After the pilot test, slight revisions of the wordings were made to ensure the questions were comprehensible to the respondents. Feedback from the experienced academicians, tour operators, and escort guides was evaluated to revise and finalise the survey instrument.

To conclude, the pilot study allowed for the modification of the questionnaire for the quantitative research phase. These modifications were consistent with the intent of the original measures whilst improving the validity of the questionnaire through reduction in respondent confusion. Accordingly, with these minor modifications and significant preliminary results, the final questionnaire (see Appendix 3) was suitable to be employed on a larger sample size to further investigate the relationships among tourist personality, affective responses, and tourist satisfaction.

Methods of Quantitative Data Analysis—SEM

Data were analysed following the principles and procedures of SEM. SEM was used as the primary approach to quantitative data analysis in this study. SEM is a statistical technique that allows the simultaneous modelling of relationship between multiple independent and dependent constructs. SEM incorporates new developments of two standard statistical methodologies: factor analysis and path analysis (Hair et al. 2010). SEM has become one of the techniques of choice for researchers across disciplines and increasingly is a "must" for researchers in the social sciences.

According to Kaplan (2008), SEM can perhaps be best defined as a class of methodologies. The essence of applying SEM is to handle structural relationships, especially relationship between latent constructs and variables(Nachtigall et al. 2003). More specifically, factor analysis, especially CFA, contributes to the understanding of the measurement part of the complete structural model. In most cases, when applying SEM only measurement models are discussed. Therefore, CFA can be regarded as the core of SEM and sometimes a proxy of SEM. However, when dealing with a structural model, CFA cannot resolve all problems. It should be used with the incorporation of path analysis techniques. Path analysis, sometimes termed simultaneous equation modelling, contributes to the identification of various types of effects (e. g. direct versus indirect) and the magnitude of these effects among variables in the model. Path analysis differentiates itself from regression in that it can simultaneously estimate all path coefficients in the model from the observed data. By combining the two statistical traditions, SEM overcomes methodological limitations of both factor and path analysis. More importantly, SEM provides a useful analytical tool for understanding relationships among several latent variables.

Practically, conventional statistical procedures, including reliability analysis, and descriptive statistics were performed using SPSS. CFA and SEM were used to test the conceptual model that examined the antecedents of tourist satisfaction. The SEM analysis was conducted using AMOS 20 to examine the hypothesised relationships among the latent constructs. The analysis procedures were divided into several steps. First, the fit and validity of individual measurement models were examined. The observed variables were tested using the CFA procedures to generate acceptable measurement models for three research constructs of personality traits, affect, and satisfaction. These individual measurement models were subsequently integrated into the overall measurement model for testing. After the overall measurement model incorporating personality, affect, and satisfaction had been validated with the CFA technique, the structural relationships among exogenous and endogenous variables were estimated by testing the hypothesised structural causal model with the entire sample.

Chapter Synopsis

In this chapter, methodological issues of the study were elaborated and discussed in terms of research paradigms, research design, research methods, data collection and analysis. Three research paradigms (i. e. positivism, interpretivism, and pragmatism) were introduced first, setting up pragmatism as the appropriate paradigm in this research. Then it provided a solid foundation for the choice of the sequential mixed-methods research method in this study by addressing the rationale for combining quantitative with qualitative research in a single study. In the qualitative exploration phase, focus group discussions were conducted to collect data and thematic analysis was used to analyse qualitative data. Next, in the quantitative investigation phase, a questionnaire survey was administered to examine the relationships among the research constructs in the conceptual framework; the instrument development was discussed and the pilot study was reported. Finally, the methods of data analysis were reported with descriptions and discussions of the SEM techniques adopted for analysing the data.

5

Chinese Tourists' Affective Experiences in Australia

The previous chapter addressed the methodological issues and provided a detailed description of the mixed-methods sequential design adopted in this study. This chapter focuses on the qualitative phase of the overall research study. As aforementioned, many destination marketers all over the world are seeking guidance from academia on how to accommodate Chinese outbound tourists as a newly emerging market. However, a review of the existing literature on Chinese outbound tourism indicates that few empirical studies have been undertaken to investigate Chinese outbound tourists' affective responses as a vital antecedent to their overall satisfaction. In addition, the rapid development of Chinese outbound tourism has necessitated exploring the nature of this phenomenon. For this purpose, qualitative research has an absolute advantage because it is ideal for identifying context-related information and thoroughly investigating emerging issues (Zhang & Albrecht 2010). More specifically, the qualitative study was designed to examine and categorise mainland Chinese outbound tourists' affective responses during their long-haul package tours to Australia. Accordingly, the qualitative phase of this study was exploratory in nature. Using the data gathered through focus group interviews, the qualitative phase aimed to achieve the following objective, as addressed in Chapter 1,

　　1) to identify and document Chinese outbound tourists' salient affective responses characterised as either positive or negative, during their trips to Australia.

Firstly, this chapter commences with an explanation of the procedures undertaken to collect the data in the qualitative research phase through focus group interviews. Questions raised in the focus group interviews cover the same research constructs as those in the survey, which has dual benefits. On the one hand, it provides an in-depth understanding of Chinese outbound tourists' affective responses when travelling in a group package tour. On the other hand, it serves as a useful pilot study to find out the issues and validate the measurement items in the subsequent questionnaire survey. Secondly, the procedures undertaken to analyse the qualitative data are discussed. Thirdly, the findings of data analysis and results pertaining to the research questions are presented. Fourthly, this chapter concludes with a summary of the qualitative phase of the study.

Data Collection

As explained in the research design in Chapter 3, the data generated from the qualitative phase serves to identify salient affective responses which will be further examined with personality traits and tourist satisfaction in the subsequent quantitative phase. Due to the exploratory nature of qualitative research, the focus group discussion (FGD) was conducted to provide insights into the understanding of Chinese outbound tourists' affective responses during their long-haul group travel to Australia. This section details the procedures of recruiting the sample group and conducting the FGDs.

Profile of FGD Participants

It has been widely accepted that researchers should select the appropriate contexts and individuals that can provide information relevant to the specific research questions (Maxwell 2005). Following this ground rule, purposive sampling was employed as the most effective sampling strategy to recruit FGD participants. For a qualitative exploratory study, homogenous sampling can "bring focus to a sample, reduce variation, simplify analysis, and facilitate group interviewing" (Patton 2005, p. 127). The qualitative phase of the study aimed to explore tourists' affective responses in the context of mainland Chinese outbound tourists to Australia; therefore, it called for a sample matching this population.

Four criteria had been pre-formulated before data collection in order to target the most eligible participants for the study. The first screening criterion was that participants had to be mainland Chinese citizens aged over 18 who visited Australia on a group package tour. Secondly, the potential participants were asked whether they had visited Australia recently, and how many times they had visited. Those who had visited Australia more than once were excluded from this study because their recent affective responses might have been biased by their previous travel experiences. Thirdly, collecting retrospective information about affective responses can be problematic (Faullant et al. 2011); therefore, the timing for data collection was carefully chosen. To guarantee the optimal timeframe of data collection, the tourists were invited to participate in the FGD within three days of their return home. At that time, the tourists' affective responses to their travel experiences in Australia were still fresh and easily accessible. Fourthly, since the different travel experiences were likely to generate dynamic variations and fluctuations in affective responses among tourists, the sample only focused on the tourists who paid their first visit to Australia, all consuming an identical travel product, i. e. an 8-day package holiday tour, sequentially visiting Sydney, Brisbane, Gold Coast, and

Melbourne (see Appendix 1).

Adopting the purposive sampling performs an essential function in the quality of data gathered (Krueger & Casey 2009); thus, reliability and competence of the participants can be guaranteed. To enhance validity, multi-source data from different tour operators were collected. As the qualitative study explores a relatively under-researched area, there is no universal rule for the number of FGDs required for this study (Guest, Bunce & Johnson 2006). Consequently, four sessions of FGD, each with eight participants, were believed to be able to provide adequate sample size for the exploratory qualitative study.

As shown in Table 5.1, a total of 32 participants consisting of 16 males and 16 females were recruited into four focus groups. The majority of participants (62.5%) were between 30 and 49 years old and the married accounted for 84.3% of the sample. With regard to their personal monthly income, 50% of respondents earned between RMB 6,000 and RMB 9,999 (approximately US $923 and US $1,538). The average per capita income of Chinese urban residents in 2011 was RMB 1998 (approximately US $307) (National Bureau of Statistics of China 2012). A university degree or above was held by 68.8% of the respondents, and another 21.9% had a college diploma. In addition to demographic information, respondents were also asked with whom they travelled to Australia. Of the respondents, 62.5% travelled with their families or relatives.

Table 5.1　Demographic Profiles of Focus Group Participants ($n = 32$)

		G1	G2	G3	G4	Total
Gender	Male	5	4	4	3	16
	Female	3	4	4	5	16
Age (years)	18 – 29		1		1	2
	30 – 39	2	2	2	2	8
	40 – 49	4	2	3	3	12
	50 – 59	1	2	2	1	6
	60 or older	1	1	1	1	4
Marital status	Unmarried		2	1	1	4
	Married	8	6	7	6	27
	Not specified				1	1

Continued

		G1	G2	G3	G4	Total
Occupation	Businessperson	2		3	1	6
	Civil servant		2	2		4
	Teacher		2		1	3
	Clerk/White-collar worker	5	2	3	3	13
	Blue-collar worker					
	Retired		1		1	2
	Unemployed	1			1	2
	Students		1		1	2
Education	Primary school or less					
	High school		1	2		3
	2-to-3-year college	2	2	1	2	7
	4-year university	6	3	3	4	16
	Postgraduate or above		2	2	2	6
Personal monthly income	No income	1	1		2	4
	Less than ¥2,000					
	¥2,000－3,999	1	1			2
	¥4,000－5,999	1	2	1		4
	¥6,000－7,999	2	2	2	4	10
	¥8,000－9,999		2	2	2	6
	¥10,000－14,999	2		1		3
	More than ¥15,000	1		2		3
Family size	1 person			1	1	2
	2－3 persons	7	6	6	6	25
	4－5 persons	1	2		1	4
	6 persons and over			1		1
Travel companion	Alone	1	1			2
	Family/Relatives	4	5	6	5	20
	Colleagues	2	1	2	2	7
	Friends	1	1		1	3

Implementation of the Focus Group

FGD Time and Location

On 8 March and 15 March 2012, four rounds of semi-structured FGDs in total were conducted in Nanjing by the researcher whose native language is Mandarin Chinese. The sequential data collection provided the opportunity for the researcher to refine the structure of FGDs and improve interview techniques as a FGD moderator. To maintain their fresh memories of affective responses to their travel experiences in Australia, all the group members participated in the discussion within three days of finishing the identical package holiday tour in Australia. Nanjing, as the capital of Jiangsu Province in China, was selected as the place for data collection because it is the top source market generating outbound tourists in the Province. Being convenient for the participants residing in Nanjing, it could save them time and effort and therefore increase their willingness to participate in this research. To guarantee that the FGD environment was quiet and safe without any interruption and disturbance (Bryman, Alan & Bell 2011), the FGDs were conducted in the meeting room of Nanjing Stone Marketing Research Company, a specifically designed venue for conducting FGDs. A round table was configured so that participants and the researcher could be seated around it to create a friendly and comfortable environment for eliciting genuine interactions. Overall, the FGD time and location for this qualitative exploratory study were carefully designed and chosen to make them appropriate for generating reliable information.

FGD Procedures

The FGD began with an introduction in which the researcher/moderator gave a brief overview of the background and purpose of the research project, and explained the FGD procedures as well as some ground rules (e. g. participants were encouraged to speak out their real thoughts and feelings; there were no right or wrong answers; the anonymity, confidentiality, and the voluntary nature of their involvement would be ensured). In order to better retain information and facilitate transcription, all the FGDs were audio-recorded with the permission of each participant. Thus, at the beginning of each FGD, participants were asked to read the participant information sheet carefully and then sign the consent form. In the introductory section, by stating his past experiences of working as a travel consultant in Nanjing before embarking on his PhD journey in Australia, the researcher managed to build trust and rapport with the participants.

The second section focused on probing the participants and eliciting responses to the main questions relevant to the antecedents and consequences of participants' affective responses to their travel experiences in Australia. This was done in three sub-stages, i. e. warm-up questions, affective responses, and tourist satisfaction (see Appendix 3). To begin with, the researcher posed four warm-up questions. Starting with an ice-breaker, he then asked them their thoughts about the most impressive features of their visit, what their travel motivations were, and whether they would consider further independent travel to Australia. Open-ended questions were used in the FGDs to stimulate discussion amongst the participants. Each participant was encouraged to express their opinions in turn and others were asked whether they had different views. As focus group participants formed a homogeneous group of outbound tourists who had travelled to Australia on the same itinerary in the past week, they felt quite at ease in the exchange of opinions and thoughts, thus maximising disclosure amongst them. Then participants were requested to give holistic affective evaluations on their whole travel experience in Australia. More probing and specific questions were subsequently raised to collect retrospective information about participants' emotional responses to their travel episodes in Australia. According to Oliver (1997), this method is advisable when various affective responses have to be measured during a specified timeframe. Based on the differentiation between positive affect and negative affect, these affective evaluations were further elaborated and discussed, which is the core focus of this qualitative exploratory study. Participants were ultimately asked to evaluate their entire trip to Australia and identify the factors that might influence their assessments of overall satisfaction. As addressed in the research methodology, the qualitative exploration serves the quantitative investigation in this study. More specifically, by asking probing questions, the researcher also aimed to inquire into the possible relationships among tourist personality, affective responses, and tourist satisfaction.

The FGD concluded with the researcher delivering a debriefing to urge participants to raise additional questions and provide more comments and feedback. In addition, demographic questions including gender, age, occupation, education and personal annual income, were collected. At the end of each FGD session, the researcher distributed the envelopes containing the gift money of RMB 150 (about US $25) among the participants as a sign of appreciation for their efforts and time.

Each FGD session lasted approximately 90 minutes and the researcher gave careful consideration to time allocation for three sections, namely, 10 minutes for the opening part, 70 minutes for the question-probing part, and 10 minutes for the closing part. During the FGDs, the moderator was responsible for covering a set of pre-determined questions within the time allotted so as to solicit the maximum amount of information needed from the group. Following the recommendation of Denzin and Lincoln (2005), the moderator plays a vital role in the success of a FGD and he/she should demonstrate no evaluations or judgements of participants' responses to maintain neutrality and avoid participant bias. Therefore, on the one hand, the researcher acted as an attentive listener after introducing each topic of inquiry; on the other hand, the researcher appropriately managed group dynamics by getting all participants actively involved in the discussion, thereby providing abundant qualitative data for further analysis.

Data Analysis Procedures

As addressed in Chapter 4, thematic analysis was performed to analyse focus group data. Data analysis began with the researcher transcribing the contents of four FGD sessions in order to make participants' affective evaluations easily verifiable. By means of the qualitative data analysis software NVivo 10, the codes were constructed from transcripts in a systematic process as the most basic segments of focus group data. Based on the different codes generated across the entire data set, the themes and sub-themes were identified and further refined to capture participants' salient affective response features during their trips to Australia. Finally, focus group data were analysed and interpreted with selected extracts. This following section describes the actual sequence of the data display, reduction, and interpretation.

Data Transcription

In the qualitative research phase, the researcher collected data through dynamic interaction with FGD participants, which gave the researcher some preliminary knowledge of the data or initial analytic thoughts. As the first step in qualitative analytical procedures, transcribing FGDs is "a key phase of data analysis within interpretative qualitative methodology" (Bird 2005, p. 227). In the process of converting the verbal account into written texts, the researcher had another opportunity to be immersed in the four FGD sessions and got acquainted with the depth and breadth of the content (Braun & Clarke 2006), thus developing a more thorough understanding of the qualitative data.

Transcription creates a mapping from sound to script, which is designed to be as true to the verbal account as possible. However, different research objectives and analysis approaches require different levels of detail in the transcripts. Pragmatically, there are no fixed guidelines to follow when transcribing verbal data (Bazeley & Jackson 2013). For example, it is suggested that rigorous verbatim transcripts are suited to conversation analysis, narrative analysis, and discourse analysis (Oliver, Serovich & Mason 2005), which captures both verbal and nonverbal communications to provide a true account of both the "what" and "how" of speech, including all the utterances, emotional responses (e. g. laughter and sighs), hand gestures, pauses, filler words like "ums", "mmms", "ers", and so on. By contrast, for conducting thematic analysis, a denaturalised transcription approach can be adopted to present interpretative explanations, rather than copies or representation of original audio recordings (Kvale & Brinkmann 2009). The qualitative phase followed the denaturalised approach to highlight the meanings and perceptions within the verbal data, as well as "the accuracy of the information content" (MacLean, Meyer & Estable 2004, p. 116). The fundamental principle was to transcribe the essence of FGDs in as much detail as possible so that the researcher could grasp complete information about participants' individual affective evaluations of their trips to Australia.

As the four FGD sessions were conducted in Mandarin, all the transcripts were produced correspondingly in Chinese so as to save time and maintain the vivid meaning of the data. In general, it took the researcher approximately seven hours to transcribe a 1.5-hour FGD. In order to avoid any potential confusion, a particular label was assigned to represent each anonymous participant at multiple sessions (e. g. the seventh participant in group 1 would be labelled as G1.7); focus groups were transcribed promptly while the session was still fresh. The researcher conducted the four FGD sessions and transcribed the audio recordings in person; therefore, he knew exactly what to transcribe and what to omit. The researcher also checked the transcripts against the audiotape for accuracy. These steps were taken to help interpret the focus group data more accurately and maintain consistency in the data analysis procedures. Once the data transcription was confirmed and finalised, the transcripts of FGDs, coupled with the field notes, constituted the raw data of the qualitative phase intended for further systematic analysis.

Data Coding

In thematic analysis, codes represent "the most basic segment, or element, of the raw data or information that can be assessed in a meaningful way regarding the phenomenon" (Boyatzis 1998, p. 63). Correspondingly, coding is an analytical process in which the raw data are categorised into significant groups to help identify and develop themes (Guest, MacQueen & Namey 2011). As indicated in Chapter 3, this research adopted the method of integrating deductive with inductive approaches to develop codes. Therefore, the coding scheme that the researcher constructed not only conformed to the theoretical paradigm underlying the qualitative phase, but was also strongly linked to the data itself.

According to Hay's (2005) two-step process, data coding begins with the fundamental coding scheme to identify primary themes, followed by a more focused coding in which specific patterns can be conceptualised and summarised as sub-themes from the FGD data. Based on a systematic review of extant literature on the structure of affect (see Chapter 2), especially in the travel and tourism context, Chinese outbound tourists' affective responses to their travel experiences in Australia were pre-established into two main themes in the coding framework: positive or negative. In addition, the affective responses that had been identified in previous studies on tourist behaviour were employed as codes to generate an initial coding structure. Bearing in mind these guidelines, the researcher, in the first round of coding, carefully perused all the focus group transcripts and field notes, and then modified the coding structure through supplementing or revising codes and sub-codes. Thus, a draft codebook was developed to document the guidelines on coding processes as recommended by Boyatzis (1998), which contained the label for each code and sub-code, the definition of the codes and sub-codes whose labels were not self-explanatory, the description of rules applying to the whole coding process, and the examples of how to code those codes and sub-codes whose labels were not self-explanatory.

The computer-assisted qualitative data analysis software NVivo 10 was thereafter employed to facilitate the further coding process. NVivo is designed to help categorise, sift, organise, and analyse non-numerical or unstructured information. Consequently, it contributes to systematically managing the coding process by means of creating and assigning codes (Bazeley & Jackson 2013). In NVivo, coding is represented by nodes which act as "a collection of references about a specific theme, place, person or other area of interest" (Bryman, Allan & Bell 2007, p. 598). The second round of coding was conducted by importing all focus group transcripts and field notes into NVivo 10 as well as putting the modified codes and sub-codes as tree nodes into the software. During this process, the codebook was readjusted accordingly.

For identifying the sub-themes under the two broad themes of positive affect and negative affect, Chinese tourists' traditional assessment criteria for their travel activities in six dimensions—"catering, lodging, transportation, tour, shopping, and entertainment (食、住、行、游、购、娱; *shi, zhu, xing, you, gou, yu*)" (Zhai 2006; Kang & Ma 2009; Wang & Chen 2013)—were employed as the pre-constructed categories (parent nodes) prior to the data coding process. Additionally, through examining the FGD transcripts, a series of child nodes were developed to help distinguish and characterise parent nodes. Participants' situational emotional responses occurring at different child nodes regarding these six dimensions accumulated gradually to form the overall affective responses to their travel experiences in Australia, which provided evidence for the researcher's conceptualisations of affective responses as the core construct in the research framework.

In this study, special care was given to increase the reliability and validity of data coding. According to Boyatzis's (1998) strategy for data reliability, the process of data coding should be consistent and reasonably stable over time and across researchers. Therefore, the researcher coded the transcripts again two weeks after the second round of coding to ensure that the same codes were applied to the same text passages. In essence, coding was developed and defined throughout

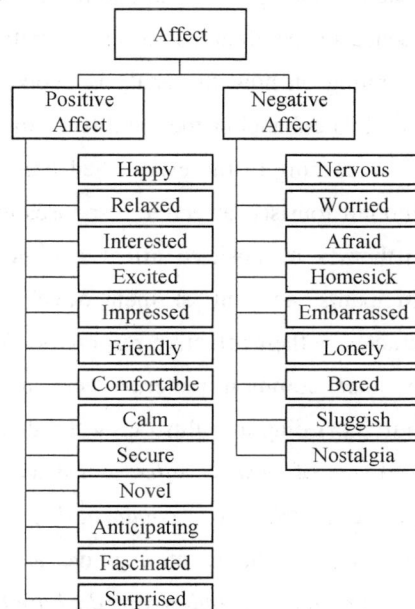

Figure 5.1　Final Coding Scheme

the entire analysis. To minimise the bias possibly arising from the researcher as the sole coder, the researcher's supervisors and peer scholars in tourism management helped check the coding structure and the codebook, focusing especially on the categorisation of the sub-themes (i. e. diverse positive or negative affective responses) as well as the codes and sub-codes whose labels were not self-explanatory. Their concerns and suggestions were incorporated into the ultimate codebook. By doing so, the final coding scheme (see Figure 5.1) for Chinese outbound tourists' affective responses during their visit to Australia provided saturation coverage while avoiding overlaps.

Data Interpretation

FGD transcripts and field notes provided a descriptive record of the qualitative research, and the data coding process helped the researcher sift and sort information to better make sense of the data. Based on these two steps, the final data analysis stage was to interpret the data with NVivo 10 and provide an explanation of Chinese outbound tourists' affective responses to their travel experiences in Australia. NVivo software is a tool which allows researchers to develop interpretative themes or sub-themes at any time during the analysis process, thus increasing the rigor of data analysis (Crowley, Harré & Tagg 2002). Two important principles were adopted in interpreting the data: 1) it presents "a concise, coherent, logical, non-repetitive, and interesting account" of the data within and across themes; 2) the analytic narrative needs to "go beyond description of the data and make an argument" in relation to the research questions (Braun & Clarke 2006, p. 93). In addition, some vivid and compelling quotes were chosen as convincing evidence in the findings to demonstrate the prevalence of themes and sub-themes. In short, by elaborating on how the analysis evolved, the flow of interpretation can be traced from the raw data, thus enhancing the validity of the inferential process in the qualitative exploration stage.

According to the established conceptualisations of affect in the existing literature, Chinese outbound tourists' affective responses to their travel experiences in Australia were interpreted into two themes of positive affect and negative affect within the qualitative data. Based on the participants' account of their travel experiences, a number of adjectives were identified to characterise their affective responses. Similar affective responses were grouped into one category and those common patterns were interpreted as different sub-themes. Figure 5.1 shows a hierarchical diagram illustrating the themes and sub-themes constructed from the qualitative data. The theme of *positive affect* consisted of 13 sub-themes: *happy, relaxed, interested, excited, impressed, friendly, comfortable, calm, secure, novel, anticipating, fascinated,* and *surprised*; the theme of negative affect comprised 9 sub-themes: *nervous, worried, afraid, homesick, lonely, embarrassed, bored, sluggish,* and *nostalgia*. The specific themes and sub-themes are addressed respectively in the next section.

Findings and Results

With four rounds of FGDs conducted, the in-depth and rich exploratory data were collected and analysed through a thematic approach. What types of affective responses did Chinese visitors associate with Australia as a tourist destination? Why were these affective responses triggered and formed during their travel to Australia? What effects would these affective responses have on tourist behaviour? In exploring these questions concerning the "what", "why", and "so what" of participants' affective responses, abundant evidence emerged to illustrate and support the FGD findings with selected quotations referenced; moreover, it provided a general structure for reporting the findings and discussing the results. Because FGDs primarily focused on participants' affective responses that have been conceptualised as positive affect (often interchangeable with positive affective response in this study) and negative affect (often interchangeable with negative affective response in this study), the report of findings in the qualitative phase began with an exploration of the participants' holistic affective responses in the context of Chinese outbound tourists to Australia, subsequently followed by another two subsections—positive affective responses and negative affective responses separately.

In the current study, Australia as a tourist destination is regarded as a synthesis of many ingredients such as environment, tourist attractions, transportation, hotels, food, shopping, and so on. From a marketing perspective, these travel components are consumed in a sequence of different episodes, thus constituting an overall travel experience of destination. In a sense, the travel experience can be perceived as an extended service transaction in which tourists interact with service providers or other tourists in different scenarios (Hosany & Gilbert 2010). Not surprisingly, diverse affective responses were elicited spontaneously by the travel experience along the service process. As a consequence, the retrospective approach was adopted in this study to evaluate participants' holistic affective responses to their travel experiences in Australia.

Affective Responses

As addressed in Chapter 2, emotions are direct, intense mental reactions to a specific event or stimulus (Beedie, Terry & Lane 2005), and are therefore transient and situational in nature. Generally speaking, emotions can be perceived as a subset of the larger domain of affective states that embrace moods and other feelings (Lambie & Marcel 2002). Emotions arising from travel experiences deposit affective memory traces, thus forming affective responses. Correspondingly, even momentary emotions can, to a certain extent, reflect one's general affective level. The frequencies and dynamics of each specific short-lived emotional response can contribute to shaping overall affective responses. Therefore, it is important to note that, for the purpose of this study, affective responses are conceptually distinguished from emotional responses, which represent a more generalised evaluation of affective states lasting for a relatively longer time. In addition, previous studies of individual affective experiences have demonstrated that both positive and negative affect can be evoked concurrently in everyday life (Westbrook 1987), suggesting that individuals may have both positive and negative affective responses to the same travel experiences.

The FGDs began with a warm-up discussion about their personality and interests, which served as an icebreaker to encourage them to share insights and experiences with others. With due consideration to the influence of personality variables, participants were asked to give an overall affective evaluation of their travel experiences in Australia. Since participants' specific affective responses were highly individual, their quick and straightforward replies, together with the narratives of their own personal travel experiences, revealed personality-related and context-related factors as two significant predictors of affective responses. Fourteen overall affective responses were summarised to capture the prevalence of participants' affective responses. Based on the initial framework of these 14 holistic affective responses, specific emotional responses triggered by different travel episodes were subsequently explored in-depth to provide supplementary evidence for the formation of overall affective responses. Finally, holistic tourist satisfaction was assessed in relation to participants' overall affective responses. In short, Chinese outbound tourists' overall affective responses were further illustrated through in-depth analysis of their emotional responses to specific travel episodes during their trip.

Based on the literature review of the differentiation between positive affect and negative affect, holistic affective responses were categorised into positive and negative affective responses accordingly. Table 5.2 reports overall affective responses engendered by participants' travel experiences of the package tour to Australia, incorporating nine positive affective responses (*happy*, *relaxed*, *interested*, *excited*, *impressed*, *friendly*, *comfortable*, *calm*, and *secure*) and five negative affective responses (*nervous*, *worried*, *homesick*, *afraid*, and *embarrassed*). The frequencies were listed in terms of the number of individuals who delineated the same affective responses, not for statistical purposes, but for reflecting the popularity and relative importance of each affective response in participants' minds.

Following the discussion of overall affective responses, participants were encouraged to recall in detail vivid moments of specific emotional responses to various travel episodes in Australia, which documented the pattern formation of prevailing affective responses. The retrospective appraisal of past affective experiences involves recalling and integrating the moments of transient emotional experiences (Fredrickson 2001). Correspondingly, the retrospective evaluation of participants' overall affective responses is based on the accumulation of a certain number of single emotional moments. From this point of view, the holistic assessment of an experienced affective response is best predicted by the occurrence frequency of all single moments of the emotional counterpart. A detailed analysis of participants' emotional responses shed light on mechanisms underlying the dimensions of affective responses.

Table 5.2　Overall Affective Responses Identified by Participants

Positive Affective Response	Individuals	Negative Affective Response	Individuals
1. Happy	27	1. Nervous	8
2. Relaxed	25	2. Worried	7
3. Interested	24	3. Homesick	6
4. Excited	22	4. Afraid	6
5. Impressed	20	5. Embarrassed	5
6. Friendly	17		
7. Comfortable	16		
8. Calm	8		
9. Secure	7		

With regard to how to measure positive and negative affect in tourism research, Pearce (1981) proposed adding up the frequency of positive or negative experiences, while Nawijn (2011a, 2011b) used the approach of "Affect Balance" by which the average negative affect score is subtracted from the average positive affect score. Following Pearce's (2009) proposition that affect can be the summation of emotional happenings, the researcher adopted the frequency analysis to tally participants' number of mentions of each specific emotional response over their 8-day tour in Australia. Over a time period, some momentary emotional responses may occur repeatedly and then develop into enduring affective responses, while others may be elicited only at that moment and then fade quickly from tourists' affective experiences. Therefore, the dynamic of each specific affective response was operationalised by measuring the frequency of its corresponding emotional responses.

The prevalence of emerging sub-themes among participants is exhibited in Table 5.3. The frequencies were listed according to the number of mentions of the same emotional response as well as the number of individuals who delineated this emotional response, not for statistical purposes, but for reflecting the participants' pronounced affective responses elicited by their travel experiences in Australia. More specifically, the "Individual" column indicates the number of participants who referred to the same emotional response triggered by the specific travel experiences regarding six categories of catering, lodging, transportation, tour, shopping, and entertainment. As an emotional response may have more than one occurrence during a travel experience, the "Number of mentions" column presents the number of mentions of the same emotional response shared by all the participants. Apparently, the higher the occurrence frequency of an emotional response among participants, the more likely it is that this emotional response would evolve into the relatively lasting affective response pervading their long-haul package tour to Australia.

Table 5.3　Prevalence of Emerging Subthemes among Participants

Theme	Sub-theme	Category	Individual($N=32$)	Number of mentions
Positive Affect	Happy	*a. b. c. d. e. f.*	27	56
	Relaxed	*a. b. c. d. f.*	25	48
	Interested	*a. c. d. e. f.*	24	51
	Excited	*a. c. d. e. f.*	22	49
	Impressed	*a. c. d. e. f.*	20	43
	Friendly	*a. b. d. e. f.*	17	38
	Comfortable	*c. d. e. f.*	16	34
	Calm	*a. d.*	8	16
	Secure	a. e.	7	16
	Novel	*a. d.*	6	13
	Anticipating	*a. d.*	4	7
	Fascinated	*d.*	4	6
	Surprised	*d.*	2	3
Negative Affect	Nervous	*c. d. f.*	8	19
	Worried	*c. d. f.*	7	17
	Afraid	*c. d. f.*	6	16
	Homesick	*a. b. f.*	6	15
	Embarrassed	*d. e. f.*	5	13
	Lonely	*b. d. f.*	4	13
	Bored	*b. e. f.*	4	12
	Sluggish	*a. d.*	2	6
	Nostalgia	*b. d.*	2	5

Note:*a.* catering;*b.* lodging;*c.* transportation;*d.* tour;*e.* shopping;*f.* entertainment

Descriptions of travel episodes in Australia generated 496 responses from 32 participants characterised as positive or negative emotional responses. Such an in-depth examination of specific emotional responses aimed to provide substantial evidence to support participants' holistic affective responses to their travel experiences in Australia, because transient emotional responses might occur frequently and eventually evolve into relatively lasting affective responses. Consequently, the detailed analysis of participants' emotional responses might predict or reflect the happenings of holistic affective responses. By conducting the two-step process of investigating both holistic affective responses and situational emotional responses, the understanding of affective responses was enriched. The major overall affective responses identified by the participants in Table 5.2 were further corroborated through a thorough investigation of participants' emotional responses to different travel episodes relating to six tourism elements (catering, lodging, transportation, tour, shopping, and entertainment).

Traditionally, there has been a consensus in Chinese tourism literature that the framework of six basic tourism elements has been the most effective tool for interpreting tourism phenomena, understanding tourism industry, and even revealing the essence of tourism (Kang & Ma 2009). They have provided a fundamental paradigm for constructing the tourism industry chain (Zhai 2006). These six elements as the essential dimensions of tourist activities have also been commonly employed by Chinese tourists to evaluate the tour quality and travel experiences (Tse & Zhang 2013). The prevalence of a specific emotional response throughout the journey can be significantly reflected by the tourism elements eliciting this emotional response. The more tourism elements an emotional response is associated with, the more prevalent it will be. The prevailing emotional response with a high occurrence frequency seems likely to develop into a relatively lasting affective response. For instance, as shown in Table 5.3, the travel episodes regarding all six tourism elements may generate the positive emotional response, *happy*. In other words, *happy* can be conceptualised as a prevailing affective response throughout all travel activities. Specifically, the majority of tourists gained happiness not only through tasting the kangaroo meat (*catering*), staying at the well-equipped accommodation (*lodging*), and taking the comfortable tourist coach (*transportation*), but also through participating in different travel activities (*tour*), shopping for Australian specialities and souvenirs (*shopping*), and enjoying some challenging entertainment activities at theme parks (*entertainment*). Conversely, another positive emotional response, *surprised* was related with only one tourism element, *tour*. Only in the travel activities did few tourists feel surprised at witnessing the vast Australian landscapes and encountering the Australian native animals (i.e. kangaroos and koalas) in the wild. Apparently, *surprised* cannot be conceptualised as a salient affective response.

As reiterated above, the main focus of this qualitative phase is to identify participants' salient affective responses while the analysis of specific emotional responses only serves as the supporting evidence for the formation of affective responses. Consequently, affective responses were further elaborated and presented as positive and negative ones. Overall, positive affective responses largely outweighed negative ones in terms of the frequency and prevalence, which is in line with earlier findings in tourist settings by Zins (2002), Hosany and Gilbert (2010), and Nawijn (2011b). As reported by participants, the formation of these affective responses had been influenced by their individual personality traits and personal travel experiences in Australia. Both positive and negative affective responses, as two major psychological variables, would play an important role in the formation of tourist satisfaction. Hence, to have a better understanding of the aforementioned "why" and "so what" questions of holistic affective responses, detailed descriptions of positive and negative affective responses will be provided respectively in the following two subsections.

Positive Affective Responses

Graburn (2001) characterised affective responses that motivated tourists as "something positive... that they cannot easily experience at home" (p. 43). Reviewing in retrospect the holistic affective responses to their travel experiences during the package tour to Australia in the past week, most participants tended to hold a positive affect toward Australia as a tourist destination. This was strikingly documented by many direct quotes from participants showcasing high levels of positive affect: "having a great time travelling in Australia", "overall, feeling happy and relaxed", "lovely wildlife animals", "unforgettable travel experience", "the sights are impressive! Nice weather and friendly people", and "this is the best overseas trip I've had so far!". Chinese outbound tourists to Australia, in their own words, described the nature of their positive affective responses to indicate they had enjoyed their trip to Australia. As shown in Table 5.2, nine main positive affective responses (*happy*, *relaxed*, *interested*, *excited*, *impressed*, *comfortable*, *friendly*, *calm*, and *secure*) were identified across the focus groups. Thus, the following analysis of specific positive affective responses was organised accordingly.

Happy

In travel and tourism settings, it is reasonable to associate travelling with the experience of freedom and relaxation. Both of these subjective states would elicit an affective response of being happy. Not surprisingly, "*happy*" as a salient affective response was explicitly described and mentioned with the maximum number of participants. Most participants felt quite happy to be on the 8-day package tour. This has corroborated the findings of other studies that tourists generally feel happy during their holiday (e.g. De Bloom et al. 2009; Nawijn 2011a). Participants noted that many attributes or dimensions of their travel experiences in Australia evoked the affective reaction of joy, including the agreeable weather, good social order, a "no-worry" lifestyle, pristine natural environments, friendly local people, unique wildlife encounters, superb iconic architecture, and so on. For instance, a 46-year-old lady in Group 4 stated:

> To be frank, the only way to describe my feeling of setting foot in Australia was simply happy and pleased, because I immediately experienced brilliant sunshine, fresh air, and beautiful weather as what I had expected. Being happy lasted throughout the whole trip and I did enjoy unspoilt natural landscapes, pristine beaches, and lovely wildlife animals there. I would like to share my happy experiences in Australia with others. (G 4.2, female)

It is worth mentioning that some participants highlighted the benefits of participating in group-package tours for visiting long-haul outbound destination countries. Such a well-arranged tour to Australia yielded pleasurable feelings of joy among participants, because it involved different tourist attractions and activities at multiple destination cities, which not only delivered better value for money but also enhanced participants' happy travel experiences in Australia. For example, a male in his late fifties in Group 3 shared the following views:

> Different from those FITs, I prefer package travel. A group-package tour to Australia with a reasonable price has brought me a lot of convenience. I am sort of extrovert guy. Being with many travel companions in an English-speaking country made me feel pleasant and at ease. I enjoy talking with people of different ages on the trip to enrich my life experience. We learned together how to greet local people in English. With the assistance of my group members, I managed to communicate with an old Australian couple in simple English and with body languages. Such a small moment added to my happiness during the whole trip. This kind of joy will strengthen my sense of attachment to Australia as a tourist destination and make me feel satisfied. I think I shall revisit Australia in the future. (G 3. 3, male)

Relaxed

Relaxation was ranked second in terms of its prevalence among the participants. It was assumed to arise mainly from the lifestyle in Australia, because the majority of participants seemed to have a high opinion of the local lifestyle. Some participants claimed that other significant sources of relaxation lay in less population and a sense of quietness:

> Before I visited Australia, I had been told by my friend who had migrated to Australia that local people feel proud of their laid-back and easy-going lifestyle. Since our plane landed in Australia, I had been feeling very relaxed throughout the entire trip. Seeing clusters of white clouds drifting across the blue sky, I forgot all my worries and work pressure in an instant and began to enjoy local residents' easy lifestyle. In contrast to the stressful and hectic city life in Nanjing, life in Australia is most relaxing and slow-paced. I do appreciate the most commonplace saying in Australia, i. e. "no worries; be happy", which fully implies Australian life attitude. (G 1. 7, male)
>
> I always felt relaxed in Australia. I have got used to the hustle and bustle of city life in China, crowded and noisy. However, when I walked in downtown Sydney, I saw many people enjoying a cup of coffee at the café or doing running exercises under brilliant sunshine. I felt a sense of inner quietness instead of feeling rushed or under pressure. It seemed that I did not visit Australia, but lived it. (G 2. 3, female)

Interested

Interest can motivate people to pursue novel information and experiences (Fredrickson 1998). Participants visited different cities in Australia (Sydney, Brisbane, Gold Coast, and Melbourne), which provided many changes and challenges. For instance, the visit to The Rocks area draws tourists' attention to convict-era Australia, while the guided tour of Sydney Opera House caters for tourists interested in a more modern slice of Sydney; a walk to the Botanical Gardens or along famous Bondi Beach convinces tourists of Sydney's high reputation as one of the most liveable cities in the world. In summary, most participants were interested in experiencing a great variety of beautiful natural environments, spectacular coastal scenery, lovely Australian native wildlife, relaxing farm life, and unique aboriginal culture. Interested participants could learn and absorb useful knowledge from these travel experiences.

I am open-minded and willing to experience anything that can arouse my interest. It was my first time to visit Australia and what I read about Australia before interested me quite a lot. Since Australia is situated on the southern hemisphere, I was interested in experiencing the season opposite to that of my residence only after 9-hour flight. I sought to experience Western culture and lifestyle in Australia. Especially, I had strong interest in the Aussie farm tour in Gold Coast, for I grew up in the city of Nanjing and never had experienced such a farm life before. Having been informed that people are encouraged to have kangaroo meat, I tasted it. I think it was tasty, tender, and juicy with a reasonable price. (G 1.5, a male college student)

Excited

Many participants had experienced short trips to Asian countries with cultural backgrounds and value systems similar to those of China. First-time visitors experienced a state of great excitement when travelling in Australia—a long-haul outbound tourist destination in the Western world. Also, there is substantial evidence that wildlife encounters can generate significantly higher levels of emotional and affective responses, such as excitement and pleasure (e. g. Farber & Hall 2007). Furthermore, most participants felt excited and satisfied with the theme parks and beach/sports activities on the Gold Coast. They expressed their willingness to participate in more entertainment or recreational activities organised by the tour operators in hopes of adding more fun and value to their experiences in Australia. In short, whether it was for Australia's vast landscapes, pristine beaches, or wildlife, most participants noted that travelling in Australia comprised a series of exciting episodes throughout:

I felt excited travelling in Australia, because it was my first time to go abroad. I have learnt English for many years, but I never had the chance to live or study in an English-speaking country. My foreign teacher at college came from Australia. To me, visiting an

English-speaking country like Australia was simply breathtaking because that was my dream in schooldays. I felt excited using English to communicate with local residents, though not very fluent. I learnt to greet strangers with "G'day, mate". Haha! I was curious about everything I did not know, especially for those Australian aboriginal cultures and indigenous wildlife animals. I was excited to see kangaroos hopping away in the wild. They are so cute. Especially, I felt very excited when cuddling the koala. She attached herself to my body, so lovely and so sweet, just like a little baby. (G 4.4, a female clerk)

Impressed

Participants shared the view that travelling in Australia was an impressive experience. They exemplified the affective response, "impressed" in many regards, such as the aroma of coffee in the street, the open land, spectacular scenery, natural environment, and even Australians' integrity and equality. Many participants were deeply impressed by spatial and ecological dimensions in Australia, and reached a consensus on the impressiveness of the spectacular landscape of the Great Ocean Road, especially of the grandeur of the "Twelve Apostles".

Australians like drinking coffee and there are so many cafés in Australia that you can even smell the aroma of coffee in the street. That's quite impressive to me. Also I was impressed by the staff's professionalism in the service industry. By contrast with the service staff in China, I think they are more confident and dedicated to their work, because their shining smiles and professional manners would leave you a deep impression. Besides, I was deeply impressed by Australians' integrity. I lost my purse with a large amount of cash in it at fish market in Sydney. There were so many people dining at the market that I nearly gave up the idea of finding my purse. Finally with the help of the tour guide, I found my purse with all the cash at the office of Lost and Found in the market. (G 2.6, female)

The open land, spectacular scenery, and unspoiled ecological environments offered me a sense of freedom and equality. They have existed for centuries and remain intact in Australia without any man-made sabotage. It seems that they are endowed with their own right and deserve respect. From this point of view, I think Australians have assumed their responsibility of maintaining the ecological sustainable development. The most impressive thing was to witness the Great Ocean Road. It was beyond my imagination. Also, the Twelve Apostles were amazing, which presented magnified landscapes in different directions. It was such an unforgettable experience that had affected me on a deep level. (G 3.2, a 45-year-old man)

Friendly

Participants generally experienced local people's friendliness and hospitality and a sense of being respected in Australia. Actually, it was one of the important determinants in the process of

Chinese outbound tourists' destination choice (Huang & Gross 2010; Li et al. 2011). Apart from the local residents' warmth and hospitality, some participants claimed that they even harboured a sense of friendliness from wild fauna and flora (e. g. booming flowers, birds, and wildlife animals) in such a harmonious society as Australia:

> *People in Australia are friendly, straightforward, and open-minded. Their sense of mateship and their no-worries attitude make our visitors feel welcome. Our coach driver is a very humorous local guy. Although he could only speak "nihao" (hello) and "xiexie" (thank you) in Chinese, we can still sense his kindness and respect from his sincere smiles and service behaviour. Interestingly, even the birds were willing to come close to you; kangaroos were browsing quietly not far from you; a vast area of parklands and botanic gardens with various kinds of booming flowers seemed to embrace you. Those encounters can generate a sense of friendliness at the bottom of my heart. (G 3.4, a female)*

Comfortable

Participants felt that travelling in Australia was a comfortable experience, because of its agreeable climate, local lifestyle, public order, travel environment, friendly people, and so on. They felt comfortable upon their arrival, because free brochures in Chinese were provided for their convenience at Australian international airports. Participants felt comfortable and pleased when shopping at duty-free shops with Chinese-speaking staff because they felt staff not only understood the Chinese language, but also had a better understanding of their genuine wants and needs.

> *I felt comfortable and agreeable in Australia. I like its amiable weather, natural environment, and friendly people. Well-maintained lawn as well as unspoiled vegetation and forests can be seen everywhere in Australia. I can see many Asian faces in Australian big cities, despite the fact that many of them speak English only. All these made me feel comfortable and familiar. Moreover, I can sense peace and harmony everywhere, especially the harmony between human beings and animals. (G 3.6, a female)*

Calm

Several participants depicted the affective response of calmness during their visit to Australia. Calmness is often experienced jointly along with relaxation and contentment and prompts self-reflection (Tugade & Fredrickson 2007). As discussed above, the majority of participants felt relaxed during their travel in Australia. Therefore, influenced by this affective response, some participants experienced calmness concurrently. For instance, the boundless yet peaceful ocean was mentioned as a trigger for the calmness within participants' inner hearts, which aroused their reflection on individual psychological needs. A female participant in her late thirties recalled:

I felt a sense of calmness and peacefulness when looking at the boundless ocean on a sunny afternoon in Gold Coast. The harmony of sea and sky made a beautiful picture. It was the first time for me to see that kind of unspoiled beauty. However, instead of excitement, I was overwhelmed by calmness, which resulted in my deep thinking and understanding of life. Similarly, when I was approaching the Twelve Apostles, the grandeur of the limestone stacks and the glinting ripples of sea at twilight made me feel calm and relaxed, thus leading to a sense of contentment and satisfaction. (G 1. 6, a female in her late thirties)

Secure

Participants generally felt secure when travelling in Australia because of its sound social order. Some emphasised the crucial role of the well-trained Chinese-speaking tour guides who acted as a mediator between the local community and tourists in intercultural settings. Participants felt secure in the company of their qualified tour guides who had a good command of language skills, local customs, and cultural differences. For instance, a participant in Group 3 (G 3. 3) observed: *"Being hosted by our professional tour guide helped me substantially lessen the language and cultural barriers, which made me feel secure when travelling in Australia".* Additionally, participants described the affective response, *"secure"* in two regards, i. e. the issue of food safety and counterfeit luxury products. The use of gutter oil (recycled and illegal cooking oil) has raised food safety as a high priority issue for Chinese people. The problem of counterfeit luxury products posed a threat to building trust and credibility in Chinese society:

I felt secure when dining in Australian restaurants, for there is no need to worry about gutter oil. At the fish market in Sydney, I enjoyed tasting a dozen of raw oysters with a little lemon juice squeezed on them, as recommended by the local diners. Growing in the Australian unpolluted seas, they were so fresh and tasty. Besides, our group members were nearly crazy for purchasing baby formula and UGG boots in Australia, because we believe that their qualities are trustworthy. We all felt secure about food safety and the genuineness of luxury goods in Australia. (G 4. 3, a 37-year-old female in Group 4)

Negative Affective Responses

Generally speaking, only a few participants described negative affective responses when retrospectively evaluating their travel experiences in Australia, indicating that most participants thought highly of Australia as a tourist destination. As shown in Table 5. 2, five adjective words delineating participants' main negative affective responses are *nervous, worried, homesick, afraid,* and *embarrassed.* They admitted that these negative affective responses resulted predominantly from the unfamiliarity with Australia as a tourist destination and cultural differences between China and Australia: "this is my first time to Australia", "I know nothing about English", "many people with Asian faces can only speak English", "I have experienced so many cultural differences", and "I was surprised to know Chinese food is so important to me". The following analysis of five negative affective responses was organised accordingly.

Nervous

Participants described the affective response of being nervous, mostly due to language and cultural barriers as well as their personality attributes. Different from those Asian destination countries that share similar cultural backgrounds and value norms with China, Chinese people acknowledge Australia to be a Western long-haul tourist destination. The majority of local people in Australia prefer living in the suburbs in order to escape from the hustle and bustle of cities. Sometimes there are few pedestrians on the road outside the city. In addition, most participants cannot communicate with local people in English and do not possess good cross-cultural consciousness either. Therefore, it is understandable that travelling in such an unfamiliar environment led to some participants' nervousness. One female participant in her fifties in Group 1 commented:

> I am sort of person who may easily feel nervous in a strange situation. Although I travelled to Australia in a group with my families, I still could not help feeling nervous. I know nothing about English and I could not communicate with others in any language other than Mandarin. If I got lost, how could people help me out? There is nothing worse than feeling helpless in a foreign country and not knowing what you can do to sort it out. I got used to seeing many people in the city. Travelling to those areas which are sparsely populated may make me feel nervous and uncomfortable. (G1.2, a female in her fifties)

Worried

Most people felt secure and peaceful when travelling in Australia, while some participants, influenced by the negative report that Chinese people had been attacked in Australia, felt a little worried about their safety in Australia. Moreover, although more than half of the participants felt curious about local nightlife experiences, such as drinking at pubs, show-watching or gambling at casinos, some respondents felt worried about the safety of going out at night to participate in these activities. Also, tourists felt worried about getting lost.

> I felt worried when I was left alone during my stay in Australia, for I could not speak English. In case I will get lost, the old-fashioned way is to write down the name and address of my accommodation before I venture out. Even if I can't speak the local language, the piece of paper will work for me. If I was really stuck, I would walk into the nearest hotel, present the card of my hotel, and ask them for help—the very least they might do is to call me a cab. (G4.7, a male in his fifties)

Homesick

The subjective experience of homesickness can be conceptualised as a self-reported tendency to experience anxiety or discomfort in times of separation from the familiar environment (Verschuur, Eurelings-Bontekoe & Spinhoven 2004). Participants mentioned homesickness with regard to food and accommodation. On the one hand, some participants expressed their strong desire to try local cuisine and wine, especially Australian seafood and kangaroo meat, but they also indicated that they still preferred having Chinese food once a day (either lunch or dinner). Most participants felt pleased when Chinese cuisine/restaurants were provided. If they had not had Chinese food for two or three days, they claimed that they began to feel homesick. On the other hand, some participants commented on their accommodation experiences in Australia:

The hotels in Australia were beyond my expectations. We were advised to stay at 4-star hotels. To be frank, I never imagined the 4-star hotel in developed countries like Australia was just comparable to a 2-star economical hotel or a 3-star hotel in China, a developing country. A 4-star hotel in China should be equipped with many modern facilities and a magnificent lobby. In addition, all the TV programs used the languages I could not understand. I did not feel at home living in such a hotel. Naturally I came up with the feeling of being homesick. (G 2.1, a female)

I agree with that lady. The tailor-made service could compensate our negative impression on the hotel infrastructure. The genuine respect and hospitality from staff would make us feel better. The hotel could provide some hot water for drinking at restaurants because we Chinese prefer drinking hot tea, especially in winter. If they really care about Chinese market, it would be better to provide toothbrush, toothpaste, and some toiletries that are basic requirements in Chinese hotels. All these measures would make me feel at home away from home by creating a familiar environment for me. (G 2.5, a male)

Afraid

Tourists may experience being afraid in mild forms when travelling in unfamiliar scenarios. Long-haul outbound travel, which as noted above may generate positive affective response of excitement, may also engender fear or anxiety. Tourists may generate different affective responses when facing wilderness, and the vastness and desolation of the Australian landscape. A participant stated that "there was a sense of exhilaration about being alone on an empty beach", while another voice claimed that "I felt the strangest sensation of fear on an empty beach". It suggested that tourists' emotional and affective responses were closely associated with their personality traits. Some tourists were inclined to feel afraid when they were in a new environment with a totally different culture and language. Not surprisingly, several participants also felt afraid when walking under conditions which were believed to be personally threatening (e. g. a deserted road at night). Participants' educational background and their past overseas travel experiences might have also served as triggers for the fear. One female in Group 3 noted:

> I knew from the media that there were attacks toward Chinese people which caused deaths and injuries in Sydney. I understood those were only rare incidents that could happen anywhere in the world. However, when I was in a narrow road with few people present, I felt afraid from the bottom of my heart. I reckon it was partly because I was strange to Australian local surroundings. Cultural differences and language barriers would make this situation even worse to me. (G 3.2, a female)

Embarrassed

Aware of the cultural differences, though not having a sound knowledge of it, some participants felt embarrassed when they were insufficiently confident about whether they had behaved properly or not. Few participants mentioned the sense of distance between tourists and locals, and claimed it was hard for them to get close to the local residents. For instance, the Chinese always bargain with the seller when shopping, which does not seem to be common in Australia. A female respondent said, "Unaware of Australian business norms, I kept bargaining at one shop as I usually did in China; the shop owner was irritated and refused to sell anything to me in the end. I felt very embarrassed". One senior respondent recalled, "A local youth attempted to drive me to Chinatown in Sydney when I lost my way, but I misjudged him as an unreliable guy by the tattoo all over his body. Later I realised I was totally wrong and I felt extremely embarrassed". The differences in social conventions as well as laws and regulations may have engendered embarrassment. One male respondent noted:

> Having known the ban on smoking indoors in Australia, I went out of the hotel and smoked on the porch of the hotel. The doorkeeper came over to me and asked me not to smoke there. I argued why I could not smoke in that public outdoor waiting area. I did not understand what he explained to me. I thought he was unfriendly to Chinese tourists. Later the tour guide explained that in Australia, it is forbidden to smoke in any open waiting area covered with a roof, such as the porch, sheltered bus or train stops. Misjudging the doorkeeper made me feel embarrassed. Besides, when we were leaving that hotel, the tour guide got on the coach and asked whose room number was 807. There was an unsettled bill for pay-TV service. I had got no oral or written notice in Chinese from both the hotel and the tour guide that some TV programmes were charged by hours. A couple of tourists made a joke at me and asked whether I enjoyed any special movie last night. I had to get off the coach in public and paid 80 Australian dollars for seeing an adult movie for 20 minutes. I felt extremely embarrassed at that moment. (G 3.8, a male)

Discussion Based on Findings

The qualitative phase of the study concentrated on Chinese outbound tourists' affective responses elicited by their travel experiences in Australia, and the analysis of rich qualitative data revealed a variety of positive and negative affective responses. By showing how the analysis and findings evolved in the preceding sections, the flow of the researcher's interpretation could be traced from the raw data, and therefore the influence of the researcher's conceptualisation of the qualitative findings could be effectively demonstrated to support the inferential validity (Creswell 2009). Theoretically, findings mainly supported previous research on tourists' affective responses (e. g. Thompson 2007; Del Bosque & San Matin 2008; Jang et al. 2009; Pearce & Packer 2013) and helped conceptualise affective responses in the context of Chinese outbound tourists to Australia. Results also revealed the underlying causes of several particular affective responses incongruent with the extant literature on tourists' affective structure, thus enriching the tourism scholarship on Chinese tourists' psychology and behaviour in the context of international tourism.

Following the presentation of FGD findings about tourists' holistic affective responses, this section provides a discussion with reference to the primary objective in the qualitative phase of this research, i. e. to identify the salient positive and negative affective responses to be employed as questionnaire items for the subsequent quantitative investigation. First of all, as depicted in Table 5.4, the interview-based affective responses were collated with literature review-based counterparts to identify the overlapping affective responses as common and salient ones shared by mass tourists. Then the researcher focused on the major discrepancies and analysed those particular affective responses derived exclusively from FGDs. Based on these two steps, a list of Chinese outbound tourists' salient affective responses was eventually confirmed as the affective items in the final questionnaire.

Table 5.4 Affective Responses Identified from Two Sources

Literature review-based	Interview-based
· **Positive Affect**: · happy, relaxed, interested, enjoyable, upbeat, calm, peaceful, cheerful, impressed, surprised, friendly, enchanted, pleased	· **Positive Affect**: · happy, relaxed, interested, calm, excited, impressed, friendly, anticipating, surprised, comfortable, novel, fascinated, secure
· **Negative Affect**: · bored, displeased, disappointed, angry, nervous, sad, restless, fidgety, fearful, lonely, depressed, worried	· **Negative Affect**: · nervous, worried, afraid, homesick, lonely, embarrassed, bored, sluggish, nostalgia

Some affective responses derived from the tourism literature review were selected in the left column. Pearce and Packer (2013) argued that 13 affective responses generated from consumption situations could be used to capture how tourists respond to diverse experiences, including *happy*, *contented*, *optimistic*, *pleased*, *worried*, *frustrated*, *tense*, *lonely*, *unfulfilled*, *discontented*, *irritated*, *sad*, and *depressed*. Kahneman et al. (2004) identified four positive affects (*happy*, *competent/capable*, *warm/friendly*, and *enjoying myself*) and eight negative ones (*impatient*, *frustrated/annoyed*, *depressed/blue*, *hassled/ pushed around*, *angry/hostile*, *worried/anxious*, *criticized/put down*, and *tired*) from travel experiences. Using Taiwanese seniors as the study sample, Jang et al. (2009) found a group of salient affective items, incorporating *calm and peaceful*, *cheerful*, *excited*, *nervous*, *sad*, *restless*, and *fidgety*. Del Bosque and San Matin (2008) adopted four positive affects (*pleased*, *enchanted*, *impressed*, and *surprised*) and four negative affects (*bored*, *displeased*, *disappointed*, and *angry*) proposed from previous studies to evaluate tourists' affective responses. Yarnal and Kerstetter's (2005) study of a group cruise experience revealed five salient affective responses: *upbeat*, *enjoyable*, *comfortable*, *interested*, and *relaxing*.

All the interview-based affective responses in Table 5.4 were listed in the right column. By comparing the affective responses from these two sources, it can be concluded that five positive affective responses (*secure*, *novel*, *anticipating*, *fascinated*, and *surprised*) and four negative affective responses (*homesick*, *embarrassed*, *sluggish*, and *nostalgia*) were derived from the focus group interviews, but were incongruent with the tourism literature. The next step was to examine whether they could be perceived as salient affective responses in the context of Chinese outbound tourists to Australia. In terms of the number of participants who mentioned the same affective item, some responses, strictly speaking, should not be conceptualised as affective responses, but rather emotional responses. The salient affective responses refer to those most frequently experienced in a wide range of travel situations in Australia, which could be verified from three factors, i. e. the number of participants who mentioned the specific affective response, the number of mentions of the corresponding emotional response, and the number of tourism elements the corresponding emotional response were associated with.

By comparing overall positive affective responses in Table 5.2 with positive affect (i. e. positive emotional responses) in Table 5.3, four sub-themes (*novel*, *anticipating*, *fascinated*, and *surprised*) were found to be new items. Following the aforementioned criteria, it can be inferred that they were less frequent positive emotional responses. Six participants explicitly reported the emotional response, "*novel*" 13 times, covering only two tourism elements: *catering* and *tour*. They felt curious about the differences in culture and lifestyle between China and Australia. These people indicated in their narratives that something new or unexpected gave rise to unique experiences. A young college student in Group 4 said:

> *I always felt novel travelling in Australia, because it was my first time to go abroad and be in an English-speaking country. I was curious about everything I did not know,*

especially for those Australian indigenous wildlife animals such as koala, kangaroo, echidna, etc. Also, I had the chance to experience Australian Aboriginal culture. (G 4.2, a young college student)

Four participants used *"anticipating"* to describe their emotional responses seven times, covering two tourism elements: *catering* and *tour*. A variety of experiences such as the beach, theme parks, nature-based parks, and wildlife contributed to their anticipation or longing for different travel activities during their 8-day tour. For example, a male in Group 2 indicated, *"Overall, it was a pleasant journey. To my great delight, I authentically experienced the Aussie farm life in Gold Coast. I was quite anticipating on a daily basis"*. Only four participants mentioned the emotional response, *"fascinated"* six times, covering the tourism element of *tour*. The picturesque scenery and the natural environment fascinated them. Only two participants mentioned the emotional response, *"surprised"* three times during their stay in Australia.

With a low occurrence frequency, these four positive emotional responses could not represent the Chinese outbound tourists' salient positive affective responses; therefore they should be excluded from the further quantitative investigation. When Table 5.3 was re-examined, two sub-themes, *"calm* and secure" attracted the research's attention. Although they were identified by participants as two overall affective responses in Table 5.2, it was noted that 16 participants mentioned the emotional response, *"comfortable"* 34 times, covering four tourism elements, i.e. *transportation, tour, shopping,* and *entertainment*, while 8 participants mentioned the emotional response *"calm"* 16 times, covering two tourism elements: *catering* and *tour*. There was a sharp decline between *"comfortable"* and *"calm"* in terms of the number of participants who mentioned them respectively, the number of their respective mentions, as well as the number of tourism elements they were related to. To reduce the bias, these two less prevalent affective responses were removed from the final questionnaire items. As a consequence, seven holistic affective responses were retained for the subsequent quantitative investigation, including *happy, relaxed, interested, excited, impressed, friendly,* and *comfortable*.

Similarly, by comparing overall negative affective responses in Table 5.2 with the negative affects (i.e. negative emotional responses) in Table 5.3, four sub-themes (*lonely, bored, sluggish,* and *nostalgia*) were found to be new items. Following the aforementioned criteria, it can be inferred that they were less frequent negative emotional responses. The plausible explanation is related to their travel mode; they chose the group package tour and most of them travelled with their friends or relatives. Four participants mentioned the emotional response, *"lonely"* 13 times, covering three tourism elements: *lodging, tour,* and *entertainment*. As to the unspoiled wilderness, a female respondent depicted her vivid mental picture of the Australian

landscape: "*Once I saw one or two trees with bare branches on the horizon, I was impressed by the vastness of the land. However, the negative affect 'loneliness' and 'monotony' emerged in my mind at the same time*". It is noteworthy that these four negative affects may not so relevant in group package tours and that future research can lay emphasis on free independent travellers' affective responses to their travel experiences at a destination.

Four respondents mentioned the emotional response, "*bored*" 12 times, covering three tourism elements: *lodging*, *shopping*, and *entertainment*. For instance, "*Life in Australia is not like in our Asian countries. Shops were closed very early and night markets were hardly found. I cannot imagine the life of watching TV at home every night. How boring it is!*". One respondent pointed out they would have felt more satisfied if the hotel and restaurants were located in the city centre because it would have been more convenient for them to participate in recreational activities at night, or just go shopping at the supermarket. Two participants depicted the emotional response, "*sluggish*" six times, covering two tourism elements: *catering* and *tour*. Many participants enjoyed the relaxing life in Australia; however, there were two participants claiming, "*I think life in Nanjing is very dynamic while life in Australia left me an impression of sluggishness and monotony*". They expressed their concern that young people, influenced by this lifestyle, would be likely to give up their ambitions.

Two participants mentioned the emotional response, "*nostalgia*" five times, covering the tourism elements: *lodging* and *tour*. "*Nostalgia*" is used to describe affective reminiscence of a familiar object or environment, representing a psychological phenomenon elicited by both objective and subjective perceptions (Chen, Yeh & Huan 2014). It was thought to be a neutral affect, including both positive and negative connotations. On the one hand, it can be interpreted as a bittersweet longing for things, persons, or situations of the past (Holbrook 1993). On the other hand, it might be interpreted as the condition of being homesick. Weather and lifestyle can be strong triggers of nostalgia. Interestingly, one lady in her sixties in Group 4 said:

> *Witnessing the white clouds in the blue sky made me recall my childhood and I tended to be nostalgic for the good old days. At that time, our sky was as blue as the Australian one with little pollution. However, several big cities in China are suffering from fog and haze due to air pollution. In old times, as many Australian do nowadays, people in China lived in their own houses with courtyards instead of flats or apartments in the skyscrapers. At that time people could enjoy close neighbourhood while we are unlikely to know who our neighbours are in Nanjing. What a pity!* (G 4.8, female)

Being nostalgia reveals the sharp contrast between Australia and China in terms of the living environment. Therefore, it was viewed as a negative emotional response in the present context.

Following the reasoning chain above, participants did not mention these four negative emotional responses as the overall negative affective responses; thereby they should be excluded from the final questionnaire. However, when Table 5.3 was re-examined, it was noted that there was a sharp decline between " *bored* " and " *sluggish* " in terms of the number of participants who mentioned them respectively, the number of their respective mentions, as well as the number of tourism elements they were related to. It would be possible for two emotional responses, " *lonely* " and " *bored* " to become more salient if the sample size was amplified. Extreme caution should be exercised when designing the questionnaire. In order to reduce the potential bias, it was decided that these two items should be kept in the final questionnaire. As a consequence, seven holistic affective responses were adopted in the subsequent quantitative investigation, including *nervous, worried, afraid, homesick, embarrassed, lonely, and bored*.

Based on the empirical evidence from focus group discussions and a comprehensive review of the tourism literature, the final structure of salient affective responses was developed for the further quantitative investigation of the correlations among tourist personality, affective responses, and tourist satisfaction. Figure 5.2 presents 14 positive and negative affective responses adopted in the final questionnaire.

As discussed above, the qualitative exploration has provided meaningful outcomes, including 1) capturing the main attributes of Chinese outbound tourists' affective responses to their travel experiences in Australia; 2) offering an insight into a complicated dynamic process of tourists' affective responses and identifying tourist personality and tourist satisfaction as an antecedent and consequence of tourists' affective responses respectively; and 3) confirming the questionnaire items of affective responses in preparation for the subsequent quantitative investigation.

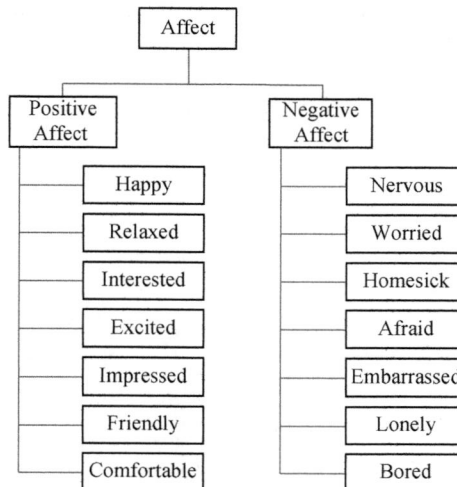

Figure 5.2　A List of Fourteen Affective Responses Adopted in the Final Questionnaire

Chapter Synopsis

Based on the description of the qualitative data collection and analysis procedures, this chapter has reported the qualitative study findings. Four sessions of FGDs involving 32 participants were conducted to collect the qualitative data. By means of the qualitative data analysis software NVivo 10, thematic analysis was then performed to analyse focus group data. The findings were presented with participants' selected quotations referenced in three sections: *affective responses*, *positive affective responses*, and *negative affective responses*. Based on the qualitative findings and results, a discussion was developed with reference to the overarching objective in the qualitative phase of this study, i. e. to identify and document Chinese outbound tourists' salient affective responses characterised as either positive or negative during their trip to Australia. Additionally, according to the information provided by participants about their personality traits and overall satisfaction with Australia as a tourist destination, findings contributed to conceptualising relationships among tourist personality, affective responses, and tourist satisfaction, as illustrated in the research framework (see Chapter 3).

As part of a rigorous research design, the qualitative exploration also refines the measurement items of affective responses, serving as the foundation for the subsequent quantitative investigation. Fourteen affective responses identified in the qualitative phase were incorporated into the survey questionnaire to be completed by Chinese group tourists to Australia in the quantitative research phase. The research construct of affective responses was examined on a large scale not only to generalise the conceptualisations of affective responses in the context of the international tourism, but also to advance the systematic understanding of the correlations among tourist personality, affective responses, and tourist satisfaction.

6

The Impact of Personality and Affect on Satisfaction

The previous chapter reported the findings from the qualitative data generated from focus group interviews. While qualitative research helps explore the behaviour and experiences of mainland Chinese outbound tourists from an interpretative perspective, it is constrained by the capacity to statistically generalise findings across a larger sample (Denzin & Lincoln 2005). Although the Chinese outbound tourists participating in the focus group interviews revealed that their affective responses triggered by their unique experiences during their trip to Australia supported the PANAS conceptualisations underlying the two variables of positive and negative affect in this research, it is not known whether the identified relationships can withstand close examination. To address this, a quantitative study was conducted in the second stage of this research. This was more confirmatory in nature because the phenomenon under study was explored by the qualitative interviews and partly confirmed by the previous studies in the literature.

The overall aim of the quantitative research was to understand the relationships among mainland Chinese outbound tourists' personality traits, affective responses, and overall satisfaction. In order to probe the relationships between these research constructs, data were collected via a questionnaire survey and used to empirically test the proposed model. Thus, the study is empirical in nature. Using the data collected via a questionnaire survey, this quantitative research aimed to achieve the following four objectives, as highlighted in Chapter 1:

2) to identify the underlying structure of Five Factors model (FFM) personality traits as applied to Chinese respondents in the context of outbound travel to Australia;

3) to examine how each dimension of the FFM contributes to the formation of tourists' positive and negative affective responses;

4) to test how positive and negative affective responses associated with specific and holistic experiences of a travel trip influence tourists' overall satisfaction with a destination; and

5) to examine how tourists' personality traits, coupled with positive and negative affective responses, can contribute to the formation of tourist satisfaction with a destination.

Data Preparation

From 10 December 2012 to 28 August 2013, the researcher conducted the questionnaire survey with the support and assistance of local outbound tour operators based in the Yangtze River Delta Region, China. According to the research design, all the questionnaires should be filled in by mainland Chinese tourists to Australia on their return flights to China, because the data collected right after the trip can accurately reveal their overall satisfaction with Australia as a tourist destination. The period from December 2012 to February 2013 (Christmas, the New Year, and the Spring Festival) was identified as the peak season for Chinese outbound tourists to Australia. After that, there was a sharp drop in the number of Chinese travel groups to Australia. Eventually, the data collection was finalised during the period of July and August, another peak season for Chinese parents to take school students on holidays to Australia. Altogether, 600 questionnaires were distributed and 563 returned. Nevertheless, some questionnaires were invalid because the respondents ticked all the boxes on the far left or right of the scale without carefully reading and understanding the questions. In addition, a few cases were deleted on account of an unacceptable percentage of missing information (more than 20%). Consequently, 493 cases were available for data analysis. The valid response rate of 82.2% was attributed to the researcher's efforts to supervise and motivate tour operators to focus on data collection. Without the support of local travel agencies and experienced escort guides, the researcher could not get access to the respondents.

The survey data were entered into the software SPSS 20 by the researcher. A case number was designated to each questionnaire to keep track of the original data. In Part A (measuring personality traits, see Appendix 3), 16 items of 44-item BFI were reverse-scored in the process of data entry. Scores for items in Part B (measuring affective responses, see Appendix 3) and Part C (measuring overall tourist satisfaction, see Appendix 3) were directly entered into the program. Answers to the demographic questions were re-coded and then entered into the system. After loading each case, the scores and codes of each item in SPSS were re-inspected against the original questionnaire. Data screening and corrections were performed carefully in this process to guarantee the dataset was appropriate for data analysis.

Profile of Survey Respondents

Respondents' demographic data were analysed by descriptive statistics using SPSS. Table 6.1 shows the demographic profile of the survey respondents. Female respondents (50.5%) slightly outnumbered their male counterparts (49.5%). The majority of participants (68.8%)

were between 30 and 49 years old and the married accounted for 79.9% of the sample. Clerks/ White-collar workers comprised 31.2% of the sample. The second-largest occupation category was businessperson, accounting for 14.6% of the sample. Nearly half of the respondents (46. 2%) had a university education; another 24.7% had three years of college education; another 12.8% had a postgraduate education. In total, 83.7% of the respondents were educated at the college level or above. With regard to their personal monthly income, nearly half (48.1%) of the respondents earned a monthly income between 6,000 and 9,999 *yuan* (approximately US $ 923 – US $1,538); another 16.6% earned a monthly income of over 10,000 *yuan* (over US $1,538). The average per capita monthly income of Chinese urban residents in 2011 was RMB 1,998 (approximately US $307) (National Bureau of Statistics of China 2012). In addition to demographic information, respondents were also asked with whom they had travelled to Australia. Of the respondents, 76.5% had travelled with their families or relatives.

As shown in Table 6.1, the demographic profile of respondents indicated that survey participants were relatively young, married, well-educated, and moderately well paid in white-collar jobs. There was a balanced gender distribution between male and female respondents among first-time visitors to Australia. The demographic profile of respondents showed a high degree of consistency with general visitor characteristics of the mainland Chinese outbound market (TRA 2013), as recorded by the Australian official statistics. In terms of demographic characteristics such as gender, the demographic profile of respondents in this study indicated that the first-time Jiangsu visitors to Australia did not appear to deviate much from the overall population of mainland Chinese outbound tourists to Australia in 2013. Thus, the composition of the sample was consistent with previous Chinese outbound tour groups in general and those visiting Australia in particular (TRA 2013).

Table 6.1   Profiles of the Survey Respondents

		Valid *N*	Percentage/%
Gender	Male	244	49.5
	Female	249	50.5
Age	18 – 29	91	18.5
	30 – 39	206	41.8
	40 – 49	133	27.0
	50 – 59	44	8.9
	60 or older	19	3.9
Marital status	Single	96	19.5
	Married	394	79.9
	Others	3	0.6

		Valid N	Percentage/%
Occupation	Student	45	9.1
	Teacher	65	13.2
	Civil Servant	56	11.4
	Businessperson	72	14.6
	Clerk/White-collar worker	154	31.2
	Blue-collar worker	23	4.7
	Retired	41	8.3
	Housewife	29	5.9
	Others	8	1.6
Education	Junior middle school	17	3.4
	Senior middle/vocational school	63	12.8
	3-year college diploma	122	24.7
	4-year university degree	228	46.2
	Postgraduate or above	63	12.8
Personal monthly income	No income	64	13
	Less than ¥2,000	3	0.6
	¥2,000−3,999	29	5.9
	¥4,000−5,999	53	10.8
	¥6,000−7,999	108	21.9
	¥8,000−9,999	129	26.2
	¥10,000−14,999	44	8.9
	Over ¥15,000	38	7.7
	Prefer not to answer	25	5.1
Household size	1 person	12	2.2
	2 persons	34	6.9
	3 persons	288	58.4
	4 persons	61	12.4
	5 persons	78	15.8
	6 persons or more	11	2.2
	Prefer not to answer	11	2.2

Data Normality

SPSS descriptive statistics analysis was conducted to examine the univariate normality by reviewing the skewness and kurtosis values of each variable in the output. According to Kline (2005), data sets with absolute values for the univariate skewness index greater than 3.0 could be described as "extremely" skewed by some researchers, while absolute values of the univariate kurtosis index from 8.0 to over 20.0 have been described as indicating "extreme" kurtosis. As shown in Table 6.2, the univariate normality assumption has been met, for the skewness (SK) and kurtosis (KU) values of almost all scaled variables ranged between −1 and +1. However, from a multivariate perspective, the data normality assumption is violated. In this study, assessment of multivariate normality was based on the "Mardia Coefficient of Multivariate Kurtosis" (Mardia 1970, 1974) in the AMOS output. A Mardia coefficient greater than 3 suggests that the data might be multivariate non-normal. If the Mardia coefficient is greater than 10, this suggests multivariate non-normality is present in the data (Cunningham 2007). Kline (2005) argued that slight departures from normality could be statistically significant in a large sample. If the data violates the multivariate normality to an "extreme" extent, one can choose to transform the non-normal data into normal data by several mathematical operations.

When using Maximum Likelihood (ML) estimation, a main assumption is that the data are multivariate normal. Any violations of multivariate normality may cause the ML estimation results to be inaccurate (Kline 2005). Although the data exhibits slight deviations from normal distribution, it is appropriate for ML estimation to be applied because all the absolute values are less than 3.0 for skewness and 10.0 for Kurtosis (Kline 2005). One way of dealing with multivariate non-normality is to remove any outliers from the data and then re-run the analysis without the excluded cases. An outlier is a case with scores that are very different from the rest of the cases (Kline 2005). Examination of the Mahalanobis distance statistic (Mahalanobis d-squared) generated in the AMOS output helps to identify any cases in the dataset that may be outliers. Another method of dealing with a multivariate non-normal sample is to use bootstrapping. This includes using bootstrapped parameter estimates and using the Bollen-Stine p (Bollen & Stine 1992) instead of the conventional Chi-square statistic. Bootstrapping is described as a "statistical re-sampling method" (Kline 2005) in which the original sample is considered as the best representation of the target population. The main advantage of using the bootstrapping method is that "it allows researchers to assess the stability of parameter estimates and thereby report their values with greater degree of accuracy" (Byrne 2009, p. 270). "Bootstrap estimates for a measurement model were generally less biased compared with those from standard ML estimation under conditions of non-normality and for sample size of $N \geqslant 200$" (Nevitt & Hancock 2001). When data are non-normal, bootstrap-obtained parameter estimates are superior to ordinary ML-based estimates (Bollen & Stine 1990; Byrne 2009). Considering that the univariate normality had been met with a slight deviation from the normal multivariate distribution, and that the sample size ($n = 493$) was large enough, it was decided to use both ML and bootstrapping in the subsequent CFA and SEM analysis in order to secure a more accurate data analysis result.

Table 6.2 Univariate and Multivariate Normality Test Results (63 items; $n = 493$)

Item	Description	Skewness	c. r.	Kurtosis	c. r.
Extraversion					
EXT1	is talkative	−.319	−2.891	−.564	−2.555
EXT2	is reserved (R)	.361	3.272	−.726	−3.290
EXT3	is full of energy	−.409	−3.710	−.201	−.913
EXT4	generates a lot of enthusiasm	.138	1.252	−1.096	−4.967
EXT5	tends to be quiet (R)	−.563	−5.100	−.058	−.265
EXT6	has an assertive personality	−.182	−1.651	−.578	−2.622
EXT7	is sometimes shy, inhibited (R)	.557	5.047	−.141	−.637
EXT8	is outgoing, sociable	−.253	−2.291	−.402	−1.820
Agreeableness					
AGR1	tends to find fault with others (R)	−.053	−.483	−.919	−4.167
AGR2	is helpful and unselfish with others	−.284	−2.577	.070	.315
AGR3	starts quarrels with others (R)	−1.019	−9.239	.278	1.259
AGR4	has a forgiving nature	−.417	−3.778	.258	1.171
AGR5	is generally trusting	−.317	−2.871	.668	3.026
AGR6	can be cold and aloof (R)	−.634	−5.743	−.524	−2.374
AGR7	is considerate and kind to almost everyone	−.175	−1.583	−.028	−.126
AGR8	is sometimes rude to others (R)	−.565	−5.126	−.514	−2.330
AGR9	likes to cooperate with others	−.511	−4.632	−.065	−.297
Conscientiousness					
CON1	does a thorough job	−.392	−3.551	−.227	−1.029
CON2	can be somewhat careless (R)	.059	.532	−.830	−3.762
CON3	is a reliable worker	−.264	−2.392	−.341	−1.545
CON4	tends to be disorganised (R)	−.323	−2.930	−.599	−2.715
CON5	tends to be lazy (R)	−.509	−4.613	−.675	−3.061
CON6	perseveres until the task is finished	−.315	−2.859	−.365	−1.655
CON7	does things efficiently	−.109	−.989	−.298	−1.353
CON8	makes plans and follows through with them	.056	.508	−.259	−1.173
CON9	is easily distracted (R)	−.239	−2.165	−.944	−4.278

Continued

Item	Description	Skewness	c. r.	Kurtosis	c. r.
Neuroticism					
NEU1	is depressed, blue	.711	6.449	− .322	− 1.458
NEU2	is relaxed, handles stress well (R)	.558	5.059	− .004	− .019
NEU3	can be tense	− .213	− 1.929	− .199	− .904
NEU4	worries a lot	.185	1.676	− 1.032	− 4.677
NEU5	is emotionally stable, not easily upset (R)	.477	4.323	− .364	− 1.649
NEU6	can be moody	.481	4.360	− 1.019	− 4.618
NEU7	remains calm in tense situations (R)	.315	2.854	− .262	− 1.187
NEU8	gets nervous easily	.008	.076	− .039	− .178
Openness					
OPE1	is original, comes up with new ideas	− .277	− 2.508	.252	1.143
OPE2	is curious about many different things	− .178	− 1.612	− .322	− 1.460
OPE3	is ingenious, a deep thinker	− .012	− .109	− .403	− 1.828
OPE4	has an active imagination	.043	.388	− .091	− .414
OPE5	is inventive	− .136	− 1.234	.460	2.086
OPE6	values artistic, aesthetic experiences	− .419	− 3.798	− .484	− 2.193
OPE7	prefers work that is routine (R)	.432	3.920	− .919	− 4.164
OPE8	likes to reflect, play with ideas	− .172	− 1.555	− .310	− 1.407
OPE9	has few artistic interests (R)	− .244	− 2.214	− .898	− 4.071
OPE10	is sophisticated in art, music, or literature	− .245	− 2.219	− .685	− 3.103
Positive Affect					
PA1	relaxed	− .371	− 3.366	− .287	− 1.302
PA2	happy	− .242	− 2.193	.054	.243
PA3	excited	.127	1.148	− .582	− 2.638
PA4	interested	− .051	− .458	− .241	− 1.092
PA5	impressed	− .043	− .389	− .357	− 1.617
PA6	a sense of friendliness	− .674	− 6.112	.821	3.723
PA7	comfortable	− .158	− 1.430	− .182	− .825
Negative Affect					
NA1	nervous	.325	2.948	− .889	− 4.028
NA2	afraid	.790	7.162	.039	.175
NA3	worried	.093	.843	− 1.033	− 4.682
NA4	lonely	.891	8.075	.060	.270
NA5	bored	.075	.679	− .691	− 3.132
NA6	embarrassed	− .055	− .502	− .970	− 4.396
NA7	homesick	− .036	− .324	− .659	− 2.986

Continued

Item	Description	Skewness	c. r.	Kurtosis	c. r.
Satisfaction					
SAT1	I have really enjoyed the trip in Australia	$-.001$	$-.007$	$-.427$	-1.933
SAT2	My choice to visit Australia was a wise one	$-.231$	-2.093	$-.362$	-1.639
SAT3	The travel experience in Australia was exactly what I needed	$-.209$	-1.897	$-.533$	-2.414
SAT4	I am satisfied with my trip in Australia	$-.082$	$-.741$	$-.251$	-1.138
Multivariate (Personality)				298.957	52.165
Multivariate (Affect)				37.400	18.386
Multivariate (Satisfaction)				10.129	16.230
(R) indicates using the reverse-scored item. c. r. = critical ratio.					

Scale Reliability

After the screening procedures for the normality of data, the next step was to check for scale reliability. The reliability analysis was conducted to test the level of internal consistency for the measurements of eight constructs: extraversion, agreeableness, conscientiousness, neuroticism, openness, positive affect, negative affect, and satisfaction. The results of reliability analysis are summarized in Table 6.3.

Cronbach's alpha coefficient was used to evaluate the internal consistency of each measurement. The closer the coefficient is to 1, the better the internal consistency of the measure. Hair et al. (2010) provided a good guideline for assessing the internal consistency, suggesting that a Cronbach's alpha (reliability coefficient) value of 0.70 or higher has generally been accepted by academics as indicating a reliable measurement. If a measurement has a Cronbach's alpha below 0.70, individual items may be deleted in an effort to obtain a higher reliability level. As shown in Table 6.3, the individual Cronbach's alpha (reliability coefficient) value of the research constructs was 0.76 for extraversion, 0.72 for agreeableness, 0.78 for conscientiousness, 0.75 for neuroticism, 0.78 for openness, 0.83 for positive affect, 0.79 for negative affect, and 0.94 for satisfaction. All measurements for the eight constructs showed a reliability coefficient above 0.70, indicating that the internal consistency of all the measurements was acceptable. A close examination of the column "Item-Total Correlation" showed that the item-total correlation of four items (i.e. 0.186 for EXT6, 0.276 for AGR6, 0.199 for CON3, and 0.248 for OPEN7) was below the threshold value of 0.30 (Hair et al. 2010). It means that they could be deleted for their low correlations with the total. A further scrutiny of the column "Alpha if Item Deleted" revealed that CON3 in the conscientiousness scale and the majority of the reverse-worded items (e. g. EXT2, EXT7, AGR1, AGR6, CON2, NEU7, and OPE7) could be removed to improve the measurement reliability. The reverse-worded items appeared to have poor correlations with normally worded items. Using reversed wording items with disturbed respondents can cause confusion that reduces reliability (Conrad et al. 2004). Using reverse-worded items in the questionnaire has been controversial for several decades (Barnette 2000). Many researchers found that reverse wordings raise ambiguities, make surveys more complex and difficult for respondents, thereby leading to more unexpected measurement errors (e. g. Schriesheim & Hill 1981; Schriesheim, Eisenbach & Hill 1991; Wong, Rindfleisch & Burroughs 2003; Conrad et al. 2004). Based on the reliability analysis, it was suggested that reverse wording effects be taken into account with caution during the subsequent measurement model testing.

It should be pointed out that the Cronbach's alpha coefficient of the personality scale is noticeably lower than the 0. 83 reported in the BFI manual (John & Srivastava 1999). It may be explained in at least three regards. First, the Big-Five inventory was used to assess the personality of Chinese outbound tourists in the context of travelling in Australia. The fatigue after such a long-haul journey may possibly have led to carelessness in answering the questionnaire on their return flights. Second, some personality traits might be defined differently in Chinese cultures than they are in Western cultures. Even for the self-administered questionnaires, Chinese respondents may have modesty bias in response to some items for self-evaluation (Wu 2008). The third possible reason for some of these differences may be the tendency to be more willing to respond with a " strongly agree" response compared with a "strongly disagree" response. It seemed that the reverse wording items may have confused the respondents to some extent. However, given the heterogeneity of the items in the scale, the alpha coefficient was considered sufficient for allowing the rest of the statistical analyses to be conducted.

In summary, all of the eight constructs generally exhibit acceptable measurement reliability. However, special concern should be given to those items which can be removed from the scale to improve the reliability of the measurement, because all the modification procedures should be followed with due consideration of both statistical evidence and theoretical justification. Considering that FFM personality traits were theorised as the multi-factor construct, and that all the affective responses were based on the literature review and the findings of the preceding qualitative research (focus group interviews), all the measurement items were retained for the next stage of analysis; eventually the researcher would determine whether or not to remove those items with low values.

Table 6.3　Measurement Reliability of the Major Constructs（n = 493）

Item	Description	Item-Total Correlation	Alpha if Item Deleted	Reliability Coefficient
Extraversion				.76
EXT1	is talkative	.604	.701	
EXT2	is reserved（R）	.451	.732	
EXT3	is full of energy	.371	.745	
EXT4	generates a lot of enthusiasm	.566	.708	
EXT5	tends to be quiet（R）	.421	.737	
EXT6	has an assertive personality	.186	.777	
EXT7	is sometimes shy, inhibited（R）	.366	.747	
EXT8	is outgoing, sociable	.694	.685	
Agreeableness				.72
AGR1	tends to find fault with others（R）	.356	.705	
AGR2	is helpful and unselfish with others	.462	.688	
AGR3	starts quarrels with others（R）	.498	.674	
AGR4	has a forgiving nature	.495	.684	
AGR5	is generally trusting	.307	.710	
AGR6	can be cold and aloof（R）	.276	.725	
AGR7	is considerate and kind to almost everyone	.451	.688	
AGR8	is sometimes rude to others（R）	.448	.685	
AGR9	likes to cooperate with others	.402	.694	
Conscientiousness				.78
CON1	does a thorough job	.534	.754	
CON2	can be somewhat careless（R）	.322	.787	
CON3	is a reliable worker	.199	.790	
CON4	tends to be disorganised（R）	.555	.749	
CON5	tends to be lazy（R）	.575	.746	
CON6	perseveres until the task is finished	.600	.746	
CON7	does things efficiently	.499	.761	
CON8	makes plans and follows through with them	.456	.765	
CON9	is easily distracted（R）	.519	.755	

Continued

Item	Description	Item-Total Correlation	Alpha if Item Deleted	Reliability Coefficient
Neuroticism				**.75**
NEU1	is depressed, blue	.475	.723	
NEU2	is relaxed, handles stress well (R)	.405	.736	
NEU3	can be tense	.422	.733	
NEU4	worries a lot	.542	.709	
NEU5	is emotionally stable, not easily upset (R)	.416	.734	
NEU6	can be moody	.482	.724	
NEU7	remains calm in tense situations (R)	.340	.746	
NEU8	gets nervous easily	.545	.714	
Openness				**.78**
OPE1	is original, comes up with new ideas	.513	.755	
OPE2	is curious about many different things	.315	.776	
OPE3	is ingenious, a deep thinker	.550	.754	
OPE4	has an active imagination	.391	.768	
OPE5	is inventive	.506	.757	
OPE6	values artistic, aesthetic experiences	.596	.740	
OPE7	prefers work that is routine (R)	.248	.796	
OPE8	likes to reflect, play with ideas	.389	.769	
OPE9	has few artistic interests (R)	.542	.749	
OPE10	is sophisticated in art, music, or literature	.554	.747	
Positive Affect				**.83**
PA1	relaxed	.460	.821	
PA2	happy	.680	.789	
PA3	excited	.577	.805	
PA4	interested	.612	.797	
PA5	impressed	.634	.794	
PA6	a sense of friendliness	.423	.826	
PA7	comfortable	.653	.792	

Continued

Item	Description	Item-Total Correlation	Alpha if Item Deleted	Reliability Coefficient
Negative Affect				.79
NA1	nervous	.675	.727	
NA2	afraid	.543	.757	
NA3	worried	.667	.728	
NA4	lonely	.494	.763	
NA5	bored	.397	.780	
NA6	embarrassed	.412	.780	
NA7	homesick	.435	.776	
Satisfaction				.94
SAT1	I have really enjoyed the trip in Australia	.868	.917	
SAT2	My choice to visit Australia was a wise one	.871	.911	
SAT3	The travel experience in Australia was exactly what I needed	.843	.929	
SAT4	I am satisfied with my trip in Australia	.869	.915	

Estimation Method

The method adopted to perform the CFA analysis in AMOS was Maximum Likelihood estimation (ML). As a predominant method of estimation, ML is the default method in most SEM computer tools and the most widely used method for analyses in structural equation models (Anderson & Gerbing 1988; Kline 2005). Notably, the adoption of an estimation method instead of ML should be well justified (Hoyle 2000). ML "describes the statistical principle that underlies the deviation of parameter estimates; the estimates are the ones that maximise the likelihood (the continuous generalization) that the data (the observed covariance) were drawn from this population" (Kline 2005, p. 112).

Although there are a number of parameter estimation methods proposed and utilised in the literature of structural equation models (e.g. generalised least squares and weighted least squares), the vast majority of the published CFA studies in social science employ ML and research suggests that it produces accurate results in most situations (e.g. Fan, Thompson & Wang 1999; Levine 2005). The ML estimation method is reasonably robust to modest violations for the assumption associated with data normality.

Two primary assumptions should be met for the use of ML in the data analysis. The first assumption is that the data should be of a continuous scale. The second assumption is that the distribution of the data cannot experience severely non-normal issues (Byrne 2009). The measurement models in this study were all measured through a 7-point Likert scale ranging from 1 to 7 with 1 being "strongly disagree" and 7 being "strongly agree". Likert scales, common in survey-based research, are always ordinal and technically ordered categorically (Schreiber 2008). Previous research has generally agreed that the original Likert scales with at least 5 categories (7 is better) assume properties that resemble interval scales whose scores at different levels of a variable have meanings and are equally distant from each other (Norman 2010). In such a case, ordinal variables can be treated as continuous to meet the first assumption for using ML (Rhemtulla, Brosseau-Liard & Savalei 2012). The second assumption regarding the multivariate normal distribution of the data has been addressed in the section on data normality.

Criteria for Goodness-of-Fit Indices

Fassinger (1987) argued that the goodness-of-fit measures for a model "are obtained by comparison between the estimated population covariance matrix (based on the model as specified by the research) and the sample covariance matrix computed from the input sample data" (p. 428). Because different measures of fit only capture different elements of the model, "evaluation of model fit should derive from a variety of sources and be based on several criteria that can assess model fit from a diversity of perspectives" (Byrne 1998, p. 119). Therefore, it is essential for researchers to clearly specify the cut-off thresholds of fit indices adopted in their studies.

The Chi-square (x^2) statistic is the fundamental measure of assessing the discrepancy between the observed covariance matrix and the model covariance matrix (Kline 2005). The data can be assumed to fit the model well when the p-value of x^2 is non-significant at the 95% confidence interval ($p > 0.05$) (Bagozzi & Foxall 1996), while a significant p-value of x^2 ($p < 0.05$) indicates a poor fit. However, using the Chi-square as the only indicator of model fit has been criticised in recent years for its extreme sensitivity to sample size (Hu & Bentler 1999; Byrne 2005). In large samples, a model may still be deemed acceptable even if the p-value is significant. Relatively less sensitive to sample size, the normed Chi-square is calculated by the Chi-square index divided by the degrees of freedom. Even though there is no clear-cut guideline, the commonly accepted value for the normed ratio of Chi-square over its degree of freedom is set at 3 : 1 (Jöreskog & Sörbom 1989). However, the normed Chi-square value is not completely exempt from the influence of sample size (Kline 2005). As a result, other more sophisticated fit indices which are less affected by sample size are recommended.

Based on the review of guidelines for determining model fit, in this study it is sensible to include the following fit indices as multiple model fit criteria: Goodness of Fit Index (GFI), Comparative Fit Index (CFI), Tucker-Lewis Index (TLI), Root Mean Square Error of

Approximation (RMSEA), and Standardised Root Mean Residual (SRMR). These indices have been chosen over other indices as they have been found to be the most insensitive to sample size, model misspecification, and parameter estimates (Byrne 2009). GFI basically compares the hypothesised model with no model at all. It ranges from 0 to 1.00, with values close to 1.00 indicating a good fit. It is generally accepted that a GFI value over 0.90 would be considered a satisfactory fit (Bollen 1989; Byrne 1998). CFI and TLI belong to comparative fit indices while SRMR and RMSEA are absolute fit indices. CFI is known as an incremental index which assesses the improvement in fit of the proposed model with a baseline model (Byrne 2005). TLI is regarded as a non-normed fit index and relatively independent of sample size (Marsh, Balla & McDonald 1988). As suggested by Byrne (1998), a value over 0.90 for these two indices indicates a good fit. RMSEA takes the error of approximation in the population into account and measures the discrepancy between the model fitted covariance matrix and the population covariance matrix. Kline (2005) recommended that RMSEA values of less than 0.05 be considered as close approximate fit, and between 0.05 and 0.08 as reasonable fit. SRMR, as a popular absolute fit indicator, represents a summary measure of the fitted residuals divided by their estimated standard errors (Byrne 2005). Values for the SRMR range from 0 to 1.0 with well-fitting models obtaining values less than 0.05 (Byrne 1998; Diamantopoulos, Siguaw & Siguaw 2000); however values as high as 0.08 are deemed acceptable (Hu & Bentler 1999).

In summary, no one index can act as a manifest criterion for testing a hypothesised model, because there are so many fit indices and different fit indices assess the model fit in different aspects. Researchers are advised to depend on multiple criteria when judging the overall fit of a model. As demonstrated by MacCallum, Browne and Sugawara (1996), even under favourable conditions, models arising from specification searches must be viewed with caution.

Individual Measurement Model Testing

Before testing the overall measurement model, measurement unidimensionality of each construct can be assessed individually (e.g. Anderson & Gerbing 1988; Gursoy, Boylu & Avci 2011). Consequently, the fit and validity of individual measurement models for the constructs of *personality*, *affect*, and *satisfaction* were examined first to ensure that each of them achieves fit indices' values, thus subsequently making the overall hypothesised model fit the collected data. FFM personality traits were combined together as an individual measurement model for the personality construct; the constructs of positive affect, negative affect, and satisfaction were integrated into another individual measurement model. The observed variables were tested using the CFA procedures to confirm the factor structure and generate acceptable measurement models for the research constructs of personality, affect, and satisfaction. Afterwards, these individual measurement models were integrated into the overall measurement model for testing.

One of the purposes of performing CFA is to evaluate whether the observed variables can reflect the latent variables in a reliable and valid manner (Anderson & Gerbing 1991). Thus, there were three underlying rationales for the CFA selected in this study to identify a measurement model with a good fit for later use: 1) CFA is a theory-driven technique to validate the underlying structure, as conceptualised in Chapter 2; 2) CFA generally follows on from the exploratory research, as supported by the findings of focus group interviews in Chapter 4; 3) CFA is employed when measurement scales are mostly borrowed or adapted from pre-existing well-established scales, as detailed in Chapter 3.

During the process of CFA, standardised regression weights (factor loadings), squared multiple correlations (SMC), and composite reliability were checked for item and construct reliabilities. SMC in CFA represents the proportion of variance in an indicator variable that can be accounted for by its underlying latent variable; therefore, the higher the squared multiple correlation, the higher the reliability for the associated indicator variable (Raykov & Marcoulides 2006). The composite reliability, also known as construct reliability, refers to the ratio of explained variance to explained variance plus unexplained variance, which can be manually calculated by the following formula using standardised factor loadings and error variances (Fornell & Larcker 1981):

$$\rho_n = \Sigma \lambda_{yi}^2 / [\Sigma \lambda_{yi}^2 + \Sigma var(\varepsilon_i)]$$

Where ρ_n = composite reliability; λ = standardised regression weights; $var(\varepsilon)$ = error variance. Besides, the construct validity was examined to assess how well the items measure the corresponding construct. Convergent validity refers to the degree to which the measure is related to other measures designed to assess the same construct, while discriminant validity focuses on the degree to which the construct is distinct from other unrelated constructs. One method of evaluating discriminant validity is to use the following formula to manually calculate average variance extracted (AVE), namely, the average ratio of variance explained by construct versus variance explained by construct plus error (Fornell & Larcker 1981):

$$\rho_{ve} = \Sigma \lambda_{yi}^2 / [\Sigma \lambda_{yi}^2 + \Sigma var(\varepsilon_i)]$$

Where ρ_{ve} = discriminant validity; λ = standardised regression weights; $var(\varepsilon)$ = error variance. Discriminant validity is regarded to be obtained if the average variances extracted (AVE) by the correlated latent variables is greater than the square of the correlation between the latent variables. The minimum value of AVE should exceed 0.50 (Fornell & Larcker 1981).

As a rule of thumb, model misspecification is evaluated in terms of the standardised residuals and the modification indices (MI) (Byrne 2009). A standardised residual covariance score higher than 0.258 is considered large; accordingly the deletion of the item can be justified. Special attention should be given to the MI of above 9.0, because large MIs suggest the presence of factor cross-loadings and can thus result in the model misfit (Byrne 2009).

According to Hair et al. (2010), the standardised regression weights (factor loadings) of 0.50 between the observed indicators and latent construct in the CFA is regarded as the minimum acceptable level. Considering that correlations among the items could influence the estimates for the factor loadings between the items and the latent variable, items were removed individually in succession. After each item was deleted, a CFA was re-run with the remaining items to re-evaluate the model fit indices. The rule was followed until the measurement model achieved a satisfactory fit or no more items could be removed. However, since CFA is a theory-oriented approach, any alterations to the model should be made in combination with the theoretical justification and not merely based on the statistical evidence (Anderson & Gerbing 1988; Kline 2005). Hence, bearing all these principles in mind, CFA using a sample of Chinese package tourists to Australia was performed directly to validate the measurement models for personality and affect as well as the psychometric properties of satisfaction.

Measurement Model for Personality Traits

The well-established Big Five Inventory has been extensively used to measure personality traits in Western literature (Gosling, Rentfrow & Swann 2003; Denissen et al. 2008). Consequently, based on the underlying structure of the priori Big Five theory among the 44-item BFI, CFA was employed to assess whether the Five-Factor model could provide a good fit to the sample data in the context of Chinese group package tours to Australia. In the conceptual framework of this study, each dimension of the personality structure was regarded as the individual research construct or latent variable. Each latent variable was measured through a number of observed variables. These observed variables were the responses to the items measured on a 7-point Likert scale (1 = strongly disagree to 7 = strongly agree).

Before performing CFA to test the measurement model for personality traits, descriptive statistics were conducted to calculate the mean values and the standard deviations of all 44 items (Table 6.4). For the dimension of extraversion, both EXT3 ("*is full of energy*") and EXT4 ("*generates a lot of enthusiasm*") had a mean value as high as 5.47 and 5.14 respectively, with the smallest standard deviations among eight extraversion items. Special attention should be paid to EXT 6 ("*has an assertive personality*") and three reverse-worded items (i.e. EXT2 "*is reserved*", EXT5 "*tends to be quiet*", and EXT7 "*is sometimes shy, inhibited*"), whose mean values were relatively lower than the other four items. Nevertheless, it is worth noting that the means of three reverse-worded items after reversion were higher than the midpoint 4.0, which indicated that the scores on the items of being reserved, quiet or shy contradicted the attributes of extraversion. Therefore, these findings suggested that EXT2, EXT5, and EXT 7 could be removed from the measurement model for extraversion in the CFA analysis.

Table 6.4　Means and Standard Deviations of Personality Traits Items ($n = 493$)

Item	Description	Mean	SD
Extraversion			
EXT1	is talkative	4.92	1.34
EXT2	is reserved (R)	4.56	1.40
EXT3	is full of energy	5.47	0.99
EXT4	generates a lot of enthusiasm	5.14	1.07
EXT5	tends to be quiet (R)	4.26	1.52
EXT6	has an assertive personality	4.39	1.28
EXT7	is sometimes shy, inhibited (R)	4.30	1.29
EXT8	is outgoing, sociable	4.81	1.27
Agreeableness			
AGR1	tends to find fault with others (R)	3.34	1.38
AGR2	is helpful and unselfish with others	5.38	0.87
AGR3	starts quarrels with others (R)	2.23	1.28
AGR4	has a forgiving nature	5.47	0.84
AGR5	is generally trusting	5.31	0.76
AGR6	can be cold and aloof (R)	2.73	1.44
AGR7	is considerate and kind to almost everyone	5.18	0.91
AGR8	is sometimes rude to others (R)	2.80	1.43
AGR9	likes to cooperate with others	5.05	1.05
Conscientiousness			
CON1	does a thorough job	5.12	1.08
CON2	can be somewhat careless (R)	4.21	1.39
CON3	is a reliable worker	5.83	0.78
CON4	tends to be disorganised (R)	3.21	1.37
CON5	tends to be lazy (R)	2.97	1.49
CON6	perseveres until the task is finished	5.39	1.06
CON7	does things efficiently	5.18	0.91
CON8	makes plans and follows through with them	4.80	0.99
CON9	is easily distracted (R)	3.57	1.39

Continued

Item	Description	Mean	SD
Neuroticism			
NEU1	is depressed, blue	2.56	1.45
NEU2	is relaxed, handles stress well (R)	5.11	1.08
NEU3	can be tense	4.70	1.14
NEU4	worries a lot	3.44	1.59
NEU5	is emotionally stable, not easily upset (R)	4.80	1.33
NEU6	can be moody	2.88	1.66
NEU7	remains calm in tense situations (R)	4.74	1.16
NEU8	gets nervous easily	3.95	1.14
Openness			
OPE1	is original, comes up with new ideas	4.82	1.00
OPE2	is curious about many different things	5.22	0.97
OPE3	is ingenious, a deep thinker	4.81	0.88
OPE4	has an active imagination	4.85	0.97
OPE5	is inventive	4.48	0.95
OPE6	values artistic, aesthetic experiences	4.17	1.46
OPE7	prefers work that is routine (R)	4.58	1.50
OPE8	likes to reflect, play with ideas	5.03	0.94
OPE9	has few artistic interests (R)	3.70	1.46
OPE10	is sophisticated in art, music, or literature	3.61	1.33

Scale: 1 = strongly disagree, 7 = strongly agree; the mean values of items with (R) were calculated before reversion.

For the dimension of agreeableness, four items (i.e. AGR2 "*is helpful and unselfish with others*", AGR4 "*has a forgiving nature*", AGR5 "*is generally trusting*", and AGR7 "*is considerate and kind to almost everyone*") had mean values of over 5.10 and standard deviations of below 1.0. Once again, the reverse-coded items (i.e. AGR1 "*tends to find fault with others*", AGR3 "*starts quarrels with others*", AGR6 "*can be cold and aloof*", and AGR8 "*is sometimes rude to others*") had low ratings after reversion. These findings were reasonable, indicating that many respondents were prone to behave themselves in a helpful, cooperative, and reconcilable manner.

For the dimension of conscientiousness, four items (i.e. CON1 "*does a thorough job*", CON3 "*is a reliable worker*", CON6 "*perseveres until the task is finished*", and CON7 "*does things efficiently*") exhibited a high mean value of over 5.10, indicating that these items appeared to be more influential as the indicator variables associated with the latent construct.

One of four reverse-worded items, CON2 "*can be somewhat careless*", was given a rating of 4. 21 after reversion, higher than the midpoint 4. 0. It contradicts the attribute of conscientiousness, being careful. This finding suggested that CON2 could be eliminated from the measurement model for conscientiousness in the CFA analysis.

For the dimension of neuroticism, all the reverse-coded items (i. e. NEU2 "*is relaxed, handles stress well*", NEU5 "*is emotionally stable, not easily upset*", and NEU7 "*remains calm in tense situations*") seemed to be the top three in mean values (above 4. 7) after reversion, which contradicted the attributes of neuroticism. Therefore, NEU2, NEU5, and NEU7 could be removed from the measurement model for neuroticism in the CFA analysis. More notably, other items except NEU3 "*can be tense*" were below the mid-point 4. 0. These findings suggested that respondents were less inclined to feel nervous and insecure. In addition, the standard deviations of all the observed variables were relatively large, indicating that respondents' opinions on these items were more diverse.

For the dimension of openness, the standard deviations of four items (i. e. OPE6 "*values artistic, aesthetic experiences*", OPE7 "*prefers work that is routine*", OPE9 "*has few artistic interests*", and OPE10 "*is sophisticated in art, music, or literature*") were relatively larger, indicating that respondents' opinions on these items were more diverse. As a reverse-worded item, the high mean value of OPE7 (4. 58) after reversion suggested that the score on the item of preferring routine work contradicted the attribute of openness. Thus, OPE7 could be removed from the measurement model for openness in the CFA analysis.

Based on the analysis of descriptive statistics, it can be summarised that the data generally represented the nature of the sample in the research context, and that all the reverse-scored items should be examined with extreme caution in the subsequent measurement model testing, which is particularly important to reaffirm at this point.

CFA using ML estimation was conducted to assess the full 44-item personality traits model (Figure 6. 1). As shown in Table 6. 5, the 44-item Five Factor model resulted in 990 sample moments, with 98 distinct parameters to be estimated and 892 (990 − 98) degrees of freedom. The Chi-square statistic was 4 009.491, $p = 0.000$; the model fit indicators GFI $= 0.645$, CFI $= 0.580$ were both far less than the recommended cut-off scores of 0. 90; RMSEA $= 0.084$, SRMR $= 0.119$ were both greater than 0. 08. These results indicated a poor model fit, which was consistent with those obtained in the previous study among Chinese adults with a smoking habit (Leung et al. 2013). The results of CFA on smokers' personality traits revealed that the Five Factor model also provided a poor fit with the data of the full 44-item BFI (Chi-square $=$ 2 311.7, degrees of freedom $= 892$, CFI $= 0.642$, RMSEA $= 0.062$, SRMR $= 0.094$). As addressed in the research objectives, this study focuses on the psychometric characteristics of the full 44-item BFI scale in order to identify an abbreviated form measuring the personality of

Chinese outbound tourists. Consequently, a number of *post hoc* modification procedures were conducted to achieve a satisfactory fit of the overall Five Factor model with the available data.

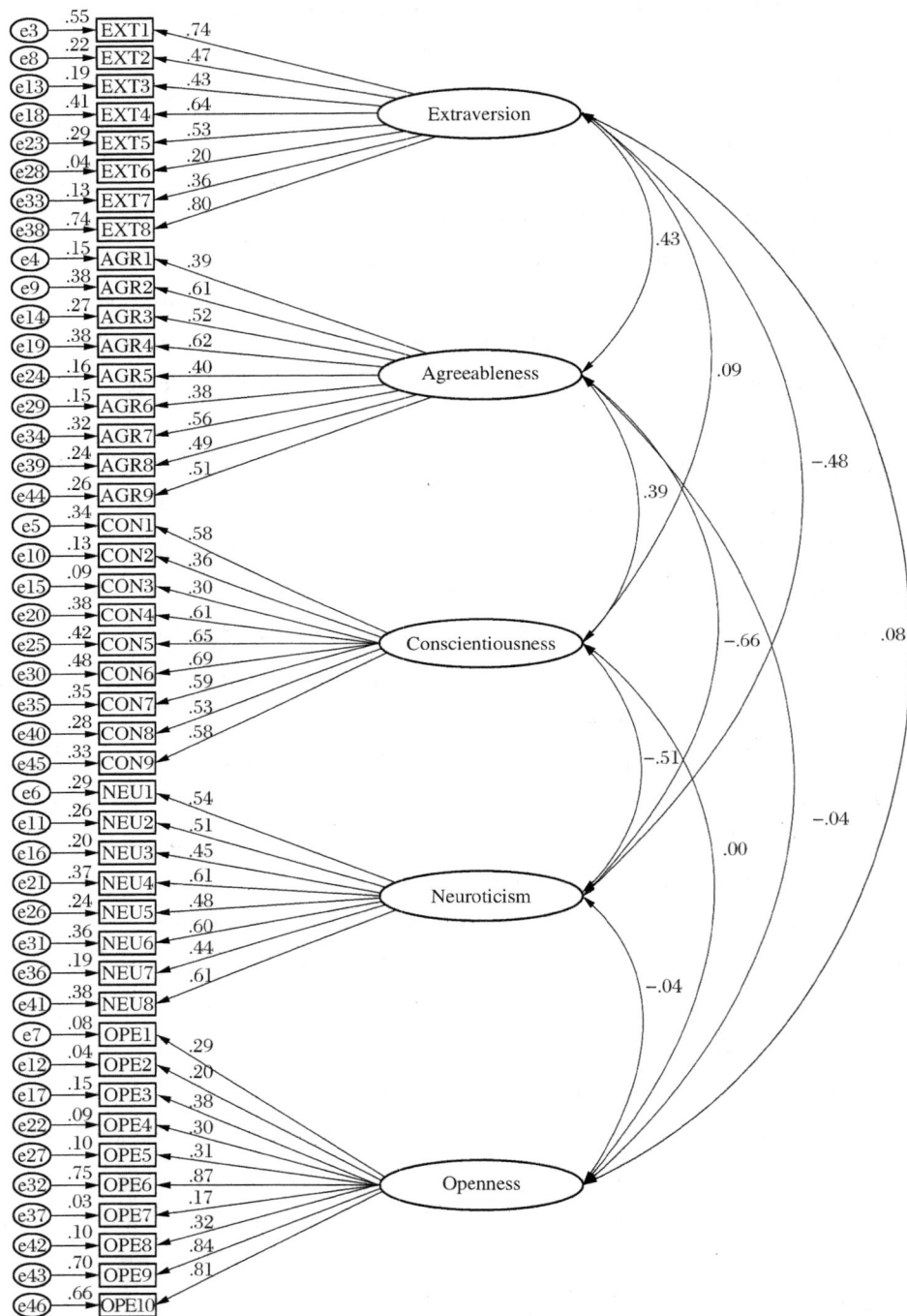

Figure 6.1　Five Factor Measurement Model with Standardised Parameter Estimates

Table 6.5 Model Summary for 44-Item Five Factor Model

Chi-square	df	ρ value	x^2/df	GFI	CFI	TLI	RMSEA	SRMR
4 009. 491	892	.000	4.495	.645	.580	.555	.084	.119

Examination of the AMOS output for the model showed a Mardia coefficient of 298. 957 (critical ratio = 52. 165), which indicated that assumption of multivariate normality might have been violated. However, examination of the Mahalanobis d-squared values for identification of outliers did not suggest deleting any cases from the analysis. Therefore, bootstrapping was utilised in the analysis to overcome the issue of multivariate non-normality in the model.

Following the aforementioned rules, items with standardised regression weights less than 0. 50 can be deleted for not having sufficient variance accounted for by their related latent variable (Hair et al. 2010). As shown in Figure 6. 1, the variables EXT2, EXT3, EXT6, and EXT7 reported a standardised factor loading of 0. 47, 0. 43, 0. 20, and 0. 36 respectively. A close examination of these four items found that EXT2 ("*is reserved*") and EXT 7 ("*is sometimes shy, inhibited*") were reverse-worded items. They could be categorised into semantic polar opposite indicators of the latent variable of extraversion. As addressed in reliability analysis and descriptive statistics results, reverse-worded items did not necessarily produce purported benefits. In addition, reverse wording effects on items should be specified for a model fitting Chinese people in a cross-cultural setting (Wu 2008). For instance, being reserved can be considered as a traditional Chinese personality attribute. People in Western culture prefer to communicate directly and frankly, and disclose themselves more while Chinese people are less open, more reserved, and communicate in a more ambiguous and indirect manner (Gudykunst & Matsumoto 1996). Not surprisingly, the differences in fundamental cultural values between the Chinese and westerners have contributed to differences in some psychometric properties. Accordingly, it can also account for why EXT6 ("*has an assertive personality*") got the lowest standardised factor loading. Furthermore, EXT3 ("*is full of energy*") in the current tourism context was not closely associated with the factor *extraversion*. Consequently, these four items were removed sequentially.

After the first run of the CFA, AGR1, AGR5, AGR6, and AGR8 reported a standardised factor loading of 0. 39, 0. 40, 0. 38, and 0. 49 respectively. Further examination found that AGR1 ("*tends to find fault with others*"), AGR6 ("*can be cold and aloof*"), and AGR8 ("*is sometimes rude to others*") were reverse-worded items, which can serve as the rationale for deleting these three items in the following analysis. Influenced by the deeply-rooted Chinese cultural and value system, the Chinese are prone to be friendly, modest, flexible, and tolerant, particularly in a group setting (Yang 2010). AGR5 ("*is generally trusting*") was found to have inadequate variance explained by the factor agreeableness in the context of group tours. Thus, the removal of these four items was justified.

For the conscientiousness factor, CON2 ("*can be somewhat careless*") and CON3 ("*is a reliable worker*") reported a low standardised factor loading of 0.36 and 0.30 respectively. CON2 was found to be a reverse-worded item and CON3 was found to have the poorest association with the factor variable conscientiousness in the context of outbound tourism. Thus, the deletion of these two items was warranted.

For the neuroticism factor, NEU3 ("*can be tense*"), NEU5 ("*is emotionally stable, not easily upset*"), and NEU7 ("*remains calm in tense situations*") reported a standardised factor loading of 0.45, 0.48, and 0.44 respectively. NEU5 and NEU7 were found to be reverse-worded items, and NEU3 may become redundant when contrasted with the more reliable item NEU8 ("*gets nervous easily*") in the context of participating in an all-inclusive package tour. Therefore, these three items were eliminated for the following analysis.

For the openness factor, OPE1 ("*is original, comes up with new ideas*"), OPE2 ("*is curious about many different things*"), OPE3 ("*is ingenious, a deep thinker*"), OPE4 ("*has an active imagination*"), OPE5 ("*is inventive*"), OPE7 ("*prefers work that is routine*"), and OPE8 ("*likes to reflect, play with ideas*") reported a very low standardised loading of 0.29, 0.20, 0.38, 0.30, 0.31, 0.17, and 0.32 respectively. Among the Five-Factor personality traits, the conceptualisation of openness has been controversial and McCrae and Costa (1997) conceded that the "concept of openness appeared to be unusually difficult to grasp" (p. 826). Cheung et al. (2008) argued that openness had the weakest psychometric properties in non-western cultures as compared to the other four factors of the FFM. Therefore, from a cross-cultural perspective, it is rather challenging to define the facets of openness to Chinese respondents, for it may vary in terms of the different research context. The statistical output directly identified three reliable items to represent the *openness* factor, i. e. OPE6 ("*values artistic, aesthetic experiences*"), OPE9 ("*has few artistic interests*"), and OPEN10 ("*is sophisticated in art, music, or literature*"), with a high standardised loading of 0.87, 0.84, and 0.81 respectively. This can be explained from two aspects. On one hand, as a tourist destination, Australia enjoys great popularity among Chinese travellers not only for its natural beauty, spectacular coastal scenery, but also for its unique multicultural environment (Yu & Weiler 2001; Huang & Gross 2010). On the other hand, respondents' demographic profile showed that a university degree or above was held by 59% of the respondents, and another 24.7% had a college diploma. A sound education background may have cultivated the sample's appreciation and enjoyment of aesthetic experiences when travelling in Australia. Beyond the five needs of the well-established hierarchical needs model, Maslow (Maslow et al. 1970) did address two other important sets of human needs, i. e. the aesthetic need, and the need to know and understand. In a tourism context, people travel to experience the beauty and gain new knowledge; therefore, both aesthetic and intellectual needs, serving concurrently as the facets of openness, far outweigh other facets, such as imagination, creativeness, and novelty. As a result, three items (OPE6, OPE9, and OPE10) were eventually retained for the subsequent measurement model testing.

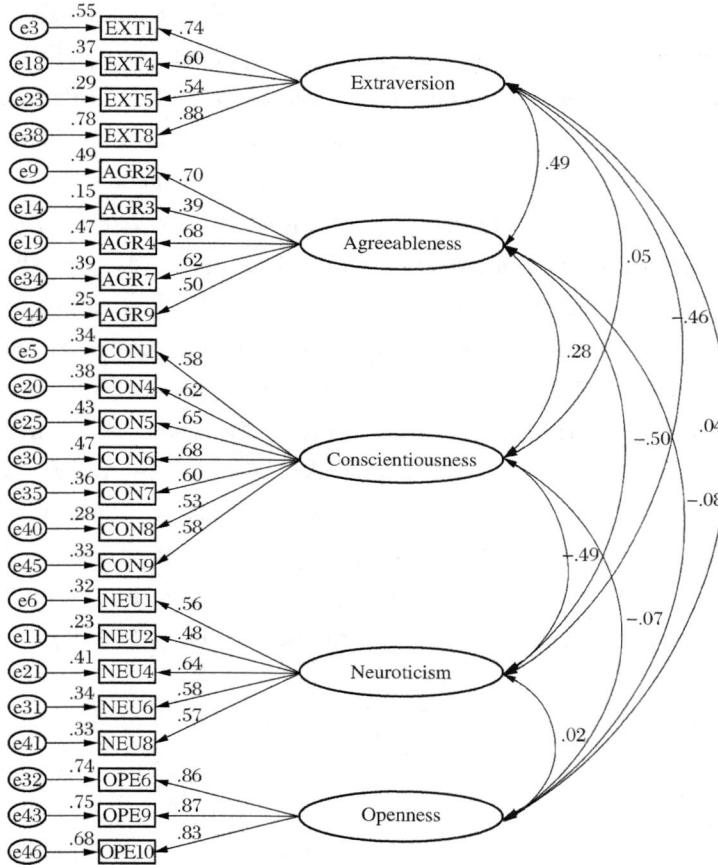

Figure 6. 2　24-Item Measurement Model with Standardised Parameter Estimates

After removing all these items sequentially, CFA was re-run on the 24-item personality measurement model to test its validity (Figure 6.2), producing results indicating an improved model fit: $x^2(242) = 887.067$, $p < 0.001$, $x^2/\text{df} = 3.666$; GFI $= 0.856$, CFI $= 0.834$; TLI $= 0.811$; RMSEA $= 0.074$ and SRMR $= 0.083$ (Table 6.6).

Table 6. 6　Model Summary for 24-Item Five Factor Model

Chi-square	df	p value	x^2/df	GFI	CFI	TLI	RMSEA	SRMR
887.067	242	.000	3.666	.856	.834	.811	.074	.083

As shown in Figure 6.2, the standardised factor loadings of AGR3 ("*starts quarrels with others*") and NEU2 ("*is relaxed, handles stress well*") were 0.39 and 0.48 respectively, below the cut-off value 0.50, so these two items were removed first. This could be justified by the fact that they were two reverse-worded items. In order to achieve an acceptable fit for the

model, the *post hoc* model fit procedures were conducted again on the Five Factors measurement model by analysing standardised residual covariances and modification indices. After further examination, it seemed that six items (EXT5, AGR9, CON4, CON8, CON9, and NEU6) had covariances with other latent variables (i. e. personality factors), either by sharing measurement error or as a direct indicator of another latent variable. Among them, EXT5 (*"tends to be quiet"*), CON4 (*"tends to be disorganised"*), and CON9 (*"is easily distracted"*) were reverse-worded items, and therefore it was decided to delete them individually in succession. After these steps, the modification indices suggested adding a path from AGR9 (*"likes to cooperate with others"*) to both extraversion and neuroticism; moreover, AGR9 had a small multiple correlation related to the other items (EXT8, EXT1, EXT4, and NEU1). Similarly, the modification indices suggested adding a path from CON8 (*"makes plans and follows through with them"*) to openness; moreover, CON8 had a small multiple correlation related to the other items (OPE9 and OPE10). The modification indices also suggested adding a path from NEU6 (*"can be moody"*) to conscientiousness; moreover, NEU6 had a small multiple correlation related to the other items (CON5 and CON6). As suggested by Little, Lindenberger and Nesselroade (1999) that dual loadings or correlated residuals were not allowed in selecting indicators for multivariate measurement and modelling with latent variables, these three items (AGR9, CON8, and NEU6) were eventually dropped. CFA was then performed again on the remaining 16-item personality measurement model to test its validity (see Figure 6.3).

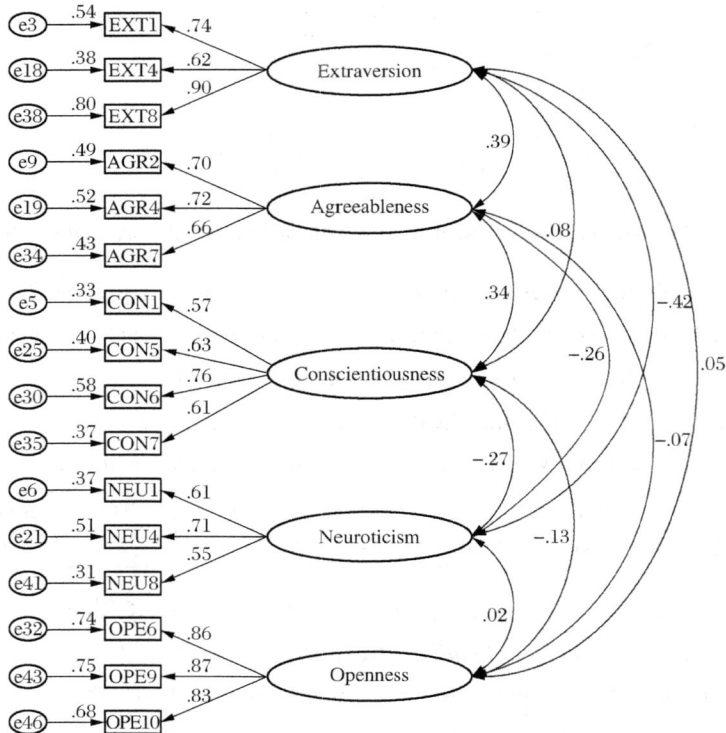

Figure 6.3　Final 16-Item Measurement Model with Standardised Parameter Estimates

Table 6.7　Model Summary for 16-Item Five Factor Model

Chi-square	df	p value	x^2/df	GFI	CFI	TLI	RMSEA	SRMR
224.210	94	.000	2.385	.946	.948	.933	.053	.050

　　The modified personality model resulted in 136 sample moments, with 42 distinct parameters to be estimated and 94 (136 − 42) degrees of freedom. The Chi-square statistic was 224.210, p = 0.000. The model fit indicators GFI = 0.946, CFI = 0.948, RMSEA = 0.053, SRMR = 0.050 indicate that the model is a good fit (Table 6.7).

　　The bootstrapping procedure involved establishing the bootstrapped standardised regression weights and SMCs for the model (Table 6.8). These estimates were bias-corrected at the 95% confidence level. The bootstrapped parameter estimates were all significant at the level of 0.001 and 0.01. Specifically, in the personality measurement model, the relationships between each observed indicator and its respective construct were all statistically significant, with standardised loading coefficients ranging from 0.553 to 0.896, thus providing support for the construct validity (Kline 2005; Hair et al. 2010). Although some of the SMC values were relatively low, more than half of them had SMC values close to or above 0.50, indicating that the latent factor could explain about half of the item's variance. A composite reliability value greater than 0.60 is regarded as desirable, while a value of 0.70 or higher suggests strong composite reliability (Bagozzi & Yi 1988). After manually calculating the composite reliability coefficients for the individual construct, it was found that the construct reliability (Extraversion = 0.80, Agreeableness = 0.73, Conscientiousness = 0.74, Neuroticism = 0.66, and Openness = 0.89) also suggested high reliability for the items. Since the final measurement model for personality produced goodness-of-fit indices, it was considered acceptable and could be used for subsequent overall measurement model testing.

Table 6.8　Bootstrapped CFA Results of Personality Model

Item	Standardised Regression Weights				SMC				Composite Reliability
	Estimate	Lower	Upper	ρ	Estimate	Lower	Upper	ρ	
EXT1	.736	.670	.793	.001	.542	.449	.629	.001	
EXT4	.615	.511	.701	.002	.379	.261	.491	.002	.80(EXT)
EXT8	.896	.825	.958	.001	.802	.681	.918	.001	
AGR2	.699	.594	.786	.001	.489	.352	.618	.001	
AGR4	.721	.642	.798	.001	.520	.412	.637	.001	.73 (AGR)
AGR7	.655	.557	.732	.001	.429	.311	.537	.001	
CON1	.573	.485	.653	.001	.328	.235	.427	.001	
CON5	.630	.535	.707	.001	.397	.286	.499	.001	.74 (CON)
CON6	.759	.669	.833	.001	.576	.447	.694	.001	
CON7	.608	.518	.685	.001	.369	.269	.469	.001	

Continued

Item	Standardised Regression Weights				SMC				Composite Reliability
	Estimate	Lower	Upper	ρ	Estimate	Lower	Upper	ρ	
NEU1	.609	.499	.709	.001	.371	.249	.503	.001	.66 (NEU)
NEU4	.712	.610	.810	.001	.507	.372	.657	.001	
NEU8	.553	.448	.643	.001	.306	.200	.414	.001	
OPE6	.860	.819	.901	.001	.740	.670	.812	.001	.89 (OPE)
OPE9	.868	.821	.910	.001	.753	.675	.828	.001	
OPE10	.826	.785	.865	.001	.683	.617	.748	.001	

Measurement Model for Affect and Satisfaction

As two endogenous variables in the conceptual framework, affect and satisfaction were integrated into a model to test its validity, for both of them can be categorised into the domain of tourist behaviour. Before running CFA to test the measurements of affect and satisfaction, descriptive statistics were calculated for 19 measurement items using SPSS. Means and standard deviation were reported in Table 6.9. The mean values of negative affect were much lower than those of positive affect. All these suggested that respondents generally possessed an abundance of positive affect during their travel to Australia. Standard deviations of negative affect were relatively larger than those of positive affect, indicating that respondents' opinions on negative affect were more diverse than on positive affect. These results were consistent with the findings of focus group interviews that positive affect was reasonably more influential than negative affect in the context of Chinese outbound tourists to Australia.

Means and standard deviations of satisfaction items were also examined. Respondents generally agreed with these four items, rating them fairly positively. All items had mean values over 5.4, together with relatively low standard deviations of these items, indicating that respondents were generally satisfied with their overall experiences of visiting Australia.

Table 6.9　Means and Standard Deviations of Affect and Satisfaction Items ($n = 493$)

Item	Description	Mean	SD
Positive Affect			
PA1	relaxed	6.03	0.75
PA2	happy	5.96	0.67
PA3	excited	5.37	0.89
PA4	interested	5.48	0.83
PA5	impressed	5.63	0.75
PA6	a sense of friendliness	5.91	0.71
PA7	comfortable	5.57	0.70

Continued

Item	Description	Mean	SD
Negative Affect			
NA1	nervous	2.91	1.30
NA2	afraid	2.20	1.03
NA3	worried	3.19	1.31
NA4	lonely	2.44	1.28
NA5	bored	3.02	1.20
NA6	embarrassed	3.26	1.33
NA7	homesick	3.66	1.39
Satisfaction			
SAT1	I have really enjoyed the trip in Australia	5.86	0.67
SAT2	My choice to visit Australia was a wise one	5.66	0.80
SAT3	The travel experience in Australia was exactly what I needed	5.45	0.90
SAT4	I am satisfied with my trip in Australia	5.83	0.68

Scale: 1 = strongly disagree, 7 = strongly agree.

CFA was performed on the 18-item combined model of affect and satisfaction using ML estimation to test its validity (Figure 6.4). The affect and satisfaction model resulted in 171 sample moments, with 39 distinct parameters to be estimated and 132 (171 − 39) degrees of freedom. The Chi-square statistic was 634.030, $p = 0.000$. The model fit indicators GFI = 0.861, CFI = 0.894, RMSEA = 0.088, SRMR = 0.079 indicated that the model was not a good fit (Table 6.10).

Table 6.10　Model Summary for 18-Item Affect and Satisfaction Model

Chi-square	df	p value	x^2/df	GFI	CFI	TLI	RMSEA	SRMR
634.030	132	.000	4.803	.861	.894	.877	.088	.079

Examination of the AMOS output for the model showed a Mardia coefficient of 37.400 (critical ratio = 18.386) for the *affect* construct, and of 10.129 (critical ratio = 16.230) for the *satisfaction* construct, a little higher than the threshold value of 10. These indicated that assumption of multivariate normality may have been violated. However, examination of the Mahalanobis d-squared values did not suggest deleting any cases from the analysis. Therefore, bootstrapping was utilised in the analysis to overcome the issue of multivariate non-normality in the model.

In order to achieve an acceptable fit for the model, the *post hoc* model fit procedures conducted on the Five Factors personality model were used in the adjustment of the affect model. As shown in Figure 6.4, the variables *lonely*, *bored*, *embarrassed*, and *homesick* reported a standardised factor loading of 0.48, 0.38, 0.41, and 0.49 respectively. These four

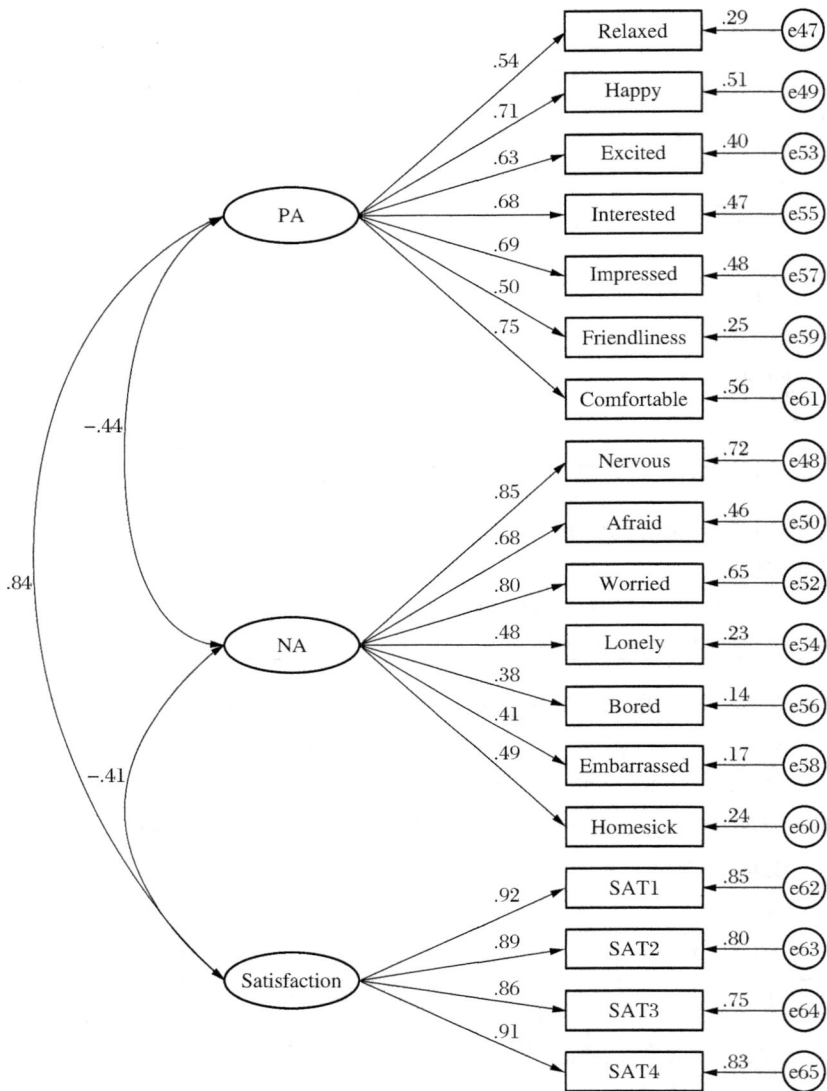

Figure 6.4 Affect & Satisfaction Measurement Model with Standardised Parameter Estimates

items with standardised regression weights less than 0.50 can be deleted for not having sufficient variance explained by their related latent variable (Hair et al. 2010). However, any alteration to the measurement model should always be made in combination with the theoretical justification instead of merely relying on the statistical output (Hair et al. 2010). These exploratory affective items, generated from the findings of the qualitative research (focus group interviews), were integrated into the final questionnaire to verify their representativeness of the sample. Based on the empirical evidence and the underlying structure of affective theories in the tourism context, three items (*lonely*, *bored*, and *embarrassed*) were removed to improve internal reliability in the model, while *homesick* was retained at this stage for two reasons. It was a relatively salient negative affective response mentioned by interview participants;

moreover, its standardised coefficient (0.49) was very close to the threshold level of 0.50.

　　Following the rule previously addressed, items were removed sequentially. Analysis of standardised residual covariances and modification indices was then conducted, revealing that *relaxed* had sizable standardised residuals. The modification indices suggested adding a path from *relaxed* to negative affect; moreover, *relaxed* had a small multiple correlation related to the other items (*homesick*, *worried*, *afraid*, and *nervous*). Similarly, the modification indices suggested *friendliness* had a small multiple correlation related to the other items (*interested*, *excited*, *comfortable*, and *SAT1*). The modification indices suggested adding a path from *comfortable* to *satisfaction*; moreover, *comfortable* had a small multiple correlation related to the other items (*happy*, *exited*, and *SAT3*). The modification indices suggested an item redundancy in satisfaction items, because *SAT1* ("*I have really enjoyed the trip in Australia*") had a multiple correlation related to the other items (*SAT2* "*My choice to visit Australia was a wise one*" and *SAT4* "*I am satisfied with my trip to Australia*"). As suggested by Little, Lindenberger and Nesselroade (1999), these four items (i. e. *relaxed*, *friendliness*, *comfortable*, and *SAT1*) were dropped to improve internal reliability in the model. The final CFA measurement model for affect and satisfaction is presented in Figure 6.5.

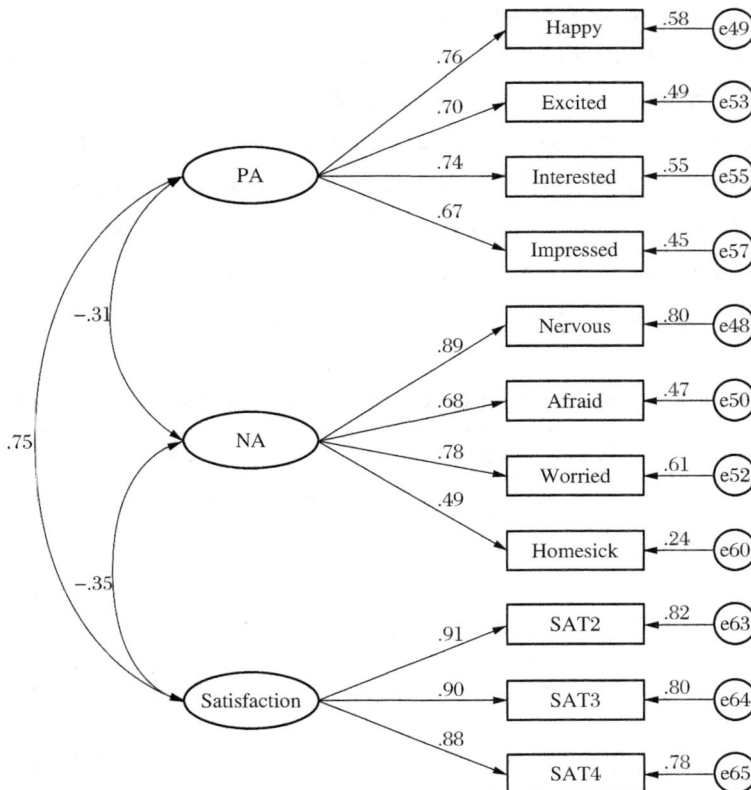

Figure 6.5　Final Measurement Model for Affect and Satisfaction

Table 6.11   Model Summary for Final Affect & Satisfaction Measurement Model

Chi-square	df	p value	x^2/df	GFI	CFI	TLI	RMSEA	SRMR
88.889	41	.000	2.168	.969	.983	.977	.049	.040

The 11-item measurement model resulted in 66 sample moments, with 25 distinct parameters to be estimated and 41 (66 − 25) degrees of freedom. The Chi-square statistic was 88.889, $p = 0.000$. The model fit indicators GFI = 0.969, CFI = 0.983, RMSEA = 0.049, SRMR = 0.040 demonstrated a good fit with the data (Table 6.11).

The bootstrapping procedure involved establishing the bootstrapped standardised regression weights and SMCs for the model (Table 6.12). These estimates were bias-corrected at the 95% confidence level. The bootstrapped parameter estimates were all significant at the level of 0.001 and 0.01. Specifically, in the measurement model for affect and satisfaction, the relationships between each observed indicator and its respective construct were all statistically significant, with standardised loading coefficients ranging from 0.485 to 0.907. All items except *homesick* and *afraid* in the scale displayed a standardised loading above the preferred level of 0.70 on the latent construct, indicating that these items were highly reliable. Although the standardised loading of the item *homesick* on the latent construct (i.e. negative affect) was marginally lower than the minimum acceptance level of 0.50, it was still retained in the final measurement model on account of its conceptual importance based on the findings of focus group interviews. The majority of SMC values were close to or above 0.50, indicating that the latent factor could explain about half of the item's variance. Composite reliability coefficients (Positive Affect = 0.81, Negative Affect = 0.81, Satisfaction = 0.92) also suggested high reliability for the items. Since the final measurement model for affect and satisfaction produced goodness-of-fit indices, it was considered acceptable and could be used for subsequent overall measurement model testing.

Table 6.12   Bootstrapped CFA Results of Affect & Satisfaction Model

Item	Standardised Regression Weights				SMC				Composite Reliability
	Estimate	Lower	Upper	p	Estimate	Lower	Upper	p	
Happy	.759	.708	.803	.001	.576	.502	.645	.001	
Excited	.700	.634	.758	.001	.490	.402	.574	.001	
Interested	.744	.671	.807	.001	.554	.450	.651	.001	.81 (PA)
Impressed	.669	.580	.739	.002	.448	.337	.546	.002	
Nervous	.893	.850	.932	.001	.797	.722	.868	.001	
Afraid	.685	.628	.737	.001	.469	.395	.544	.001	
Worried	.783	.716	.834	.001	.613	.513	.696	.001	.81 (NA)
Homesick	.485	.395	.566	.001	.235	.156	.320	.001	

Continued

Item	Standardised Regression Weights				SMC				Composite Reliability
	Estimate	Lower	Upper	p	Estimate	Lower	Upper	p	
SAT2	.907	.882	.930	.001	.823	.778	.864	.001	
SAT3	.895	.866	.921	.001	.802	.751	.849	.001	.92 (SAT)
SAT4	.881	.850	.905	.002	.777	.723	.819	.002	

Overall Measurement Model Testing

After assessing the unidimensionality of each construct individually to ensure the validity and fit of each measurement model, the overall measurement model can be estimated, combing all the constructs together (e. g. Anderson & Gerbing 1988; Gursoy, Boylu & Avic 2011). Specifically, once an acceptable "model fit" has been achieved for each measurement model, the causal (structural) relationships between the eight latent constructs of extraversion, agreeableness, conscientiousness, neuroticism, openness, positive affect, negative affect, and satisfaction can be tested. When the measurement models indicate good fit, the findings from the full structural model can be presented with confidence (Byrne 2009). Hence, allowing the latent variables to be freely correlated, the overall measurement model was tested using CFA. Bootstrapping was again utilised in the analysis to overcome the issue of multivariate non-normality in the model. It was presented with standardised parameter estimates (Figure 6.6).

Table 6.13 Model Summary for Overall Measurement Model

Chi-square	df	p value	x^2/df	GFI	CFI	TLI	RMSEA	SRMR
553.827	296	.000	1.871	.922	.955	.946	.042	.049

The overall measurement model resulted in 378 sample moments, with 82 distinct parameters to be estimated and 296 (378 − 82) degrees of freedom. The Chi-square statistic was 553.827, p = 0.000. The model fit indicators GFI = 0.922, CFI = 0.955, RMSEA = 0.042, SRMR = 0.049 indicated that the overall measurement model was a good fit with the data (Table 6.13).

The bootstrapping procedure involved establishing the bootstrapped standardised regression weights and SMCs for the model (Table 6.14). These estimates were bias-corrected at the 95% confidence level. All the bootstrapped parameter estimates were 0.50 and higher and significant at the level of 0.001 and 0.01, suggesting construct validity as proposed by Hair et al. (2010). Both standardised regression weights and SMC values in the overall measurement model exhibited slight variations from those in the individual measurement models. In addition, as shown in Table 6.14, all the composite reliability coefficients for each construct maintained the

same as those in the individual measurement models, indicating strong composite reliability.

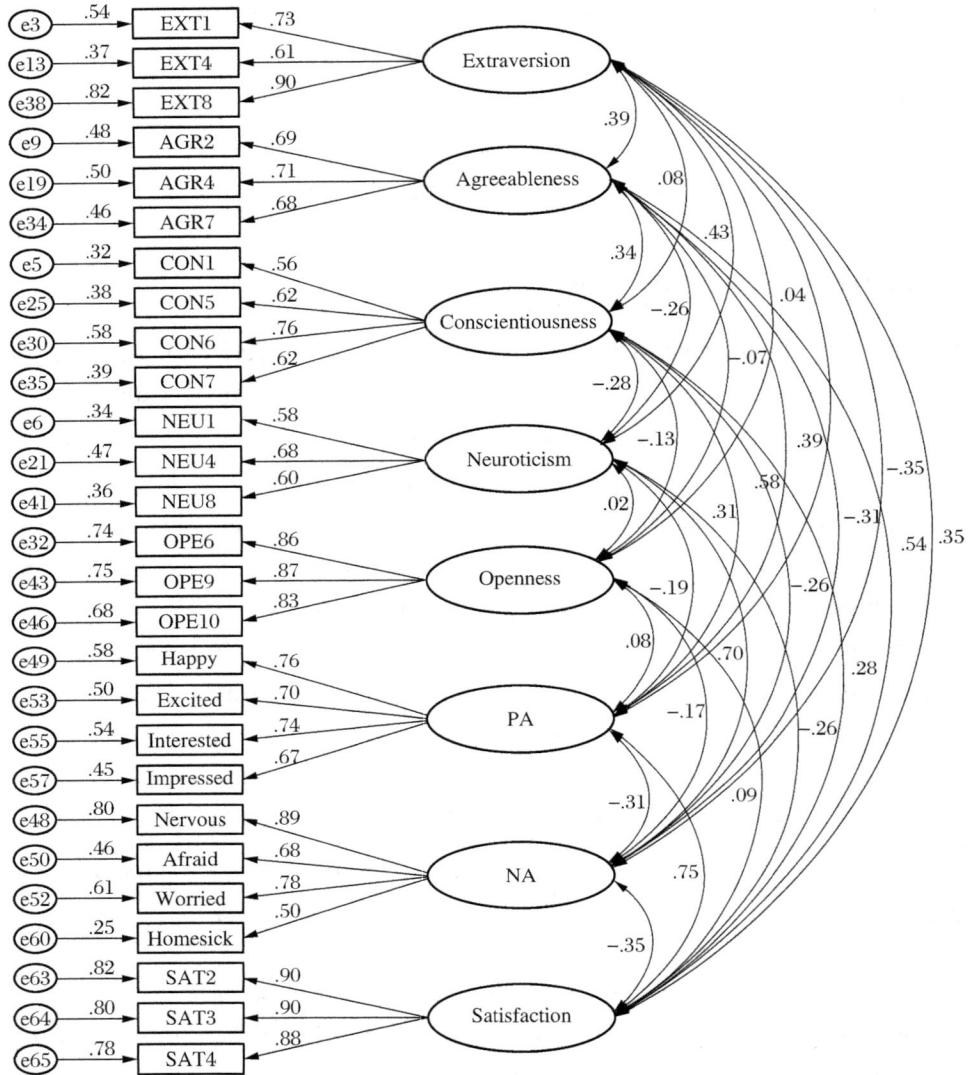

Figure 6.6　Overall Measurement Model with Standardised Parameter Estimates

Table 6.14　Bootstrapped CFA Results of Overall Measurement Model

Item	Standardised Regression Weights				SMC				Composite Reliability
	Estimate	Lower	Upper	ρ	Estimate	Lower	Upper	ρ	
EXT1	.731	.664	.788	.001	.535	.441	.621	.001	
EXT4	.609	.508	.694	.002	.371	.258	.482	.002	.80（EXT）
EXT8	.903	.836	.964	.001	.816	.698	.929	.001	

Continued

Item	Standardised Regression Weights				SMC				Composite Reliability
	Estimate	Lower	Upper	ρ	Estimate	Lower	Upper	ρ	
AGR2	.694	.594	.780	.001	.481	.353	.609	.001	
AGR4	.707	.636	.776	.001	.500	.404	.602	.001	.73 (AGR)
AGR7	.676	.585	.755	.001	.457	.342	.570	.001	
CON1	.565	.475	.646	.001	.319	.226	.417	.001	
CON5	.619	.523	.698	.001	.383	.274	.487	.001	.74 (CON)
CON6	.761	.671	.833	.001	.579	.450	.693	.001	
CON7	.623	.531	.707	.001	.388	.282	.500	.001	
NEU1	.580	.467	.677	.001	.336	.218	.458	.001	
NEU4	.684	.593	.758	.002	.467	.352	.575	.002	.66 (NEU)
NEU8	.603	.509	.678	.001	.363	.259	.459	.001	
OPE6	.860	.817	.901	.001	.740	.668	.811	.001	
OPE9	.869	.824	.910	.001	.754	.680	.828	.001	.89 (OPE)
OPE10	.826	.784	.864	.001	.682	.615	.746	.001	
Happy	.762	.711	.807	.001	.581	.506	.651	.001	
Excited	.704	.640	.762	.001	.496	.410	.581	.001	.81 (PA)
Interested	.737	.665	.799	.001	.543	.443	.639	.001	
Impressed	.669	.579	.742	.001	.447	.335	.550	.001	
Nervous	.893	.852	.929	.001	.797	.726	.863	.001	
Afraid	.680	.619	.732	.001	.463	.383	.536	.001	.81 (NA)
Worried	.783	.716	.834	.001	.609	.516	.689	.001	
Homesick	.500	.415	.580	.001	.250	.172	.337	.001	
SAT2	.905	.880	.927	.001	.818	.774	.860	.001	
SAT3	.897	.868	.923	.001	.804	.753	.853	.001	.92 (SAT)
SAT4	.883	.852	.906	.002	.779	.726	.821	.002	

Discriminant validity was then examined by checking the correlation matrix among the latent variables in the overall measurement model (Table 6.15). Low correlations among latent variables would provide evidence of discriminant validity. Results showed that 24 of the 28 elements in the correlation matrix had a value below 0.50, suggesting that the measurement model had generally achieved discriminant validity. However, the correlation between positive affect and satisfaction was 0.752 and between neuroticism and negative affect it was 0.701,

which indicates that the constructs may not be sufficiently differentiated from each other. According to Fornell and Larcker (1981), discriminant validity is obtained if the AVE by the correlated latent variables is greater than the square of the correlation between the latent variables. The squared correlation estimate between positive affect and satisfaction was 0.566, and the calculated AVE reported a high score of 0.80. Furthermore, the squared correlation estimate between neuroticism and negative affect was 0.491, and the calculated AVE reported a high score of 0.53. Thus, the discriminant validity was confirmed. Since the overall measurement model for the study produced goodness-of-fit indices, it was considered acceptable and could be used for subsequent structural model testing.

Table 6.15　Correlation Matrix of Latent Variables in the Overall Measurement Model

Satisfaction	Extraversion	Agreeableness	Conscientiousness	Neuroticism	Openness	Positive	Positive Affect	Negative Affect
Extraversion	1.00							
Agreeableness	0.386	1.000						
	* * *							
Conscientiousness	0.083	0.344	1.000					
	0.164	* * *						
Neuroticism	−0.425	−0.260	−0.281	1.000				
	* * *	* * *	* * *					
Openness	0.044	−0.072	−0.131	0.020	1.000			
	0.442	0.242	0.036	0.802				
Positive Affect	0.394	0.580	0.311	−0.187	0.085	1.000		
	* * *	* * *	* * *	* *	0.102			
Negative Affect	−0.351	−0.314	−0.260	0.701	−0.167	−0.312	1.000	
	* * *	* * *	* * *	* * *	* *	* *		
Satisfaction	0.355	0.538	0.275	−0.255	0.085	0.752	−0.352	1.000
	* * *	* * *	* * *	* * *	0.076	* * *	* * *	

Structural Model Testing

After the overall measurement model incorporating personality, affect, and satisfaction had been validated with the CFA technique, the structural relationships between exogenous and endogenous variables were estimated by testing the hypothesised structural causal model with the entire sample ($n = 493$). ML estimation was adopted to assess the structural model. This process helped "specify the causal relations of the constructs to one another, as posited by some theory" (Anderson & Gerbing 1988, p. 411). As proposed in the conceptual framework (see Chapter 2), the structural relationships focused on the collective impacts of personality and affect on satisfaction. The exogenous variables were represented by five factors of personality traits (i. e. extraversion, agreeableness, conscientiousness, neuroticism, openness) and the endogenous variables were represented by positive affect, negative affect, and satisfaction. The structural model was tested using AMOS 20 to examine the hypothesised relationships among the latent constructs (Figure 6. 7).

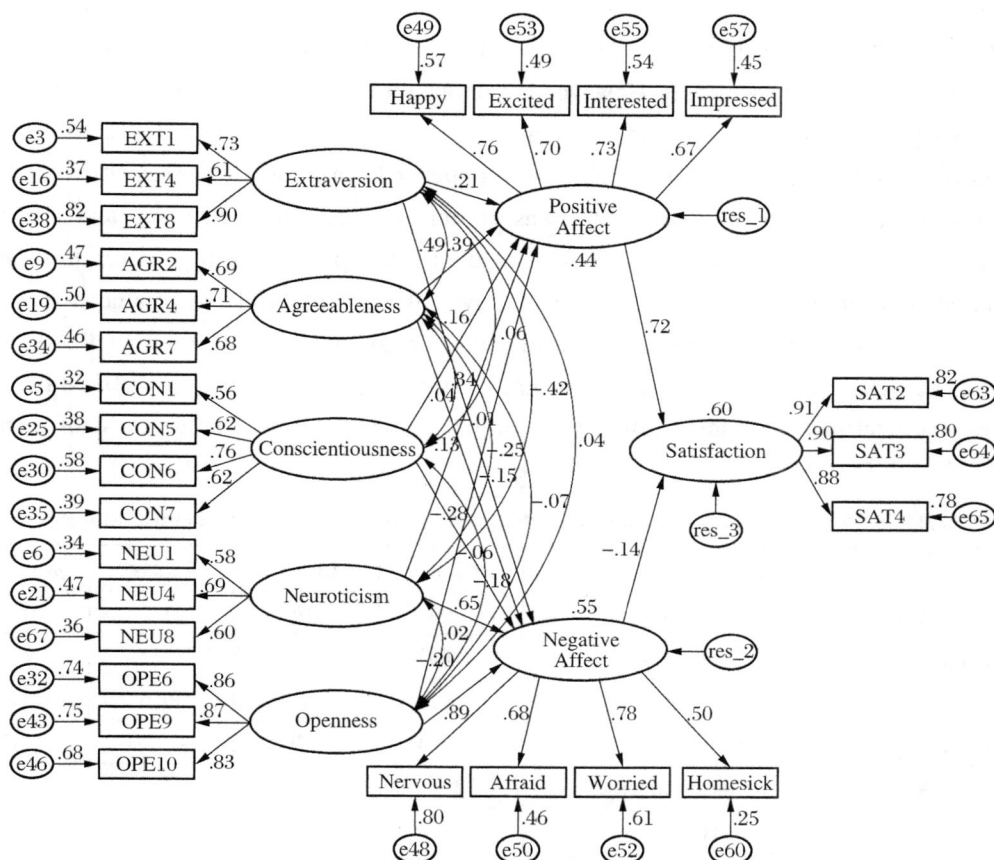

Figure 6. 7　Standardised Parameter Estimates for Structural Model

Table 6. 16　Model Summary for Structural Model

Chi-square	df	p value	x^2/df	GFI	CFI	TLI	RMSEA	SRMR
562. 611	302	. 000	1. 863	. 921	. 954	. 947	. 042	. 050

The analysis of the structural model resulted in 378 sample moments, with 76 distinct parameters to be estimated and 302 (378 − 76) degrees of freedom. The Chi-square statistic was 562. 611, p = 0. 000. The model fit indicators GFI = 0. 921, CFI = 0. 954, RMSEA = 0. 042, SRMR = 0. 050 indicated that the model was a good fit (Table 6. 16). As shown in Figure 6. 7, the values of both standardised factor loadings and SMCs were found to be nearly identical to the ones in the overall measurement model, suggesting the robustness of the measurements for each construct in the structural model. Therefore, no further modifications were conducted because all fit indices reported a level of pre-set threshold values. Blindly following the over-fitted model may run the risk of capitalising on chance, thus resulting in more statistical bias (Silvia & MacCallum 1988).

Further examination of the AMOS output showed the Mardia statistic for the structural model was 90.870 (critical ratio = 25.493). This indicated that assumption of multivariate normality may have been violated. However, examination of the Mahalanobis d-squared values did not suggest deleting any outstanding outlier cases from the analysis. Therefore, it was decided to keep the 493 cases and to utilise bootstrapping to overcome the issue of multivariate non-normality in the model. The model was re-run with 2,000 bootstraps, and the bias-corrected bootstrapped parameter estimates (standardised regression weights) for this model were all significant at 95% confidence intervals, with the exception of the parameter estimates between extraversion and negative affect (standardised regression weight or $\gamma = -0.007$, $\rho = 0.909$), between conscientiousness and negative affect ($\gamma = -0.056$, $\rho = 0.388$), and between neuroticism and positive affect ($\gamma = 0.041$, $\rho = 0.450$). These are highlighted in Table 6.17.

Table 6.17 Bootstrapped Standardised Regression Weights for Full Structural Model

Parameter			Estimate	Lower	Upper	ρ Value
Positive Affect	←	Extraversion	.209	.079	.343	.001
Negative Affect	←	Extraversion	**−.007**	−.141	.135	**.909**
Positive Affect	←	Agreeableness	.492	.357	.616	.001
Negative Affect	←	Agreeableness	−.154	−.303	−.004	.047
Positive Affect	←	Conscientiousness	.160	.038	.285	.010
Negative Affect	←	Conscientiousness	**−.056**	−.178	.074	**.388**
Positive Affect	←	Neuroticism	**.041**	−.080	.178	**.450**
Negative Affect	←	Neuroticism	.646	.503	.795	.002
Positive Affect	←	Openness	.133	.039	.225	.008
Negative Affect	←	Openness	−.199	−.284	−.105	.002
Satisfaction	←	Positive Affect	.724	.654	.790	.001
Satisfaction	←	Negative Affect	−.139	−.223	−.048	.004
EXT8	←	Extraversion	.903	.833	.960	.002
EXT4	←	Extraversion	.609	.508	.695	.001
EXT1	←	Extraversion	.732	.666	.788	.001
AGR7	←	Agreeableness	.679	.588	.757	.001
AGR4	←	Agreeableness	.707	.636	.776	.001

Continued

Parameter			Estimate	Lower	Upper	ρ Value
AGR2	←	Agreeableness	.689	.589	.776	.001
CON7	←	Conscientiousness	.623	.531	.707	.001
CON6	←	Conscientiousness	.761	.670	.832	.001
CON5	←	Conscientiousness	.619	.523	.698	.001
CON1	←	Conscientiousness	.565	.475	.646	.001
NEU8	←	Neuroticism	.600	.508	.674	.001
NEU4	←	Neuroticism	.685	.595	.760	.002
NEU1	←	Neuroticism	.584	.474	.679	.001
OPE10	←	Openness	.826	.783	.863	.001
OPE9	←	Openness	.868	.824	.910	.001
OPE6	←	Openness	.861	.817	.901	.001
Impressed	←	Positive Affect	.669	.578	.743	.001
Interested	←	Positive Affect	.734	.664	.797	.001
Excited	←	Positive Affect	.701	.637	.759	.001
Happy	←	Positive Affect	.756	.707	.801	.001
Nervous	←	Negative Affect	.894	.853	.930	.001
Afraid	←	Negative Affect	.679	.619	.732	.001
Worried	←	Negative Affect	.779	.718	.829	.001
Homesick	←	Negative Affect	.500	.415	.580	.001
SAT2	←	Satisfaction	.905	.880	.927	.001
SAT3	←	Satisfaction	.896	.866	.922	.001
SAT4	←	Satisfaction	.882	.851	.906	.002

In the hypothesised structural model, the variables of personality and affect can be considered as two antecedents that affect overall tourist satisfaction among Chinese outbound tourists to Australia. Therefore, the bootstrapped SMCs were also assessed to reveal the amount of variance in each endogenous variable that was accounted for by the antecedent variables in the relevant structural equation. Cohen(1988) suggested that SMC values of 0.01, 0.09, and 0.25 could be used to denote "small", "medium", and "large" effects respectively in behavioural sciences. The SMCs of negative affect, positive affect, and satisfaction are 0.55, 0.44, and 0.60 respectively, significant at the 95% confidence interval (Table 6.18). Specifically, the structural relationships between the exogenous variables and endogenous variables in the final model explain 55% of the total variation in negative affect, 44% of the total variation in positive affect, and finally both personality and affect explain 60% of the total variation in overall tourist satisfaction. Obviously, five factors of personality traits as exogenous variables, together with the mediating variable affect, had a substantial joint effect on overall tourist satisfaction. Consequently, it can be reasonably inferred that using the SMC coefficients as the indicator, the hypothesised structural model would be able to exercise a strong statistical power to predict mainland Chinese package tourists' affective responses travelling in Australia, and their overall satisfaction with Australia as a tourist destination.

Table 6.18　Structural Model—Bootstrapped Squared Multiple Correlations

Parameter	Estimate	Lower	Upper	p-Value
Negative Affect	.552	.417	.664	.004
Positive Affect	.436	.315	.534	.004
Satisfaction	.598	.512	.673	.002
SAT4	.778	.724	.820	.002
SAT3	.802	.750	.850	.001
SAT2	.819	.774	.860	.001
Nervous	.799	.728	.864	.001
Afraid	.461	.383	.535	.001
Worried	.607	.515	.687	.001
Homesick	.250	.172	.336	.001
Impressed	.448	.334	.551	.001
Interested	.539	.440	.635	.001
Excited	.491	.406	.576	.001
Happy	.572	.499	.642	.001
OPE6	.741	.668	.811	.001
OPE9	.754	.679	.828	.001
OPE10	.681	.614	.746	.001
NEU1	.341	.224	.461	.001
NEU4	.470	.354	.577	.002
NEU8	.360	.258	.454	.001
CON1	.319	.226	.417	.001
CON5	.383	.273	.488	.001
CON6	.579	.449	.692	.001
CON7	.388	.282	.500	.001
AGR2	.475	.347	.602	.001
AGR4	.499	.405	.602	.001
AGR7	.461	.346	.573	.001
EXT1	.536	.443	.622	.001
EXT4	.371	.258	.483	.001
EXT8	.815	.694	.922	.002

Hypotheses Testing

Since the structural model was found to fit the sample data adequately, the hypotheses proposed in the conceptual framework in Chapter 3 were examined to find out whether they were supported or not. One of the advantages of adopting SEM is its capability to estimate structural relations among the latent variables simultaneously (Hair et al. 2010). Therefore, the hypotheses can be tested by directly examining the statistical significance of path coefficients among the constructs. Figure 6.8 shows the structural model combined with the standardised regression weights. The results of the hypotheses testing are further illustrated in Figure 6.8.

Hypothesis 1a posited that extraversion has a positive impact on positive affect experienced at a destination. The hypothesis was tested by studying the path coefficients between extraversion and positive affect. As shown in Figure 6.8, the path coefficient of 0.21 from extraversion to positive affect was positive and significant at the 0.001 level, thus supporting Hypothesis 1a. Hypothesis 1b posited that extraversion has a negative impact on negative affect experienced at a destination. Evidence indicated that the negative impact of extraversion on negative affect was not significant. Therefore, Hypothesis 1b is not supported.

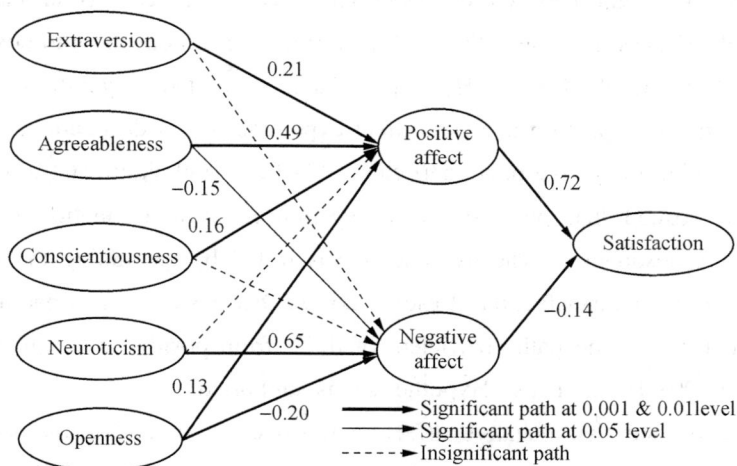

Figure 6.8 Structural Model with Estimated Path Coefficients

Hypothesis 2a posited that neuroticism has a negative impact on positive affect experienced at a destination. Model test results indicated that the negative impact of neuroticism on positive affect was not significant. Thus, Hypothesis 2a is not supported. Hypothesis 2b posited that neuroticism has a positive impact on negative affect experienced at a destination. Path coefficient of 0.65 from neuroticism to negative affect, significant at the 0.01 level, indicated that neuroticism had a strong positive impact on negative affect. Thus, Hypothesis 2b is supported.

Hypothesis 3a posited that agreeableness has a positive impact on positive affect experienced at a destination. The hypothesis was tested by studying the path coefficients between agreeableness and positive affect. The path coefficient of 0.49, significant at the 0.001 level, indicated that agreeableness had a strong positive impact on positive affect in the context of Chinese group package tour to Australia. Thus, Hypothesis 3a is supported. Hypothesis 3b posited that agreeableness has a negative impact on negative affect experienced at a destination. This hypothesis is supported, with a negative path coefficient of -0.15 from agreeableness to negative affect and significant at the 0.05 level.

Hypothesis 4a posited that conscientiousness has a positive impact on positive affect experienced at a destination. Although not as salient as the impact of agreeableness on positive affect, the positive impact of conscientiousness on positive affect did exist. The path coefficient from conscientiousness to positive affect was 0.16, significant at the 0.01 level. Therefore, Hypothesis 4a is supported. Hypothesis 4b posited that conscientiousness has a negative impact on negative affect experienced at a destination. Results showed that the negative impact of conscientiousness on negative affect was not significant statistically. Therefore, Hypothesis 4b is not supported.

Hypothesis 5a posited that openness has a positive impact on positive affect experienced at a destination. Path coefficient between openness and positive affect was checked to test this hypothesis. Results showed that the path coefficient of 0.13 from openness to positive affect was significant at the 0.01 level. Hence, Hypothesis 5a is supported. Hypothesis 5b posited that openness has a negative impact on negative affect experienced at a destination. This hypothesis is also supported, with a negative path coefficient of -0.20 and significant at the 0.01 level.

Hypothesis 6 posited that positive affect experienced at a destination positively affects satisfaction with the destination. The hypothesis was tested by examining the path coefficient between positive affect and satisfaction. Results showed that positive affect had a strong positive impact on satisfaction, for the path coefficient of 0.72 from positive affect to satisfaction was significant at the 0.001 level. Thus, Hypothesis 6 is supported.

Hypothesis 7 posited that negative affect experienced at a destination negatively affects satisfaction with the destination. The hypothesis was tested by examining the path coefficient between negative affect and satisfaction. The path coefficient of -0.14 from negative affect to satisfaction was significant at the 0.01 level. Thus, the hypothesis is also supported.

As shown in Figure 6.8, it is worth noting that affect plays an important mediating role between personality dimensions and satisfaction. More specifically, except for neuroticism, other factors of FFM personality traits (i. e. extraversion, agreeableness, conscientiousness, and openness) had a positive impact on positive affect. In addition, since none of modification suggestions were found to add paths from latent factors of any Five-Factor personality traits to satisfaction during the modification procedures, it could be logically inferred that Five-Factor personality traits had no direct effect on satisfaction. Therefore, it appears that positive affect plays a complete mediating role between these four factors and satisfaction. Similarly, negative affect plays a full mediating role between three factors of personality traits (i. e. agreeableness, neuroticism, and openness) and satisfaction. On the other hand, as shown by their path coefficients, both extraversion and conscientiousness had no significant negative impact on negative affect; thus, negative affect did not mediate between these two personality factors and satisfaction. As is the case with negative affect, positive affect did not mediate neuroticism and satisfaction either.

Table 6. 19　Hypotheses Testing Results

Hypothesis	Path	Standardised Coefficient	p Value	Result
H1: Impact of Extraversion on Affect	a) EXT→PA	0. 21	. 001	Supported
	b) EXT→NA	− 0. 01	. 909	Not supported
H2: Impact of Neuroticism on Affect	a) NEU→PA	0. 04	. 450	Not supported
	b) NEU→NA	0. 65	. 002	Supported
H3: Impact of Agreeableness on Affect	a) AGR→PA	0. 49	. 001	Supported
	b) AGR→NA	− 0. 15	. 047	Supported
H4: Impact of Conscientiousness on Affect	a) CON→PA	0. 16	. 010	Supported
	b) CON→NA	− 0. 06	. 388	Not supported
H5: Impact of Openness on Affect	a) OPE→PA	0. 13	. 008	Supported
	b) OPE→NA	− 0. 20	. 002	Supported
H6: Impact of Positive Affect on Satisfaction	PA →SAT	0. 72	. 001	Supported
H7: Impact of Negative Affect on Satisfaction	NA →SAT	− 0. 14	. 004	Supported

To sum up, it was found that Hypotheses 1a, 2b, 3a, 3b, 4a, 5a, 5b, 6, and 7 are supported, and that Hypotheses 1b, 2a, 4b are not supported at all (Table 6. 19). Although three hypotheses were rejected, most of the hypotheses developed on the basis of the literature review, coupled with the findings of the foregoing qualitative research (focus group interviews), were supported in the quantitative study. Consequently, the final structural model has been further validated.

Chapter Synopsis

This chapter focused on the quantitative investigation phase of this research. It provided detailed information about the data analysis procedures. Surveys were conducted among Chinese outbound tourists to Australia departing from Jiangsu Province. In the surveys, respondents' personality traits, their individual positive or negative affect triggered by their travel experiences, and their overall satisfaction with Australia as a tourist destination were quantitatively assessed. The data analysis process commenced with data screening to ensure the underlying assumptions pertaining to normality, and outliers were met. Bootstrapping was employed to deal with the multivariate non-normal issues. Based on the survey data, CFAs were then performed on the constructs and measurement models related to Five-Factor personality traits, positive and negative affect, and satisfaction. Based on the responses from the sample, a 16-item Chinese-language BFI was identified from the full 44-item inventory. Four positive affects (i.e. *happy*, *excited*, *interested*, and *impressed*), four negative affects (i.e. *nervous*, *worried*, *afraid*, and *homesick*), and a 3-item satisfaction construct were reported to generate a measurement model with a satisfactory fit with the data. Then two individual measurement models were integrated into the overall measurement model for testing. The results confirmed the construct reliability and validity.

After the overall measurement model was determined to be satisfactory, the structural models proposing the relationships among eight latent variables were tested. This chapter presented the quantitative findings. The hypothesised path relationships, as outlined in Chapter 3, were mostly corroborated by the structural model. The quantitative findings also suggested that the positive affective responses triggered by tourists' travel experiences played a complete mediating role between four factors of FFM personality traits (i.e. extraversion, agreeableness, conscientiousness, and openness) and overall tourist satisfaction. As is the case with positive affect, negative affect fully mediated three personality factors (i.e. agreeableness, neuroticism, and openness) and satisfaction. The implications of these results from the quantitative research, together with the findings of the qualitative research (focus group interviews), are further discussed in the following chapter.

7

Psychological Analysis of Tourist Satisfaction

The previous chapter empirically investigated the theoretical model incorporating relationships among personality traits, affective responses (both positive and negative), and tourist satisfaction in the context of mainland Chinese group tourists visiting Australia. The structural model underpinning the research was confirmed with regards to the relationships among eight research variables. A new relationship was also identified, mediating the effect of affective responses on the relationship between tourist personality and tourist satisfaction. Based on these quantitative findings, a detailed discussion combining both the focus group interview findings and questionnaire survey results are presented in this chapter. These results are discussed in relation to both the research objectives and hypotheses to identify to what extent they have been achieved. This chapter commences with an overview of the study and a review of key findings. It discusses the research constructs of personality traits and affective responses independently, followed by the interpretations of structural relationships among tourist personality, positive or negative affective responses, and tourist satisfaction.

Tourist Satisfaction

Research Overview and Review of Findings

Most research on tourist behaviour involves travel motivation, travel experience, tourist satisfaction, and destination loyalty, and investigating the impact of situational variables on tourist behaviour. In the past decade, a number of previous studies have focused on how situational factors influence tourist behaviour, including atmospherics, physical surroundings, social surroundings, temporal perspective, and transient conditions or temporary affective responses (e. g. Farber & Hall 2007; Yüksel & Yüksel 2007; Lee et al. 2008; Prayag, Hosany & Odeh 2013; Tan & Tang 2013; Lee 2014; Prayag et al. 2015). Recently, growing recognition of limitations in utilising personality and affect to explain variations in tourist behaviour (e. g. Cohen & Cohen 2012; Pearce 2012; Pearce & Packer 2013) has prompted appeals to examine the influences of individual psychological characteristics on tourist satisfaction, such as tourist personality and affective responses (e. g. Gountas & Gountas 2007; Faullant et al. 2011). There is a need for both researchers and industry practitioners to provide fresh insights into the role of tourist personality, as a relatively consistent and enduring response to one's environment, in determining tourists' affective responses as influenced by situational destination factors and tourists' overall satisfaction.

Although it has been acknowledged that personality orientations and affective experiences are important variables in tourist behaviour research (e. g. Mueller & Peters 2008; Coghlan & Pearce 2010; Tung & Ritchie 2011; Brunner-Sperdin, Peters & Strobl 2012; Hosany 2012; Ong & Musa 2012; Hosany & Prayag 2013), the literature has not presented a clear picture on the psychological (personality traits and affective responses) processes that may help account for tourist behaviour. The roles of specific affective responses in experiential consumption and the role of individual differences in shaping those travel-related affective responses have not been adequately investigated or tested empirically. Satisfaction increasing through tourist destination interactions can be viewed from a psychophysical perspective where a quantitative relationship between tourists' personality characteristics and tourists' affective responses can be established (Chhetri, Arrowsmith & Jackson 2004). With few exceptions (Gountas & Gountas 2007; Faullant et al. 2011), research into the joint impact of personality traits and affective responses on tourist satisfaction remains underexplored in the tourism research.

To address such a gap, the current research linked enduring personality traits with situational affective responses to examine their joint impacts on tourists' overall satisfaction formation in the context of mainland Chinese package tourists to Australia. It aimed to develop and empirically test a structural model explaining the impact of tourist personality and experience-elicited affective responses on the formation of tourists' overall satisfaction by integrating personality traits as measured by the Big Five Inventory (John, Donahue & Kentle 1991) and affective responses characterised as either positive or negative. This study adopted a sequential mixed-methods approach consisting of both qualitative and quantitative research stages. The step-by-step procedures in data analysis and results reporting reflect the methodological rigor in the study.

In the qualitative exploration phase, four sessions of focus group interviews were performed to collect data and then the interview data were thematically analysed to identify the structure of 14 salient affective responses (seven positive items: *happy*, *relaxed*, *interested*, *excited*, *impressed*, *friendly*, and *comfortable*; and seven negative items: *nervous*, *worried*, *homesick*, *afraid*, *embarrassed*, *lonely*, and *bored*), thus guiding the development of the questionnaire design for the second stage. In the quantitative investigation phase, a theoretical model incorporating psychological constructs of tourist personality, affective responses, and tourist satisfaction was tested with a valid sample of 493 Chinese package tourists to Australia. The structural model substantiated four salient positive affective responses (*happy*, *excited*, *interested*, and *impressed*) and four salient negative affective responses (*nervous*, *afraid*, *worried*, and *homesick*).

More importantly, the SEM analysis offered support for the interrelationships among the research constructs included in the proposed structural model. The structural relations can be described as follows: (1) Extraversion had a significant positive effect on positive affect, but its effect on negative affect was insignificant; (2) Agreeableness had a significant positive effect on positive affect and a significant negative effect on negative affect; (3) Conscientiousness had a significant positive effect on positive affect, but its effect on negative affect was insignificant; (4) Although neuroticism did not significantly affect positive affect, it did have a strong positive effect on negative affect; (5) Openness had a significant positive effect on positive affect and a significant negative effect on negative affect; (6) Positive affect had a strong positive effect on tourist satisfaction; (7) Negative affect had a significant negative effect on tourist satisfaction. These interesting findings have triggered an in-depth analysis of the proposed relationships among eight research variables. Further examination of prior studies and interpretation of the current study are needed to explain why extraversion and conscientiousness only affected positive affect, but not negative affect; why agreeableness and openness affected both positive affect and negative affect; and why neuroticism only affected negative affect, but not positive affect.

In addition, SEM analysis also substantiated the full mediation role positive affect played between four personality factors (extraversion, agreeableness, conscientiousness, and openness) and overall satisfaction, as well as the full mediation role negative affect played between three personality factors (agreeableness, neuroticism, and openness) and overall satisfaction. In other words, the mediating role of affective responses in the structural model was mainly embodied in the indirect effect of personality traits on tourist satisfaction through affective response. Overall, the findings confirmed that tourist satisfaction was influenced by tourist personality and experience-elicited affective responses, consistent with the personality-affect-satisfaction scheme suggested by the literature review. More importantly, the fact that mediated by affective responses, tourist personality can predict tourist satisfaction supports the notion that personality is an important determinant of individual behaviour during a holiday. This study highlights the need for researchers to incorporate tourist personality and affective responses as components of the integrative model of tourist satisfaction. To reiterate, the following sections address the five research objectives respectively.

Personality Traits

The first research objective was to identify the underlying structure of the FFM as applied to Chinese respondents in the context of outbound travel to Australia. In this study, tourists' personality traits were assessed using John et al. 's (1991) Big Five Inventory (BFI). However, the widely-used 44-item BFI proved to be too lengthy for many research purposes. The need for brief but efficient measures of the Big Five factors continues to grow due to many constraints within the survey context. Many researchers have sought to develop an abbreviated form of the Five Factor personality scales. In addition, the increasing acceptance of the Big Five as a model for delineating the structure of core personality traits has called for the need to assess the Big Five personality dimensions in both cross-cultural and cross-disciplinary settings (e. g. Rammstedt 2007; Denissen et al. 2008). The most common personality assessment instruments used in Asian countries are based on English-language paper-and-pencil questionnaires (Cheung 2004). The cross-cultural equivalence of personality assessment has to be demonstrated in order to test the universal generalisability of personality dimensions (Van de Vijver & Poortinga 1997).

This study achieved the first research objective by identifying and developing a short Chinese 16-item Big Five Inventory (BFI-SC), an abbreviated version of the well-established 44-item Big Five Inventory. While maintaining the validity and reliability of the BFI, the BFI-SC helps reduce respondents' confusion, especially confusion caused by reverse-worded items, and eliminate items irrelevant to the essential core of the construct as applied in the international tourism context. The BFI-SC can contribute to quick, but reliable estimations of the Big Five personality constructs as applied to Chinese respondents in the context of outbound travel to Australia. In previous studies, an ultra-short 10-item personality inventory (TIPI) has been developed and tested as a scale of the Big Five personality domains (e. g. Gosling et al. 2003; Romero et al. 2012), based on such popular instruments as the 44-item BFI and the 60-item NEO Personality Inventory (NEO-FFI, Costa & McCrae 1992). Rammstedt and John (2007) abbreviated the 44-item BFI to a 10-item version (BFI-10) in both English and German for cross-cultural research. However, extremely brief scales of Big Five factors with two or only one item each may not be suitable for each latent variable in factor analysis and SEM. The minimum three items for each dimension can identify the five-factor structure of personality traits (Gagne & Hancock 2006). In alignment with this fundamental requirement, a short 15-item German adoption of the BFI Version (BFI-S) was confirmed as a suitable scale for large-scale multidisciplinary surveys, and this brief measure has been adopted in international ongoing longitudinal panel studies in Great Britain, Australia, and Germany (Lang et al. 2011).

The current study evaluated the factor structure and reliability of the Chinese version of the 44-item BFI (BFI-C) and reduced it to a 16-item measure of the Big Five dimensions with the satisfactory psychometric properties, which proved to be applicable to the sample of Chinese group tourists to Australia. Previously, Leung et al. (2013) modified the Chinese version of the 44-item BFI and confirmed the Chinese translation of the abbreviated 29-item BFI as a useful and practical tool for measuring personality traits among Chinese adults who had a smoking habit. Short instruments could "eliminate item redundancy and therefore reduce the fatigue, frustration, and boredom associated with answering highly similar questions repeatedly" (Robins et al. 2001, p. 152). Therefore, the 16-item BFI-SC would reduce respondents' burden while maintaining reliability and improving validity. It is understood that long-haul tourists would not expect to be disturbed by a lengthy and annoying questionnaire. As illustrated in Table 7.1, a detailed item comparison of three short forms of the BFI has been provided to demonstrate that the brevity of the 16-item BFI-SC will be more appealing to researchers who are concerned about expending the time and energy of their Chinese participants. It will also contribute to the current personality literature on the BFI across different cultures.

In recognition of the uniqueness of different cultures, it is of great significance to explore the common characteristics of personality across cultures (Triandis & Suh 2002; Wang, Cui & Zhou 2005). Ten items in bold font of the 16-item BFI-SC in Table 7.1 overlap with their counterparts in the 15-item German adoption of the BFI Version (BFI-S, Lang et al. 2011) and Big Five Inventory-10 (BFI-10). Only two negatively-worded items were retained in the final short form of the 16-item BFI-SC, which corresponds to many researchers' conclusions that participants might have interpreted the positively and negatively worded items differently in the BFI-44. Inclusion of both item types may reduce response bias but it also introduces systematic bias in the form of undesirable components and complicates the factor structure (Horan, DiStefano & Motl 2003).

Table 7.1 A Summary of Three Short Forms of the Abbreviated BFI

	16-Item	15-Item	10-Item
Extraversion	**is talkative**	**is talkative**	
	is outgoing, sociable	**is outgoing, sociable**	**is outgoing, sociable**
	generates a lot of enthusiasm	*is reserved (R)*	*is reserved (R)*
Agreeableness	**has a forgiving nature**	**has a forgiving nature**	
	is considerate and kind to almost everyone	**is considerate and kind to almost everyone**	
	is helpful and unselfish with others	is sometimes rude to others (R)	is generally trusting
			tends to find fault with others (R)

Continued

	16-Item	15-Item	10-Item
Conscientiousness	does a thorough job	does a thorough job	does a thorough job
	tends to be lazy（R）	tends to be lazy（R）	tends to be lazy（R）
	does things efficiently	does things efficiently	
	perseveres until the task is finished		
Neuroticism	worries a lot	worries a lot	
	gets nervous easily	gets nervous easily	gets nervous easily
	is depressed, blue	remains calm in tense situations（R）	is relaxed, handles stress well（R）
Openness	value artistic, aesthetic experiences	value artistic, aesthetic experiences	
	has few artistic interests（R）	is original, comes up with new ideas	has few artistic interests（R）
	is sophisticated in art, music, or literature	has an active imagination	has an active imagination

A personality scale developed in a specific context may not be applicable to another context with similar reliability and validity (Denissen et al. 2008). Consequently, the BFI which originated in the west may not be directly applicable to the Chinese setting. Cronbach's alpha coefficients for the constructs of extraversion (0.80), agreeableness (0.73), and conscientiousness (0.74) in this study are relatively consistent with previously reported Cronbach's alpha coefficients (e. g. John & Srivastava 1999; Elanain 2007; Stanway 2010; Leung et al. 2013). However, the neuroticism construct reliability (0.66) in this study is lower than the counterpart (0.81) in a Chinese sample of smokers receiving cessation treatment (Leung et al. 2013) and the counterpart (0.82) in an Australian sample of full-time dancers in training (Stanway 2010). Neuroticism items refer to being low in spirits (*is depressed, blue*), being anxious (*worries a lot*), and a kind of mental state (*gets nervous easily*). In general, these dispositional features should be less associated with the sample who are willing to challenge themselves by taking a long-haul outbound travel to a non-Asian tourist destination. According to Plog's (1974) travel personality framework, allocentric tourists who are intellectually curious and eager to explore the world prefer exotic destinations. Therefore, it can be reasonably inferred that the sample may show a tendency to be less neurotic.

Also, the composite reliability for openness (0.89) in this study was higher than the counterparts (0.77) in two other studies (Stanway 2010; Leung et al. 2013). The openness items refer to being art-loving (*values artistic, aesthetic experiences*), open to arts [*has few artistic interests (R)*], and cultural appreciation (*is sophisticated in arts/literature*). It can be interpreted from two perspectives. On one hand, it may be attributed to the sample characteristics. Respondents' demographic profile revealed that a university degree or above was held by 59% of the respondents, and another 24.7% had a college diploma. Sound educational background of the sample has cultivated their appreciation and enjoyment of aesthetic experiences in international tourism. Beyond the five needs of the well-established hierarchical needs model, Maslow (1970) did address two other important sets of human needs, i. e. the aesthetic need, and the need to know and understand. Australia enjoys great popularity among Chinese travellers not only for its natural beauty, spectacular coastal scenery, but also for its unique multicultural atmosphere as the salient "pull" factors of travel motivations for a tourist destination (e. g. Yu & Weiler 2001; Huang & Gross 2010). The sample in an international tourism context chose to take a vacation in Australia to satisfy their aesthetic and intellectual needs, thus indicating the conceptual consistency of openness.

On the other hand, openness is the most controversial dimension from a cross-cultural perspective (Cheung et al. 2008). From lexical studies of openness, the predominant features are imagination, creativity or unconventionality (McCrae & Costa 2004). However, when these measurement items were deleted from the scale until only the three items were finally kept, the reliability coefficient of openness rose from 0. 78 to 0. 89, indicating that not all facets of openness might be equally important in every culture. For instance, the need for variety in activities has been proved not to be a central part of openness in Chinese culture (McCrae & Costa 2003). Even though the five factors are observed in both Western and Eastern cultures, "major differences have been recognised in their relative importance and social desirability" (Schultz & Schultz 2009, p. 283). There are both universal and culture-specific aspects of variation in personality (Triandis & Suh 2002). For example, Eastern societies are likely to be more introverted than Western societies. Chinese college students living in Hong Kong are likely to be more introverted than those Chinese students living in Canada (Schultz & Schultz 2009). Japanese respondents exhibit higher level of neuroticism, and lower conscientiousness and extraversion levels than US respondents (Matsumoto 2006). Consequently, although a large body of literature suggests that the Big Five personality factors emerge in various cultures, caution is required in arguing for such universality, for most studies have not included culture-specific traits.

Affective Responses

The second research objective was to identify and document Chinese package tourists' salient positive and negative affective responses during their trip to Australia. Numerous studies have operationalised affect/emotion as high-level positive or negative dimensions, and investigated the impact of affective responses on tourist behaviour, such as travel motivation, tourist satisfaction, and behavioural intentions (e. g. McGoldrick & Pieros 1998; Zeelenberg & Pieters 2004; Martínez Caro & Martínez García 2007; Ladhari, Brun & Morales 2008; Jang et al. 2009; Grappi & Montanari 2011).

Based on the empirical evidence from the focus group discussions and a comprehensive review of tourism literature, the final structure of 14 salient affective responses was developed in Chapter 4 for the subsequent quantitative investigation of the structural relationships. These include seven positive affective responses (*happy*, *relaxed*, *interested*, *excited*, *impressed*, *friendly*, and *comfortable*) and seven negative affective responses (*nervous*, *worried*, *afraid*, *homesick*, *embarrassed*, *lonely*, and *bored*). When the sample size was amplified in the quantitative phase, those affective responses with standardised regression weights less than 0. 50 could not be counted as the most salient ones because of insufficient variance explained by their related latent variable (Hair et al. 2010). Consequently, the SEM analysis results confirmed empirically that Chinese outbound tourists mainly possess four positive affective response (*happy*, *interested*, *excited*, and *impressed*) and four negative ones (*nervous*, *worried*, *afraid*, and *homesick*), and that these basic affective responses are important to tourists' experiences and to their resulting satisfaction.

These findings conform to previous studies on affective responses in the domains of psychology, marketing, and tourism. During the same stay individuals may experience positive and negative affect because they have multiple interactions with the resources of the destination. By exploring the affective responses prompted by a wide range of consumption situations, Derbaix and Pham (1991) reported that respondents possess more positive than negative affective responses, and that negative experiences are thought to be more salient, are perceived with greater intensity, and are expressed with greater variety. However, in the context of Chinese package tourists to Australia, the current study revealed that respondents are generally high in hedonic level of affect, with positive affect exceeding negative affect, and that respondents hold a high level of overall satisfaction with Australia as a tourist destination. These findings are consistent with previous research, suggesting that travellers are unlikely to feel strong negative affect simultaneously when they experience positive affect during the vacation (e. g. Nawijn 2011a; Tung & Ritchie 2011). Tourists are inclined to mitigate negative occurrences in their retrospective assessments of travel experiences and magnify positive experiences (Lee & Kyle 2013). The balance of positive to negative affect has been perceived as particularly important in recent positive psychology studies (Pearce 2009). Some experimental research on group behaviour indicates that a ratio of more than three positive affects for every one negative emotion is required for individuals to feel good (Fredrickson & Losada 2005). These findings call for in-depth explorations of more dimensions of affective responses to international travel engagements, which may be generalised to tourism more broadly.

Positive Affective Responses

Reviewing in retrospect the holistic affective responses of the trip to Australia, most participants tended to hold a positive affect toward Australia as a tourist destination. It is consistent with the fact that vacation is characterised as a set of positive experiential processes (Mannell & Iso-Ahola 1987; Nawijn 2011b), primarily consumed for hedonic purposes (Otto & Ritchie 1996). Tourists seek pleasurable and memorable experiences through the consumption of their vacation (Hosany 2012). The structural model demonstrated that four affective responses were engendered through the international tourism experience, i. e. *happy* (Mean = 5. 96, standardised factor loading or $\lambda = 0.756$), *interested* (Mean = 5.48, $\lambda = 0.734$), *excited* (Mean =5. 37, $\lambda = 0.701$), and *impressed* (Mean = 5. 63, $\lambda = 0.669$). These results are partly consistent with Richins' (1997) CES in product consumption contexts, where a set of positive emotions such as *joy*, *pride*, and *contentment* was most strongly expressed.

The findings replicated the results of previous studies that have investigated emotions elicited in other tourism product consumption situations (Bigné, Andreu & Gnoth 2005; Lee & Kyle 2013). Tourists are motivated to travel in anticipation of experiencing positive emotions during their vacation (Sirgy 2010; Nawijn 2011a). As indicated by participants in the focus group interviews, tourists felt excited, interested, happy, and impressed while making some individual connections with kangaroos and koalas in Australia, which was consistent with previous findings that memorable wildlife encounters which involved being close to animals generated feelings of intimacy and excitement (Chapman 2003; Myers, Saunders & Birjulin 2004).

The positive affect of *happy* is the most salient among respondents followed by *excited*, *interested*, and *impressed*. Adopting a rigorous scale development procedure, EFA and CFA, Hosany and Gilbert (2010) developed the Destination Emotion Scale (DES2) involving three salient dimensions, namely, *joy*, *love*, and *positive surprise*, demonstrating that *joy/happiness* is a key element of tourists' affective experiences. The three dimensions of the DES2 are measured by their corresponding scale items respectively, namely, *joy* (cheerful, pleasure, joy, enthusiasm, delight, enjoyment, happiness, entertained, and comfortable), *love* (tenderness, love, caring, affection, warm-hearted, sentimental, romantic, compassionate, and passionate), and *positive surprise* (amazement, astonishment, fascinated, inspired, and surprise).

Apparently, the four salient positive affective responses (*happy*, *interested*, *excited*, and *impressed*) identified in this study can not be fully accounted for with the DES2. Due to the differences in the specific cultural context, DES2 is unable to cover Chinese package tourists' salient affective responses to their travel experiences in Australia. Thus, the current study further enriches the structure of visitors' positive affective responses to tourist destinations in the international tourism setting. Most importantly, tourists' emotional responses in the DES2 were measured only in terms of a holistic evaluation, while in the qualitative phase of this study, tourists' emotional responses at various episodes or encounters during the vacation were investigated to understand how in turn aggregate emotional responses shape overall affective responses. This process echoes Dubé and Morgan's (1998) proposition that emotions evolve over the course of a transaction and as a result influence retrospective global judgments of affective responses. Thus, based on the comparisons with the DES2, further analysis and examination of the four items for positive affective responses is warranted.

Generally speaking, these four positive affective responses can be traced as the measurement scales for positive affect from previous studies in psychology and marketing (Donovan et al. 1994; Richins 1997). The pursuit of pleasurable experiences is a key motivational factor in tourism (e. g. Currie 1997; Goossens 2000). Carr (2002) notes tourists have a higher propensity for pleasure-seeking experiences while on holidays. A coherent body of previous studies in tourism employed *happy* and *excited* to measure the construct of positive affect (e. g. Zeelenberg & Pieters 2004; Ladhari, Brun & Morales 2008; Grappi & Montanari 2011). Graburn (2001) and Filep and Deery (2010) theorised that *joy/happiness* and *interest* are important during leisure travel. Two affective responses (i. e. *excited* and *interested*) are consistent with PANAS as the items for positive affect (Wirtz, Mattila & Tan 2000). *Interested*, theorised to be the most frequent emotion (Izard 1997), facilitates the pursuit of novel information and experiences (Fredrickson 1998, 2001). *Impressed* was adopted as one item for positive affect in carrying out an exploration of the cognitive and affective psychological process of tourist satisfaction (Del Bosque & San Martín 2008). It is noteworthy that different from *happy*, *excited*, and *interested*, the item *impressed* possesses the attribute of capturing more of the environment's impact on the person. This finding best conforms to the widespread recognition of the separate and interactive effects of traits and situations on behaviour (Faullant et al. 2011).

This study also found that the development of overall positive affect during leisure travel will lead to tourist satisfaction, and that positive affective responses are the most significant indicators of overall satisfaction assessment. Kahneman (1999) argues that overall well-being and objective happiness can be measured by tracking and later cumulating positive affect. The role of positive affect has been highlighted to serve human happiness and well-being (Pearce 2009). Leisure travel experiences are a source of positive affect in people's lives (Nawijn 2011b), while positive affect/emotions can result in valuable life outcomes (Mitas et al. 2012). Thus, this research provides empirical support for the emerging literature in tourism on the relationships between tourism and quality of life and subjective well-being (e. g. Nawijn

2011a; McCabe & Johnson 2013; Nawijn et al. 2013).

Negative Affective Responses

A small proportion of respondents reported negative affective responses during their travel to Australia. It is worth noting that the DES2 only captures positive valence emotions without negative occurrences in tourists' retrospective evaluations of the destination. Therefore, the current study extends the structure of visitors' affective responses to tourist destinations by supplementing the dimension of negative affect. The study findings documented four salient negative affective responses during the Chinese package tourists' visit to Australia, i. e. *nervous* (Mean = 2.91, λ = 0.894), *worried* (Mean = 3.19, λ = 0.779), *afraid* (Mean = 2.20, λ = 0.679), and *homesick* (Mean = 3.66, λ = 0.500). The negative affect of *nervous* was the most salient among respondents followed by *worried*, *afraid*, and *homesick*. *Nervous*, *worried*, and *afraid* are three basic negative affects in the literature of psychology, marketing, and even in tourism. This finding is in line with previous studies (e. g. Richins 1997; Zins 2002; Jang et al. 2009; Nawijn 2011b; Tung & Ritchie 2011), which further validates the structure of negative affect experienced in tourism. These three negative affect echoed an over-50-year-old female participant's retrospective thoughts of her trip in Australia: "This is my first time to travel to an English-speaking country. I have been on the alert because I think there is nothing worse than feeling helpless in a foreign country and not knowing what I can do to sort myself out".

In both consumer and tourist behaviour literature, *homesick* has been labelled as a negative affective response (e. g. Havlena & Holbrook 1986; Laros & Steenkamp 2005; Yüksel 2007; Hosany 2012). It can be noted that the standardised factor loading of *homesick* just meets the threshold value 0.50 to be recognised as one of salient negative affective responses in the current study. The finding of *homesick* in a tourism setting is initially interview-based, not literature-based. This may be attributed to the fact that the sample were consuming a long-haul non-Asian travel product for the first time. For example, some FGD participants claimed that they preferred Chinese food to Western-style food, and that they would become homesick if they had not had Chinese food for several days. Industry practitioners could take practical aspects like this into account, when trying to accommodate Chinese tourists. Another plausible explanation for homesickness is related to the nature of the tourists' long-haul international tourism experiences. As indicated by many informants, they felt very tired after eight days of touring around Australia and longed for the comfort of their own home.

Effect of Personality Traits on Affective Responses

The Big-Five framework has long been established; however, the focus of personality research has now "shifted from psychometric and structural properties of the Big Five to relations between the Big-Five dimensions and other constructs and outcomes" (Gosling, Rentfrow & Swann 2003, p. 524). In this study, personality traits as enduring individual differences are included to explain and clarify differences across tourists in the travel experience-related affective responses. In other words, the extent to which tourists experience joy or fear thus not only depends upon situational stimuli, but is also determined by tourists' personality predisposition. Thus, the third research objective was addressed to examine how each dimension of the FFM contributes to the formation of tourists' positive and negative affective responses.

According to the field theory approach, behaviour is a function of the interconnection between personal and situational factors (Beaty, Cleveland & Murphy 2001). It is well established that people elicit affective responses from their immediate environment (Machleit & Eroglu 2000). In most circumstances, a change in the affective responses of an individual may be considered as a change caused by a stimulus that usually comes from the physical or social environment and human itself (Jang et al. 2009). As explained in Chapter 2, the expression of personality can be constrained by certain cues conceptualised as "strong" and "weak" situations; the setting of a vacation tour in this study has been justified as a weak situation. The behaviour of vacation travellers is usually driven by their innate personality orientations rather than by any desired correct responses or normative expectations of behaviour. Therefore, in a weak situation, it is not the specific physical circumstances that mainly generate affective responses, but rather the unique psychological appraisal determined by individual differences in evaluating and interpreting the circumstances (Bagozzi, Gopinath & Nyer 1999).

Specifically, Yik and Russel (2001) argued that the understanding of the nature of affect is conceptually to depend on the degree to which it is more personality-dependent. For example, one type of travel experience or the same tourism product may engender different types of affective responses from different people. Conversely, different types of travel experiences may lead to the same affective response from different people. Two individuals may have different affective responses to the same event (Siemer, Mauss & Gross 2007). Obviously, personality characteristics play an important role in determining the formation of experience-elicited affective responses. As stated in Chapter 3, all the respondents in this study shared the homogeneous background of participating in the same 8-day package tour to Australia for the first time, departing from Jiangsu Province, China. Consequently, the personality variable in the current study was perceived as the main determinant of affective responses, and all other background factors (e. g. situational factors, context-related, cultural and social-economic factors) were either controlled for or randomised across the experimental conditions.

Due to the discrepancy in tourist personality, even the same travel experiences in Australia may engender different affective outcomes among different tourists. For instance, witnessing fewer people everywhere in Australia (slow-paced people) and the harmony between people and birds in public squares, some participants felt relaxed, while others felt sluggish or lonely. The discrepancies in tourist personality may account for this striking contrast. Most notably, the results of the present study have provided additional evidence supporting the stability and robustness of the relationships between personality traits and affective responses in the international tourism settings.

Effect of Extraversion &Neuroticism on Affective Responses

Extraversion and Positive Affect

Extraversion and neuroticism have long been argued in psychology, and later in marketing and tourism, as two traits defined as predispositions towards affective experiences (e. g. Eysenck 1992; Mooradian & Olver 1997; Miller, Vachon & Lynam 2009; Faullant et al. 2011). The result of the present study demonstrates the positive impact of extraversion on positive affect, and the magnitude of this relationship ($\beta = 0.21$) agrees with previous studies by Costa and McCrae (1980) ($\beta = 0.16 - 0.27$) and Izard et al. (1993) ($\beta = 0.21 - 0.35$). This finding clearly shows that being highly extraverted has a significant positive impact on the positive affective responses of the outbound Chinese tourists to their travel experience in Australia, suggesting that extraverts are particularly susceptible to positive affect with their package holiday experiences. In psychology, this finding replicates Penley and Tomaka's (2002) result that extraversion is positively associated with positive affects such as happiness, pride, and self-satisfaction, thus supporting that individuals high in extraversion are prone to experiencing positive affect. In tourism, this finding is also consistent with Faullant and his colleagues' (2011) finding that more extraverted tourists respond to intense travel experiences with higher levels of positive affective responses (joy) in experiential tourism activities such as mountaineering.

Extraverts are characterised by being energetic, enthusiastic, and excitement-seeking by nature, and they are bold and venture into the unknown with confidence (John & Srivastava 1999). These common attributes may generate and enhance their positive emotions in tourism activities. In addition, being outgoing, talkative, warm-hearted, and sociable, they show a keen interest in external events and other people and enjoy the company of others (Rose et al. 2010). Being gregarious, individuals who are high in extraversion enjoy socialising with people around them and prefer highly social activities such as parties. In line with the literature on interpersonal relationships, the consumers' need for social affiliation has been established as a preference to be with other people and to engage in relationships (Bloemer et al. 2003). Accordingly, people travel not just to undertake recreational activities but to seek socialising benefits (Yüksel 2007). Extraverts with positive attitudes enjoy interactions with people, thus contributing to positive affect experienced at the tourist destination.

Extraversion and Negative Affect

Inconsistent with what was suggested in the literature, such as Wilson and Gullone's (1999) study wherein extraversion and negative affect exhibited a weak, inverse correlation ($\beta = -0.12$) in adults, the finding did not support the negative impact of extraversion on negative affect experienced at a destination. Extraversion was found to be negatively correlated with perceived stress, fear, and self-disgust (Penley & Tomaka 2002). In examining correlations and causes of happiness and depression among adolescents, Cheng and Furnham (2003) also found that extraversion was significantly correlated with negative affect ($\beta = -0.22$). However, the current study suggests that being extravert does not seem to mitigate negative affect in the context of international group package tour. While this is potentially important finding in relation to the extraversion-NA relationship, the findings need to be interpreted in terms of the contextual specificities and trait attributes with caution.

Evidence has been found that extraverts' social interactions partially mediated the relationship between extraversion and positive affect (Srivastava, Angelo & Vallereux 2008). This argument supports the field theory approach in which personality traits like extraversion are seen as styles of actively interacting with the environment. Although the holiday tour to Australia has been justified as a weak situation, and tour attributes have been maximally controlled for experimental conditions to highlight the dominance of structural models of personality in capturing average levels of affective responses, the dynamic processes that occur between the individual and the environment cannot be neglected (Ormel, Rosmalen & Farmer 2004). Extraverts tend to engage in more social activities (Yüksel 2007), and tourism generally provides an avenue for extraverts to be involved in social participation. However, it was reported in Chapter 4 that participants from focus group interviews experienced negative affect (e. g. *embarrassed*, *lonely*, *bored*, and *homesick*) mainly due to their needs for social affiliation failing to be met because of language barriers and differences in culture and lifestyle, coupled with the constraints by the group package tour, such as less flexibility and dominance of their travel itineraries and activities. In the group package tour, each tourist has to follow the tour guide and the tour group, which may make some of them feel that they are following the herd, thus restricting communicating their conspicuous elements to other people in an effort to gain social recognition. More notably, being one of the group members is bound to prohibit them from venturing into the unknown according to their personal preferences. As a result, under such circumstances, being more or less extravert has nothing to do with negative affect at the destination.

Neuroticism and Positive Affect

In contrast to the inverse but significant correlation ($\beta = -0.30$) between neuroticism and positive affect in adults in Wilson and Gullone's (1999) study on the relationship between personality and affect over the human lifespan, the result of this study did not support the negative impact of neuroticism on positive affect experienced at a destination. Cheng and Furnham (2003) also revealed that neuroticism was significantly correlated with positive affect ($\beta = -0.24$) among adolescents. It is generally accepted that holidays are usually positively anticipated and primarily consumed for hedonic purposes (Mitchell et al. 1997). Thus, even individuals who have high neuroticism may experience pleasurable and memorable experiences through taking a holiday, thus contributing to their subjective wellbeing. Three plausible explanations relating to this finding are discussed.

First, neuroticism is associated with sensitivity to uncertainty and risk. As indicated by the prevention focus in the regulatory focus theory, neurotics individuals are concerned with security and safety (Crowe & Higgins 1997). They are more likely to be concerned about the risks relating to the tourism products they would consume (Huang, Gursoy & Xu 2014). Therefore, neurotic individuals may seek more information in order to reduce the uncertainty and risk associated with their pleasure travel (Roehl & Fesenmaier 1992). With an adequate amount of knowledge acquired, these individuals will be more familiar with tourism products and tourist destinations, thus reducing uncertainty and anxiety.

Second, given that tourists with high neuroticism may generate fluctuating affective responses ranging from negative to positive throughout their travel experiences, thus possibly leading to both negative and positive affective responses, the role of qualified tour guides has been emphasised. This finding corresponded with Weiler and Ham's (2010) proposition that tour guides' interpretation performance has been proven to potentially impact tourists' affective state (what they feel) in a wide range of tourism contexts. In the qualitative exploration phase, a number of participants reported that they were lucky to have excellent Chinese-speaking tour guides who were committed to their responsibilities, and which thus helped reduce their anxiety and worry in an exotic environment. A 58-year-old woman in the FGD said, "Our tour guide is smart, accommodating, informative, and reliable. We feel very happy and warm to have his company for the 8-day trip in Australia."

Third, according to the profiles of survey respondents, 76.5% travelled with their families or relatives. Lehto et al. (2009) empirically assessed family functioning during leisure travel, that is, the interplay of family vacation, family cohesion, and communication. Holidays may strengthen family bonds which in turn could increase satisfaction with family life (Farber & Hall 2007). Obviously, travelling with families and relatives may relieve neurotic individuals' anxiety and worry, thus contributing to their emotional well-being. Based on the above-mentioned three explanations, it can be concluded that under the influence of the contextual factors in tourism, being more neurotic does not seem to reduce positive affective responses

during or after their travel experiences. Thus, neuroticism does not seem to be related to positive affect at a destination.

Neuroticism and Negative Affect

The result of the present study demonstrated the positive impact of neuroticism on negative affect, and the magnitude of this relationship ($\beta = 0.65$) agreed with the counterparts in previous studies by Watson and Clark (1992) ($\beta = 0.52 - 0.65$) and Suh et al. (1996) ($\beta = 0.47 - 0.69$) in psychology. This finding clearly showed that neuroticism contributed to negative affective responses to package holiday experiences at a destination. The strong neuroticism-NA correlation is highly consistent with Faullant and his colleagues' (2011) finding that more neurotic tourists are more prone to experience negative affective responses (fear) in experiential tourism activities such as mountaineering. Prior research has revealed that neurotic individuals are susceptible to negative emotions (e. g. *anxiety, fear, guilt, self-disgust*, and *shame*) (Penley & Tomaka 2002), stress and burnout (Zimmerman et al. 2012), and low levels of job satisfaction and well-being (Ozer & Benet-Martinez 2006; Templer 2012). In general, individuals who are high in neuroticism are likely to be shy, worried, and pessimistic (Costa & McCrae 1992; Myers, Sen & Alexandrov 2010). Being insecure, these individuals are likely to have a higher anxiety level and be more sensitive to risks associated with their decisions (Tanford, Raab & Kim 2013). Consumption of tourism products tends to involve more risks than consumptions of most tangible products due to their intangible, heterogeneous, inseparable and perishable nature (Huang, Gursoy & Xu 2014). International tourism products tend to be highly priced and consumed in exotic communities without any tangible returns (Gursoy, McCleary & Lepsito 2007). When travelling to a new destination, tourists face certain levels of uncertainty and risk. Neurotic individuals' anxiety levels thus directly affect their affective responses to travel experiences at a destination.

Effect of Agreeableness &Conscientiousness on Affective Responses

In contrast to the frequently-examined structures of extraversion-PA and neuroticism-NA, few studies have been conducted to investigate the effects of agreeableness, conscientiousness, and openness on affect(Yik & Russell 2001). However, the trait attributes of agreeableness and conscientiousness are assumed to create situations and life experiences that, in turn, lead to powerful affective responses (Watson, David & Clark 1992). A small number of researchers have investigated relationships between all five factors of the FFM and the general measures of self-rated affect and found that both agreeableness and conscientiousness correlate positively with positive affect and negatively with negative affect in psychology (e. g. McCrae & Costa 1991; Watson, David & Clark 1992). The present study partially replicated the previous findings and provided the new insights into personality-affect relationships in the tourism context.

Agreeableness and Positive/Negative Affect

The results of this study revealed that agreeableness experienced at a destination correlated positively with positive affect ($\beta = 0.49$) and negatively with negative affect ($\beta = -0.15$). These findings are consistent with the previous research by Panaccio and Vandenberghe (2012) in which, using a longitudinal approach, the researchers demonstrated that agreeableness predicted change in organisational commitments partly through the mediating influence of positive and negative affective states, and that agreeableness was positively related to positive affect ($\beta = 0.15$) and negatively related to negative affect ($\beta = -0.18$). These can be explained by the notion that agreeable individuals' tendency to experience positive affect and control negative affect in the interpersonal context help them achieve better social acceptance (Graziano et al. 2007). These findings are consistent with the theoretical conceptualisations of agreeableness as characterised by being friendly, good-natured, flexible, reconcilable, and supportive of others (McCrae & Costa 2003). Partly through these mechanisms, agreeable people are likely to be trusted by others, and they tend to experience pleasant interactions with others because of their sound interpersonal skills (Panaccio & Vandenberghe 2012). In addition, agreeableness has been shown to influence job performance most when collaboration and cooperation amongst workers become indispensable (Witt et al. 2002). Hence, individuals with a high level of agreeableness foster the types of interpersonal bonds and social success that in turn, result in greater quality of life and higher life satisfaction (Watson, David & Clark 1992). Admittedly, high levels of agreeableness are associated with increased positive affect and decreased negative affect.

By analysing the three measurement items for agreeableness in this study, i. e. "is helpful and unselfish with others", "has a forgiving nature", and "is considerate and kind to almost everyone", it is logical to believe that a group package tour provides a particular context for demonstrating helpfulness, collaboration, and good interpersonal relationships with the tour guide and other group members. Influenced by the Eastern collectivism, people in conflict situations are primarily concerned with maintaining relationships with others, so agreeable tourists tend to have a higher tolerance for contradictions to maintain interpersonal order and harmony within the travel group or between themselves and the environment (Ji, Peng & Nisbett 2000). Chinese tourists may display a tendency to perceive others in a more positive light, show respect for senior people, abide by group decisions, and be less likely to complain about their dissatisfaction (Tse 2015). Since individuals who are high in agreeableness tend to avoid conflict and are more forgiving and tolerant (Tan & Tang 2013), they are more likely to control negative affective responses in group situations. Thus, agreeable individuals' regulation of negative affect likely reduces the possibilities of experiencing negative affect, resulting in more positive affect and less negative affect.

Conscientiousness and Positive Affect

Conscientiousness was found to have a positive impact ($\beta = 0.16$) on positive affect experienced at a destination. It was consistent with Penley and Tomaka's (2002) study on the associations among the FFM, emotional responses, and coping with acute stress in which conscientiousness was found to be positively correlated with total positive affect, compassion, happiness, hope, and pride. This finding also replicated Watson and Clark's (1992) study in psychology, which demonstrated that conscientiousness had a significant, independent relation with general positive affect entirely due to the specific affect of *attentiveness*, and that among six facets of the conscientiousness trait (*order*, *dutifulness*, *competence*, *deliberation*, *self-discipline*, and *achievement-striving*), only *achievement-striving* correlated broadly with positive affect. Following the same reasoning, tourists with high conscientiousness evaluate whether their achievement goals have been attained at the end of their holiday. If their goals are congruent with the holistic destination experiences, positive affective responses are elicited. Conscientiousness is characterised as being self-disciplined, well-organised, responsible, thorough, and achievement-oriented (Costa & McCrae 1992; Rose et al. 2010). When people succeed in their achievement goals, they experience positive affects such as cheerfulness (Perugini & Bagozzi 2001). The achievement-related success that conscientiousness creates may contribute to greater quality of life and overall subjective well-being, and higher life satisfaction (Watson, David & Clark 1992). Similarly, recent studies have shown a relationship between tourism and life satisfaction/well-being in different contexts (McCabe & Johnson 2013). Consequently, individuals with high conscientiousness can elicit more positive experiences through tourism engagements.

Interestingly, previous research has established conscientiousness as a predictor of longevity (e. g. Friedman et al. 1995; Martin & Friedman 2000). One plausible explanation for the underlying mechanisms lies in that conscientious individuals' persistence and self-discipline might motivate them to stick to a healthy lifestyle, such as exercise regularly, and no smoking or excessive drinking. Another explanation can be built upon Besser and Shackelford's (2007) findings that conscientiousness affects longevity through its effects on stress management and coping strategies, and that conscientious individuals' strength in avoiding stress and enjoying life can contribute to positive physical and psychological well-being. In addition, a planned vacation can serve as a good opportunity for high conscientious individuals to refresh themselves and relax, away from work demands and routine life, thus resulting in more positive affect.

Conscientiousness and Negative Affect

Inconsistent with what was suggested in Penley and Tomaka's (2002) study wherein conscientiousness was demonstrated to be negatively correlated with perceived stress and fear, the finding did not support the negative impact of conscientiousness on negative affect experienced at a destination. Penley and Tomaka (2002) argued that individuals high in conscientiousness perceived themselves as able to meet situational demands in stress and coping processes, thus leading to more positive affect and less negative affect. This notion can be accounted for by two salient trait attributes of conscientiousness, i. e. self-disciplined and achievement-oriented. Being efficient and organised, conscientious individuals exhibit a tendency to be dependable, punctual, rule abiding, and act dutifully (Barrick, Mount & Judge 2001). They display planned rather than spontaneous behaviour, including such elements as carefulness, thoroughness, and deliberation; they tend to think carefully before acting (Thompson 2008).

Therefore, it is logical to believe that conscientious individuals tend to plan and prioritise activities, leading to extra time to accomplish tasks and less procrastination (Gellatly 1996; Kelly, Johnson & Miller 2003). Accordingly, individuals high in conscientiousness may plan a vacation well and use their vacation time efficiently, which generates less stress and increases positive affect. In a sense, conscientiousness is an additional dimension of personality specifically relevant to understanding subjective well-being. As explained with regard to the relationship between extraversion and negative affect, one disadvantage of participating in the group package tour is that tourists are constrained to follow the tour guide and the set travel itinerary. They are not allowed to plan their travel activities and control the time spent at each tourist attraction in terms of their own preferences. Endowed with the attributes of being organised, conscientious tourists themselves tend to be rule abiding and punctual in the group tour, but they can not dictate whether or not other group members could act effectively in accordance with group travel arrangements. Uncontrolled contextual factors such as these may engender tourists' negative affective responses. Hence, in the circumstances, being more or less conscientious does not seem to be associated with negative affect at a destination.

Effect of Openness on Affective Responses

The results of this study indicated that openness experienced at a destination correlated positively with positive affect ($\beta = 0.13$) and negatively with negative affect ($\beta = -0.20$). These findings are consistent with the partial results of previous research by Matzler et al. (2006) and Penley and Tomaka (2002) respectively. In exploring the relationships among openness, hedonic value, brand affect and loyalty, Matzler et al. (2006) demonstrated that in marketing, openness directly influence brand affect which in turn drives attitudinal and purchase loyalty. Brand affect was measured with three items indicating positive affect: "I feel good when I use this brand", "This brand makes me happy", and "This brand gives me pleasure". The results suggest that customers who score high on openness respond stronger to affective stimuli. The more open customers are, the more positive affect they will experience.

Conversely, in psychology, openness was found to be negatively related to perceived stress, fear and shame in linking associations among the FFM, emotional responses, and coping with acute stress (Penley & Tomaka 2002). In other words, the more open individuals are, the less negative affect they will experience.

Openness is associated with active imagination, aesthetic sensitivity, attentiveness to inner feelings, preference for variety, intellectual curiosity, and independence of judgment(McCrae & Costa 2003). By further examining the three items for measuring openness in the context of Chinese package tourists to Australia: "values artistic, aesthetic experiences", "has few artistic interests (R)", and "is sophisticated in art, music, or literature", openness was found to be conceptualised as being aesthetic, artistic, and intellectual among the sample. In a tourism setting, people travel to experience the beauty and gain new knowledge; therefore, both aesthetic and intellectual needs, serving concurrently as the two facets of openness, far outweigh other facets, such as imagination, creativeness, and novelty. Beyond the five needs of the well-established hierarchical needs model, Maslow et al. (1970) addressed another two important sets of human needs, i. e. aesthetic needs, and the need to know and understand. Thus, the shift of attention to the high-level spiritual needs can be perceived as another plausible explanation for high levels of openness being related to more positive affect and less negative affect, eventually contributing to subjective well-being.

Moreover, novelty seeking, as one of well-established travel motivations, can be closely related to the openness trait due to such common inherent attributes as being curious, insightful, and attentive to inner feelings (Rose et al. 2010). Based on the concept of an optimal stimulation level (McAlister & Pessemier 1982), when an environment on which people rely for living or working can only provide low stimulation, below the optimal level, the individual becomes bored and the desire for increased stimulation rises (Menon & Kahn 1995). These circumstances may motivate open individuals to explore internally and seek novelty. Individuals high in openness may travel to other destinations, seeking to increase stimulation from the new environment, through which positive affect is induced along with stimulation, thus reducing negative affect.

Further Discussion on Personality-Affect Relation

Prior studies have established prominent correlations of neuroticism-NA and extraversion-PA structures with robustness and stability in psychology, marketing, and tourism (e. g. Mooradian & Olver 1997; Rusting & Larsen 1997; McNiel & Fleeson 2006; Faullant et al. 2011). In response to the call for a shift in research emphasis from unidimensional personality traits to all the core and stable dimensions of the FFM (Pearce & Packer 2013; Cohen, Prayag & Moital 2014), the current study examined how each dimension of the FFM contributed to the formation of affective responses either positive or negative. The results of this study have provided additional evidence supporting the stability and robustness of the personality-affect relationships in the international tourism setting. The strong correlations between neuroticism and negative affect and extraversion and positive affect are consistent with the findings of most previous studies (e. g. Wilson & Gullone 1999; Srivastava, Angelo & Vallereux 2008; Miller, Vachon & Lynam 2009).

In the current study, neuroticism had the strongest positive association with negative affect ($\beta = 0.65$), followed by agreeableness' ($\beta = 0.49$) and extraversion's ($\beta = 0.21$) positive associations with positive affect. It is worth noting that the path coefficient from agreeableness to positive affect being much higher than that from extraversion to positive affect suggests that agreeableness is a better predictor than extraversion in generating tourists' positive affective responses in the tourism context. This result would be of interest to researchers because it is contrary to the previous studies in which a tendency to experience positive affect is one of the defining features of extraversion because of their robust correlations (Watson, David & Clark 1997; Srivastava, Angelo & Vallereux 2008). This inconsistency can be explained by the conspicuous attribute of extraversion in the research context of Chinese group tourists to Australia. To those extraverted/agreeable tourists in mass tourism, group dynamics had significant impacts on the affective responses elicited during the whole travel experience in Australia. The particular affective responses evoked varied depending on the nature of the interaction and the particular people involved. Therefore, it is of significance that future research would investigate which relationship is more pronounced between extraversion-PA and agreeableness-PA among free independent travellers who are less affected by group dynamics. Tourist personality has proved to be associated with affective responses, although people did not have expectations about which would be most prevalent or in what combinations they would be described (Farber & Hall 2007).

In short, these findings have revealed the reliable and significant links between personality and affect. This study has also established the capacity of enduring personality traits to explain cross-tourist differences in the experience of temporary basic affective responses, and the robust nature of those connections regardless of situational factors. However, the findings are questionable as to what the precise relation is between affect and any specific personality trait, and the extent of that relation (Yik & Russell 2001). Further empirical studies on affective responses across measures and methods as well as diverse cultures and contexts are warranted.

Effect of Affective Reponses on Tourist Satisfaction

Numerous studies have investigated the impact of affective responses on customer satisfaction. Studies in marketing (e. g. Mooradian & Olver 1997; Ladhari 2007; Walsh et al.

2011) and tourism (e. g. Bigné et al. 2005; Yüksel & Yüksel 2007) confirm a relationship between affect and satisfaction, indicating that affective responses are significant direct predictors influencing consumer or tourist satisfaction. Positive affects such as joy (Faullant et al. 2011), happiness, excitement, and pleasure (Grappi & Montanari 2011) have a favourable influence on satisfaction. Negative affects such as fear (Faullant et al. 2011), boredom, anger (Grappi & Montanari 2011), annoyance, frustration, disappointment, and irritation (Han & Jeong 2013) have a negative effect on satisfaction (Prayag, Hosany & Odeh 2013). Thus, in this section, the fourth research objective is addressed to test how positive and negative affective responses associated with specific and holistic experiences of a travel trip influence tourists' overall satisfaction with a destination. The results confirm empirically that experience-elicited affective responses are important to tourists' resulting satisfaction. While positive affective responses increase overall satisfaction with travel experiences at a destination, the opposite is true for negative affective responses.

A direct positive relationship between positive affect and tourist satisfaction was corroborated, which is consistent with previous studies in demonstrating that affective responses are powerful antecedents of tourist satisfaction (e. g. Del Bosque & San Martín 2008; Hosany & Prayag 2013; Prayag et al. 2015). The more happy, interested, excited, and impressed tourists felt, the higher their satisfaction levels. From an affective perspective, the cumulative effect of positive affective responses contributes to overall tourist satisfaction. Theoretically, this approach has somehow echoed the attribute satisfaction theory (Hsu 2003) which conceptualises tourist satisfaction from a cognitive perspective, that is, the cumulative effect of all attribute level satisfaction in turn leads to or shapes overall tourist satisfaction. In addition, findings also suggest that in tourism, positive affective responses and tourist satisfaction are related but distinct constructs, consistent with environmental psychology literature and tourist satisfaction literature.

In contrast to Hosany and Gilbert's (2010) DES2, this study has enriched the tourism literature pertinent to the effect of negative affective responses on tourist satisfaction with a destination. Due to the discrepancies in personality orientations, different consumption situations may elicit different affective responses. For a destination, tourists may experience both positive and negative affective responses. It can be claimed as one of DES2's shortcomings, as it does not contain any negative affect felt at a destination. Except for the PA-satisfaction relationship, the findings also substantiated a negative impact of negative affect on tourist satisfaction. The results of this study also align with both marketing (Westbrook 1987; Phillips & Baumgartner 2002) and tourism studies (Del Bosque & San Martin 2008; Grappi & Montanari 2011), suggesting that negative affective responses will reduce tourist satisfaction levels. Besides, the current study confirmed that respondents generally rated negative affective responses lower than positive affective responses, and hence, overall satisfaction with tourist destination is still positive.

This study provides further evidence to support the relationship between experience-elicited affective responses and tourist satisfaction identified in the literature (Zins 2002; Bigné et al. 2005; Del Bosque & San Martin 2008; Grappi & Montanari 2011; Lee et al. 2008; Yüksel & Yüksel 2007). In line with previous studies (e. g. Hosany & Gilbert 2010; Hosany & Prayag 2013), the ability for positive/negative affective responses to predict tourist satisfaction highlights the need for researchers to understand the affective drivers of tourist satisfaction. Drawing on insights of affective responses experienced at a tourist destination and theories of tourist satisfaction formation, the findings of this study can be further interpreted from the perspective of positive psychology. A consideration of the role of affective responses in subjective well-being and human development has been gaining momentum in recent positive psychology research (Pearce 2009). Overall, positive or negative affects in one's life are significant predictors of subjective well-being (Weiss 2002). Positive affective responses arising from the holiday experience enhance an individual's sense of well-being and contribute significantly to one's overall happiness with life (Gilbert & Abdullah 2004; Sirgy 2010).

Effect of Personality Traits and Affective Responses on Tourist Satisfaction

This section addresses the fifth research objective of examining how tourists' personality traits, coupled with positive and negative affective responses, can contribute to the formation of tourist satisfaction with a destination. As illustrated in Chapter 5, the structural relationship between the exogenous variables and endogenous variables in the final model explain 55% of the variance in negative affect, 44% of the variance in positive affect, and finally both personality and affect explain 60% of the total variation in overall tourist satisfaction. Results identify tourist personality and experience-elicited affective responses as the main determinants of holistic tourist satisfaction. In addition, the intervening constructs of positive and negative affective responses are indicative measures of the process through which tourist personality traits are thought to impact tourist satisfaction. However, the result does not imply that personality alone can fully explain the formation of tourist satisfaction. It establishes the capacity of enduring personality traits to explain overall tourist satisfaction through the mediation of temporary affective responses. The relationship between personality traits and tourist satisfaction is consistent with previous scarce studies in tourism which used the Big Five personality traits to predict specific emotions and satisfaction (Faullant et al. 2011). From the perspective of consumer behaviour, Mooadian and Olver (1997) argued that extraversion and neuroticism affected customer satisfaction through the mediation of positive or negative emotional response systems respectively.

Nevertheless, since respondents had to rate study variables in the questionnaire using retrospective self-report measures, it should be acknowledged that data might be susceptible to common method variance (Lindell & Whitney 2001) and memory bias. Memory is a constructive rather than faithful accurate process. Therefore, it is arguable that personality traits may influence the process of creating memories. From this perspective the satisfaction evaluation of a holiday must be related to personality because personality influences how memory is constructed. In order to reduce the bias of retrospective measures for affective responses and tourist satisfaction to the minimum, a more generalised evaluation of affective responses and tourist satisfaction as a summative overall construct were conceptualised and operationalised in the current study; moreover, the quantitative data were collected on respondents' return flights to their home country.

In line with this result, the present study also found that Chinese visitors' overall satisfaction with Australia as a travel destination was generally high, with only a very small proportion of visitors expressing dissatisfaction with their overall travel experiences. The results of means and standard deviations for satisfaction items showed that respondents generally agreed with the four measurement items, rating them fairly positively. All items had mean values over 5.4, together with relatively low standard deviations of these items, indicating that respondents were satisfied with their overall experiences of visiting Australia. For such a high satisfaction level, the common method variance bias of self-reported data should be acknowledged (Lindell & Whitney 2001). Regardless of the overwhelming compliments, different voices can still be heard from the focus group discussions. The fact that none of the mean scores fell between "satisfied" and "strongly satisfied" indicates that visitors were only moderately satisfied. In other words, the tourist products and services in Australia were not considered outstanding or perfect in this study. In particular, there was some degree of dissatisfaction with "food", "shopping", and "tour itinerary".

As stated above, both personality and affect explain 60% of the total variation in overall tourist satisfaction. It is a little higher compared with the past study conducted by Westbrook (1987) in marketing research. He integrated "affective responses" with the confirmation/disconfirmation model and found that positive and negative consumption-related emotions contributed directly and significantly to the explanation of variance in consumer satisfaction beyond the variance explained by the cognitions, concluding that "affective variables alone … explain almost as much variance in satisfaction judgments as do the cognitive/semantic belief variables" (pp. 265-266). It indicates that the affective approach is equally important to the cognitive approach in evaluating customer satisfaction. The current study endeavoured to investigate the psychological determinants of tourist satisfaction but without considering such controlled variables as cognitive evaluations, and cultural and socio-economic influences.

Many studies have examined the direct effects of affective responses on tourist satisfaction, but there is no study that evaluates the direct effects of tourist personality on tourist satisfaction in the destination context. Mediation analysis assesses the extent to which the effect of the independent variables on the dependent variable is direct or indirect via the mediator(Iacobucci, Saldanha & Deng 2007). Personality dimensions can predict tourist satisfaction indirectly via their associations with affective responses. In other words, affective responses serve as the full mediators of the relationship between tourist personality and tourist satisfaction. This research converges with the related study conducted by Faullant et al. (2011) which evaluated the indirect effects of personality on satisfaction via joy and fear in the mountaineering context. It showed that joy and fear mediated the relationship between personality (extraversion and neuroticism) and satisfaction. Another previous study attempted to prioritise the direct and/or indirect effects of affective responses on the relationship between personality and satisfaction (Gountas & Gountas 2007). A recent study on food-related personality traits in hospitality and tourism recognises the important role of personality with regard to satisfaction and loyalty (Kim, Suh & Eves 2010).

This study developed a theoretical model integrating both tourist personality and affective response theories and tourist satisfaction theories and tested it with Chinese package tourists in the setting of outbound travel to Australia. The conceptual model builds a link among tourist personality, affective responses, and tourist satisfaction, which has not been explicitly examined in the tourism literature despite its importance in the tourism industries, especially in the context of outbound group package tours. Building on psychological variables, it illustrates some new approaches to tourist satisfaction. Thus, incorporating tourist personality and tourist affective responses in integrative models of tourist satisfaction in future studies not only extends existing models of tourist satisfaction but also enriches tourist behaviour theory.

Chapter Synopsis

This chapter focused on the structural analysis of the impact of tourist personality and positive or negative affective responses on tourist satisfaction. Affective responses acted as fully mediating variables between tourist personality and tourist satisfaction. Mediated by positive affective responses, *extraversion*, *agreeableness*, *openness*, and *conscientiousness* can predict tourist satisfaction; mediated by negative affective responses, *agreeableness*, *neuroticism*, and *openness* can also explain tourist satisfaction. The structural relationship between the exogenous variables and endogenous variables in the final model explain 55% of the total variance of negative affect, 44% of the total variance of positive affect, and finally both personality and affect explain 60% of the total variation in overall satisfaction.

8

Tourist Satisfaction Research: Concluding Remarks

This chapter addresses theoretical contributions and practical implications of the study, and provides marketing- and management-related recommendations for travel destinations, followed by the limitations of the present study and future research directions. The final section of this chapter presents concluding remarks, highlighting the theoretical significance of this study.

Theoretical Contributions

This study sought to identify and document Chinese outbound tourists' positive and negative affective responses generated during their outbound travel engagement in Australia, and to examine the impact of two psychological variables (i. e. tourist personality and affective responses) on overall tourist satisfaction. One of the most important theoretical contributions of this study is that it advances the framework for tourist satisfaction by integrating personality traits and affective responses. It confirms that personality traits are predictors (antecedents) of tourist satisfaction through the mediation of affective responses. From a theoretical perspective, most previous studies have concentrated largely on cognitive approaches to assess whether the perceived quality meets or exceeds expectation, while other studies define satisfaction as an affective state derived from travel experiences. Few recent studies have incorporated both cognitive and affective antecedents to model tourist satisfaction (e. g. Del Bosque & San Martin 2008). However, aside from cognitive and affective variables, other psychological factors such as tourist personality may contribute to different levels of satisfaction. In addition, personality differences may cause tourists to elicit different affective responses to their travel experiences at a destination. Growing recognition of the deficiencies in understanding personality as a predictor of tourist behaviour has called for more research efforts. Therefore, an in-depth examination of these variables and their interrelationships in the process of tourist satisfaction formation is required for a better understanding of the conceptual underpinnings of satisfaction.

Firstly, personality traits are widely recognised as important factors that influence tourists' decision-making (Moutinho 1987; Um & Crompton 1990; Yoo & Gretzel 2011; Tan & Tang 2013). However their relationship with other consumer characteristics is seldom examined (Nunkoo, Ramkissoon & Gursoy 2013). A variety of psychological factors can be identified from past studies, among which the current study refined two constructs hypothesised to influence tourist satisfaction, i. e. affective responses and personality traits. Correspondingly, many contributions in the marketing literature have taken personality traits and emotions into consideration(Mooradian & Olver 1997); however, their relevance and impact on customer satisfaction, especially in the tourism setting, are as yet only little understood. In addition, although many other interrelated psychological influences may exist concurrently, it is generally understood that the Big Five personality domains account for an important portion of the variance in explaining or predicting tourist behaviour. A review on the role of personality in the tourism and hospitality industry identified that the majority of the tourism literature which employs the Big Five model either for data analysis or as part of the research framework has focused on analysing service staff personality (Leung & Law 2010) rather than tourist personality. To date there has been surprisingly little research employing the Big Five model to evaluate tourist satisfaction. Therefore, by exploring the joint impact of enduring personality traits and temporary affective responses on the formation of overall satisfaction in the context of mainland Chinese outbound tourists to Australia, this study was designed to develop and empirically test a model explaining tourist satisfaction with a destination. It makes a unique contribution by testing the theoretical relationships among the psychological constructs of personality, affect, and satisfaction in the context of international tourism.

Secondly, this research has made a contribution to the measurement scale for Big Five personality by identifying and developing a short Chinese 16-item Big Five Inventory (BFI-SC), an abbreviated version of the well-established 44-item Big Five Inventory. It assesses each of the five personality dimensions with three or four items on a 7-point Likert scale from 1 (strongly disagree) to 7 (strongly agree). BFI-SC can contribute to quick, but reliable estimations of the Big Five personality constructs as applied to Chinese respondents in the context of outbound travel to Australia. The increasing acceptance of the Big Five as a model for delineating the structure of core personality traits has called for the need to assess the Big Five personality dimensions in both cross-cultural and cross-disciplinary settings (e. g. Rammstedt 2007; Denissen et al. 2008). The 44-item BFI, as a widely-used instrument, proved to be too lengthy for many research purposes. As a consequence, the need for brief but efficient measures of the Big Five factors continues to grow due to many constraints of the survey context. In response to this call, three short-form scales of personality traits have been developed and tested as the scale of the Big Five personality domains, namely, TIPI (e. g. Gosling, Rentfrow & Swann 2003; Romero et al. 2012), BFI-10 (Rammstedt & John 2007), and BFI-S (Lang et al. 2011). Because these three short-form scales of personality traits need to be further validated in large-scale multidisciplinary and cross-cultural research, the current study evaluates the factor structure and reliability of the Chinese version of the 44-item BFI (BFI-C) and reduces it to a 16-item measure of the Big Five dimensions with the satisfactory psychometric properties, which proves to be applicable to the sample of Chinese outbound tourists to Australia. Such a short instrument could mitigate Chinese respondents' fatigue, frustration, and boredom resulting from answering highly similar questions repeatedly. Therefore, the brevity of the 16-item BFI-SC will be more appealing to researchers who are concerned about expending the time and energy of their Chinese participants. It will contribute to the current personality literature on the BFI across the different cultures.

Thirdly, the differentiation between affect and emotion has been addressed, for there is considerable ambiguity about the differences between these two terms in psychology and marketing. This study calls for some elaboration on the clear conceptualisations of these terms in tourism and hospitality. Findings from the qualitative stage of this study mainly support previous research on consumers' affective responses (e. g. Jun et al. 2001) and help conceptualise affective responses in the context of Chinese package tourists to Australia. It will not only enrich the tourism literature on positive and negative affective responses associated with specific and overall experiences of a travel trip, but also contribute to a good theoretical understanding of consumer behaviour in general. In addition, this study demonstrates the application of field theory from psychology to the tourism domain. Field theory examines patterns of interaction between the individual and the environment. It emphasises individual personalities and situational variables and proposes that behaviour is the result of the individual and their environment. In viewing a person's social environment and its impact on their dynamic field, it was found that a person's psychological state influences their social behaviour (Beaty, Cleveland & Murphy 2001). The on-site travel experience is normally considered as a non-ordinary time that transforms the individuals into tourists with the exotic touristic environment. Enduring personality traits have been linked to the temporary affective outcomes of a tourism experience (Lin et al. 2014). Thus, it well interprets that enduring tourist personality and situational affective responses during a trip can work together to influence tourists' travel behaviour.

Fourthly, this study has enriched the personality-affect relationship in the tourism literature. The rationale for this comprehensive investigation of the relationship between each personality trait and positive or negative affect stems from the pressing needs to extend our understanding of personality-affect relationships in tourism, and further inform the efforts to conceptualise and theorise the influences of personality traits on affective responses. In a weak situation, personality is assumed to be a main predictor for regulating positive and negative affect, irrespective of situational factors. Furthermore, instead of simply viewing isolated dimensions of personality traits, such as extraversion and neuroticism, this study breaks new ground by employing all five factors of the FFM as five independent variables in the Chinese context to examine how each dimension of the FFM contributes to the formation of tourists' positive and negative affective responses. In addition, empirical studies on the role of affect/emotion in the context of tourist destinations remain sparse (Hosany & Gilbert 2010). To address such a gap, this study sought to conceptualise and document Chinese package tourists' salient positive and negative affective responses during their trip to Australia.

Last but not least, this study highlights the application of positive psychology in the context of international mass tourism. Positive psychology is an area of study that seeks to highlight the role of positive affect, character strengths, and positive institutions serving human happiness and well-being(Pearce 2009). Although there has been a rapid rise in prominence in this area of psychology since the year 2000, tourism studies have not yet made as many connections to the new study area as might be expected. To address the under-researched area, this study also contributes to the tourism literature by substantiating the role of travel experience-engendered positive affective responses on tourists' happiness and well-being.

Practical Implications

Managerial Implications

This study offers managerial implications for both mass tourists and industry practitioners. From the perspective of mass tourists, due to the influence of personality differences, the same travel products and destination environments may elicit different affective responses. His study offers several managerial implications for both mass tourists and industry practitioners. It is because of the distinct psychological variables as represented by personality traits and affective responses that the judgment of the determinants in satisfaction formation can be individualistic and diverse. Therefore, having a good command of the satisfaction formation mechanism from the psychological perspective, mass tourists would be able to learn how to regulate their affective responses to the travel experiences at the destination based on their individual personality orientations. Self-managing affective responses in terms of individual personality traits may help generate more positive affective responses and lead to a high level of tourist satisfaction. In turn this may help produce physical and mental health benefits through tourism engagements. Eventually, this will be conducive to enhancing tourists' subjective well-being and improving their quality of life.

The findings also suggest that destination managers should capture tourists' personality characteristics and affective responses as part of destination surveys to better understand psychological orientations of visitors. Given that both positive and negative affect impact on tourist satisfaction, tourism operators should attend to travel experiences more carefully to generate more positive affective responses. The findings also suggest the need for destination marketers to better understand negative affective responses, as negative affective responses derived from the tourist destination and social environment interactions are difficult to predict and manage. However, negative affective responses from service failures involving face-to-face interactions with tour guides are relatively controllable, so they should be avoided from the management perspective. Consequently, tour managers have to recognise the strategic importance of training qualified tour guides and learn how to empower them to facilitate tourists' positive affective responses and react in an empathic way to minimise tourists' negative affective responses, resulting in maximum satisfaction levels. For tour operators, a thorough tour preparation and communication before starting the tour will help the guides to get a picture of the personality of their customers, and will enable them to better act as a cultural translator for those package tourists who will encounter language barriers and who lack travel experience to exotic destinations. For service staff like tour guides, it is of crucial importance to optimise the service encounter. A trustworthy, well-organised, and warm-hearted tour guide will be highly favoured by neurotic, agreeable, and conscientious tourists. Through tour guides' tailor-made services, tourists with different personality orientations can experience more positive affect, thus resulting in high levels of satisfaction.

The practical findings from focus group discussions in the qualitative phase of this study offer valuable implications for Western tourism and hospitality practitioners and destination marketers. The findings have contributed to a better understanding of Chinese consumers in modern society and this study is thus able to propose useful recommendations on how to manage their affective responses. Despite China's trend towards urbanisation and modernisation, Chinese people are staying true to their Eastern values. Chinese people are becoming modern, but not thoroughly westernised. It has been evidenced that when consuming international tourism products, Chinese tourists are remaining culturally and ethically Chinese, instead of adopting Western values. Having Chinese food and drinking hot tea or water are much favoured by Chinese tourists. They may be frugal at home, but spend a large amount of money buying gifts for their friends and relatives.

The findings can help tourism marketers understand who the target markets for certain tourism products are and what specific needs they have. For example, extraverts enjoy interaction and prefer those travel activities that allow them to express themselves while being social (e. g. interactive activities with local people, free markets or night markets); some challenging experiential activities such as skydiving, bungee jumping, mountaineering, and white water rafting can be provided and organised. Before departing from the home country, tour operators should invest time in organising a detailed briefing with outbound tourists in order to provide them with a realistic view of the cultural and social differences that they will experience at the destination country. For those who are high in neuroticism, these practices will help them get more familiar with the tourism product and the destination country in the form of pictures, videos, travel blogs, and brochures, thus mitigating or reducing their anxiety and nervousness. Besides, for those high in neuroticism, on the one hand, guiding services from a well-trained tour guide is of particular importance to their travel experiences; on the other hand, tourism products suitable for the family vacation could serve as good personalised recommendations to facilitate their travel decision-making. For those open tourists, they are likely to participate in culture-related activities to gain more knowledge, as well as nature-based activities to satisfy their aesthetic needs.

Marketing Implications

The results also offer a series of marketing implications for travel destinations. A study on mainland Chinese visitors' satisfaction with Australia as a tourist destination is not only valuable to Australian tourism marketing and planning organisations, but also provides useful information to other destination countries who want to expand their market share of Chinese outbound travel. This study provided insights into the motivators of satisfaction and the causes of dissatisfaction among Chinese tourists; this could help Australian industry practitioners better understand Chinese visitors so that they can make appropriate decisions to target and attract this important market segment. In order for Australia to sustain its competitive advantage as a tourist destination and attract more Chinese visitors, tourism providers should strive to generate positive affect (*happy*, *excited*, *interested*, and *impressed*) to create delightful and unforgettable experiences. Furthermore, destination marketers could manipulate their advertising messages to activate, stimulate, and promote these positive affects, such as using refined photography and videos which tap into particular personality traits. For example, simple, understandable, and detailed information about the destination and its attributes can be provided to neurotic tourists to assist them in making their vacation decisions.

The notions of experience economy and experiential marketing (Pine & Gilmore 2011) have been widely adopted by DMOs and tourism research, respectively; however, there is still a lack of research that would allow destination promoters to recognise the crucial components of tourism experiences (Lee & Kyle 2013). A sound understanding of tourists' personality characteristics, affective responses, and the related tourist satisfaction will aid in the formulation of strategic marketing, segmentation, and communication efforts. Results identify tourist personality and experience-elicited affective responses as the main determinants of holistic tourist satisfaction. Destination marketers should strive to understand this tourist satisfaction model and create pleasant experiences in order to consistently elicit positive affective responses and high levels of tourist satisfaction. Specifically, this study provided marketing implications in the following three regards.

Firstly, different personality traits were found to have a positive or negative impact on tourists' affective responses associated with specific and holistic experiences of a travel trip. Linking the product features to tourist personality, tourism marketers need to provide Chinese travellers with some tailor-made tourism products and services designed to accommodate their varying needs and travel preferences. Providing tailor-made services based on tourist personality will enable destinations to better serve the individual tourists' needs in different market segments. Personality knowledge allows marketers to segment the specific markets based on their personality traits. Marketers cannot change tourists' personality to match their products, but understanding which specific characteristics elicit positive responses can help marketers to appeal to these traits in their target audiences. Hence, travel products and services could be customised to meet the needs of tourists with different personality traits. Travel consultants or tour guides can ask some basic questions at the start of their interactions with tourists to probe their personality before directing them to the appropriate tourism products or services.

Secondly, identifying the underlying causes of generating positive or negative affective responses could help decision-makers adopt proactive measures to minimise the negative effects of these psychological factors. During the same stay individuals may experience positive and negative affect because they have multiple interactions with the resources of the destination. It is significant to create affective associations between visitors and the destination. This affective association can result from sentimental memories and socialisation experienced post-visit (Grisaffe & Nguyen 2011). Hence, marketing strategies that foster and increase affective associations with a destination over time will meaningfully impact tourist satisfaction with a destination. As a destination matures, the challenge of retaining existing visitors and attracting new ones intensifies; marketing measures can be designed for achieving tourists' affective attachment to the destination. By understanding the visitors' affective responses, destinations such as Australia can remain competitive and ensure sustainable development of their tourism industry.

Thirdly, since the interrelationships among personality, affect, and satisfaction are clarified, it would assist tourism marketers in developing appropriate tourism products and launching effective campaigns so as to gain positive WOM, to enhance tourist loyalty to a destination, and eventually to secure more repeat visitors. As this study only covered respondents who were first-time visitors to Australia, the findings would have great implications for Australian marketers, because these visitors' overall satisfaction with Australia would determine their revisit intention. The profile of Chinese visitors to Australia in 2012 indicated that repeat visitors account for 47% of total visitors. In the long term, Australia is likely to remain a destination for repeat visitations from mainland China among all ADS destinations due to its unspoilt natural environment and laid back lifestyle, coupled with its close economic and political connections with China. To sum up, in today's competitive environment, industry practitioners would be able to better serve an emerging market if they develop better understanding of the market and target customers. Such knowledge would be of particular significance in identifying predictor variables of tourist satisfaction and developing more appropriate marketing strategies to suit individual personality orientations.

Limitations and Future Research

The study has some limitations, which suggest avenues for future research. As such, a discussion of the key limitations of this study is presented in conjunction with the directions for future research. First of all, the most prominent limitation of this study to be addressed resides in that the types of the sampling are homogeneous. The study used Chinese package tourists departing from Jiangsu Province to Australia as a convenience sample, exclusive of mainland travellers living in other parts of China. This may affect the strength and generalisability of the results. Thus, future research may attempt to use more representative samples to further validate the results of this study. Moreover, the research findings are specific to only one culture. People of different cultures and languages categorise personality traits and affective responses in different ways (Russell 1991). Previous studies have found that the measurement of personality traits (BFI) and positive or negative affect (PANAS) are culture specific (e. g. Thompson 2007; Denissen et al. 2008). An area of future research is to replicate this study using respondents from different cultures/nationalities. Furthermore, it would be of significance to further explore and compare the differences using samples visiting other destinations, such as the USA, European countries, Africa and Southeast Asia. A lack of comparisons of Australia with similar destinations in the study may have missed useful information. Similarly, the sample covers Chinese tourists in a group package tour to Australia; therefore, the conclusions need to be regarded with caution and should not be generalised to the increasing market segment of free independent tourists (FIT) in Chinese outbound tourism. Therefore, further comparative study on FITs' personality traits, affective responses, and their joint impact on tourist satisfaction is warranted.

Another limitation concerns the measurement and operationalization of affective responses, which may involve conscious and unconscious affective responses making the measurement using standardised surveys difficult. Some affective responses, assumed to be conscious, might be hard to express in words. Other affective responses might only be expressed by facial reactions. Interviewers with a psychological background and other methods like facial coding, should therefore be included in future research (Brunner-Sperdin, Peters & Strobl 2012). Future studies should also attempt to capture unconscious affective responses that can provide unbiased portrayals of individuals' initial affective reactions when exposed to a stimulus (Li, Scott & Walters 2015).

This study used retrospective self-report measures to collect the data, which is subject to criticisms of reliability. It is arguable that asking tourists to recall their emotional responses even from a few days ago will lead to a cognitive rather than affective response. Although the quantitative data were arranged to be collected on respondents' return flights to China to reduce the bias to the minimum from the perspective of the research design, emotional responses vary across time and episodes, and it is still debated how well people can recall their prior emotional responses. In any event, respondents are asked to recall what activates their memory. It should be acknowledged that since memory is reconstructive, recalled affect may be biased by personality rather than being an accurate reflection of holiday afffect as it occurs. Future studies should attempt to capture every on-site tourists' emotional response by the aid of the emotional-recording apparatus without interruptions and compare the results with post hoc global evaluations of affective responses. Alternatively, future research could collect longitudinal data to more precisely measure changes across time and the direction of causality among relationships (Chi & Qu 2008). Besides, in the weak situation of a vacation tour, this study highlights the role of the personality variable in the formation of tourists' affective responses, rather than those situational factors and cultural and socio-economic differences whose profound impacts on affective responses should also be evaluated in future studies. It should be noted that this study utilised the cross-sectional retrospective self-report survey to assess tourist personality, affective responses, and tourist satisfaction, which may have inflated the correlations among research constructs because of common method variance bias (Lindell & Whitney 2001; Prayag et al. 2015). Future studies should adopt a more diverse methodology such as peer ratings to provide a fuller picture of research constructs and the correlations among them.

Despite its limitations, this study advances and enriches the development of the tourist satisfaction model in tourism. Tourist satisfaction plays a crucial role in successful destination marketing, which influences the choice of destination and the decision to return (Yoon & Uysal 2005). Thus, a high level of satisfaction derived at the destination encourages individual tourists to revisit the destination, and leads to positive WOM advertising and destination loyalty (e. g. Prayag, Hosany & Odeh 2013; Su & Hsu 2013). Conversely, the characteristics of tourists' negative affective responses should also be investigated to determine how they affect tourist behaviour, such as negative word of mouth and complaining. While this study shed light on the influence of tourist personality traits and affective responses, either generated by neural stimulation or triggered by travel experiences, with regard to overall satisfaction with a destination, more research is needed to inform a better understanding of the interrelationships among personality traits, affective responses, tourist satisfaction, and potential behavioural intentions. Future research agendas could be directed at integrating the cognitive and affective determinants with other psychological variables to establish a more comprehensive theoretical framework for understanding tourist satisfaction.

Finally, Pearce and Packer (2013) pointed out the need to assess more thoughtfully the interplay for tourists between their individual satisfaction and the satisfaction of other members of their travel party. The dominant tradition in satisfaction research is to ask individuals for their own evaluations of their travels. Diener and Biswas-Diener (2008) observe that some respondents in Asian cultures see their happiness and satisfaction as entirely bound up with and dependent on the good times had by their travel companions. Collecting the perspectives of individuals on how other members of their travel party have enjoyed the experience as well as recording their own evaluations might enrich the way tourist behaviour is assessed in an interconnected social world.

Concluding Remarks

In response to a call for tourism researchers (e. g. Coghlan & Pearce 2010; Pearce, Philip 2012; Pearce & Packer 2013) to focus on the psychological variables of tourist satisfaction, the main objective of this book was to examine the relationships among tourist personality, affective responses, and tourist satisfaction. In particular, the proposed framework allowed the identification of relationships between (1) specific personality traits and positive affect; (2) specific personality traits and negative affect; and (3) positive or negative affect and tourist satisfaction. One of the most significant theoretical contributions of this study is that its findings confirm the importance of such psychological predictors as tourist personality and affective responses in determining overall tourist satisfaction. This is especially valid in the context of international tourism in which tourists' overall satisfaction seems more reliant on psychological determinants due to the cultural and socio-economic discrepancies between home and destination countries. It is noteworthy that it has been necessary to compare the findings from this study with those of studies conducted in very different contexts. This demonstrates the importance of the contribution that has been made to better understand the role of personality in tourism.

The current study advances the framework for the tourist satisfaction model by integrating tourist personality traits with experience-elicited affective responses as two important predictor variables of tourist satisfaction. In the structural model, *extraversion*, *neuroticism*, *conscientiousness*, *agreeableness*, and *openness* served as exogenous variables in the model, while positive and negative affective responses were demonstrated to act as fully mediating endogenous variables between personality traits and tourist satisfaction. The structural relationship between the exogenous variables and endogenous variables in the final model explain

55% of the total variation in negative affect, and 44% of the total variation in positive affect, and finally both personality and affect explain 60% of the total variation in overall tourist satisfaction. The results corroborated personality traits and affective responses as the main determinants of holistic tourist satisfaction. The strong statistical power of the final model suggested that this study could serve as a basis for further research into psychological and affective determinants of tourist satisfaction.

This study contributes to the tourism literature by revealing how tourist personality traits, through the mediation of positive and negative affective responses, explain tourist satisfaction with travel experiences at a destination. Most importantly, this study also extends the understanding of personality-affect and affect-satisfaction relationships in the tourism context. In summary, the current study has confirmed the need for the application of more comprehensive and more sophisticated frameworks to conceptualise and evaluate tourist satisfaction. Having a good command of these psychological variables of tourist satisfaction may improve the monitoring and the management of tourism experiences and maximise tourists' subjective well-being.

References

Aaker, JL 1997, "Dimensions of brand personality", *Journal of Marketing Research*, vol. 34, no. 3, pp. 347-356.

Acar, AS & Polonsky, M 2007, "Online social networks and insights into marketing communications", *Journal of Internet Commerce*, vol. 6, no. 4, pp. 55-72.

Agrusa, J, Kim, SS & Wang, KC 2011, "Mainland Chinese tourists to Hawaii: Their characteristics and preferences", *Journal of Travel & Tourism Marketing*, vol. 28, no. 3, pp. 261-278.

Alegre, J & Cladera, M 2006, "Repeat visitation in mature sun and sand holiday destinations", *Journal of Travel Research*, vol. 44, no. 3, pp. 288-297.

Anderson, EW, Fornell, C & Lehmann, DR 1994, "Customer satisfaction, market share, and profitability: Findings from Sweden", *The Journal of Marketing*, vol. 4, no. 4, pp. 53-66.

Anderson, EW 1998, "Customer satisfaction and word of mouth", *Journal of Service Research*, vol. 1, no. 1, pp. 5-17.

Anderson, JC & Gerbing, DW 1988, "Structural equation modeling in practice: A review and recommended two-step approach", *Psychological Bulletin*, vol. 103, no. 3, pp. 411-422.

Anderson, JC & Gerbing, DW 1991, "Predicting the performance of measures in a confirmatory factor analysis with a pretest assessment of their substantive validities", *Journal of Applied Psychology*, vol. 76, no. 5, pp. 732-740.

Arlt, WG 2006, *China's outbound tourism*, Routledge, New York.

Arora, R & Singer, J 2006, "Cognitive and affective service marketing strategies for fine dining restaurant managers", *Journal of Small Business Strategy*, vol. 17, pp. 51-61.

Arthur, S & Nazroo, J 2003, "Designing fieldwork strategies and materials", *Qualitative research practice: A guide for social science students and researchers*, pp. 109-137.

Ashton, MC 2007, "Self-reports and stereotypes: A comment on McCrae et al", *European Journal of Personality*, vol. 21, no. 8, pp. 983-986.

Assaker, G & Hallak, R 2013, "Moderating effects of tourists' novelty-seeking tendencies on destination image, visitor satisfaction, and short- and long-term revisit intentions", *Journal of Travel Research*, vol. 52, no. 5, pp. 600-613.

Australian Bureau of Statistics 2015, *Overseas Arrivals and Departures* (*cat. no.* 3401. 0), viewed July 31, 2015, < http://www. abs. gov. au/ausstats/abs@. nsf/mf/3401. 0 >.

Babin, BJ & Griffin, M 1998, "The nature of satisfaction: An updated examination and analysis", *Journal of Business Research*, vol. 41, no. 2, pp. 127-136.

Bagozzi, R, Gopinath, M & Nyer, P 1999, "The role of emotions in marketing", *Journal of the Academy of Marketing Science*, vol. 27, no. 2, pp. 184-206.

Bagozzi, RP & Yi, Y 1988, "On the evaluation of structural equation models", *Journal of the Academy of Marketing Science*, vol. 16, no. 1, pp. 74-94.

Bagozzi, RP & Foxall, GR 1996, "Construct validation of a measure of adaptive-innovative cognitive styles in consumption", *International Journal of Research in Marketing*, vol. 13, no. 3, pp. 201-213.

Bagozzi, RP, Gopinath, M & Nyer, PU 1999, "The role of emotions in marketing", *Journal of the Academy of Marketing Science*, vol. 27, no. 2, pp. 184-206.

Bakker, AB, Van Der Zee, KI, Lewig, KA & Dollard, MF 2006, "The relationship between the big five personality factors and burnout: A study among volunteer counselors", *The Journal of Social Psychology*, vol. 146, no. 1, pp. 31-50.

Barnett, LA 2006, "Accounting for leisure preferences from within: The relative contributions of gender, race or ethnicity, personality, affective style, and motivational orientation", *Journal of Leisure Research*, vol. 38, no. 4, pp. 445-474.

Barnette, JJ 2000, "Effects of stem and Likert response option reversals on survey internal consistency: If you feel the need, there is a better alternative to using those negatively worded stems", *Educational and Psychological Measurement*, vol. 60, no. 3, pp. 361-370.

Barrash, DI & Costen, WM 2007, "Getting along with others: The relationship between agreeableness and customer satisfaction in the foodservice industry", *Journal of Human Resources in Hospitality & Tourism*, vol. 7, no. 1, pp. 65-83.

Barrick, MR & Mount, MK 1991, "The big five personality dimensions and job performance: A meta-analysis", *Personnel Psychology*, vol. 44, no. 1, pp. 1-26.

Barrick, MR, Mount, MK & Gupta, R 2003, "Meta-analysis of the relationship between the five-factor model of personality and Holland's occupational types", *Personnel Psychology*, vol. 56, pp. 45-74.

Barrick, MR, Mount, M & Judge, T 2001, "The FFM personality dimensions and job performance: Meta-analysis of meta-analyses", *International Journal of Selection and Assessment*, vol. 9, no. 1/2, pp. 9-30.

Barsky, J & Nash, L 2002, "Evoking emotion: Affective keys to hotel loyalty", *The Cornell Hotel and Restaurant Administration Quarterly*, vol. 43, no. 1, pp. 39-46.

Basala, SL & Klenosky, DB 2001, "Travel-style preferences for visiting a novel destination: A conjoint investigation across the novelty-familiarity continuum", *Journal of Travel Research*, vol. 40, no. 2, pp. 172-182.

Bazeley, P & Jackson, K 2013, *Qualitative data analysis with NVivo*, Sage Publications, London.

Beaty Jr, JC, Cleveland, JN & Murphy, KR 2001, "The relation between personality and contextual performance in 'strong' versus 'weak' situations", *Human Performance*, vol. 14, no. 2, pp. 125-148.

Beedie, C, Terry, P & Lane, A 2005, "Distinctions between emotion and mood", *Cognition & Emotion*, vol. 19, no. 6, pp. 847-878.

Besser, A & Shackelford, TK 2007, "Mediation of the effects of the big five personality dimensions on negative mood and confirmed affective expectations by perceived situational stress: A quasi-field study of vacationers", *Personality and Individual Differences*, vol. 42, no. 7, pp. 1333-1346.

Bigné, JE, Andreu, L & Gnoth, J 2005, "The theme park experience: An analysis of pleasure, arousal and satisfaction", *Tourism Management*, vol. 26, no. 6, pp. 833-844.

Bigné, JE & Andreu, L 2004, "Emotions in segmentation: An empirical study", *Annals of Tourism Research*, vol. 31, no. 3, pp. 682-696.

Bird, CM 2005, "How I stopped dreading and learned to love transcription", *Qualitative Inquiry*, vol. 11, no. 2, pp. 226-248.

Block, J 1995, "A contrarian view of the five-factor approach to personality description", *Psychological Bulletin*, vol. 117, no. 2, pp. 187-198.

Bloemer, J & De Ruyter, K 1998, "On the relationship between store image, store satisfaction and store loyalty", *European Journal of Marketing*, vol. 32, no. 5/6, pp. 499-513.

Bloemer, J, Odekerken-Schröder, G & Kestens, L 2003, "The impact of need for social affiliation and consumer relationship proneness on behavioural intentions: An empirical study in a hairdresser's context", *Journal of Retailing and Consumer Services*, vol. 10, no. 4, pp. 231-240.

Bollen, KA 1989, "A new incremental fit index for general structural equation models", *Sociological Methods & Research*, vol. 17, no. 3, pp. 303-316.

Bollen, KA & Stine, R 1990, "Direct and indirect effects: Classical and bootstrap estimates of variability", *Sociological Methodology*, vol. 20, no. 1, pp. 115-140.

Bollen, KA & Stine, RA 1992, "Bootstrapping goodness-of-fit measures in structural equation models", *Sociological Methods & Research*, vol. 21, no. 2, pp. 205-229.

Bolton, RN & Drew, JH 1991, "A multistage model of customers' assessments of service quality and value", *Journal of Consumer Research*, pp. 375-384.

Bolton, RN & Lemon, KN 1999, "A dynamic model of customers' usage of services: Usage as an antecedent and consequence of satisfaction", *Journal of Marketing Research*, vol. 16, no. 5, pp. 171-186.

Bowen, D 2001, "Antecedents of consumer satisfaction and dis-satisfaction (CS/D) on long-haul inclusive tours—a reality check on theoretical considerations", *Tourism Management*, vol. 22, no. 1, pp. 49-61.

Bowen, D & Clarke, J 2002, "Reflections on tourist satisfaction research: Past, present and future", *Journal of Vacation Marketing*, vol. 8, no. 4, pp. 297-308.

Bowen, D & Clarke, J 2009, *Contemporary tourist behaviour: Yourself and others as tourists*, Cabi, Wallingford, UK.

Boyatzis, RE 1998, *Transforming qualitative information: Thematic analysis and code development*, Sage, Thousand Oaks, CA.

Braun, V & Clarke, V 2006, "Using thematic analysis in psychology", *Qualitative Research in Psychology*, vol. 3, no. 2, pp. 77-101.

Brislin, RW 1976, "Comparative research methodology: Cross-cultural studies", *International Journal of Psychology*, vol. 11, no. 3, pp. 215-229.

Brown, KW & Ryan, RM 2003, "The benefits of being present: Mindfulness and its role in psychological well-being", *Journal of Personality and Social Psychology*, vol. 84, no. 4, pp. 822-832.

Brown, TJ, Mowen, JC, Donavan, DT & Licata, JW 2002, "The customer orientation of service workers: Personality trait effects on self- and supervisor performance ratings", *Journal of Marketing Research*, vol. 39, no. 1, pp. 110-119.

Brunner-Sperdin, A, Peters, M & Strobl, A 2012, "It is all about the emotional state: Managing tourists' experiences", *International Journal of Hospitality Management*, vol. 31, no. 1, pp. 23-30.

Bryman, A 2006, "Paradigm peace and the implications for quality", *International Journal of Social Research Methodology*, vol. 9, no. 2, pp. 111-126.

Bryman, A & Bell, E 2007, *Business research strategies*, Oxford University Press, London.

Bryman, A 2008, *Social research methods*, 3rd edn, Oxford University Press, New York.

Bryman, A & Bell, E 2011, *Business Research Methods*, 3rd edn, Oxford University Press, Oxford.

Byrne, BM 1998, *Structural equation modeling with LISREL, PRELIS, and SIMPLIS: Basic concepts, applications, and programming*, Erlbaum, Mahwah, NJ.

Byrne, BM 2001, "Structural equation modeling with AMOS, EQS, and LISREL: Comparative approaches to testing for the factorial validity of a measuring instrument", *International Journal of Testing*, vol. 1, no. 1, pp. 55-86.

Byrne, BM 2005, "Factor analytic models: Viewing the structure of an assessment instrument from three perspectives", *Journal of Personality Assessment*, vol. 85, no. 1, pp. 17-32.

Byrne, BM 2009, *Structural equation modeling with AMOS: Basic concepts, applications, and programming*, 2nd edn, Lawrence Erlbaum Associates, Mahwah, NJ.

Cai, LA, Boger, C & O'Leary, J 1999, "The Chinese travelers to Singapore, Malaysia, and Thailand: A unique Chinese outbound market", *Asia Pacific Journal of Tourism Research*, vol. 3, no. 2, pp. 2-13.

Cai, LA, Li, M & Knutson, BJ 2007, "Research on China outbound market: A meta-review", *Journal of Hospitality & Leisure Marketing*, vol. 16, no. 1/2, pp. 5-20.

Cameron, R & Molina-Azorin, JF 2011, "The acceptance of mixed methods in business and management research", *International Journal of Organizational Analysis*, vol. 19, no. 3, pp. 256-271.

Carr, N 2002, "The tourism-leisure behavioural continuum", *Annals of Tourism Research*, vol. 29, no. 4, pp. 972-986.

Carver, CS & Scheier, MF 2008, "Feedback processes in the simultaneous regulation of action and affect", in Shah, JY & L, GW (eds), *Handbook of Motivation Science*, The Guilford Press, New York, pp. 308-324.

Carver, CS, Sutton, SK & Scheier, MF 2000, "Action, emotion, and personality: Emerging conceptual integration", *Personality and Social Psychology Bulletin*, vol. 26, no. 6, pp. 741-751.

Cervone, D & Pervin, LA 2010, *Personality: Theory and research*, 11th. edn, Wiley, Hoboken, NJ.

Chandler, JA & Costello, CA 2002, "A profile of visitors at heritage tourism destinations in East Tennessee according to Plog's lifestyle and activity level preferences model", *Journal of Travel Research*, vol. 41, no. 2, pp. 161-166.

Chang, JC 2008, "Tourists' satisfaction judgments: An investigation of emotion, equity, and attribution", *Journal of Hospitality & Tourism Research*, vol. 32, no. 1, pp. 108-134.

Chapman, R 2003, "Memorable wildlife encounters in Elk Island National Park", *Human Dimensions of Wildlife*, *vol.* 8, no. 3, pp. 235-236.

Chebat, JC & Michon, R 2003, "Impact of ambient odors on mall shoppers' emotions, cognition, and spending: A test of competitive causal theories", *Journal of Business Research*, vol. 56, no. 7, pp. 529-539.

Chen, CF & Tsai, D 2007, "How destination image and evaluative factors affect behavioral intentions?", *Tourism Management*, vol. 28, no. 4, pp. 1115-1122.

Chen, CF & Chen, FS 2010, "Experience quality, perceived value, satisfaction and behavioral intentions for heritage tourists", *Tourism Management*, vol. 31, no. 1, pp. 29-35.

Chen, HB, Yeh, SS & Huan, TC 2014, "Nostalgic emotion, experiential value, brand image, and consumption intentions of customers of nostalgic-themed restaurants", *Journal of Business Research*, vol. 67, no. 3, pp. 354-360.

Chen, Y, Mak, B & McKercher, B 2011, "What Drives People to Travel: Integrating the Tourist Motivation Paradigms", *Journal of China Tourism Research*, vol. 7, no. 2, pp. 120-136.

Cheng, H & Furnham, A 2003, "Personality, self-esteem, and demographic predictions of happiness and depression", *Personality and Individual Differences*, vol. 34, no. 6, pp. 921-942.

Cheung, FM 2004, "Use of western and indigenously developed personality tests in Asia", *Applied Psychology*, vol. 53, no. 2, pp. 173-191.

Cheung, FM, Cheung, SF, Zhang, J, Leung, K, Leong, F & Huiyeh, K 2008, "Relevance of Openness as a Personality Dimension in Chinese Culture Aspects of its Cultural Relevance", *Journal of Cross-Cultural Psychology*, vol. 39, no. 1, pp. 81-108.

Chhetri, P, Arrowsmith, C & Jackson, M 2004, "Determining hiking experiences in nature-based tourist destinations", *Tourism Management*, vol. 25, no. 1, pp. 31-43.

Chi, CG-Q & Qu, H 2008, "Examining the structural relationships of destination image, tourist satisfaction and destination loyalty: An integrated approach", *Tourism Management*, vol. 29, no. 4, pp. 624-636.

China Daily 2013, *Affluent tourists "go it alone"; seek culture, good food*, viewed 21 January, 2014, < http://usa. chinadaily. com. cn/business/2013-08/22/content_16912831. htm > .

China National Tourism Administration (CNTA) 2001-2015, *The yearbook of China tourism statistics*, China Travel & Tourism Press, Beijing.

China National Tourism Administration (CNTA) 2013, *List of approved destination for Chinese citizens*, viewed December 31, 2013, < http://www. cnta. gov. cn/html/2009-5/2009-5-13-10-53 -54953. html > .

China Tourism Academy (CTA) 2014, *China's tourism performance: Review & forecast (2013 - 2014)*, China Travel & Tourism Press, Beijing.

Chon, K-S 1989, "Understanding recreational traveler's motivation, attitude and satisfaction", *The Tourist Review*, vol. 44, no. 1, pp. 3-7.

Chow, I & Murphy, P 2008, "Travel activity preferences of Chinese outbound tourists for overseas destinations", *Journal of Hospitality Marketing & Management*, vol. 16, no. 1, pp. 61-80.

Coghlan, A & Pearce, P 2010, "Tracking affective components of satisfaction", *Tourism and Hospitality Research*, vol. 10, no. 1, pp. 42-58.

Cohen, E & Cohen, SA 2012, "Current sociological theories and issues in tourism", *Annals of Tourism*

Research, vol. 39, no. 4, pp. 2177-2202.

Cohen, J 1988, *Statistical power analysis for the behavioral sciences*, 2nd edn, Lawrence Erlbanm Associates, Hillsdale, NJ.

Cohen, JB & Areni, CS 1991, "Affect and consumer behavior", *Handbook of Consumer Behavior*, no. 7, pp. 188-240.

Cohen, JB & Areni, CS 1991, "Affect and consumer behavior", *Handbook of consumer behavior*, vol. 4, no. 7, pp. 188-240.

Cohen, SA, Prayag, G & Moital, M 2014, "Consumer behaviour in tourism: Concepts, influences and opportunities", *Current Issues in Tourism*, vol. 17, no. 10, pp. 872-909.

Conrad, KJ, Wright, BD, McKnight, P, McFall, M, Fontana, A & Rosenheck, R 2004, "Comparing traditional and Rasch analyses of the Mississippi PTSD Scale: Revealing limitations of reverse-scored items", *Journal of applied measurement*, vol. 5, no. 1, pp. 15-30.

Costa, PT & McCrae, RR 1980, "Influence of extraversion and neuroticism on subjective well-being: Happy and unhappy people", *Journal of Personality and Social Psychology*, vol. 38, no. 4, pp. 668-678.

Costa, PT & McCrae, RR 1992, *NEO Personality Inventory-Revised (NEO PI-R)*, Professional Manual, Psychological Assessment Resources, Odessa.

Costa, PT & McCrae, RR 1992, *Revised neo personality inventory (neo pi-r) and neo five-factor inventory (neo-ffi)*, Psychological Assessment Resources, Odessa.

Costa, PT, McCrae, RR & Holland, JL 1984, "Personality and vocational interests in an adult sample", *Journal of Applied Psychology*, vol. 69, no. 3, pp. 390-408.

Crawford, JR & Henry, JD 2004, "The Positive and Negative Affect Schedule (PANAS): Construct validity, measurement properties and normative data in a large non-clinical sample", *British Journal of Clinical Psychology*, vol. 43, no. 3, pp. 245-265.

Creswell, JW & Plano Clark, VL 2007, *Designing and conducting Mixed Methods Research*, Sage Publications, Thousand Oaks, CA.

Creswell, JW 2009, *Research design: Qualitative, quantitative, and mixed methods approaches*, 3rd edn, Sage Publications, Thousand Oaks, CA.

Crompton, JL & Love, LL 1995, "The predictive validity of alternative approaches to evaluating quality of a festival", *Journal of Travel Research*, vol. 34, no. 1, pp. 11-24.

Crouch, GI 2004, *Consumer psychology of tourism, hospitality and leisure*, Cabi, London.

Crowe, E & Higgins, ET 1997, "Regulatory focus and strategic inclinations: Promotion and prevention in decision-making", *Organizational behavior and human decision processes*, vol. 69, no. 2, pp. 117-132.

Crowley, C, Harré, R & Tagg, C 2002, "Qualitative research and computing: methodological issues and practices in using QSR NVivo and NUD * IST", *International journal of social research methodology*, vol. 5, no. 3, pp. 193-197.

Cunningham, E 2007, *Structural equation modelling using AMOS, stateline*, Education & Statistics Consultancy, Brunswick, Victoria.

Currie, RR 1997, "A pleasure-tourism behaviors framework", *Annals of Tourism Research*, vol. 24, no. 4, pp. 884-897.

De Bloom, J, Kompier, M, Geurts, S, De Weerth, C, Taris, T & Sonnentag, S 2009, "Do we recover from vacation? Meta-analysis of vacation effects on health and well-being", *Journal of Occupational Health*, vol. 51, no. 1, pp. 13-25.

De Rojas, C & Camarero, C 2008, "Visitors' experience, mood and satisfaction in a heritage context: Evidence from an interpretation center", *Tourism Management*, vol. 29, no. 3, pp. 525-537.

Del Bosque, IR & San Martín, H 2008, "Tourist satisfaction a cognitive-affective model", *Annals of Tourism Research*, vol. 35, no. 2, pp. 551-573.

DeNeve, KM & Cooper, H 1998, "The happy personality: A meta-analysis of 137 personality traits and subjective well-being", *Psychological Bulletin*, vol. 124, no. 2, pp. 197 – 229.

Denissen, JJ, Geenen, R, Van Aken, MA, Gosling, SD & Potter, J 2008, "Development and validation of a Dutch translation of the Big Five Inventory (BFI)", *Journal of Personality Assessment*, vol. 90, no. 2, pp. 152-157.

Denscombe, M 2008, "Communities of practice a research paradigm for the mixed methods approach", *Journal of Mixed Methods Research*, vol. 2, no. 3, pp. 270-283.

Denzin, NK & Lincoln, YS 2005, *The Sage handbook of qualitative research*, 3rd edn, Sage, Thousands Oaks, CA.

Derbaix, C & Pham, MT 1991, "Affective reactions to consumption situations: A pilot investigation", *Journal of Economic Psychology*, vol. 12, no. 2, pp. 325-355.

DeVellis, RF 2012, *Scale development: Theory and applications*, 3rd edn, Sage Publications, Thousand Oaks, CA.

Diamantopoulos, A, Siguaw, JA & Siguaw, JA 2000, *Introducing LISREL: A guide for the uninitiated*, Sage Publications, London.

Diener, E 2000, "Subjective well-being: The science of happiness and a proposal for a national index", *American Psychologist*, vol. 55, no. 1, pp. 34-48.

Diener, E & Biswas-Diener, R 2008, *Happiness: Unlocking the mysteries of psychological wealth*, Blackwell Publishing, Oxford.

Donovan, RJ, Rossiter, JR, Marcoolyn, G & Nesdale, A 1994, "Store atmosphere and purchasing behavior", *Journal of Retailing*, vol. 70, no. 3, pp. 283-294.

Du, J & Dai, B 2005, *Annual report of China outbound tourism development* 2004, China Tourism Education Press, Beijing.

Dubé, L & Morgan, MS 1998, "Capturing the dynamics of in-process consumption emotions and satisfaction in extended service transactions", *International Journal of Research in Marketing*, vol. 15, no. 4, pp. 309-320.

Easterbrook, G 2003, *The progress paradox: How life gets better while people feel worse*, Random House, New York.

Edell, JA & Burke, MC 1987, "The power of feelings in understanding advertising effects", *Journal of Consumer Research*, pp. 421-433.

Elanain, HA 2007, "Relationship between personality and organizational citizenship behavior: Does personality influence employee citizenship", *International Review of Business Research Papers*, vol. 3, no. 4, pp. 31-43.

Engeset, MG & Elvekrok, I 2015, "Authentic concepts: Effects on tourist satisfaction", *Journal of Travel Research*, vol. 54, no. 4, pp. 456-466.

Epstein, S 1979, "The stability of behavior: On predicting most of the people much of the time", *Journal of Personality and Social Psychology*, vol. 37, no. 7, pp. 1097-1108.

Eusébio, C & Vieira, AL 2013, "Destination attributes' evaluation, satisfaction and behavioural intentions: a structural modelling approach", *International Journal of Tourism Research*, vol. 15, no. 1, pp. 66-80.

Eysenck, HJ 1992, "A reply to Costa and McCrae. P or A and C—the role of theory", *Personality and Individual Differences*, vol. 13, no. 8, pp. 867-868.

Fan, X, Thompson, B & Wang, L 1999, "The effects of sample size, estimation methods, and model specification on SEM indices", *Structural Equation Modeling*, vol. 6, no. 1, pp. 56-83.

Farber, ME & Hall, TE 2007, "Emotion and environment: Visitors' extraordinary experiences along the Dalton highway in Alaska", *Journal of Leisure Research*, vol. 39, no. 2, pp. 248-270.

Fassinger, RE 1987, "Use of structural equation modeling in counseling psychology research", *Journal of Counseling Psychology*, vol. 34, no. 4, pp. 425-436.

Faullant, R, Matzler, K & Mooradian, TA 2011, "Personality, basic emotions, and satisfaction: Primary emotions in the mountaineering experience", *Tourism Management*, vol. 32, no. 6, pp. 1423-1430.

Fereday, J & Muir-Cochrane, E 2006, "The role of performance feedback in the self-assessment of competence: A research study with nursing clinicians", *Collegian*, vol. 13, no. 1, pp. 10-15.

Filep, S & Deery, M 2010, "Towards a picture of tourists' happiness", *Tourism Analysis*, vol. 15, no. 4, pp. 399-410.

Fleeson, W 2004, "Moving personality beyond the person-situation debate the challenge and the opportunity of within-person variability", *Current Directions in Psychological Science*, vol. 13, no. 2, pp. 83-87.

Fornell, C & Larcker, DF 1981, "Evaluating structural equation models with unobservable variables and measurement error", *Journal of Marketing Research*, vol. 18, no. 1, pp. 65-78.

Fournier, S & Mick, DG 1999, "Rediscovering satisfaction", *The Journal of Marketing*, pp. 5-23.

Fredrickson, BL 1998, "What good are positive emotions?", *Review of General Psychology*, vol. 2, no. 3, pp. 300-308.

Fredrickson, BL 2000, "Extracting meaning from past affective experiences: The importance of peaks, ends, and specific emotions", *Cognition & Emotion*, vol. 14, no. 4, pp. 577-606.

Fredrickson, BL 2001, "The role of positive emotions in positive psychology: The broaden-and-build theory of positive emotions", *American Psychologist*, vol. 56, no. 3, pp. 218-221.

Fredrickson, BL & Losada, MF 2005, "Positive affect and the complex dynamics of human flourishing", *American Psychologist*, vol. 60, no. 7, pp. 678-693.

Friedman, HS, Tucker, JS, Schwartz, JE, Martin, LR, Tomlinson-Keasey, C, Wingard, DL & Criqui, MH 1995, "Childhood conscientiousness and longevity: health behaviors and cause of death", *Journal of Personality and Social Psychology*, vol. 68, no. 4, pp. 696-703.

Friedman, HS & Schustack, MW 2009, *Personality: Classic theories and modern research*, 4th edn,

Pearson, Boston.

Frew, EA & Shaw, RN 1999, "The relationship between personality, gender, and tourism behavior", *Tourism Management*, vol. 20, no. 2, pp. 193-202.

Fuchs, M & Weiermair, K 2004, "Destination benchmarking: An indicator-system's potential for exploring guest satisfaction", *Journal of Travel Research*, vol. 42, no. 3, pp. 212-225.

Funder, DC 2009, "Persons, behaviors and situations: An agenda for personality psychology in the postwar era", *Journal of Research in Personality*, vol. 43, no. 2, pp. 120-126.

Gagne, P & Hancock, GR 2006, "Measurement model quality, sample size, and solution propriety in confirmatory factor models", *Multivariate Behavioral Research*, vol. 41, no. 1, pp. 65-83.

Galloway, G, Mitchell, R, Getz, D, Crouch, G & Ong, B 2008, "Sensation seeking and the prediction of attitudes and behaviours of wine tourists", *Tourism Management*, vol. 29, no. 5, pp. 950-966.

Gardner, MP 1985, "Mood states and consumer behavior: A critical review", *Journal of Consumer Research*, pp. 281-300.

Gellatly, IR 1996, "Conscientiousness and task performance: Test of cognitive process model", *Journal of Applied Psychology*, vol. 81, no. 5, pp. 474-482.

Gilbert, D & Abdullah, J 2004, "Holidaytaking and the sense of well-being", *Annals of Tourism Research*, vol. 31, no. 1, pp. 103-121.

Giluk, TL 2009, "Mindfulness, Big Five personality, and affect: A meta-analysis", *Personality and Individual Differences*, vol. 47, no. 8, pp. 805-811.

Glesne, C & Peshkin, A 1999, *Becoming qualitative researchers: An introduction*, 2nd edn, Longman White Plains, New York.

Gnoth, J, Andreu, L, Kozak, M, Dmitrovic, T, Knezevic Cvelbar, L, Kolar, T, Makovec Brencic, M, Ograjenšek, I & Zabkar, V 2009, "Conceptualizing tourist satisfaction at the destination level", *International Journal of Culture, Tourism and Hospitality Research*, vol. 3, no. 2, pp. 116-126.

Goldberg, LR 1990, "An alternative 'description of personality': The Big-Five factor structure", *Journal of Personality and Social Psychology*, vol. 59, no. 6, pp. 1216-1229.

Goldberg, LR 1992, "The development of markers for the Big-Five factor structure", *Psychological assessment*, vol. 4, no. 1, pp. 26-42.

Goossens, C 2000, "Tourism information and pleasure motivation", *Annals of Tourism Research*, vol. 27, no. 2, pp. 301-321.

Gosling, SD, Rentfrow, PJ & Swann Jr, WB 2003, "A very brief measure of the Big-Five personality domains", *Journal of Research in Personality*, vol. 37, no. 6, pp. 504-528.

Gountas, J & Gountas, S 2007, "Personality orientations, emotional states, customer satisfaction, and intention to repurchase", *Journal of Business Research*, vol. 60, no. 1, pp. 72-75.

Graburn, NH 2001, "Secular ritual: A general theory of tourism", in Smith, VL & Brent, M (eds), *Hosts and guests revisited: Tourism issues of the 21st century*, Cognizant Communications Corporation, Elmsford, NY, pp. 42-50.

Grant, S, Langan-Fox, J & Anglim, J 2009, "The big five traits as predictors of subjective and psychological well-being", *Psychological Reports*, vol. 105, no. 1, pp. 205-231.

Grappi, S & Montanari, F 2011, "The role of social identification and hedonism in affecting tourist re-patronizing behaviours: The case of an Italian festival", *Tourism Management*, vol. 32, no. 5, pp. 1128-1140.

Graziano, WG, Habashi, MM, Sheese, BE & Tobin, RM 2007, "Agreeableness, empathy, and helping: A person × situation perspective", *Journal of Personality and Social Psychology*, vol. 93, no. 4, pp. 583-598.

Gretzel, U, Mitsche, N, Hwang, YH & Fesenmaier, DR 2004, "Tell me who you are and I will tell you where to go: use of travel personalities in destination recommendation systems", *Information Technology & Tourism*, vol. 7, no. 1, pp. 3-12.

Grisaffe, DB & Nguyen, HP 2011, "Antecedents of emotional attachment to brands", *Journal of Business Research*, vol. 64, no. 10, pp. 1052-1059.

Gross, JJ, Sutton, SK & Ketelaar, T 1998, "Affective-reactivity views", *Personality and Social Psychology Bulletin*, vol. 24, no. 13, pp. 279-287.

Gudykunst, WB & Matsumoto, Y 1996, "Cross cultural variability of communication in personal relationships", *Communication in personal relationships across cultures*, pp. 19-56.

Guest, G, Bunce, A & Johnson, L 2006, "How many interviews are enough? An experiment with data saturation and variability", *Field Methods*, vol. 18, no. 1, pp. 59-82.

Guest, G, MacQueen, KM & Namey, EE 2011, *Applied thematic analysis*, Sage, Thousand Oaks, CA.

Guo, W, Turner, LW & King, BE 2002, "The emerging golden age of Chinese tourism and its historical antecedents: A thematic investigation", *Tourism Culture & Communication*, vol. 3, no. 3, pp. 131-146.

Guo, Y, Kim, SS & Timothy, DJ 2007, "Development characteristics and implications of mainland Chinese outbound tourism", *Asia Pacific Journal of Tourism Research*, vol. 12, no. 4, pp. 313-332.

Gursoy, D, Boylu, Y & Avci, U 2011, "Identifying the complex relationships among emotional labor and its correlates", *International Journal of Hospitality Management*, vol. 30, no. 4, pp. 783-794.

Gursoy, D, McCleary, KW & Lepsito, LR 2007, "Propensity to complain: Effects of personality and behavioral factors", *Journal of Hospitality & Tourism Research*, vol. 31, no. 3, pp. 358-386.

Gutiérrez, JLG, Jiménez, BM, Hernández, EG & Pcn, C 2005, "Personality and subjective well-being: Big five correlates and demographic variables", *Personality and Individual Differences*, vol. 38, no. 7, pp. 1561-1569.

Hair, JF, Black, WC, Babin, BJ, Anderson, RE & Tatham RL 2010, *Multivariate data analysis*, 7th edn, Pearson Prentice Hall, Upper Saddle River, NJ.

Hall, CM 1997, *Tourism in the Pacific Rim: Development, impacts, and markets*, 2nd edn, Addison Wesley Longman, Melbourne.

Han, H & Back, KJ 2007, "Assessing customers' emotional experiences influencing their satisfaction in the lodging industry", *Journal of Travel & Tourism Marketing*, vol. 23, no. 1, pp. 43-56.

Han, H, Back, KJ & Barrett, B 2010, "A consumption emotion measurement development: A full-service restaurant setting", *The Service Industries Journal*, vol. 30, no. 2, pp. 299-320.

Han, H & Jeong, C 2013, "Multi-dimensions of patrons' emotional experiences in upscale restaurants and their role in loyalty formation: Emotion scale improvement", *International Journal of Hospitality Management*, vol. 32, pp. 59-70.

Hattrup, K & Jackson, S 1996, "Learning about individual differences by taking situations seriously", in

Murphy, KR (ed), *Individual differences and behavior in organizations*, Jossey-Bass, san Francisco, pp. 507-547.

Havlena, WJ & Holbrook, MB 1986, "The varieties of consumption experience: Comparing two typologies of emotion in consumer behavior", *Journal of Consumer Research*, pp. 394-404.

Hay, I 2005, *Qualitative research methods in human geography*, 2nd edn, Oxford University Press, Oxford.

Haynes, SN, Richard, D & Kubany, ES 1995, "Content validity in psychological assessment: A functional approach to concepts and methods", *Psychological Assessment*, vol. 7, no. 3, pp. 238-249.

He, Y & Song, H 2009, "A mediation model of tourists' repurchase intentions for packaged tour services", *Journal of Travel Research*, vol. 47, no. 3, pp. 317-331.

Heung, VC 2000, "Satisfaction levels of mainland Chinese travelers with Hong Kong hotel services", *International Journal of Contemporary Hospitality Management*, vol. 12, no. 5, pp. 308-315.

Heung, VC, Wong, M & Qu, H 2002, "A Study of Tourists' Satisfaction and Post-Experience Behavioral Intentions in Relation to Airport Restaurant Services in the Hong Kong SAR", *Journal of Travel & Tourism Marketing*, vol. 12, no. 2-3, pp. 111-135.

Hirsh, JB & Dolderman, D 2007, "Personality predictors of consumerism and environmentalism: A preliminary study", *Personality and Individual Differences*, vol. 43, no. 6, pp. 1583-1593.

Hirsh, JB 2010, "Personality and environmental concern", *Journal of Environmental Psychology*, vol. 30, no. 2, pp. 245-248.

Hogan, J & Holland, B 2003, "Using theory to evaluate personality and job-performance relations: a socioanalytic perspective", *Journal of Applied Psychology*, vol. 88, no. 1, pp. 100-112.

Holbrook, MB & Westwood, RA 1989, "The role of emotion in advertising revisited: Testing a typology of emotional responses", *Cognitive and Affective Responses to Advertising*, pp. 353-371.

Holbrook, MB 1993, "Nostalgia and consumption preferences: Some emerging patterns of consumer tastes", *Journal of Consumer Research*, pp. 245-256.

Homburg, C, Koschate, N & Hoyer, WD 2005, "Do satisfied customers really pay more? A study of the relationship between customer satisfaction and willingness to pay", *Journal of Marketing*, vol. 69, no. 2, pp. 84-96.

Horan, PM, DiStefano, C & Motl, RW 2003, "Wording effects in self-esteem scales: Methodological artifact or response style?", *Structural Equation Modeling*, vol. 10, no. 3, pp. 435-455.

Hosany, S & Gilbert, D 2010, "Measuring tourists' emotional experiences toward hedonic holiday destinations", *Journal of Travel Research*, vol. 49, no. 4, pp. 513-526.

Hosany, S & Witham, M 2010, "Dimensions of cruisers' experiences, satisfaction, and intention to recommend", *Journal of Travel Research*, vol. 49, no. 3, pp. 351-364.

Hosany, S 2012, "Appraisal determinants of tourist emotional responses", *Journal of Travel Research*, vol. 51, no. 3, pp. 303-314.

Hosany, S & Prayag, G 2013, "Patterns of tourists' emotional responses, satisfaction, and intention to recommend", *Journal of Business Research*, vol. 66, no. 6, pp. 730-737.

Hosany, S, Prayag, G, Deesilatham, S, Causevic, S & Odeh, K 2015, "Measuring tourists' emotional experiences: further validation of the destination emotion scale", *Journal of Travel Research*, vol. 54, no. 4, pp. 482-495.

Hough, LM & Schneider, R 1996, "Personality traits, taxonomies, and applications in organizations", in Murphy, KR (ed), *Individual differences and behavior in organizations*, Jossey-Bass, San Francisco, pp. 31-88.

Hoxter, AL & Lester, D 1988, "Tourist behavior and personality", *Personality and Individual Differences*, vol. 9, no. 1, pp. 177-178.

Hoyle, RH 2000, "Confirmatory factor analysis", in Tinsley, HE & Brown, SD (eds), *Handbook of applied multivariate statistics and mathematical modeling*, Academic Press, Cambridge, Massachusetts, pp. 465-497.

Hsu, C & Lam, T 2003, "Mainland Chinese travelers's motivations and barriers of visiting Hong Kong", *Journal of Academy of Business and Economics*, vol. 2, no. 1, pp. 60-67.

Hsu, CH 2003, "Mature motorcoach travelers' satisfaction: A preliminary step toward measurement development", *Journal of Hospitality & Tourism Research*, vol. 27, no. 3, pp. 291-309.

Hsu, CH & Kang, SK 2007, "CHAID-based segmentation: International visitors' trip characteristics and perceptions", *Journal of Travel Research*, vol. 46, no. 2, pp. 207-216.

Hsu, CH & Song, H 2012, "Projected images of major Chinese outbound destinations", *Asia Pacific Journal of Tourism Research*, vol. 17, no. 5, pp. 577-593.

Hsu, CHC, Cai, LA & Li, M 2010, "Expectation, motivation, and attitude: A tourist behavioral model", *Journal of Travel Research*, vol. 49, no. 3, pp. 282-295.

Hu, LT & Bentler, PM 1999, "Cutoff criteria for fit indexes in covariance structure analysis: Conventional criteria versus new alternatives", *Structural Equation Modeling: A Multidisciplinary Journal*, vol. 6, no. 1, pp. 1-55.

Hua, Y & Yoo, JE 2011, "Travel motivations of mainland Chinese Travellers to the United States", *Journal of China Tourism Research*, vol. 7, no. 4, pp. 355-376.

Huang, J & Hsu, CH 2009, "The impact of customer-to-customer interaction on cruise experience and vacation satisfaction", *Journal of Travel Research*, vol. 49, no. 1, pp. 79-92.

Huang, JH & Yang, YC 2010, "The relationship between personality traits and online shopping motivations", *Social Behavior and Personality: An International Journal*, vol. 38, no. 5, pp. 673-679.

Huang, L, Gursoy, D & Xu, H 2014, "Impact of personality traits and involvement on prior knowledge", *Annals of Tourism Research*, vol. 48, pp. 42-57.

Huang, SS & Gross, MJ 2010, "Australia's destination image among mainland Chinese travellers: An exploratory study", *Journal of Travel & Tourism Marketing*, vol. 27, no. 1, pp. 63-81.

Huang, SS & Hsu, CH 2005, "Mainland Chinese residents' perceptions and motivations of visiting Hong Kong: Evidence from focus group interviews", *Asia Pacific Journal of Tourism Research*, vol. 10, no. 2, pp. 191-205.

Huang, SS, Hsu, CH & Chan, A 2010, "Tour guide performance and tourist satisfaction: A study of the package tours in Shanghai", *Journal of Hospitality & Tourism Research*, vol. 34, no. 1, pp. 3-33.

Huang, SS & Sun, XM 2014, *Economy hotels in China: A glocalized innovative hospitality sector*,

Routledge, London.

Huang, SS & Weiler, B 2010, "A review and evaluation of China's quality assurance system for tour guiding", *Journal of Sustainable Tourism*, vol. 18, no. 7, pp. 845-860.

Huang, SS, Weiler, B & Assaker, G 2015, "Effects of interpretive guiding outcomes on tourist satisfaction and behavioral intention", *Journal of Travel Research*, vol. 54, no. 3, pp. 344-358.

Huh, J, Uysal, M & McCleary, K 2006, "Cultural/heritage destinations: Tourist satisfaction and market segmentation", *Journal of Hospitality & Leisure Marketing*, vol. 14, no. 3, pp. 81-99.

Hui, TK, Wan, D & Ho, A 2007, "Tourists' satisfaction, recommendation and revisiting Singapore", *Tourism management*, vol. 28, no. 4, pp. 965-975.

Iacobucci, D, Saldanha, N & Deng, X 2007, "A meditation on mediation: Evidence that structural equations models perform better than regressions", *Journal of Consumer Psychology*, vol. 17, no. 2, pp. 139-153.

Inman, JJ, Dyer, JS & Jia, J 1997, "A generalized utility model of disappointment and regret effects on post-choice valuation", *Marketing Science*, vol. 16, no. 2, pp. 97-111.

Izard, CE 1977, *Human emotions*, Plenum Press, New York.

Izard, CE, Libero, DZ, Putnam, P & Haynes, OM 1993, "Stability of emotion experiences and their relations to traits of personality", *Journal of Personality and Social Psychology*, vol. 64, pp. 847-860.

Izard, CE 1997, "Emotions and facial expressions: A perspective from Differential Emotions Theory", *The Psychology of Facial Expression*, vol. 2, pp. 57-77.

Jang, SS, Bai, B, Hu, C & Wu, C-ME 2009, "Affect, travel motivation, and travel intention: A senior market", *Journal of Hospitality & Tourism Research*, vol. 33, no. 1, pp. 51-73.

Jang, SS & Namkung, Y 2009, "Perceived quality, emotions, and behavioral intentions: Application of an extended Mehrabian-Russell model to restaurants", *Journal of Business Research*, vol. 62, no. 4, pp. 451-460.

Jayanti, RK 1998, "Affective responses towards service providers: a categorization theory perspective", *Journal of Consumer Satisfaction Dissatisfaction and Complaining Behavior*, vol. 11, pp. 51-61.

Jeng, S-P & Teng, C-I 2008, "Personality and motivations for playing online games", *Social Behavior and Personality: An International Journal*, vol. 36, no. 8, pp. 1053-1060.

Jennings, G 2001, *Tourism research*, John Wiley and Sons, Sydney.

Ji, LJ, Peng, K & Nisbett, RE 2000, "Culture, control, and perception of relationships in the environment", *Journal of Personality and Social Psychology*, vol. 78, no. 5, pp. 943-956.

Jiang, S, Scott, N, Ding, P & Zou, TT 2012, "Exploring Chinese outbound tourism motivation using means-end chains: A conceptual model", *Journal of China Tourism Research*, vol. 8, no. 4, pp. 359-372.

Jin, N, Lee, S & Gopalan, R 2012, "How do individual personality traits (D) influence perceived satisfaction with service for college students (C) in a casual restaurant setting (I)?: The CID framework", *Journal of Hospitality Marketing & Management*, vol. 21, no. 6, pp. 591-616.

Jin, L, Watkins, D & Yuen, M 2009, "Personality, career decision self-efficacy and commitment to the career choices process among Chinese graduate students", *Journal of Vocational Behavior*, vol. 74, no. 1, pp. 47-52.

Jin, X & Wang, Y 2016, "Chinese outbound tourism research: A review", *Journal of Travel Research*, vol. 55, no. 4, pp. 440-453.

Johanson, MM 2008, "The outbound mainland China market to the United States: Uncovering motivations for future travel to Hawaii", *Journal of Hospitality & Leisure Marketing*, vol. 16, no. 1-2, pp. 41-59.

John, OP, Donahue, EM & Kentle, RL 1991, *The big five inventory—versions 4a and 54*, Institute of Personality and Social Research, University of California, Berkerley.

John, OP & Gross, JJ 2004, "Healthy and unhealthy emotion regulation: Personality processes, individual differences, and life span development", *Journal of Personality*, vol. 72, no. 6, pp. 1301-1334.

John, OP & Srivastava, S 1999, "The Big Five trait taxonomy: History, measurement, and theoretical perspectives", in Pervin, LA, & John, OP (ed), *Handbook of Personality: Theory and Research*, vol. 2, Guilford Press, New York, pp. 102-138.

Johns, N, Avcí, T & Karatepe, OM 2004, "Measuring service quality of travel agents: Evidence from Northern Cyprus", *The Service Industries Journal*, vol. 24, no. 3, pp. 82-100.

Johnson, RB & Onwuegbuzie, AJ 2004, "Mixed methods research: A research paradigm whose time has come", *Educational Researcher*, vol. 33, no. 7, pp. 14-26.

Jöreskog, KG & Sörbom, D 1989, *LISREL 7: A guide to the program and applications*, 2nd edn, Spss Publications, Chicago.

Joshanloo, M & Afshari, S 2011, "Big five personality traits and self-esteem as predictors of life satisfaction in Iranian Muslim University students", *Journal of Happiness Studies*, vol. 12, no. 1, pp. 105-113.

Josselson, R 2007, "The ethical attitude in narrative research: Principles and practicalities", in Clandinin, DJ (ed), *Handbook of narrative inquiry: Mapping a methodology*, Sage Publications, Thousand Oaks: CA, pp. 537-567.

JSChina 2015, *The number of Jiangsu outbound tourists in 2014*, viewed June 8, 2015, < http://tour. jschina. com. cn/system/2015/2/05/022827597. shtml >.

Judge, TA, Locke, EA, Durham, CC & Kluger, AN 1998, "Dispositional effects on job and life satisfaction: The role of core evaluations", *Journal of Applied Psychology*, vol. 83, no. 1, pp. 17-26.

Jun, S, Hyun, YJ, Gentry, JW & Song, CS 2001, "The relative influence of affective experience on consumer satisfaction under positive versus negative discrepancies", *Journal of Consumer Satisfaction, Dissatisfaction and Complaining Behaviour*, vol. 14, pp. 141-153.

Kahneman, D 1999, "Objective happiness", in Kahneman, D, Diener, E & Schwartz, N (eds), *Well-being: Foundations of hedonic psychology*, Russell Sage Foundation, New York, pp. 3-5.

Kahneman, D, Krueger, AB, Schkade, DA, Schwarz, N & Stone, AA 2004, "A survey method for characterizing daily life experience: The day reconstruction method", *Science*, vol. 306, no. 5702, pp. 1776-1780.

Kamdar, D & Van Dyne, L 2007, "The joint effects of personality and workplace social exchange relationships in predicting task performance and citizenship performance", *Journal of Applied Psychology*, vol. 92, no. 5, pp. 1286-1299.

Kang, X & Ma, Y 2009, "Rethinking six components in tourism", *Tourism Forum*, vol. 2, no. 4, pp. 475-478.

Kaplan, D 2008, *Structural equation modeling: Foundations and extensions*, 2nd edn, Sage Publications,

Thousand Oaks.

Kassin, SM 2003, *Essentials of psychology*, Prentice Hall, New York.

Kau, AK & Lim, PS 2005, "Clustering of Chinese tourists to Singapore: An analysis of their motivations, values and satisfaction", *International Journal of Tourism Research*, vol. 7, no. 4 5, pp. 231-248.

Kau, AK & Lim, PS 2005, "Clustering of Chinese tourists to Singapore: An analysis of their motivations, values and satisfaction", *International Journal of Tourism Research*, vol. 7, no. 4-5, pp. 231-248.

Keating, B & Kriz, A 2008, "Outbound tourism from China: Literature review and research agenda", *Journal of Hospitality and Tourism Management*, vol. 15, no. 2, pp. 32-41.

Keating, B, Huang, S, Kriz, A & Heung, V 2015, "A systematic review of the Chinese outbound tourism literature: 1983-2012", *Journal of Travel & Tourism Marketing*, vol. 32, no. 1-2, pp. 2-17.

Kelly, WE, Johnson, JL & Miller, MJ 2003, "Conscientiousness and the prediction of task duration", *North American Journal of Psychology*, vol. 5, no. 3, pp. 56-67.

Kim, SS, Guo, Y & Agrusa, J 2005, "Preference and positioning analyses of overseas destinations by mainland Chinese outbound pleasure tourists", *Journal of Travel Research*, vol. 44, no. 2, pp. 212-220.

Kim, WG, Cai, LA & Jung, K 2004, "A profile of the Chinese casino vacationer to South Korea", *Journal of Hospitality & Leisure Marketing*, vol. 11, no. 2-3, pp. 65-79.

Kim, YG, Suh, BW & Eves, A 2010, "The relationships between food-related personality traits, satisfaction, and loyalty among visitors attending food events and festivals", *International Journal of Hospitality Management*, vol. 29, no. 2, pp. 216-226.

Kline, RB 2005, *Principles and practice of structural equation modeling*, 2nd edn, Guilford Press, New York.

Kozak, M 2000, "A critical review of approaches to measure satisfaction with tourist destinations", *Tourism Analysis*, vol. 5, no. 2/4, pp. 191-196.

Kozak, M & Rimmington, M 2000, "Tourist satisfaction with Mallorca, Spain, as an off-season holiday destination", *Journal of Travel Research*, vol. 38, no. 3, pp. 260-269.

Kozak, M 2001, "Repeaters' behavior at two distinct destinations", *Annals of Tourism Research*, vol. 28, no. 3, pp. 784-807.

Krueger, RA & Casey, MA 2009, *Focus groups: A practical guide for applied research*, 4th edn, Sage Publications, Thousand Oaks, CA.

Kvale, S & Brinkmann, S 2009, *Interviews: Learning the craft of qualitative research interviewing*, 2nd edn, SAGE Publications, Thousand Oaks.

Kwortnik Jr, RJ & Ross Jr, WT 2007, "The role of positive emotions in experiential decisions", *International Journal of Research in Marketing*, vol. 24, no. 4, pp. 324-335.

Kwortnik, RJ & Ross, WT 2007, "The role of positive emotions in experiential decisions", *International Journal of Research in Marketing*, vol. 24, no. 4, pp. 324-335.

Ladhari, R 2007, "The effect of consumption emotions on satisfaction and word-of-mouth communications", *Psychology & Marketing*, vol. 24, no. 12, pp. 1085-1108.

Ladhari, R, Brun, I & Morales, M 2008, "Determinants of dining satisfaction and post-dining behavioral intentions", *International Journal of Hospitality Management*, vol. 27, no. 4, pp. 563-573.

Lambie, JA & Marcel, AJ 2002, "Consciousness and the varieties of emotion experience: A theoretical framework", *Psychological Review*, vol. 109, no. 2, pp. 219-259.

Landers, RN & Lounsbury, JW 2006, "An investigation of Big Five and narrow personality traits in relation to Internet usage", *Computers in Human Behavior*, vol. 22, no. 2, pp. 283-293.

Lang, FR, John, D, Lüdtke, O, Schupp, J & Wagner, GG 2011, "Short assessment of the Big Five: Robust across survey methods except telephone interviewing", *Behavior Research Methods*, vol. 43, no. 2, pp. 548-567.

Laros, FJ & Steenkamp, JBE 2004, "Importance of fear in the case of genetically modified food", *Psychology & Marketing*, vol. 21, no. 11, pp. 889-908.

Laros, FJ & Steenkamp, JBE 2005, "Emotions in consumer behavior: A hierarchical approach", *Journal of Business Research*, vol. 58, no. 10, pp. 1437-1445.

LaTour, SA & Peat, NC 1979, "Conceptual and methodological issues in consumer satisfaction research", *Advances in Consumer Research*, vol. 6, no. 1, pp. 15-23.

Lazarus, RS 1991, "Progress on a cognitive-motivational-relational theory of emotion", *American Psychologist*, vol. 46, no. 8, pp. 819-826.

LeDoux, J 2000, "Emotion circuits in the brain", *Annual Review of Neuroscience*, vol. 23, pp. 155-184.

Lee, B & Shafer, CS 2002, "The dynamic nature of leisure experience: An application of affect control theory", *Journal of Leisure Research*, vol. 34, no. 3, pp. 290-301.

Lee, CK, Yoon, YS & Lee, SK 2007, "Investigating the relationships among perceived value, satisfaction, and recommendations: The case of the Korean DMZ", *Tourism Management*, vol. 28, no. 1, pp. 204-214.

Lee, JS, Lee, CK & Choi, Y 2010, "Examining the role of emotional and functional values in festival evaluation", *Journal of Travel Research*, vol. 50, no. 6, pp. 685-696.

Lee, J & Kyle, GT 2013, "The measurement of emotions elicited within festival contexts: A psychometric test of a Festival Consumption Emotions (FCE) scale", *Tourism Analysis*, vol. 18, no. 6, pp. 635-649.

Lee, J 2014, "Visitors' emotional responses to the festival environment", *Journal of Travel & Tourism Marketing*, vol. 31, no. 1, pp. 114-131.

Lee, JJ & Kyle, GT 2013, "The measurement of emotions elicited within festival contexts: A psychometric test of a Festival Consumption Emotions (FCE) Scale", *Tourism Analysis*, vol. 18, no. 6, pp. 635-649.

Lee, JW 2009, "Relatinship between consumer personality and brand personality as self-concept: From the case of Korean automobile brands", *Academy of Marketing Studies Journal*, vol. 13, no. 1, pp. 25-44.

Lee, S, Jeon, S & Kim, D 2011, "The impact of tour quality and tourist satisfaction on tourist loyalty: The case of Chinese tourists in Korea", *Tourism Management*, vol. 32, no. 5, pp. 1115-1124.

Lee, YK, Lee, CK, Lee, SK & Babin, BJ 2008, "Festivalscapes and patrons' emotions, satisfaction, and loyalty", *Journal of Business Research*, vol. 61, no. 1, pp. 56-64.

Leech, NL & Onwuegbuzie, AJ 2009, "A typology of Mixed Methods Research designs", *Quality & Quantity*, vol. 43, no. 2, pp. 265-275.

Lehto, XY, Choi, S, Lin, Y-C & MacDermid, SM 2009, "Vacation and family functioning", *Annals of Tourism Research*, vol. 36, no. 3, pp. 459-479.

Leiper, N 1995, *Tourism management*, TAFE Publications, Collingwood, Victoria.

Lepp, A & Gibson, H 2008, "Sensation seeking and tourism: Tourist role, perception of risk and destination choice", *Tourism Management*, vol. 29, no. 4, pp. 740-750.

Leung, DY, Wong, EM, Chan, SS & Lam, T 2013, "Psychometric properties of the Big Five Inventory in a Chinese sample of smokers receiving cessation treatment: A validation study", *Journal of Nursing Education & Practice*, vol. 3, no. 6, pp. 1-10.

Leung, R & Law, R 2010, "A review of personality research in the tourism and hospitality context", *Journal of Travel & Tourism Marketing*, vol. 27, no. 5, pp. 439-459.

Levine, TR 2005, "Confirmatory factor analysis and scale validation in communication research", *Communication Research Reports*, vol. 22, no. 4, pp. 335-338.

Li, G, Song, H, Chen, JL & Wu, DC 2012, "Comparing mainland Chinese tourists' satisfaction with Hong Kong and the UK using tourist satisfaction index", *Journal of China Tourism Research*, vol. 8, no. 4, pp. 373-394.

Li, JW & Carr, N 2004, "Visitor satisfaction: An analysis of mainland Chinese tourists on the Australian Gold Coast", *International Journal of Hospitality & Tourism Administration*, vol. 5, no. 3, pp. 31-48.

Li, M 2007, "Modeling the travel motivation of mainland Chinese outbound tourists", Purdue University.

Li, M, Zhang, H, Mao, I & Deng, C 2011, "Segmenting Chinese outbound tourists by perceived constraints", *Journal of Travel & Tourism Marketing*, vol. 28, no. 6, pp. 629-643.

Li, S, Scott, N & Walters, G 2015, "Current and potential methods for measuring emotion in tourism experiences: A review", *Current Issues in Tourism*, vol. 18, no. 9, pp. 805-827.

Li, XR, Lai, C, Harrill, R, Kline, S & Wang, L 2011, "When east meets west: An exploratory study on Chinese outbound tourists' travel expectations", *Tourism Management*, vol. 32, no. 4, pp. 741-749.

Lin, IY & Mattila, AS 2010, "Restaurant servicescape, service encounter, and perceived congruency on customers' emotions and satisfaction", *Journal of Hospitality Marketing & Management*, vol. 19, no. 8, pp. 819-841.

Lin, LY 2010, "The relationship of consumer personality trait, brand personality and brand loyalty: An empirical study of toys and video games buyers", *Journal of Product & Brand Management*, vol. 19, no. 1, pp. 4-17.

Lin, YH & Lin, KQ 2006, "Assessing mainland Chinese visitors' satisfaction with shopping in Taiwan", *Asia Pacific Journal of Tourism Research*, vol. 11, no. 3, pp. 247-268.

Lin, Y, Kerstetter, D, Nawijn, J & Mitas, O 2014, "Changes in emotions and their interactions with personality in a vacation context", *Tourism Management*, vol. 40, pp. 416-424.

Lindell, MK & Whitney, DJ 2001, "Accounting for common method variance in cross-sectional research designs", *Journal of Applied Psychology*, vol. 86, no. 1, pp. 114-128.

Little, TD, Lindenberger, U & Nesselroade, JR 1999, "On selecting indicators for multivariate measurement and modeling with latent variables: When 'good' indicators are bad and 'bad' indicators are good", *Psychological Methods*, vol. 4, no. 2, pp. 192-201.

Litvin, SW 2006, "Revisiting Plog's model of allocentricity and psychocentricity one more time", *Cornell Hotel and Restaurant Administration Quarterly*, vol. 47, no. 3, pp. 245-253.

Liu, CM & Chen, KJ 2006, "Personality traits as antecedents of employee customer orientation: A case study in the hospitality industry", *International Journal of Management*, vol. 23, no. 3, pp. 478-485.

Lucas, RE, Diener, E, Grob, A, Suh, EM & Shao, L 2000, "Cross-cultural evidence for the fundamental features of extraversion", *Journal of Personality and Social Psychology*, vol. 79, no. 3, pp. 452-465.

Lucas, RE & Fujita, F 2000, "Factors influencing the relation between extraversion and pleasant affect", *Journal of Personality and Social Psychology*, vol. 79, no. 6, pp. 1039-1052.

Ma, J, Gao, J, Scott, N & Ding, P 2013, "Customer delight from theme park experiences: The antecedents of delight based on cognitive appraisal theory", *Annals of Tourism Research*, vol. 42, pp. 359-381.

MacCallum, RC, Browne, MW & Sugawara, HM 1996, "Power analysis and determination of sample size for covariance structure modeling", *Psychological Methods*, vol. 1, no. 2, pp. 130-139.

Machleit, KA & Eroglu, SA 2000, "Describing and measuring emotional response to shopping experience", *Journal of Business Research*, vol. 49, no. 2, pp. 101-111.

MacLean, LM, Meyer, M & Estable, A 2004, "Improving accuracy of transcripts in qualitative research", *Qualitative Health Research*, vol. 14, no. 1, pp. 113-123.

Madrigal, R 1995, "Cognitive and affective determinants of fan satisfaction with sporting event attendance", *Journal article by Robert Madrigal*; *Journal of Leisure Research*, vol. 27, pp. 35-48.

Mak, B 2013, "The influence of political ideology on the outbound tourism in China", *Journal of China Tourism Research*, vol. 9, no. 1, pp. 1-26.

Mannell, RC & Iso-Ahola, SE 1987, "Psychological nature of leisure and tourism experience", *Annals of Tourism Research*, vol. 14, no. 3, pp. 314-331.

Mano, H & Oliver, RL 1993, "Assessing the dimensionality and structure of the consumption experience: Evaluation, feeling, and satisfaction", *Journal of Consumer Research*, vol. 20, no. 3, pp. 451-466.

Mardia, KV 1970, "Measures of multivariate skewness and kurtosis with applications", *Biometrika*, vol. 57, no. 3, pp. 519-530.

Mardia, KV 1974, "Applications of some measures of multivariate skewness and kurtosis in testing normality and robustness studies", *Sankhyā: The Indian Journal of Statistics, Series B*, pp. 115-128.

Marsh, HW, Balla, JR & McDonald, RP 1988, "Goodness-of-fit indexes in confirmatory factor analysis: The effect of sample size", *Psychological Bulletin*, vol. 103, no. 3, pp. 391-399.

Martin, D, O'neill, M, Hubbard, S & Palmer, A 2008, "The role of emotion in explaining consumer satisfaction and future behavioural intention", *Journal of Services Marketing*, vol. 22, no. 3, pp. 224-236.

Martin, LL & Tesser, A 1996, *Striving and feeling: Interactions among goals, affect, and self-regulation*, Psychology Press, London.

Martin, LR & Friedman, HS 2000, "Comparing personality scales across time: An illustrative study of validity and consistency in life-span archival data", *Journal of Personality*, vol. 68, no. 1, pp. 85-110.

Martínez Caro, L & Martínez García, JA 2007, "Cognitive-affective model of consumer satisfaction: An exploratory study within the framework of a sporting event", *Journal of Business Research*, vol. 60, no. 2, pp. 108-114.

Maslow, AH, Frager, R, Fadiman, J, McReynolds, C & Cox, R 1970, *Motivation and personality*, Harper & Row New York.

Mason, MC & Paggiaro, A 2012, "Investigating the role of festivalscape in culinary tourism: The case of food and wine events", *Tourism management*, vol. 33, no. 6, pp. 1329-1336.

Matsumoto, D 2006, "Are cultural differences in emotion regulation mediated by personality traits?", *Journal of Cross-Cultural Psychology*, vol. 37, no. 4, pp. 421-437.

Matzler, K, Faullant, R, Renzl, B & Leiter, V 2005, "The relationship between personality traits (extraversion and neuroticism), emotions and customer self-satisfaction", *Innovative Marketing*, vol. 1, no. 2, pp. 32-39.

Matzler, K, Bidmon, S & Grabner-Kräuter, S 2006, "Individual determinants of brand affect: The role of the personality traits of extraversion and openness to experience", *Journal of Product & Brand Management*, vol. 15, no. 7, pp. 427-434.

Matzler, K, Renzl, B, Müller, J, Herting, S & Mooradian, TA 2008, "Personality traits and knowledge sharing", *Journal of Economic Psychology*, vol. 29, no. 3, pp. 301-313.

Maxwell, JA 2005, *Qualitative Research Design: An Interactive Approach*, 2nd edn, Sage Publications, Thousand Oaks, CA.

Mayer, KJ, Johnson, L, Hu, C & Chen, S 1998, "Gaming customer satisfaction: An exploratory study", *Journal of Travel Research*, vol. 37, no. 2, pp. 178-183.

McAlister, L & Pessemier, E 1982, "Variety seeking behavior: An interdisciplinary review", *Journal of Consumer Research*, pp. 311-322.

McCabe, S & Johnson, S 2013, "The happiness factor in tourism: Subjective well-being and social tourism", *Annals of Tourism Research*, vol. 41, pp. 42-65.

McCrae, R & Costa, P, Jr 1997, "Conceptions and correlates of openness to experience", in Hogan R., JJ, Briggs S. (ed), *Handbook of personality psychology*, Academic Press, San Diego, pp. 825-847.

McCrae, RR & Costa, PT 1991, "Adding Liebe und Arbeit: The Full Five-Factor Model and Well-Being", *Personality and Social Psychology Bulletin*, vol. 17, no. 2, April 1, 1991, pp. 227-232.

McCrae, RR & John, OP 1992, "An introduction to the five-factor model and its applications", *Journal of Personality*, vol. 60, no. 2, pp. 175-215.

McCrae, RR & Costa, PT 1997, "Personality trait structure as a human universal", *American Psychologist*, vol. 52, no. 5, pp. 509-519.

McCrae, RR & Costa, PT 2003, *Personality in adulthood: A five-factor theory perspective*, Guilford Press, New York.

McCrae, RR & Costa, PT 2004, "A contemplated revision of the NEO Five-Factor Inventory", *Personality and Individual Differences*, vol. 36, no. 3, pp. 587-596.

McGoldrick, PJ & Pieros, CP 1998, "Atmospherics, pleasure and arousal: The influence of response moderators", *Journal of Marketing Management*, vol. 14, no. 1-3, pp. 173-197.

McKercher, B 2005, "Are psychographics predictors of destination life cycles?", *Journal of Travel & Tourism Marketing*, vol. 19, no. 1, pp. 49-55.

McNiel, JM & Fleeson, W 2006, "The causal effects of extraversion on positive affect and neuroticism on negative affect: Manipulating state extraversion and state neuroticism in an experimental approach", *Journal of Research in Personality*, vol. 40, no. 5, pp. 529-550.

Mehrabian, A & Russell, JA 1974, *An approach to environmental psychology*, M. I. T. Press, Cambridge.

Meng, F, Turk, ES & Altintas, V 2012, "Tour operators' service quality and efficacy of satisfaction measurement", *Tourism Analysis*, vol. 17, no. 3, pp. 325-342.

Menon, S & Kahn, BE 1995, "The impact of context on variety seeking in product choices", *Journal of Consumer Research*, pp. 285-295.

Meyer, WU, Reisenzein, R & Schützwohl, A 1997, "Toward a process analysis of emotions: The case of surprise", *Motivation and Emotion*, vol. 21, no. 3, pp. 251-274.

Millán, Á & Esteban, A 2004, "Development of a multiple-item scale for measuring customer satisfaction in travel agencies services", *Tourism Management*, vol. 25, no. 5, pp. 533-546.

Miller, DJ, Vachon, DD & Lynam, DR 2009, "Neuroticism, negative affect, and negative affect instability: Establishing convergent and discriminant validity using ecological momentary assessment", *Personality and Individual Differences*, vol. 47, no. 8, pp. 873-877.

Ministry of Commerce of the People's Republic of China 2014, *Jiangsu's gross product in 2013 reaching nearly RMB 6 trillion; per capita GDP over US $12 thousand*, viewed May 8, 2014, < http://www. mofcom. gov. cn/article/resume/n/201401/20140100473531. shtml > .

Mischel, W 1977, "The interaction of person and situation", in Magnusson, D & Endler, NS (eds), *Personality at the crossroads: Current issues in interactional psychology*, vol. 3, Lawrence Erlbaum Associates, Inc. , Hillsdale, NJ, pp. 333-352.

Mitas, O, Yarnal, C, Adams, R & Ram, N 2012, "Taking a 'peak' at leisure travelers' positive emotions", *Leisure Sciences*, vol. 34, no. 2, pp. 115-135.

Mitchell, TR, Thompson, L, Peterson, E & Cronk, R 1997, "Temporal adjustments in the evaluation of events: The 'rosy view'", *Journal of Experimental Social Psychology*, vol. 33, no. 4, pp. 421-448.

Mooradian, T, Renzl, B & Matzler, K 2006, "Who trusts? Personality, trust and knowledge sharing", *Management Learning*, vol. 37, no. 4, pp. 523-540.

Mooradian, TA 1996, "Personality and ad-evoked feelings: The case for extraversion and neuroticism", *Journal of the Academy of Marketing Science*, vol. 24, no. 2, pp. 99-109.

Mooradian, TA & Olver, JM 1997, "'I can't get no satisfaction:' The impact of personality and emotion on postpurchase processes", *Psychology and Marketing*, vol. 14, no. 4, pp. 379-393.

Mount, M, Ilies, R & Johnson, E 2006, "Relationship of personality traits and counterproductive work behaviors: The mediating effects of job satisfaction", *Personnel Psychology*, vol. 59, no. 3, pp. 591-622.

Moutafi, J, Furnham, A & Crump, J 2006, "What facets of openness and conscientiousness predict fluid intelligence score?", *Learning and Individual Differences*, vol. 16, no. 1, pp. 31-42.

Moutinho, L 1987, "Consumer behaviour in tourism", *European Journal of Marketing*, vol. 21, no. 10, pp. 5-44.

Mueller, S & Peters, M 2008, "The personality of freestyle snowboarders: Implications for product development", *Tourism (Zagreb)*, vol. 56, no. 4, pp. 339-354.

Muller, TE, Tse, D & Venkatasubramaniam, R 1991, "Post-consumption emotions: Exploring their emergence and determinants", *Journal of Consumer Satisfaction, Dissatisfaction and Complaining Behavior*, vol. 4, pp. 13-20.

Myers, OE, Saunders, CD & Birjulin, AA 2004, "Emotional dimensions of watching zoo animals: An experience sampling study building on insights from psychology", *Curator: The Museum Journal*, vol. 47, no. 3, pp. 299-321.

Myers, S, Sen, S & Alexandrov, A 2010, "The moderating effect of personality traits on attitudes toward advertisements: A contingency framework", *Management & Marketing*, vol. 5, no. 3, pp. 3-20.

Nachtigall, C, Kroehne, U, Funke, F & Steyer, R 2003, "Pros and Cons of Structural Equation Modeling", *Methods of Psychological Research Online*, vol. 8, no. 2, pp. 1-22.

Nam, J-H & Lee, TJ 2011, "Foreign travelers' satisfaction with traditional Korean restaurants", *International Journal of Hospitality Management*, vol. 30, no. 4, pp. 982-989.

National Bureau of Statistics of China 2012, *Statistical bulletin of 2011 national economic & social development*, viewed Novembre 8, 2012, < http://www. stats. gov. cn/tjgb/ndtjgb/qgndtjg b/t20120222 _ 402786440. htm >.

National Bureau of Statistics of China 2015, *China statistical yearbook of 2014*, viewed August 3, 2015, < http://www. stats. gov. cn/tjsj/ndsj/2014/indexeh. htm >.

Nawijn, J 2011a, "Happiness through vacationing: Just a temporary boost or long-term benefits?", *Journal of Happiness Studies*, vol. 12, no. 4, pp. 651-665.

Nawijn, J 2011b, "Determinants of daily happiness on vacation", *Journal of Travel Research*, vol. 50, no. 5, pp. 559-566.

Nawijn, J, Mitas, O, Lin, Y & Kerstetter, D 2013, "How do we feel on vacation? A closer look at how emotions change over the course of a trip", *Journal of Travel Research*, vol. 52, no. 2, pp. 265-274.

Neal, JD & Gursoy, D 2008, "A multifaceted analysis of tourism satisfaction", *Journal of Travel Research*, vol. 47, no. 1, pp. 53-62.

Neuman, WL 2005, *Social research methods: Quantitative and qualitative approaches*, Allyn & Bacon, Boston, MA.

Nevitt, J & Hancock, GR 2001, "Performance of bootstrapping approaches to model test statistics and parameter standard error estimation in structural equation modeling", *Structural Equation Modeling*, vol. 8, no. 3, pp. 353-377.

Nguyen, DN, Yanagawa, Y & Miyazaki, S 2005, "University education and employment in Japan: Students' perceptions on employment attributes and implications for university education", *Quality Assurance in Education*, vol. 13, no. 3, pp. 202-218.

Nias, DK 1985, "Personality and recreational behaviour", *Individual Differences in Movement*, Springer, pp. 279-292.

Norman, G 2010, "Likert scales, levels of measurement and the 'laws' of statistics", *Advances in Health Sciences Education*, vol. 15, no. 5, pp. 625-632.

Nunkoo, R, Ramkissoon, H & Gursoy, D 2013, "Use of structural equation modeling in tourism research past, present, and future", *Journal of Travel Research*, vol. 52, no. 6, pp. 759-771.

Nyer, PU 1997, "Modeling the cognitive antecedents of post-consumption emotions", *Journal of Consumer Satisfaction Dissatisfaction and Complaining Behavior*, vol. 10, pp. 80-90.

Oliver, DG, Serovich, JM & Mason, TL 2005, "Constraints and opportunities with interview transcription: Towards reflection in qualitative research", *Social Forces*, vol. 84, no. 2, pp. 1273-1289.

Oliver, RL 1980, "A cognitive model of the antecedents and consequences of satisfaction decisions", *Journal of Marketing Research*, pp. 460-469.

Oliver, RL & Swan, JE 1989, "Consumer perceptions of interpersonal equity and satisfaction in transactions: A field survey approach", *The Journal of Marketing*, pp. 21-35.

Oliver, RL 1993, "Cognitive, affective, and attribute bases of the satisfaction response", *The Journal of Consumer Research*, vol. 20, no. 3, pp. 418-430.

Oliver, RL 1997, *Satisfaction: A behavioral perspective on the customer*, McGraw-Hill, New York.

Ong, CE & du Cros, H 2012, "The post-Mao gazes: Chinese backpackers in Macau", *Annals of Tourism Research*, vol. 39, no. 2, pp. 735-754.

Ong, TF & Musa, G 2012, "Examining the influences of experience, personality and attitude on SCUBA divers' underwater behaviour: A structural equation model", *Tourism Management*, vol. 33, no. 6, pp. 1521-1534.

Ormel, J, Rosmalen, J & Farmer, A 2004, "Neuroticism: A non-informative marker of vulnerability to psychopathology", *Social Psychiatry and Psychiatric Epidemiology*, vol. 39, pp. 906-912.

Otto, JE & Ritchie, J 1996, "The service experience in tourism", *Tourism Management*, vol. 17, no. 3, pp. 165-174.

Ozer, DJ & Benet-Martinez, V 2006, "Personality and the prediction of consequential outcomes", *Annual Review of Psychology.*, vol. 57, pp. 401-421.

Palau-Saumell, R, Forgas-Coll, S, Sánchez-García, J & Prats-Planagumà, L 2013, "Tourist behavior intentions and the moderator effect of knowledge of UNESCO World Heritage Sites: The case of La Sagrada Família", *Journal of Travel Research*, vol. 52, no. 3, pp. 364-376.

Palmer, B, Donaldson, C & Stough, C 2002, "Emotional intelligence and life satisfaction", *Personality and Individual Differences*, vol. 33, no. 7, pp. 1091-1100.

Pan, B, Li, X, Zhang, L & Smith, WW 2007, "An exploratory study on the satisfaction and barriers of online trip planning to China: American college students' experience", *Journal of Hospitality and Leisure Marketing*, vol. 16 (1-2), pp. 203-226.

Pan, GW & Laws, E 2003, "Tourism development of Australia as a sustained preferred destination for Chinese tourists", *Asia Pacific Journal of Tourism Research*, vol. 8, no. 1, pp. 37-47.

Panaccio, A & Vandenberghe, C 2012, "Five-factor model of personality and organizational commitment: The mediating role of positive and negative affective states", *Journal of Vocational Behavior*, vol. 80, no. 3, pp. 647-658.

Parrott, WG & Hertel, P 1999, "Research methods in cognition and emotion", *Handbook of Cognition and Emotion*, pp. 61-81.

Patton, MQ 2005, "Qualitative Research", in Everitt, BS & Howell, DC (eds), *Encyclopedia of statistics in behavioral science*, vol. 3, John Wiley & Sons, Chichester, pp. 1633-1636.

Pearce, PL 1981, "Environment shock: A study of tourists' reactions to two tropical islands", *Journal of Applied Social Psychology*, vol. 11, no. 3, pp. 268-280.

Pearce, PL 2005, *Tourist behaviour: Themes and conceptual schemes*, Channel View Publications,

Clevedon.

Pearce, PL 2009, "The relationship between positive psychology and tourist behavior studies", *Tourism Analysis*, vol. 14, no. 1, pp. 37-48.

Pearce, PL 2011, *The study of tourism: Foundations from psychology*, Emerald Group Publishing, Bingley.

Pearce, PL 2012, "The experience of visiting home and familiar places", *Annals of Tourism Research*, vol. 39, no. 2, pp. 1024-1047.

Pearce, PL & Packer, J 2013, "Minds on the move: New links from psychology to tourism", *Annals of Tourism Research*, vol. 40, pp. 386-411.

Penley, JA & Tomaka, J 2002, "Associations among the Big Five, emotional responses, and coping with acute stress", *Personality and Individual Differences*, vol. 32, no. 7, pp. 1215-1228.

Perugini, M & Bagozzi, RP 2001, "The role of desires and anticipated emotions in goal-directed behaviours: Broadening and deepening the theory of planned behaviour", *British Journal of Social Psychology*, vol. 40, no. 1, pp. 79-98.

Pervin, LA 1993, "Affect and personality" in Lewis, M & Haviland, JM (eds), *Handbook of emotions*, Guilford Press, New York, pp. 301-311.

Phillips, DM & Baumgartner, H 2002, "The role of consumption emotions in the satisfaction response", *Journal of Consumer Psychology*, vol. 12, no. 3, pp. 243-252.

Pine, BJ & Gilmore, JH 2011, *The experience economy*, Harvard Business Press, Boston.

Pizam, A & Ellis, T 1999, "Customer satisfaction and its measurement in hospitality enterprises", *International Journal of Contemporary Hospitality Management*, vol. 11, no. 7, pp. 326-339.

Pizam, A, Jeong, GH, Reichel, A, van Boemmel, H, Lusson, JM, Steynberg, L, Volo, S, Kroesbacher, C, Kucerova, J & Montmany, N 2004, "The relationship between risk-taking, sensation-seeking, and the tourist behavior of young adults: A cross-cultural study", *Journal of Travel Research*, vol. 42, no. 3, pp. 251-260.

Pizam, A & Milman, A 1993, "Predicting satisfaction among first time visitors to a destination by using the expectancy disconfirmation theory", *International Journal of Hospitality Management*, vol. 12, no. 2, pp. 197-209.

Pizam, A, Neumann, Y & Reichel, A 1978, "Dimentions of tourist satisfaction with a destination area", *Annals of Tourism Research*, vol. 5, no. 3, pp. 314-322.

Plog, S 2001, "Why destination areas rise and fall in popularity", *Cornell Hotel and Restaurant Administration Quarterly*, vol. 42, no. 3, pp. 13-24.

Plog, SC 1974, "Why destination areas rise and fall in popularity", *Cornell Hotel and Restaurant Administration Quarterly*, vol. 14, no. 4, pp. 55-60.

Plog, SC 2002, "The power of psychographics and the concept of venturesomeness", *Journal of Travel Research*, vol. 40, no. 3, pp. 244-251.

Plutchik, R 1980, *Emotion: A psychoevolutionary synthesis*, Harper & Row, New York.

Prayag, G, Hosany, S & Odeh, K 2013, "The role of tourists' emotional experiences and satisfaction in understanding behavioral intentions", *Journal of Destination Marketing & Management*, vol. 2, no. 2, pp. 118-127.

Prayag, G, Hosany, S, Muskat, B & Del Chiappa, G 2015, "Understanding the relationships between tourists' emotional experiences, perceived overall image, satisfaction, and intention to recommend", *Journal of Travel Research*, doi: 10.1177/0047287515620567.

Price, LL, Arnould, EJ & Deibler, SL 1995, "Consumers' emotional responses to service encounters: The influence of the service provider", *International Journal of Service Industry Management*, vol.6, no.3, pp. 34-63.

Raja, U, Johns, G & Ntalianis, F 2004, "The impact of personality on psychological contracts", *Academy of Management Journal*, vol.47, no.3, pp. 350-367.

Rammstedt, B 2007, "The 10-item big five inventory", *European Journal of Psychological Assessment*, vol.23, no.3, pp. 193-201.

Rammstedt, B & John, OP 2007, "Measuring personality in one minute or less: A 10-item short version of the Big Five Inventory in English and German", *Journal of Research in Personality*, vol.41, no.1, pp. 203-212.

Raykov, T & Marcoulides, GA 2006, "On multilevel model reliability estimation from the perspective of structural equation modeling", *Structural Equation Modeling*, vol.13, no.1, pp. 130-141.

Reisinger, Y & Mavondo, F 2004, "Exploring the relationships among psychographic factors in the female and male youth travel market", *Tourism Review International*, vol.8, no.2, pp. 69-84.

Reisinger, Y & Mavondo, F 2004, "Modeling psychographic profiles: A study of the US and Australian student travel market", *Journal of Hospitality & Tourism Research*, vol.28, no.1, pp. 44-65.

Rhemtulla, M, Brosseau-Liard, PÉ & Savalei, V 2012, "When can categorical variables be treated as continuous? A comparison of robust continuous and categorical SEM estimation methods under suboptimal conditions", *Psychological Methods*, vol.17, no.3, pp. 354-373.

Richins, ML 1997, "Measuring emotions in the consumption experience", *Journal of Consumer Research*, vol.24, no.2, pp. 127-146.

Riddick, CC & Russell, RV 2008, *Research in recreation, parks, sport, and tourism*, 2nd edn, Sagamore Publication, Champaign, IL.

Robins, RW, Hendin, HM & Trzesniewski, KH 2001, "Measuring global self-esteem: Construct validation of a single-item measure and the Rosenberg Self-Esteem Scale", *Personality and Social Psychology Bulletin*, vol.27, no.2, pp. 151-161.

Roehl, WS & Fesenmaier, DR 1992, "Risk perceptions and pleasure travel: An exploratory analysis", *Journal of Travel Research*, vol.30, no.4, pp. 17-26.

Romero, E, Villar, P, Gómez-Fraguela, JA & López-Romero, L 2012, "Measuring personality traits with ultra-short scales: A study of the Ten Item Personality Inventory (TIPI) in a Spanish sample", *Personality and Individual Differences*, vol.53, no.3, pp. 289-293.

Rose, RC, Ramalu, SS, Uli, J & Kumar, N 2010, "Expatriate performance in overseas assignments: The role of big five personality", *Asian Social Science*, vol.6, no.9, pp. 104-113.

Ross, C, Orr, ES, Sisic, M, Arseneault, JM, Simmering, MG & Orr, RR 2009, "Personality and motivations associated with Facebook use", *Computers in Human Behavior*, vol.25, no.2, pp. 578-586.

Ross, GF 1994, *The psychology of tourism*, Hospitality Press, Elsternwick.

Russell, JA & Pratt, G 1980, "A description of the affective quality attributed to environments", *Journal of Personality and Social Psychology*, vol. 38, no. 2, pp. 311-315.

Russell, JA 1991, "Culture and the categorization of emotions", *Psychological Bulletin*, vol. 110, no. 3, pp. 426-432.

Russell, JA & Barrett, LF 1999, "Core affect, prototypical emotional episodes, and other things called emotion: Dissecting the elephant", *Journal of Personality and Social Psychology*, vol. 76, no. 5, pp. 805-814.

Rusting, CL & Larsen, RJ 1997, "Extraversion, neuroticism, and susceptibility to positive and negative affect: A test of two theoretical models", *Personality and Individual Differences*, vol. 22, no. 5, pp. 607-612.

Ryan, C 1995, *Researching tourist satisfaction: Issues, concepts, problems*, Routledge, London.

Ryan, C 1997, *The tourist experience: A new introduction*, Cassell, London.

Ryan, C & Mo, X 2002, "Chinese visitors to New Zealand: Demographics and perceptions", *Journal of Vacation Marketing*, vol. 8, no. 1, pp. 13-27.

Ryan, C & Zhang, Z 2007, "Chinese students: Holiday behaviours in New Zealand", *Journal of Vacation Marketing*, vol. 13, no. 2, pp. 91-106.

Ryan, C & Gu, H 2008, *Tourism in China: Destination, cultures and communities*, Routledge, London.

Sánchez-García, I & Currás-Pérez, R 2011, "Effects of dissatisfaction in tourist services: The role of anger and regret", *Tourism Management*, vol. 32, no. 6, pp. 1397-1406.

Salgado, JF 2002, "The Big Five personality dimensions and counterproductive behaviors", *International Journal of Selection and Assessment*, vol. 10, no. 1-2, pp. 117-125.

Santrock, JW 2009, *Life-span development*, 14th edn, McGraw-Hill, Boston, MA.

Sasser, WE, Schlesinger, LA & Heskett, JL 1997, *Service profit chain*, Simon and Schuster.

Schäfer, T, Zimmermann, D & Sedlmeier, P 2014, "How we remember the emotional intensity of past musical experiences", *Frontiers in Psychology*, vol. 5, article 911, doi: 10.3389/fpsyg.20014.00911.

Schoefer, K & Diamantopoulos, A 2008, "Measuring experienced emotions during service recovery encounters: construction and assessment of the ESRE scale", *Service Business*, vol. 2, no. 1, pp. 65-81.

Schreiber, JB 2008, "Core reporting practices in structural equation modeling", *Research in Social and Administrative Pharmacy*, vol. 4, no. 2, pp. 83-97.

Schriesheim, CA & Hill, KD 1981, "Controlling acquiescence response bias by item reversals: The effect on questionnaire validity", *Educational and Psychological Measurement*, vol. 41, no. 4, pp. 1101-1114.

Schriesheim, CA, Eisenbach, RJ & Hill, KD 1991, "The effect of negation and polar opposite item reversals on questionnaire reliability and validity: An experimental investigation", *Educational and Psychological Measurement*, vol. 51, no. 1, pp. 67-78.

Schultz, DP & Schultz, SE 2009, *Theories of personality*, 9th edn, Cengage Learning, Wadsworth.

Seal, DW, Bogart, LM & Ehrhardt, AA 1998, "Small group dynamics: The utility of focus group discussions as a research method", *Group Dynamics: Theory, Research, and Practice*, vol. 2, no. 4, pp. 253-266.

Seaton, AV & Bennett, MM 1996, *The marketing of tourism products: Concepts, issues and cases*, International Thompson Business Press, London.

Shaver, P, Schwartz, J, Kirson, D & O'connor, C 1987, "Emotion knowledge: further exploration of a prototype approach", *Journal of Personality and Social Psychology*, vol. 52, no. 6, pp. 1061-1066.

Sherman, E, Mathur, A & Smith, RB 1997, "Store environment and consumer purchase behavior: Mediating role of consumer emotions", *Psychology & Marketing*, vol. 14, no. 4, pp. 361-378.

Shiota, MN, Keltner, D & John, OP 2006, "Positive emotion dispositions differentially associated with Big Five personality and attachment style", *The Journal of Positive Psychology*, vol. 1, no. 2, pp. 61-71.

Siemer, M, Mauss, I & Gross, JJ 2007, "Same situation-different emotions: How appraisals shape our emotions", *Emotion*, vol. 7, no. 3, pp. 592-604.

Silvia, ESM & MacCallum, RC 1988, "Some factors affecting the success of specification searches in covariance structure modeling", *Multivariate Behavioral Research*, vol. 23, no. 3, pp. 297-326.

Sirakaya, E, Petrick, J & Choi, H-S 2004, "The role of mood on tourism product evaluations", *Annals of Tourism Research*, vol. 31, no. 3, pp. 517-539.

Sirgy, MJ 2010, "Toward a quality-of-life theory of leisure travel satisfaction", *Journal of Travel Research*, vol. 49, no. 2, pp. 246-260.

Smith, SL 1990, "A test of Plog's allocentric/psychocentric model: Evidence from seven nations", *Journal of Travel Research*, vol. 28, no. 4, pp. 40-43.

Sohn, HK & Lee, TJ 2012, "Relationship between HEXACO personality factors and emotional labour of service providers in the tourism industry", *Tourism Management*, vol. 33, no. 1, pp. 116-125.

Song, H & Cheung, C 2010, "Factors affecting tourist satisfaction with theatrical performances: A case study of The Romance of the Song Dynasty in Hangzhou, China", *Journal of Travel & Tourism Marketing*, vol. 27, no. 7, pp. 708-722.

Song, H, Li, G, van der Veen, R & Chen, JL 2011, "Assessing mainland Chinese tourists' satisfaction with Hong Kong using tourist satisfaction index", *International Journal of Tourism Research*, vol. 13, no. 1, pp. 82-96.

Song, H, van der Veen, R, Li, G & Chen, JL 2012, "The Hong Kong tourist satisfaction index", *Annals of Tourism Research*, vol. 39, no. 1, pp. 459-479.

Spagnoli, P & Caetano, A 2012, "Personality and organisational commitment: The mediating role of job satisfaction during socialisation", *Career Development International*, vol. 17, no. 3, pp. 255-275.

Sparks, B & Pan, GW 2009, "Chinese Outbound tourists: Understanding their attitudes, constraints and use of information sources", *Tourism Management*, vol. 30, no. 4, pp. 483-494.

Spreng, RA, MacKenzie, SB & Olshavsky, RW 1996, "A reexamination of the determinants of consumer satisfaction", *The Journal of Marketing*, pp. 15-32.

Srivastava, S, Angelo, KM & Vallereux, SR 2008, "Extraversion and positive affect: A day reconstruction study of person-environment transactions", *Journal of Research in Personality*, vol. 42, no. 6, pp. 1613-1618.

Stanway, AR 2010, "An Analysis of Psychological Contract, the Five-Factor Model and Loyal Boosterism Among Full-time Dancers in Training in Australia", University of South Australia.

Stepchenkova, S & Li, XR 2012, "Chinese outbound tourists' destination image of America: Part II", *Journal of Travel Research*, p. 0047287512451137.

Su, L & Hsu, MK 2013, "Service fairness, consumption emotions, satisfaction, and behavioral intentions: The experience of Chinese heritage tourists", *Journal of Travel & Tourism Marketing*, vol. 30, no. 8, pp. 786-805.

Suh, E, Diener, E & Fujita, F 1996, "Events and subjective well-being: Only recent events matter", *Journal of Personality and Social Psychology*, vol. 70, no. 5, pp. 1091-1102.

Sun, KA & Kim, DY 2013, "Does customer satisfaction increase firm performance? An application of American Customer Satisfaction Index (ACSI)", *International Journal of Hospitality Management*, vol. 35, pp. 68-77.

Sun, X, Chi, CG-Q & Xu, H 2013, "Developing destination loyalty: The case of Hainan Island", *Annals of Tourism Research*, vol. 43, pp. 547-577.

Swarbrooke, J & Horner, S 2004, *Consumer behaviour in tourism*, Butterworth-Heinemann, Burlington, MA.

Tan, HH, Der Foo, M & Kwek, MH 2004, "The effects of customer personality traits on the display of positive emotions", *Academy of Management Journal*, vol. 47, no. 2, pp. 287-296.

Tan, WK & Tang, CY 2013, "Does personality predict tourism information search and feedback behaviour?", *Current Issues in Tourism*, vol. 16, no. 4, pp. 388-406.

Tanford, S, Raab, C & Kim, Y-S 2013, "A model of hotel defection at the purchasing stage", *Journal of Hospitality Marketing & Management*, vol. 22, no. 8, pp. 805-831.

Tashakkori, A & Teddlie, C 1998, *Mixed methodology: Combining qualitative and quantitative approaches*, Sage Publications, Thousand Oaks, CA.

Tellegen, A 1985, "Structures of mood and personality and their relevance to assessing anxiety, with an emphasis on self-report", in Tuma, AH & Maser, JD (eds), *Anxiety and the anxiety disorders*, Lawrence Erlbaum, Hillsdale, NJ, pp. 681-706.

Tellegen, A & Waller, NG 2008, "Exploring personality through test construction: Development of the Multidimensional Personality Questionnaire", *The Sage handbook of personality theory and assessment*, vol. 2, pp. 261-292.

Templer, KJ 2012, "Five-Factor model of personality and job satisfaction: The importance of agreeableness in a tight and collectivistic Asian society", *Applied Psychology*, vol. 61, no. 1, pp. 114-129.

Teng, CC 2008, "The effects of personality traits and attitudes on student uptake in hospitality employment", *International Journal of Hospitality Management*, vol. 27, no. 1, pp. 76-86.

Teng, CI, Huang, KW & Tsai, IL 2007, "Effects of personality on service quality in business transactions", *The Service Industries Journal*, vol. 27, no. 7, pp. 849-863.

Thompson, ER 2007, "Development and validation of an internationally reliable short-form of the positive and negative affect schedule (PANAS)", *Journal of Cross-Cultural Psychology*, vol. 38, no. 2, pp. 227-242.

Thompson, ER 2008, "Development and validation of an international English Big-Five mini-markers", *Personality and Individual Differences*, vol. 45, no. 6, pp. 542-548.

Thrift, N 2004, "Intensities of feeling: Towards a spatial politics of affect", *Geografiska Annaler: Series B, Human Geography*, vol. 86, no. 1, pp. 57-78.

Tourism Australia 2013, *China Market Profile*, viewed 15 December, 2013, < http://www. tourism. australia. com/documents/Markets/MP-2013_CHINA-Web. pdf > .

Tourism Australia 2015, *China Market Profile*, viewed 19 October, 2015, < http://www. tourism. australia. com/documents/Markets/Market_Profile_2015_China. pdf > .

Tourism Research Australia 2014, *Chinese Satisfaction Survey*, viewed 26 February, 2015 < http://www. tra. gov. au/documents/Chinese_Satisfaction_Survey_FULL_REPORT_FINAL_24JAN2014. pdf >.

Tourism Research Australia (TRA) 2013, *Marketing Matters-China*, viewed November 6, 2014 < http:// www. tra. gov. au/documents/amf/Marketing_Matters_China_OCT2013_FINAL_V2. pdf >.

Trentelman, CK 2009, "Place attachment and community attachment: A primer grounded in the lived experience of a community sociologist", *Society and Natural Resources*, vol. 22, no. 3, pp. 191-210.

Triandis, HC & Suh, EM 2002, "Cultural influences on personality", *Annual Review of Psychology*, vol. 53, no. 1, pp. 133-160.

Tribe, J & Snaith, T 1998, "From SERVQUAL to HOLSAT: Holiday satisfaction in Varadero, Cuba", *Tourism Management*, vol. 19, no. 1, pp. 25-34.

Truong, TH & King, B 2009, "An evaluation of satisfaction levels among Chinese tourists in Vietnam", *International Journal of Tourism Research*, vol. 11, no. 6, pp. 521-535.

Tsaur, S-H, Chiu, Y-T & Wang, C-H 2007, "The visitors behavioral consequences of experiential marketing: an empirical study on Taipei Zoo", *Journal of Travel & Tourism Marketing*, vol. 21, no. 1, pp. 47-64.

Tse, DK & Wilton, PC 1988, "Models of consumer satisfaction formation: An extension", *Journal of Marketing Research*, pp. 204-212.

Tse, T 2007, "Book Reviews", *Journal of Travel & Tourism Marketing*, vol. 22, no. 2, pp. 89-93.

Tse, TS & Zhang, EY 2013, "Analysis of blogs and microblogs: A case study of Chinese bloggers sharing their Hong Kong travel experiences", *Asia Pacific Journal of Tourism Research*, vol. 18, no. 4, pp. 314-329.

Tse, TS 2015, "A review of Chinese outbound tourism research and the way forward", *Journal of China Tourism Research*, vol. 11, no. 1, pp. 1-18.

Tugade, MM & Fredrickson, BL 2007, "Regulation of positive emotions: Emotion regulation strategies that promote resilience", *Journal of Happiness Studies*, vol. 8, no. 3, pp. 311-333.

Tung, VWS & Ritchie, JB 2011, "Exploring the essence of memorable tourism experiences", *Annals of Tourism Research*, vol. 38, no. 4, pp. 1367-1386.

Um, S & Crompton, JL 1990, "Attitude determinants in tourism destination choice", *Annals of Tourism Research*, vol. 17, no. 3, pp. 432-448.

United Nations Development Programme (UNDP) 2013, *China National Human Development Report* 2013, viewed October 19, 2014, < http://www. cn. undp. org/content/ dam/china/docs/Publications/UNDP-CH-HD-Publication-NHDR_2013_EN_final. pdf >.

United Nations World Tourism Organization (UNWTO) 2001, *Tourism 2020 Vision volume* 7: *Global forecasts and profiles of market segments*, World Tourism Organization, Madrid.

UNWTO 2013a, *UNWTO Tourism Highlights*, 2013 *Edition*, UNWTO, viewed January 8, 2014, < http://dtxtq4w60xqpw. cloudfront. net/sites/all/files/pdf/unwto_highlights13_en_hr. pd f >.

UNWTO 2013b, *The Chinese Outbound Travel Market*-2012 *Update*, viewed September 28, 2013, < http://www. e-unwto. org/content/R32620 >.

Van de Vijver, FJ & Poortinga, YH 1997, "Towards an integrated analysis of bias in cross-cultural assessment", *European Journal of Psychological Assessment*, vol. 13, no. 1, pp. 29-42.

Van Dolen, W, De Ruyter, K & Lemmink, J 2004, "An empirical assessment of the influence of customer emotions and contact employee performance on encounter and relationship satisfaction", *Journal of Business Research*, vol. 57, no. 4, pp. 437-444.

Van Heck, GL 1997, "Personality and physical health: Toward an ecological approach to health-related personality research", *European Journal of Personality*, vol. 11, no. 5, pp. 415-443.

Velting, DM 1999, "Personality and negative expectancies: Trait structure of the Beck Hopelessness Scale", *Personality and Individual Differences*, vol. 26, no. 5, pp. 913-921.

Verplanken, B & Orbell, S 2003, "Reflections on past behaviour: A self-report index of hait strength", *Journal of Applied Social Psychology*, vol. 33, no. 6, pp. 1313-1330.

Verschuur, MJ, Eurelings-Bontekoe, EH & Spinhoven, P 2004, "Associations among homesickness, anger, anxiety, and depression 1,2", *Psychological Reports*, vol. 94, no. 3c, pp. 1155-1170.

Viswesvaran, C, Ones, DS & Hough, LM 2001, "Do impression management scales in personality inventories predict managerial job performance ratings?", *International Journal of Selection and Assessment*, vol. 9, no. 4, pp. 277-289.

Walsh, G, Shiu, E, Hassan, LM, Michaelidou, N & Beatty, SE 2011, "Emotions, store-environmental cues, store-choice criteria, and marketing outcomes", *Journal of Business Research*, vol. 64, no. 7, pp. 737-744.

Wang, CY & Hsu, MK 2010, "The relationships of destination image, satisfaction, and behavioral intentions: An integrated model", *Journal of Travel & Tourism Marketing*, vol. 27, no. 8, pp. 829-843.

Wang, D, Cui, H & Zhou, F 2005, "Measuring the personality of Chinese: QZPS versus NEO PI-R", *Asian Journal of Social Psychology*, vol. 8, no. 1, pp. 97-122.

Wang, KC, Hsieh, AT & Huan, T-C 2000, "Critical service features in group package tour: An exploratory research", *Tourism Management*, vol. 21, no. 2, pp. 177-189.

Wang, L & Chen, S 2013, "An empirical study on Lhasa's tourism consumption based on the analysis of six tourism elements", *Consumer Economics*, vol. 29, no. 6, pp. 27-30.

Wang, N 2004, "The rise of touristic consumerism in urban China", *Tourism Recreation Research*, vol. 29, no. 2, pp. 47-58.

Wang, Y & Sheldon, PJ 1996, "The sleeping dragon awakes: The outbound Chinese travel market", *Journal of Travel & Tourism Marketing*, vol. 4, no. 4, pp. 41-54.

Wang, Y & Davidson, MC 2009, "Chinese leisure tourists: Perceptions and satisfaction with Australia", *Tourism Analysis*, vol. 14, no. 6, pp. 737-747.

Wang, Y & Davidson, MC 2010, "Pre- and post-trip perceptions: An insight into Chinese package holiday market to Australia", *Journal of Vacation Marketing*, vol. 16, no. 2, pp. 111-123.

Watson, D & Tellegen, A 1985, "Toward a consensual structure of mood", *Psychological Bulletin*, vol. 98, no. 2, pp. 219-225.

Watson, D, Clark, LA & Tellegen, A 1988, "Development and validation of brief measures of positive and negative affect: The PANAS scales", *Journal of Personality and Social Psychology*, vol. 54, no. 6, pp. 1063-1070.

Watson, D & Clark, LA 1992, "On traits and temperament: General and specific factors of emotional experience and their relation to the five-factor model", *Journal of Personality*, vol. 60, no. 2, pp. 441-476.

Watson, D & Hubbard, B 1996, "Adaptational style and dispositional structure: Coping in the context of the five-factor model", *Journal of Personality*, vol. 64, no. 4, pp. 737-774.

Watson, D & Clark, LA 1997, "Extraversion and its positive emotional core", in Hogan, R & Johnson, JA (eds), *Handbook of social psychology*, 4th edn, vol. 2, McGraw-Hill, New York, pp. 446-496.

Weaver, DB 2012, "Psychographic insights from a South Carolina protected area", *Tourism Management*, vol. 33, no. 2, pp. 371-379.

Weiler, B & Ham, SH 2010, "Development of a research instrument for evaluating the visitor outcomes of face-to-face interpretation", *Visitor Studies*, vol. 13, no. 2, pp. 187-205.

Weiss, HM 2002, "Introductory comments: Antecedents of emotional experiences at work", *Motivation and Emotion*, vol. 26, no. 1, pp. 1-2.

Wellington, J & Szczerbinski, M 2007, *Research methods for the social sciences*, Continuum International Publication Group, London.

Westbrook, RA 1980, "A rating scale for measuring product/service satisfaction", *The Journal of Marketing*, pp. 68-72.

Westbrook, RA & Reilly, MD 1983, "Value-percept disparity: An alternative to the disconfirmation of expectations theory of consumer satisfaction", *Advances in Consumer Research*, vol. 10, no. 1. pp. 53-59.

Westbrook, RA 1987, "Product/Consumption-Based affective responses and postpurchase processes", *Journal of Marketing Research*, vol. 24, no. 3, pp. 258-270.

Westbrook, RA & Oliver, RL 1991, "The dimensionality of consumption emotion patterns and consumer satisfaction", *Journal of Consumer Research*, pp. 84-91.

Wilson, K & Gullone, E 1999, "The relationship between personality and affect over the lifespan", *Personality and Individual Differences*, vol. 27, no. 6, pp. 1141-1156.

Wirtz, J & Bateson, JE 1999, "Consumer satisfaction with services: Integrating the environment perspective in services marketing into the traditional disconfirmation paradigm", *Journal of Business Research*, vol. 44, no. 1, pp. 55-66.

Wirtz, J, Mattila, AS & Tan, RL 2000, "The moderating role of target-arousal on the impact of affect on satisfaction—an examination in the context of service experiences", *Journal of Retailing*, vol. 76, no. 3, pp. 347-365.

Witt, L, Burke, LA, Barrick, MA & Mount, MK 2002, "The interactive effects of conscientiousness and agreeableness on job performance", *Journal of Applied Psychology*, vol. 87, no. 1, pp. 164-178.

Wong, N, Rindfleisch, A & Burroughs, JE 2003, "Do reverse-worded items confound measures in cross-cultural consumer research? The case of the Material Values Scale", *Journal of Consumer Research*, vol. 30, no. 1, pp. 72-91.

Wright, TA & Staw, BM 1999, "Affect and favorable work outcomes: Two longitudinal tests of the happy-productive worker thesis", *Journal of Organizational Behavior*, vol. 20, no. 1, pp. 1-23.

Wu, CH 2008, "An examination of the wording effect in the Rosenberg Self-Esteem Scale among culturally Chinese people", *The Journal of Social Psychology*, vol. 148, no. 5, pp. 535-552.

Xiang, Y 2013, "The characteristics of independent Chinese outbound tourists", *Tourism Planning &*

Development, vol. 10, no. 2, pp. 134-148.

Xie, Y & Li, M 2009, "Development of China's outbound tourism and the characteristics of its tourist flow", *Journal of China Tourism Research*, vol. 5, no. 3, pp. 226-242.

Xu, H, Ding, P & Packer, J 2008, "Tourism research in China: Understanding the unique cultural contexts and complexities", *Current Issues in Tourism*, vol. 11, no. 6, pp. 473-491.

Yüksel, A 2007, "Tourist shopping habitat: Effects on emotions, shopping value and behaviours", *Tourism Management*, vol. 28, no. 1, pp. 58-69.

Yüksel, A & Akgül, O 2007, "Postcards as affective image makers: An idle agent in destination marketing", *Tourism management*, vol. 28, no. 3, pp. 714-725.

Yüksel, A & Yüksel, F 2007, "Shopping risk perceptions: Effects on tourists' emotions, satisfaction and expressed loyalty intentions", *Tourism Management*, vol. 28, no. 3, pp. 703-713.

Yamagata, S, Suzuki, A, Ando, J, Ono, Y, Kijima, N, Yoshimura, K, Ostendorf, F, Angleitner, A, Riemann, R, Spinath, FM, Livesley, WJ & Jang, KL 2006, "Is the genetic structure of human personality universal? A cross-cultural twin study from North America, Europe, and Asia", *Journal of Personality and Social Psychology*, vol. 90, no. 6, pp. 987-998.

Yang, JF 2010, "Cross-Cultural personality assessment: The revised neo personality inventory in China", *Social Behavior and Personality: An International Journal*, vol. 38, no. 8, pp. 1097-1104.

Yarnal, CM & Kerstetter, D 2005, "Casting off an exploration of cruise ship space, group tour behavior, and social interaction", *Journal of Travel Research*, vol. 43, no. 4, pp. 368-379.

Yik, MS & Russell, JA 2001, "Predicting the Big Two of affect from the Big Five of personality", *Journal of Research in Personality*, vol. 35, no. 3, pp. 247-277.

Yoo, KH & Gretzel, U 2011, "Influence of personality on travel-related consumer-generated media creation", *Computers in Human Behavior*, vol. 27, no. 2, pp. 609-621.

Yoon, Y & Uysal, M 2005, "An examination of the effects of motivation and satisfaction on destination loyalty: A structural model", *Tourism Management*, vol. 26, no. 1, pp. 45-56.

Yu, L & Goulden, M 2006, "A comparative analysis of international tourists' satisfaction in Mongolia", *Tourism Management*, vol. 27, no. 6, pp. 1331-1342.

Yu, X & Weiler, B 2001, "Mainland Chinese pleasure travelers to Australia: a leisure behavior analysis", *Tourism Culture & Communication*, vol. 3, no. 2, pp. 81-91.

Yüksel, A 2007, "Tourist shopping habitat: Effects on emotions, shopping value and behaviours", *Tourism Management*, vol. 28, no. 1, pp. 58-69.

Yüksel, A & Akgül, O 2007, "Postcards as affective image makers: An idle agent in destination marketing", *Tourism Management*, vol. 28, no. 3, pp. 714-725.

Yüksel, A & Yüksel, F 2001, "Measurement and management issues in customer satisfaction research: Review, critique and research agenda: Part one", *Journal of Travel & Tourism Marketing*, vol. 10, no. 4, pp. 47-80.

Yüksel, A, Yüksel, F & Bilim, Y 2010, "Destination attachment: Effects on customer satisfaction and cognitive, affective and conative loyalty", *Tourism management*, vol. 31, no. 2, pp. 274-284.

Zajonc, RB 1980, "Feeling and thinking: Preferences need no inferences", *American Psychologist*, vol.

35, no. 2, pp. 151-155.

Zajonc, RB 1984, "On the primacy of affect", *American Psychologist*, vol. 39, no. 2, pp. 117-123.

Zajonc, RB & Markus, H 1985, "Must all affect be mediated by cognition?", *Journal of Consumer Research*, vol. 12, no. 3, pp. 363-368.

Zeelenberg, M & Pieters, R 2004, "Beyond valence in customer dissatisfaction: A review and new findings on behavioral responses to regret and disappointment in failed services", *Journal of Business Research*, vol. 57, no. 4, pp. 445-455.

Zhai, Fd 2006, "Probe into the six components in tourism", *Tourism Tribune*, vol. 4, no. 21, pp. 18-22.

Zhang, G 2006, *China's Outbound Tourism: An Overview*, viewed August 26, < http://torc. linkbc. ca/ torc/downs1/china%20outbound. pdf >.

Zhang, HQ & Heung, VCS 2002, "The emergence of the mainland Chinese outbound travel market and its implications for tourism marketing", *Journal of Vacation Marketing*, vol. 8, no. 1, pp. 7-12.

Zhang, HQ & Chow, I 2004, "Application of importance-performance model in tour guides' performance: Evidence from mainland Chinese outbound visitors in Hong Kong", *Tourism Management*, vol. 25, no. 1, pp. 81-91.

Zhang, Lf 2006, "Thinking styles and the big five personality traits revisited", *Personality and Individual Differences*, vol. 40, no. 6, pp. 1177-1187.

Zhang, Y & Albrecht, C 2010, "The role of cultural values on a firm's strategic human resource management development: A comparative case study of Spanish firms in China", *The International Journal of Human Resource Management*, vol. 21, no. 11, pp. 1911-1930.

Zimmerman, RD, Boswell, WR, Shipp, AJ, Dunford, BB & Boudreau, JW 2012, "Explaining the pathways between approach-avoidance personality traits and employees' job search behavior", *Journal of Management*, vol. 38, no. 5, pp. 1450-1475.

Zins, AH 2002, "Consumption emotions, experience quality and satisfaction: A structural analysis for complainers versus non-complainers", *Journal of Travel & Tourism Marketing*, vol. 12, no. 2-3, pp. 3-18.

Appendix 1 Itinerary for 8-day Tour in Australia

	Itinerary & Main Attractions	Meals
Day 1	**Shanghai/Sydney**　　　**On Board** 	Dinner Break- fast
Day 2	**Sydney – the Blue Mountains – Sydney** 　　　After arrival in Sydney, the capital of New South Wales, then one and a half hours' drive to [the Blue Mountains], a UNESCO World Heritage Area (approximately 100 kilometers west of Sydney). The Blue Mountains consists mainly of a sandstone plateau filled with tall forests, canyons, sandstone cliffs, bush land and rainforests. It derives its name from a blue haze that falls over the mountains and which is actually a mist of oil released by the eucalyptus trees. You can choose to take the world's steepest [cable-driven funicular railway nearly parallel to 90-degree slope] into the depth of the Blue Mountains to stroll in the subtropical rainforest. Then take another thrilling cable car [SKYWAY] across the primitive valley and the stunning waterfalls to reach [the Three Sisters], a massive rock trio named after an aboriginal legend and eroded into interesting and dramatic shapes. (All the cable car fees around AU $35/pax are at your own cost.) A complimentary 20-minute lingering in the town [Leura] where you can have a cup of Cappuccino while experiencing the easygoing life in Australia. On the way back to Sydney, pay a 30-minute visit to the [2000 Olympic Village] to relive the Olympic atmosphere. Afterwards, return to Sydney and check-in at the 4-star hotel after the dinner.	Lunch Dinner

Itinerary & Main Attractions	Meals
Sydney Day 3 The Sydney urban sightseeing starts after breakfast. First pay a 30-minute visit to the one kilometre long [Bondi Beach], the significant historical sports center for surfers in Australia. Sightsee the [Rose Bay] and the [Double Bay] on the bus, two affluent harbourside eastern suburbs of Sydney. A 20-minute tour to [the Rocks], an historic area and well-preserved colonial district with its side streets filled with boutique shops, restaurants and pubs as well as quaint buildings. Then at noon visit the famous [Fish Market] (60 minutes) where you can buy and enjoy a yummy fresh seafood meal on the wharf overlooking the water (meals excluded). Afterwards, visit the attractive [the Royal Botanic Gardens] (30 minutes) and appreciate the iconic [Sydney Opera House] (25 minutes). Then visit the duty-free shop [JTH Pty Ltd] for local specialities (60 minutes). At dusk, take the cruise to appreciate the amazing nocturnal view of the Opera House and the legendary [Harbour Bridge] while enjoying the Australian western-style dinner (75 minutes). Afterwards, take the optional activities (Sydney Night Tour) or alternatively return to the hotel (4-star). Optional Self-financed Activities: Sydney Night Tour (Climbing [the Sydney Tower], the highest tower on the southern hemisphere, giving you a bird's eye view of Sydney's night view; take the monorail sightseeing train around the city; the coach will pass through [Kings Cross], the Red Light area in Sydney.) AU $90/pax	Break- fast Dinner
Sydney – Brisbane – Gold Coast Day 4 Fly to Brisbane after breakfast and then pay a 30-minute visit to [the South Bank Parklands], the site of World Expo 88; the coach will take you to [Kangaroo Point] via the [Story Bridge] where you can take a 15-minute walk to appreciate the beautiful scenery of the Brisbane River. Complimentary tour to the [Mount Coot-tha] (15 minutes), overlooking a superb panorama of Brisbane. Afterwards, drive to Gold Coast. Stop at the [Surfers Paradise] to take a walk on the golden beach stretching for 73 kilometres. Take one of the fastest lift in the world before dusk to the 77th level [Sky point Observation Deck] to have a 360 degree bird's-eye view of the attractive beach scenery. Back to the hotel (4-star) after dinner.	Break- fast Lunch Dinner

Itinerary & Main Attractions		Meals
Day 5	**Gold Coast** After breakfast, drive to the 【Dreamworld Theme Park】(3. 5 hours), where you can experience a variety of thrilling amusement facilities. Thunder River Rapids Ride, a white water rafting, will take you to travel down a foamy water track past the dark mine tunnel deserted in the Gold Rush Country; and 360-degree rotary oscillation will bring you a series of pleasant sensations through the turbulent rapids. Also, you can feed the kangaroos, cuddle the koalas (extra cost involved) and experience the life on the Australian farm with live sheep shearing show. (Lunch excluded). Twelve recreation areas in the Dreamworld await your arrival with a lot of fun and fantastic programs. Afterwards, visit the duty-free shop for local specialities 【Dabalong Pty Ltd】(60 minutes), and【Australian Opal Factory Outlet】(40 minutes). After dinner, take the optional activities (Gold Coast Night Tour) or alternatively return to the hotel (4-star). Optional Self-financed Activities: Gold Coast Night Tour (Board the luxury cruise to appreciate the intoxicating nocturnal view of Gold Coast and witness the outer appearance of the residences of billionaires; visit the local middle-class family to gain an insight into their lives; hearty night snacks included, such as kangaroo meat, oyster, quail, organic vegetable, etc.) AU $90/pax	Break-fast Dinner
Day 6	**Gold Coast/Melbourne** After breakfast, fly to Melbourne, a city of the most typical European style. Stroll around the spectacular 【Royal Botanic Gardens】(60 minutes) where there are 51,000 kinds of plants and black swans assembling along the lakeside, and so on. Visit the most popular sites for wedding photography in Melbourne (30 minutes), the【Fitzroy Gardens】and the【Captain Cottage】. Built in 1755 by Captain Cook's parents, the Cottage chronicled the growth of Captain Cook who discovered Australia. Visit the Gothic 【St. Patrick's Cathedral】(20 minutes), the symbol of Melbourne's architectural splendour. Then stroll around the 【Federation Square】(20 minutes) located at the bank of the【Yarra River】, and visit 【Victorian Arts Centre】(10 minutes), one of Melbourne's landmarks, etc. Check-in at the hotel (4-star) after dinner.	Break-fast Lunch Dinner

Itinerary & Main Attractions	Meals
Day 7 **Melbourne – Great Ocean Road – Melbourne** Take the scenic drive to the world-famous【Great Ocean Road】, renowned as the gem of Victoria. Especially【the twelve Apostles】(30 minutes) is the most representative attraction. The limestone pillars that rise out of the ocean have been carved into the current natural wonders over time by the waves, wind and rain. Regrettably, there remain only seven rocks at present. Another complimentary tour to the【London Bridge】(20 minutes); tourists from all over the world are stunned by the blue water and these peculiar rocks embracing each other. Afterwards, return to Melbourne and visit the duty-free shop【Palicon Duty Free】for local specialities (60 minutes). Check-in at the hotel after dinner. 	Break-fast Lunch Dinner
Day 8 **Melbourne /Shanghai** **On Board** Back to Shanghai	Break-fast Lunch

The itinerary is subject to change according to the arrangement of local tour operators.

Appendix 2 Preliminary Questionnaire

> **The Impact of Personality and Affect on Tourist Satisfaction: The Case of Mainland Chinese Tourists to Australia**

No.			

> You are invited to participate in a questionnaire survey examining how mainland Chinese tourists' personality traits and affective responses triggered by their travel experiences influence their level of overall satisfaction with Australia as a destination. The survey will take roughly 15 minutes of your time. There is no correct or wrong answer. Participants are expected to answer all the questions seriously.
>
> If you encounter any problem about the survey, please ask your tour escort for help and clarification.

Screening Questions

1. Are you a mainland Chinese citizen?
   - ☐ YES
   - ☐ NO   (terminate)

2. Are you over 18 years old?
   - ☐ YES
   - ☐ NO   (terminate)

3. Have you been living in Yangtse River Delta (YRD, referring to Shanghai, Southern Jiangsu Province and northern Zhejiang Province) for over one year?
   - ☐ YES

     Please specify which city you are currently living in _____.
   - ☐ NO   (terminate)

4. Is this your first visit to Australia?
   - ☐ YES
   - ☐ NO   (terminate)

Part A: Personality Traits

Here are a number of characteristics that may or may not apply to you. For example, do you agree that you are someone who likes to spend time with others? Please tick a number to indicate the extent to which you agree or disagree with that statement（the number 1-7 indicating *strongly disagree* to *strongly agree*）.

I see myself as someone who... ☞Please tick（√）one response on each line	Strongly Disagree	Disagree	Somewhat Disagree	Neutral	Somewhat Agree	Agree	Strongly Agree
5. is talkative	1	2	3	4	5	6	7
6. tends to find fault with others	1	2	3	4	5	6	7
7. does a thorough job	1	2	3	4	5	6	7
8. is depressed, blue	1	2	3	4	5	6	7
9. is original, comes up with new ideas	1	2	3	4	5	6	7
10. is reserved	1	2	3	4	5	6	7
11. is helpful and unselfish with others	1	2	3	4	5	6	7
12. can be somewhat careless	1	2	3	4	5	6	7
13. is relaxed, handles stress well	1	2	3	4	5	6	7
14. is curious about many different things	1	2	3	4	5	6	7
15. is full of energy	1	2	3	4	5	6	7
16. starts quarrels with others	1	2	3	4	5	6	7
17. is a reliable worker	1	2	3	4	5	6	7
18. can be tense	1	2	3	4	5	6	7
19. is ingenious, a deep thinker	1	2	3	4	5	6	7
20. generates a lot of enthusiasm	1	2	3	4	5	6	7
21. has a forgiving nature	1	2	3	4	5	6	7
22. tends to be disorganized	1	2	3	4	5	6	7
23. worries a lot	1	2	3	4	5	6	7
24. has an active imagination	1	2	3	4	5	6	7
25. tends to be quiet	1	2	3	4	5	6	7
26. is generally trusting	1	2	3	4	5	6	7
27. tends to be lazy	1	2	3	4	5	6	7
28. is emotionally stable, not easily upset	1	2	3	4	5	6	7
29. is inventive	1	2	3	4	5	6	7
30. has an assertive personality	1	2	3	4	5	6	7
31. can be cold and aloof	1	2	3	4	5	6	7
32. perseveres until the task is finished	1	2	3	4	5	6	7

I see myself as someone who... ☞Please tick (√) one response on each line	Strongly Disagree	Disagree	Somewhat Disagree	Neutral	Somewhat Agree	Agree	Strongly Agree
33. can be moody	1	2	3	4	5	6	7
34. values artistic, aesthetic experiences	1	2	3	4	5	6	7
35. is sometimes shy, inhibited	1	2	3	4	5	6	7
36. is considerate and kind to almost everyone	1	2	3	4	5	6	7
37. does things efficiently	1	2	3	4	5	6	7
38. remains calm in tense situations	1	2	3	4	5	6	7
39. prefers work that is routine	1	2	3	4	5	6	7
40. is outgoing, sociable	1	2	3	4	5	6	7
41. is sometimes rude to others	1	2	3	4	5	6	7
42. makes plans and follows through with them	1	2	3	4	5	6	7
43. gets nervous easily	1	2	3	4	5	6	7
44. likes to reflect, play with ideas	1	2	3	4	5	6	7
45. has few artistic interests	1	2	3	4	5	6	7
46. likes to cooperate with others	1	2	3	4	5	6	7
47. is easily distracted	1	2	3	4	5	6	7
48. is sophisticated in art, music, or literature	1	2	3	4	5	6	7

Part B: Affective Experience

Thinking about your affective experiences during this trip to Australia, please indicate to what extent you generally felt (Please tick one number among the number 1 −7 indicating *never* to *always*).

	Never Always						
49. anticipating	1	2	3	4	5	6	7
50. jittery	1	2	3	4	5	6	7
51. excited	1	2	3	4	5	6	7
52. scared	1	2	3	4	5	6	7
53. pleasant	1	2	3	4	5	6	7
54. nostalgic	1	2	3	4	5	6	7
55. relaxing	1	2	3	4	5	6	7
56. distressed	1	2	3	4	5	6	7
57. interested	1	2	3	4	5	6	7
58. embarrassed	1	2	3	4	5	6	7

Part C: Tourist Satisfaction

Please indicate your level of AGREEMENT with the following statements describing your satisfaction with your travel experience in Australia (Please tick one number among the number 1 - 7 indicating *strongly disagree* to *strongly agree*).

	Never Always						
59. This is one of the best outbound destinations I have visited	1	2	3	4	5	6	7
60. I am satisfied with my decision to visit Australia	1	2	3	4	5	6	7
61. My choice to visit Australia is a wise one	1	2	3	4	5	6	7
62. I have really enjoyed travelling in Australia	1	2	3	4	5	6	7
63. I am sure it is the right thing to visit Australia	1	2	3	4	5	6	7

Part D: Demographic Information

Please answer the following questions by ticking the box before appropriate items.

64. Your gender:
    ☐ Male   ☐ Female

65. Your age:
    ☐ 18 - 24 yrs   ☐ 25 - 34 yrs   ☐ 35 - 44 yrs
    ☐ 45 - 54 yrs   ☐ 55 - 64 yrs   ☐ 65 yrs or older

66. Your marital status:
    ☐ Single   ☐ Married   ☐ Others _____

67. Occupation:
    ☐ Student   ☐ Teacher   ☐ Businessperson   ☐ Clerk/white-collar worker
    ☐ Civil Servant   ☐ Blue-collar worker ☐ Retired   ☐ Unemployed, housewife
    ☐ Others (Please specify) _____

68. Education:
    ☐ Primary school or below   ☐ Junior Middle School   ☐ Senior middle/vocational school
    ☐ Associate Degree   ☐ University Degree   ☐ Postgraduate or above

69. Your personal monthly income (in RMB):
    ☐ No income   ☐ Less than 1,000 ☐ 1,001 - 1,999 ☐2,000 - 2,999 ☐ 3,000 - 3,999
    ☐ 4,000 - 4,999   ☐ 5,000 - 5,999   ☐ 6,000 - 6,999 ☐7,000 - 7,999   ☐ 8,000 - 10,000

☐ 10,001 – 15,000　　☐ Over 15,000　　☐ Not specified

70. Your household size：

☐ 1 person　　　☐ 2 persons　　　☐ 3 persons　　☐ 4 persons　　☐ 5 persons
☐ 6 persons or more　　　　　☐ Not specified

71. Have you travelled overseas purely for leisure and pleasure in recent two years?

☐ YES

Please indicate the countries _____

☐ NO

72. Whom are you travelling with in this trip to Australia?

☐ Alone　　　　☐ Parents　　　☐ Children　　☐ Colleagues　　☐ Friends
☐ Spouse in honeymoon / Boy or girl friend
☐ Others（Please specify _____ ）

☺ THANK YOU VERY MUCH FOR YOUR TIME ☺

Please return the completed questionnaire to your tour escort
on the return flight back to China.

Appendix 3 Final Questionnaire Used in Survey

> You are invited to participate in a questionnaire survey examining mainland Chinese tourists' overall satisfaction with Australia as a tourist destination. The survey will take you roughly 15 minutes. There is no right or wrong answer—only your opinion counts. Participants are expected to answer all the questions truthfully. If you encounter any problem about the survey, please ask your tour escort for help and clarification.

Are you a mainland Chinese citizen over 18 years old?

☐ YES （Please continue）

☐ NO （The survey stops, thank you）

Is this your first visit to Australia?

☐ YES

☐ NO （Please indicate how many times you have visited Australia: _____ ）

Part A: Personality Traits

Here are a number of characteristics to describe you. Please tick a number to indicate the extent to which you agree or disagree with the following statements (the number 1 - 7 indicating *strongly disagree* to *strongly agree*).

I see myself as someone who... ☞Please tick (√) one response on each line	Strongly Disagree	Disagree	Somewhat Disagree	Neutral	Somewhat Agree	Agree	Strongly Agree
1. is talkative	1	2	3	4	5	6	7
2. tends to find fault with others	1	2	3	4	5	6	7
3. does a thorough job	1	2	3	4	5	6	7
4. is depressed, blue	1	2	3	4	5	6	7
5. is original, comes up with new ideas	1	2	3	4	5	6	7
6. is reserved	1	2	3	4	5	6	7
7. is helpful and unselfish with others	1	2	3	4	5	6	7
8. can be somewhat careless	1	2	3	4	5	6	7
9. is relaxed, handles stress well	1	2	3	4	5	6	7
10. is curious about many different things	1	2	3	4	5	6	7

I see myself as someone who... ☞Please tick (√) one response on each line	Strongly Disagree	Disagree	Somewhat Disagree	Neutral	Somewhat Agree	Agree	Strongly Agree
11. is full of energy	1	2	3	4	5	6	7
12. starts quarrels with others	1	2	3	4	5	6	7
13. is a reliable worker	1	2	3	4	5	6	7
14. can be tense	1	2	3	4	5	6	7
15. is ingenious, a deep thinker	1	2	3	4	5	6	7
16. generates a lot of enthusiasm	1	2	3	4	5	6	7
17. has a forgiving nature	1	2	3	4	5	6	7
18. tends to be disorganized	1	2	3	4	5	6	7
19. worries a lot	1	2	3	4	5	6	7
20. has an active imagination	1	2	3	4	5	6	7
21. tends to be quiet	1	2	3	4	5	6	7
22. is generally trusting	1	2	3	4	5	6	7
23. tends to be lazy	1	2	3	4	5	6	7
24. is emotionally stable, not easily upset	1	2	3	4	5	6	7
25. is inventive	1	2	3	4	5	6	7
26. has an assertive personality	1	2	3	4	5	6	7
27. can be cold and aloof	1	2	3	4	5	6	7
28. perseveres until the task is finished	1	2	3	4	5	6	7
29. can be moody	1	2	3	4	5	6	7
30. values artistic, aesthetic experiences	1	2	3	4	5	6	7
31. is sometimes shy, inhibited	1	2	3	4	5	6	7
32. is considerate and kind to almost everyone	1	2	3	4	5	6	7
33. does things efficiently	1	2	3	4	5	6	7
34. remains calm in tense situations	1	2	3	4	5	6	7

I see myself as someone who... ☞Please tick (√) one response on each line	Strongly Disagree	Disagree	Somewhat Disagree	Neutral	Somewhat Agree	Agree	Strongly Agree
35. prefers work that is routine	1	2	3	4	5	6	7
36. is outgoing, sociable	1	2	3	4	5	6	7
37. is sometimes rude to others	1	2	3	4	5	6	7
38. makes plans and follows through with them	1	2	3	4	5	6	7
39. gets nervous easily	1	2	3	4	5	6	7
40. likes to reflect, play with ideas	1	2	3	4	5	6	7
41. has few artistic interests	1	2	3	4	5	6	7
42. likes to cooperate with others	1	2	3	4	5	6	7
43. is easily distracted	1	2	3	4	5	6	7
44. is sophisticated in art, music, or literature	1	2	3	4	5	6	7

Part B: Affective Experiences

Reviewing in retrospect your own holistic affective responses of the trip to Australia in the past week, please tick a number to indicate the extent to which you agree or disagree with the following statements (the number 1−7 indicating *strongly disagree* to *strongly agree*).

Overall, regarding my travel experiences in Australia in the past week, I felt...	Strongly Disagree	Disagree	Somewhat Disagree	Neutral	Somewhat Agree	Agree	Strongly Agree
45. relaxed	1	2	3	4	5	6	7
46. nervous	1	2	3	4	5	6	7
47. happy	1	2	3	4	5	6	7
48. afraid	1	2	3	4	5	6	7
49. excited	1	2	3	4	5	6	7
50. worried	1	2	3	4	5	6	7
51. interested	1	2	3	4	5	6	7
52. lonely	1	2	3	4	5	6	7
53. impressed	1	2	3	4	5	6	7
54. bored	1	2	3	4	5	6	7
55. a sense of friendliness	1	2	3	4	5	6	7
56. embarrassed	1	2	3	4	5	6	7
57. comfortable	1	2	3	4	5	6	7
58. homesick	1	2	3	4	5	6	7

Part C: Tourist Satisfaction

Please indicate your level of AGREEMENT with the following statements describing your overall satisfaction with your travel experience in Australia (Please tick one number among the number 1 – 7 indicating *strongly disagree* to *strongly agree*).

	Strongly Disagree	Disagree	Somewhat Disagree	Neutral	Somewhat Agree	Agree	Strongly Agree
59. I have really enjoyed the trip in Australia	1	2	3	4	5	6	7
60. My choice to visit Australia was a wise one	1	2	3	4	5	6	7
61. The travel experience in Australia was exactly what I needed	1	2	3	4	5	6	7
62. I am satisfied with my trip in Australia	1	2	3	4	5	6	7

Part D: Demographic Information

Please answer the following questions by ticking the box before appropriate items.

63. Your gender:
 □ Male   □ Female

64. Your age:
 □ 18 – 29 yrs   □ 30 – 39 yrs   □ 40 – 49 yrs
 □ 50 – 59 yrs   □ 60 yrs or older

65. Your marital status:
 □ Single   □ Married   □ Others _____

66. Occupation:
 □ Student   □ Teacher   □ Civil Servant   □ Businessperson
 □ Clerk/white-collar worker   □ Blue-collar worker   □ Retired
 □ Housewife   □ Others (Please specify) _____

67. Education:
 □ Primary school or below   □ Junior Middle School
 □ Senior middle/vocational school   □ Three-year college diploma
 □ Four-year University Degree   □ Postgraduate or above

68. Your personal monthly income (in RMB):
 □ No income   □ Less than 2,000   □ 2,000 – 3,999   □ 4,000 – 5,999
 □ 6,000 – 7,999   □ 8,000 – 9,999   □ 10,000 – 14,999   □ Over 15,000

□ Prefer not to answer

69. Your household size：

□ 1 person　　　　□ 2 persons　　　　□ 3 persons　　　　□ 4 persons

□ 5 persons　　　□ 6 persons or more　□ Prefer not to answer

70. Whom are you travelling with in this trip to Australia?

□ Alone　　　　□ Parents　　　　□ Children　　　　□ Colleagues

□ Friends　　　□ Spouse / Partner

□ Others（Please specify _____ ）

71. Did you travel overseas during the past 5 years?

□ Yes（Please specify the countries _____ ）

□ No

☺ THANK YOU VERY MUCH FOR YOUR TIME ☺

Please return the completed questionnaire to your tour escort
on the return flight back to China.